THE MOCKINGBIRD DEVOTIONAL

Good News for Today
(and Every Day)

A Resource from Mockingbird Ministries

Edited by Ethan Richardson and Sean Norris

MOCKINGBIRD

Copyright © 2013 by Mockingbird Ministries
Mockingbird Ministries
100 West Jefferson Street
Charlottesville, VA 22902
www.mbird.com

Cover design by Stephanie Fishwick. Editing by Ethan Richardson and Sean Norris. Copy editing and book layout by William McDavid in Archer by Hoefler & Frere-Jones and Goudy Bookletter 1911 by Barry Schwartz. Published 2013 and printed by Createspace.com in the United States of America.

ISBN-13: 978-0-9907927-1-0

A big thank you to David Zahl for making this project possible, as well as to the wider Mockingbird community—individuals, churches and ministries who have contributed to or helped shape this substantial and significant project. Special thanks to Kate Norris, Claire Veligdan and Aaron Zimmerman for their edits in the early stages of this project, as well as to Will McDavid and Ken Wilson for the masterful detail-work that has made all the difference with this edition. Also thanks to John Zahl, for his meticulous and helpful installment of our liturgical calendar appendix. And most importantly, thanks to all the authors for bringing their heartfelt insights home to all of us.

CONTENTS

FOREWORD

On the Ministry of Encouragement

John Morley (1838-1923) claimed that "human nature is good" and that "it is the key that secularizes the world."[*] He believed that the evil of the world is the fruit of bad education and bad institutions. Reinhold Niebuhr called secularism "this-world-is-all-there-is-ism" and it has replaced Christianity as the predominant religion of Western Civilization. This trust in man and history, without God, produces arrogant hubris begging for judgment, dangerous naïveté regarding human nature, and tragic human discouragement in the face of increasingly frightening reality.

As one of the contributors to this work reminds us, "reality is an ally to God." The Holy Spirit speaks to our discouragement through some 365 commentaries on texts from Genesis to Revelation by more than sixty diverse, talented, and scholarly contributors. Diverse, yes, but unified in three counter-cultural themes.

First, a sure and confident trust that we do indeed have a gracious and awesome God pervades these messages. In the face of tradition's fear of antinomianism the most depressed, despairing, undeserving sinner is shown again and again that God initiates, God forgives, God accepts, and God redeems. This good news tends to be obscured and often denied in

---

[*] Owen Chadwick, *The Secularization of the European Mind in the 19th Century*, 152.

all traditions. The irrefutable evidence for this can be found in the dictionary definitions of "preach": "to give advice in an offensive or obtrusive manner on religious or moral grounds," "to give religious or moral instruction, especially in a drawn-out tiresome manner." Similar definitions of "sermon" are little more than exhortations. Virtually no definition is given for either "preach" or "sermon" that mentions any reassuring good news for discouraged sinners. When one reflects on the fact that dictionaries do not tell us what words should mean but what they do mean, then we can appreciate the urgent need for the clear and unmistakable comfort and encouragement given by the Holy Spirit through scripture and the hearts of these contributors.

Second, a sure and confident trust in scripture as revealing God's word pervades these messages. When scripture is studied without trust, its grace and power are inaccessible. Anselm's wisdom is forgotten: I must believe in order to know.

Professor Richard Hays at Duke University shows the need for trust that these authors have so fruitfully used to approach scripture: "I want to argue that a hermeneutic of trust is both necessary and primary."[*] The many authors of this work have been given the trust to open scripture for God's word to flow.

Third, a unifying principle of this work is one in which the compilers expressed with candor (and humor) that each is an undeserving sinner who is free from condemnation by the law only because of the sacrifice of Christ upon the cross. They know they were not "born free," as the secular world and their sinful natures teach. They know they were born bound and that sin is not an expression of freedom but an example of bondage (John 8:34). Freedom is a synonym for salvation,[†] something we do not naturally have but is uniquely God's gift. Trusting in a gracious God who frees us by the blood of Christ from condemnation, even for yet remaining sin, these authors read scripture seeing themselves as dry deserts needing the irrigation of God. They look on others sinners not with condemnation but with compassion. They share in God's love for this desperate world. Their hearts are open to hear the poignant cries of the world in movies, events, and lyrics of the day.

---

[*] "Salvation by Trust? Reading the Bible Faithfully," *The Christian Century*, Feb. 26, 1997, 218.
[†] C. K. Barrett, *The Gospel According to St. John*, 285.

A gratifying result in pondering these meditations can be expressed in one word: encouragement. Living in a post-Christian world where there is no resurrection, where we are finally bereft of justice, mercy, or meaning, and where nothing will ever be right, is both depressing and discouraging. The disarming acknowledgment of debilitating sin in the confession of undeserved favor by their forgiveness in Christ renders these authors as winsome windows to behold our gracious God. Here can be seen the grounds of hope for justice, mercy and meaning.

It has been for me a most encouraging experience to receive God's word in passages from Genesis through Revelation aided by the insight and experience of many who are less than half my age. If the readers tire of the word "encourage" let them ponder 2 Corinthians 1:3-7, where St. Paul used the word ten times in only five verses. The operative word, alternately translated "comfort," translates the Greek word *parakaleo*, the very work of the Holy Spirit, the Paraclete. The crucial text is verse four "...to encourage those who are in any affliction, with the encouragement with which we are encouraged by God."

None of these contributors tried to encourage with their own encouragement. One would have found that unhelpful or even off-putting. They merely encourage with "the encouragement with which they have been encouraged." It is the Holy Spirit who speaks.

—C. FitzSimons Allison, Bishop of South Carolina (ret.), 2009

INTRODUCTION

In 2011, an undrafted, minor league Erie BayHawks guard was brought into the National Basketball Association to play for an injury-plagued team on a heavy losing streak. Because the NBA was in lockout, the New York Knicks claimed Jeremy Lin on waivers, and he slept on his brother's couch in the Lower East Side before his first game. On February 4, just a week before the Knicks were planning to release him, Lin, fourth on the "depth chart" for his position, scored a career high 25 points, and in the next three games scored 28, 23, and 38 points, the last one outscoring his Lakers' defender, the famed Kobe Bryant. This wild accident propelled an electric fever known as "Linsanity." New York fans became rejuvenated by a no-name hero they didn't know they'd been waiting for: his jerseys filled the streets, e-books were written within weeks of his first game, his face shown on the cover of *Time* magazine. Suddenly, the initial shock had become the *story*, the myth of one boy, that Heroic Underdog, who defied the odds and arose victorious: Jeremy Lin, the Lionhearted.

Then, the very next season, he was traded. Contract up, the Knicks didn't fight the Rockets for him like expected, and he was gone. Without much melodrama, the story faded to post-season chatter, and the nerdy Harvard kid who saved his team from their horrendous start was exchanged for a faster, stronger Raymond Felton. "Linsanity," if you are a New Yorker, is now just one more story in a city full of them.

This kind of slip is not a rare thing. People crave miraculous breakthroughs and changes and renewals—this is why we get tattoos and go on vacations and look for new music to love. It is why fast food restaurants like Pizza Hut and McDonalds unveil fresh gimmicks every season such as *Pizza Sliders* (which are basically glorified Bagel Bites from the 80s). And yet, even the most miraculous renewals become tired within weeks. This is what the philosopher Martin Heidegger meant by the word "everydayness," that new words slowly lose their meaning with overuse, that work e-mails still haunt us on our beach getaway, that "passions" slowly become just "a way to pay the bills." Some events in life can be startlingly painful and others startlingly beautiful, but much of life, like the graying ink of that impulsive tattoo, can slide into the unfelt blurriness of boredom.

Author Walker Percy likens this to two men riding the commuter train home. The first man is "fat, dumb, and happy." He leads a hollow life of "work, gossip, television, and sleep"—and he feels content with it. The second man's daily routine is no different, but "he knows that something is dreadfully wrong." They quietly ride the train together, umbrellas laid across their paunch, with the same underpinning malaise. Percy then goes on to say that if a stranger were to enter their railcar and bring some good news, the man who would understand it is the man who sees himself as in deep, deep trouble. Only the second passenger could heed the stranger's good news. On the other hand, Percy describes, *neither* man will pay any attention at all if it is not *pertinent* to their situation:

> The canon of acceptance by which one rejects and another heeds... is its relevance to his predicament. The man who is dying of thirst will not heed news of diamonds. The man at home, the satisfied man, he who does not feel himself to be in a predicament, will not heed good news... The castaway will heed news relevant to his predicament.[*]

Within this illustration—a framework that Percy is borrowing from Søren Kierkegaard—the modern human must first become aware that "something is dreadfully wrong" before any hope is to be had. Only when someone sees their predicament, namely, that they are castaways awaiting "news from across the sea," can there be any possibility of salvation.

---

[*] Percy, Walker. "The Message in the Bottle" in *The Message in the Bottle* (Farrar, Straus and Giroux, 1984), p. 135.

The power of Percy's metaphor is not limited to "modern man." Its expediency extends beyond expat novelists, teenagers in *Zombieland*, and 19th century existentialists; it draws from the still-living language of God's people in the Bible. The Bible plants our human origins around two such castaways, Adam and Eve, who, after being breathed into existence by God, are sent away from home to work and to die. In fact, all the "bible heroes" are moral outcasts: crooks, liars, philanderers, drunks, prostitutes, doubters, you name it. They, too, ride the railcar in need of a stranger's good news, as the psalmist bellows:

> I cry out to God; yes, I shout. Oh, that God would listen to me! When I was in deep trouble, I searched for the Lord. All night long I prayed, with hands lifted toward heaven, but my soul was not comforted. I think of God, and I moan, overwhelmed with longing for his help (Psalm 77, NLT).

The Bible positions humanity as a species gone lost, men and women in staunch rebellion to the Law of God, lost in the wilderness with "no direction home." It speaks of wayward patriarchs and hesitant prophets, believers fashioning trinket gods in the desert and scalpers fleecing widows in the Temple. It depicts people who are fundamentally at odds with themselves: who they've said they would be stares glaring back in the harsh light of who they really are.

And so, the Bible points to us today, and not just to our continued failure before God's Law, but before all the laws of human reality. Scripture, *sui generis*, gives ground to the identity crises of our time, to that creedal American "pursuit of happiness," and to all those contemporary disciplines to eat better, invest smarter, live simpler. As much as these standards may be good in and of themselves—which is certainly even truer of God's Law—their pursuit rarely seems to generate the enduring change we long for. Ruth Whippman said it perfectly in *The New York Times*:

> ...the American approach to happiness can spur a debilitating anxiety. The initial sense of promise and hope is seductive, but it soon gives way to a nagging slow-burn feeling of inadequacy. Am I happy? Happy enough? As happy as everyone else? Could I be doing more about it? Even basic contentment feels like failure when pitched against capital-H Happiness. The goal is so elusive and

hard to define, it's impossible to pinpoint when it's even been achieved—a recipe for neurosis.[*]

The capital-H here closely represents the capital-L of God's Law. When Jesus is asked for a summation of God's Law by our first-century co-castaways, he responds with the impossible: you are to love God with everything you have, you are to love your neighbor as you love yourself (Matt 22:35-40). We are to "be perfect, therefore, as your Father in Heaven is perfect" (Matt 5:48). Talk about an elusive goal and a recipe for neurosis! And to top it off, Jesus describes (demands? defines?) how perfect, law-fulfilling living involves one's right hand not knowing what the left hand is doing—not only must we love God and neighbor with an impossible love, our love for God and neighbor must be so "second nature" that we don't know we're doing it (Matt 6). To borrow from Whippman, even "basic" human love feels like failure against this capital L.

But then there's the story of the "penitent thief," hanging on the cross beside Jesus, who seems to comprehend this failure and cries out, "I have been condemned justly, for the sentence corresponds to my crime... *but this man...*" This criminal is you and me—a stand-in for humankind's inveterate incapacity to meet God's demand—and in his plea, Jesus tells him the Kingdom is *his* (Luke 23:43). This honesty about a self and a world gone "dreadfully wrong" is merely the starting point of Christian hope. The rest of story, that "news from across the sea," rests upon the cross of Christ, in the good news of his death and resurrection. While God's Law classifies the human heart as a criminal and castaway of the first degree, it is the grace of God in Jesus Christ that frees us from its verdict. And, like Knicks fans worldwide, we have been astonished by news we didn't know we were looking for.

God's grace turns everything on its head. Nothing may change, but, simultaneously, *everything* changes. The same people may surround you but somehow social standing, the rank and file, do not matter quite as much as they once did. Empathy is born in relationships where there was once only resentment. "Five-year plans" and "visions" are willingly and liberally surrendered. You find you care less—or maybe more—you can't decide. All you know is that your knees have stopped

---

[*] Whippman, Ruth. "America the Anxious." September 22, 2012: *The New York Times Opinionator*. http://opinionator.blogs.nytimes.com/2012/09/22/america-the-anxious/

jackhammering under the table; you've let yourself listen to Van Halen again; you no longer feel quite as strong a need to change the minds of your in-laws; you decide—now that the pressure's off—you would like to cook for your friends. You find it easier to laugh at yourself and the kinds of things you say sometimes.

These are fruits of God's love and mercy. Just like Jeremy Lin and his New York minute, though, God's loving message is not impervious to human forgetfulness. Just as quickly as the "news from across the sea" washes ashore, we turn our rescue into ceremonious claptrap. It becomes another vaulted expectation. Or perhaps it begins to sound like something people just say, some confuted mixture of pretty words and old mythologies—you remember something you may have heard or felt or understood before, but you do not hear, feel, or understand it now. So it goes. We are often thankless creatures. Life doesn't permanently transfigure into some American Candyland—we don't cease being the earthly Jans and Alices and Ricks and Billys any more than we stop wishing we got paid a little more, or that the Packers hadn't gotten nabbed in the draft last year. Even if we have "seen a great light," our human disposition is naturally opposed to the Gospel world of freebies, of winning losers and losing winners. It is not that our good news has left us or failed us or ceased being what it is—it is simply that we *forget*.

It is for this reason that people throughout the ages have come to the Bible for daily comfort and encouragement, and why the idea of a "daily devotional" holds such hope for those sunk in their "everydayness." Because we forget, because new turns to old more quickly than we would like, because we turn back to illusions of control and success and self-reliance, we yearn for something with "staying power."

This is the hope of the book you hold in your hands. *The Mockingbird Devotional*, a 365-day collection of devotions from Genesis to Revelation, is meant to tell and re-tell, in fresh and illustrative ways, the message of God's grace in Jesus Christ. Inspired by the Bible itself, we have sought to address the problems and insecurities of everyday life, to bring comfort in the midst of suffering and clarity in times of confusion. Unlike the contemporary vernacular of maintenance manuals and self-help tapes and do-it-yourself blogs, this devotional looks to the repeated refrain of one story: an afflicted, obstinate people in the grip of God's equally obstinate forgiveness—most fundamentally demonstrated in the death and resurrection of Jesus Christ. With help from continental philosophy and monster B-movies (and everything in between!), *The Mockingbird Devotional* expounds on the echoes of this story throughout Scripture.

This project is the collected work of over sixty contributors from various backgrounds, ages, and vocations. Some are ordained clergy and/or theologians, while others are businessmen or nurse practitioners, mothers or grandmothers. All come together in the unifying experience of the Gospel.

For this reason, this is by no means some bookish and exhaustive concordance, nor is it a comprehensive read-the-Bible-in-a-year book. Some books of the Bible are heavily discussed, and others not as much. Each contributor chose the Scripture passages and translations they wanted to reflect on, and each contributor may have decided to focus his or her attention on one particular element of one particular passage—there were no hard-and-fast rules on how to contribute to this devotional.

Likewise, there are no rules on how to *read* this book. The reflections are short enough to absorb whenever one catches a break during the day. There are dates on the entries only to help one have a place to go; read as many as you'd like as often as you'd like—one per month, or three per day. The devotional itself is organized according to the order of the books of the Bible, and where the passages are on the longer side, we have printed a brief section and referenced the entire thing at the beginning of the reflection, for you to consult at your leisure. For those who wish to follow the church calendar or the lectionary, an appendix is provided in the back of this edition.

Most of all, we hope that these devotions communicate God's comfort to you *today*, wherever you may find yourself. This is news that never wearies, news we did not know we longed for, and we hope this book delivers that good news to you as deeply as it has to us.

—Ethan Richardson, Editor, 2013

TRANSLATIONS KEY

ASV   American Standard Version
ESV   English Standard Version
KJV   King James Version
NASB   New American Standard Bible
NIV   New International Version
NKJV   New King James Version
NLT   New Living Translation
NRSV   New Revised Standard Version
RSV   Revised Standard Version

OLD
TESTAMENT

January 1

Now the earth was formless and empty, darkness was over the surface of the deep, and the Spirit of God was hovering over the waters. And God said, "Let there be light," and there was light. God called the light 'day', and the darkness he called "night." And there was evening, and there was morning—the first day. (Genesis 1:1-5, NIV)

"Formless and empty." These are the two words that the writer of Genesis uses to describe the world, pre-creation. They are frightening words. Enter God the Creator. He brings shape and substance to the void. He creates something where there was nothing.

"Formless and empty." None of us would want these words said about our apartment. We certainly wouldn't choose these words for our epitaph. Sometimes, though, it is exactly how life feels. Emptiness often feels like the default setting, so much so that we search for things to *create* to give us shape and meaning: careers, relationships, money, children, good health. We come to realize in this passage that *true* shape and meaning are things only God can provide.

Our pursuits, the means of meaning, amplify the feelings of emptiness, hurting us and those around us. We know this from experience, religious or otherwise. Doing a good job becomes workaholism. Taking care of ourselves becomes vanity. Getting involved in good causes becomes self-righteousness. The list goes on, and no amount of self-esteem or positive thinking can help us. As Ted Boynton says in the movie *Barcelona*, "Positive thinking is fine in theory. But whenever I try it on a systematic basis... I end up really depressed."

This is the Gospel, the love of Christ found even in the creation of the world: that God brings us back to the place where our formlessness and meaninglessness is overcome. How do we know this? The most dramatic evidence is Jesus Christ, God made human. In Jesus, God comes to us even though it means death at our hands. And he overcomes death, the moment when life becomes formless and empty. He shows us his love has the power to *re*create.

Have you felt formless and empty? Have you wondered if God loves you? Have you wondered if God could exist amidst all this suffering and chaos?

Be reminded, God is pursuing you with a love that conquers all chaos, formlessness and meaninglessness. His pursuit is not dependent on what you do or fail to do. His pursuit is based in unfettered love. Jesus' death on the cross and his resurrection tell us that God's love for us is real and that He has done all the work. He is faithful to us even when our lives seem to say otherwise.

—*K. Marc Choi*

January 2

God blessed them, and God said to them, 'Be fruitful and multiply, and fill the earth and subdue it; and have dominion over the fish of the sea and over the birds of the air and over every living thing that moves upon the earth.' God said, 'See, I have given you every plant yielding seed that is upon the face of all the earth, and every tree with seed in its fruit; you shall have them for food. And to every beast of the earth, and to every bird of the air, and to everything that creeps on the earth, everything that has the breath of life, I have given every green plant for food.' And it was so. God saw everything that he had made, and indeed, it was very good. (Genesis 1:14-31, NRSV)

I If you look around your world, what do you see? People colliding into one another as they go about their daily lives, adapting and reacting. Simultaneous moments of happiness for some and catastrophe for others. Mostly bad news clips on television screens. General reminders of decay. The world often seems like an accident.

Genesis instead sees the world as a story. The story doesn't cover up or explain away all the present moments, but it is still there, no less real than our own experiences. The world in the story, however, begins not with an accident, but with creation and the repeated word "good." In the beginning, God created the heavens and the earth and the seas and the vegetation and all the living creatures, and each time, "He saw that it was good." Finally, of course, he created us, human beings, and he saw that it was "very good." This created goodness sets the stage for our story. At the very outset we are assured that creation and goodness, not disaster and chaos, is the heart of existence.

Now, to view reality through the lens of this story is a strange thing. It is hopeful in that it introduces meaning and sanity into the seeming chaos of our everyday existence, but at the same time it doesn't shield us from the pain. Knowing the height from which we have fallen, in a sense, only makes the pain worse. And we find little comfort in shrugging our shoulders and saying, "it's just a part of the story." Even as we begin to see ourselves as characters, still we cannot force the plot to our advantage. Therefore the sting of disaster is felt all the more, at least until one day it is all made new. But for that we must read on.

For now, suffice it to say, the plot is to our advantage. Augustine wrote in his Confessions, "You made us for yourself and our hearts find no peace until they rest in you." There is in the created order always a presence of goodness, even in its restless absence. Goodness is the root of reality. That's the thrilling news we get at the beginning of this great story. And, as the story tells us, we don't just find it here—He has written it all over creation. As Luther reputedly said, "This is the purpose of springtime.".".

—Ross Byrd

January 3

So God created man in his own image,
in the image of God he created him;
male and female he created them.
And God blessed them. (Genesis 1:27-28, NIV)

There are three enormous—colossal!—ideas presented right here at the Creation. And they all have colossal implications for people personally.

The first idea is that God creates us in His image. Somewhere in us is the "look" or *image* of God. It must be smothered, like the meat in a gigantic "signature" cheeseburger, with French onion rings, A-1 sauce, gorgonzola, and bacon strips. But it's there! Underneath all the built-up surfaces and rationalized cosmetic add-ons of defended selves, we are, underneath everything, made in the image of God. This gives us, and the people who love us, something to go on and work with. In the words of Joe Meek, "It's hard to believe it, but it's true."

The second idea is that the division into men and women is a primary fact of life.

So primally important is it, this distinction, that it comes only just after the statement of our founding. It is core, in other words. Now I may not particularly like this, and it might not be exactly how I might have done it if it were up to me, but it's reality. We are either men or women. Incidentally, the fissure of this fact in human history has sometimes been a kind of nightmare for Christianity. Many on the outside of faith today would say that confusion about sex, or rather, a negative attitude towards sex, is the chief obstacle to their becoming a Christian. The famous Aldous Huxley said this in the 1930s, when he wrote that the men and women of his generation who rejected Christianity had rejected it mainly because they thought it was negative toward their idea of how they wanted to live in their sexual selves. Yet Genesis is not a "no" to anyone, nor is it a judgment, but a descriptive bifurcation in the order of life.

The third idea in these verses is that God blesses man and woman who are made in His image. Now we all know that original sin is not the same as "original blessing." Personal experience has exposed to us the deep fault lines of human nature. I don't often see a lot that God—*Glorious in Majesty*—could, if He were me, desire to bless. In other words, the God of standard and law could not possibly bless the inhabitants of this Malthusian world, let alone the chief inhabitant of this Malthusian world, me. I don't deserve it, and don't see anybody else out there who could deserve it either. As far as I am concerned, the "glass" of human personality and behavior is half empty. And yet, God blesses the people He has made. He did it in the Bible's first chapter, and it's not in small print.

I think this is a word that could temper one's pessimism. Moreover, over the long term of a human life, God's blessing probably amounts to, well, God's *grace*.

—*Paul Zahl*

January 4

And the LORD God formed man of the dust of the ground, and breathed into his nostrils the breath of life; and man became a living soul. (Genesis 2:7, KJV)

At the foundation of human life lies neediness. A Golden Smog song called "Think About Yourself" (from *Another Fine Day*) goes:

Every night you close your eyes
Your head is filled with alibis and rules to play,
Everywhere I turn I see the bridges
That you've burned just to be free again.

This is so obviously a bitter-love breakup song, but it's a breakup song with theological implications—the best kind of breakup song. I actually believe God wrote this song about me! All I *do* is think about myself, and it's a surefire ending, just like the song forebodes: bridges burned, nowhere to turn, stuck on a road-blocked island of my own making. All because I thought the freedom I knew was the freedom I needed. I'm rescued time and again, without fail, yet it brings me to just one more chance to prove myself. I can do it, *autonomously*—watch!

I read a book by Henri Nouwen that talks about his experience working in a community of the mentally and physically handicapped. He describes a highly touted, upper-echelon type of career in academia, his unfulfilling success, and his move into a facility where his medals, keynote addresses, his qualified abbreviations, were a wash amidst the daily routine of feeding adults, cleaning soiled sheets, saying *nothing*. In retrospect, he describes that the experience "forced me to let go of my relevant self—the self that can do things, show things, prove things, build things—and forced me to reclaim that unadorned self in which I am completely vulnerable, open to receive and give love regardless of any accomplishments." The Spirit moves not in our self-ordained notions of autonomy, but in our naked and common *need*.

This Genesis passage narrates the beginnings of people, and it's a beginning that moves in the opposite direction of accomplishment and seclusion. At the very foundation of our existence lies the Gospel: the Spirit of God moves and breathes life into that which had no life before. It's not a narrative of elemental *potential* or *possibility*—the Scriptures don't depict a well-intentioned person with poor skills and bad tools suddenly given the tools for success. It's instead the miracle of breathing *dirt* into life and "living soul" from existential nothingness. This is the beginning—that, as Nouwen says, "God loves us not because of what we do or accomplish, but because God has created and redeemed us in love."

—*Ethan Richardson*

January 5

...This at last is bone of my bones and flesh of my flesh...
(Genesis 2:23, ESV)

Who is woman? A question asked by men and women alike, of all generations. A question I ask myself, *as a woman*, one that is all too often defined by form and function. But we cannot isolate woman from man to answer this question, because the answer to *who she is* lies in her relation to him. And often the answer seems to be not really an answer at all. She is completely similar to him, yet utterly different; she is equal yet not interchangeable; she is of the same flesh and bone, yet a different person completely; she is comfort and challenge.

The best answer I can give to "Who is Woman?" is: she is the first gift of grace. She is God's first act of intervention on behalf of man. She would not only alleviate man's loneliness, drawing him up and out of himself toward another, but would also be the means by which God would consummate His relationship to man—with them as one. Without her, there is no relationship between God and man; without her, loneliness prevails and the Bridegroom is left standing at the altar. Through this wonderful gift, God demonstrates to the whole of creation His love for this curved-in man who cannot help himself, who is otherwise stuck in his isolation.

The word used in Gen 2:18, "Helper," is the same word often used of God throughout the Old Testament. In her creation, in her name ("helper"), the themes of protecting, supporting, shielding, sustaining, delivering, comforting, and giving hope and blessing are contained. As God gently nudges Adam awake and brings Eve to him, Adam is delivered out of loneliness into communion; he is given hope and comfort. He is blessed. She imputes to him that which is intrinsically hers and that which he lacks. Apart from her, the story ends too early.

In Ephesians, Paul says about the union of man and woman, "This mystery is profound, and I am saying that it refers to Christ and the church." This truth reverberates through the books of the Old Testament and into the ears, hearts, and minds of the New Testament audience as well as into ours today. We were, like Adam, isolated, lonely, hopeless, and helpless. "But God, being rich in mercy, because of the great love with which he loved us, even when we were dead in our trespasses, made us alive together with Christ—by grace you have been saved" (Eph. 2:4-5). In Jesus, through his life, death, resurrection, and ascension, God demonstrates Himself to be our true helper. What is intrinsically His (righteousness), He imputes to us; we were estranged, yet He entered into the midst of it and called us and brought us into communion with Him at His expense. Man and woman, woman and man, we live because Jesus, being merciful and taking pity on our estate, died.

As it was in the beginning, so it is now: like Adam, we've been saved by grace.

—Lauren R.E. Larkin

January 6

Then the eyes of both were opened and they knew that they were naked. (Genesis 3:1-7, ESV)

In these verses from Genesis, a terrible thing happens. The writer says, "they knew that they were naked"—and there it is, the first moment in which shame enters the human equation. Then, from an ashamed Adam a few verses later, "I hid myself"—the first moment in which running away enters the human equation. These are the moments in which free disclosure is exchanged for the new norms of hiding and division.

Those wise theologians of the 1960s—Crosby, Stills, Nash and Young—understood our hearts well when they sang, "We got to get ourselves back to the garden." But we can't. That gate is closed with a fiery sword guarding it. It doesn't mean we don't try to get back in; we have a go at Nike's *Just Do It* swagger; we train and are trained to be those Little Engines That Could (a children's story that has driven generations of children into therapy); we repeatedly chug, "I think I can." If we just work hard enough, we say, we can restore what we've lost.

But finally, and often repeatedly, comes the "Nineteenth Nervous Breakdown" (from another wise theologian), and as we're stuck outside the gate in that age-old shame and separation, there comes the One who does for us what we can't do for ourselves.

We know the feeling of being outside the gate. Theodore Parker Ferris, Rector of Trinity Church in Boston in the early part of the last century, was having dinner with a young man, and they were talking about the young man's father, who was known to be a stern and exacting man.

The son said that when he had been in the Army, he had made a terrible mistake, gotten into trouble, and was given a dishonorable discharge. He knew that what he had done disgraced the family, and he was sure that his father would be outraged. But he also felt that he had to tell his father what had happened.

"So I did," the son said. "I wired him and told him what happened. He sent a telegram back. The telegram had three sentences in it: *I will stand by you no matter what happens. I will be there in the morning. Remember whose you are.*"

Right at this moment, outside the gate, the Lord Jesus stands with you. He is looking you in the eye. He is saying the same to you, even while you hide: "I will stand by you no matter what happens. I will be there. Remember whose you are."

—Jim Munroe

January 7

> *But the serpent said to the woman, 'You will not die, for God knows that when you eat of it your eyes will be opened, and you will be like God, knowing good and evil.' (Genesis 3:4-5, NRSV)*

At a recent rehearsal dinner, the father of the groom related *his* interpretation of this passage: "We all know there's a difference between *naked* and *nekkid*, don't we? Naked means you don't have any clothes on. *Nekkid* means you don't have any clothes on and you're up to something."

Those of us in the wedding party got a good laugh, pretending not to remember any time when that adjective might have been true for any of us. Surely it's not one of those "You had to be there" stories, because we have been there. This father's toast—to a long marriage of mutual, unashamed vulnerability, with one another and with God—was not only refreshingly genuine and to-the-point, but also it recalled those *nekkid* times of discontent, the kind of discontent Genesis presents here in Adam and Eve's predicament. Like ours, it is a predicament stemming first from the experience of *having something withheld*.

To have something withheld, or at least to be convinced that there is something being withheld, is one of the biggest impediments to trust and one of the most prodigious sowers of discontent. (Cite the prodigal son's older brother for an easy example. Also cite any fifteen-year-old denied their iPhone and a later curfew.) This is the seed sown in the Garden. In these situations the "offended" becomes wholeheartedly convinced that the withholders are, once again, trying to ruin their lives.

Of course, the gut-level discontentment often goes deeper: when prayers for a good doctor's report, a better marriage, a breakthrough, a break are left unanswered. You fill in the blank: "Why *wouldn't* God want me to have (blank) right now?" The gamut runs on forever.

For sure, inasmuch as contentment is a blessing from the hand of God, so too is discontentment. Occasionally, our discontentment leaves us on our knees, praying less for what we want, and more for peace with whatever we've been given. Our wants put aside, we are left trusting that God gives us what we need. And when we reach for it and are left unsatisfied, looking for our proverbial fig leaf, we can trust in the unwavering grace of our Father.

In a sermon on the 23rd Psalm, Frederick Buechner says, "Maybe 'I shall not want' means that, whatever else is withheld, the shepherd never withholds himself, and he is what we want more than anything else." In not getting what we want, the Lord is our Shepherd still.

—Addie Chapin

January 8

> *And he said, "I heard the sound of you in the garden, and I was afraid, because I was naked, and I hid myself."*
> *(Genesis 3:10, ESV)*

I love weddings. I love the free food and how happy everyone is and, above all, the opportunity that they afford to bring groups of people, who may have moved apart, back together. There is a Time Machine quality to many wedding celebrations that is almost a completely positive quality—*almost.*

Lurking beneath the frivolity of each wedding celebration is the fact that both bride and groom, in varying levels to various guests, are *known* quantities—and this knowing can often serve as the emotional currency thrown around during the rehearsal dinner. One can overhear statements like, "Good thing you didn't know Bob-or-Sally back during the mid-80s," "We never thought that Bob-or-Sally would even survive college," or the ever-popular "Looking at them now, you would never think Bob-or-Sally ever had a serious problem with *you-know-what.*"

These varying degrees of knowledge are what make rehearsal dinners so anxiety-producing: because in most cases, Kappa-Kappa-Phi-Brother-Danielson and Childhood-Friend-Anne-Margaret have access not merely to funny, childish stories—like that one where Bob-or-Sally ate a whole tube of toothpaste on a dare at Camp Wildfire (can you *believe* it!?)—but rather the stories which splay out deep character flaws. Fortunately, some kind of goodwill keeps the lid on these stories, but sometimes, for all sorts of reasons, there are serious errors in judgment.

Throughout each toast, Bob-or-Sally know that they are the subjects of the praising stories or the childish ones, but they are also people with histories, and thus are secretly afraid of being found out.

In many ways, that flash of fear captured in a rehearsal dinner mirrors a deeper fear that is addressed by the Gospel. Fear of exposure before God is based on a real past, with real stories that could easily come out if the wrong person grabs the microphone. This fear is not just some kind of psychologized guilt, but rather rooted in deliberate thoughts and actions that rightfully should condemn us. This is real guilt, and it breeds real, debilitating fear. This is when we go into hiding.

Into this cycle breaks the message of the Gospel, the message that, on the cross, God has levied our embarrassing stories on the innocent, in our place, so that we stand known before God without fear or hiding. While the drama surrounding rehearsal dinners may never end, the message of the Gospel speaks clearly to the fears of knowing and being known. We can rest secure, knowing we are *known* in absolution, and that the mic has never been in better hands.

—*Jady Koch*

January 9

I will put enmity between you and the woman, and between your offspring and her offspring; he shall bruise your head, and you shall bruise his heel. (Genesis 3:15, ESV)

What theologians call the "Fall" of Adam and Eve is the Bible's origin for brokenness in the world. In the mystery of the Fall, the desire to be like God takes hold of the hearts of men and women. The serpent convinces them they need only themselves; all they must do is turn from Him and in on themselves. Thus, here in the first three chapters of the Bible, after the Fall, the need for and purpose of Christ is brought to bear (Gal 4:4).

The Bible describes God as jealous for people (Zech 1:14, 8:2). He is the curiously hot-pursuing lover of sinners, harlots, and tax collectors. He is the persistent wooer of those He lost in the garden, those shepherdless sheep. The Undesirables of this world are the apple of His eye. The weak ones the world rejects, He embraces.

And this promise is for you and me. He crushes the evil one on our behalf—the Hebrew promise means, "to crush, or to batter." While we inherit the Fall's curse, God promises to strike the fatal blow upon our enemy, which He accomplishes on the cross for us. While serving as our atonement, the cross, too, is the death-dealing strike against the forces of hell.

The story starts here: this is the beginning of God's hot-blooded pursuit of His dissolute people. But the cross is the great exchange; there Jesus steals our identity as sinners and defends us from the hopelessness of hell. He is the Lamb of God that takes away the sins of the world (John 1:29). The cornerstone that crushes the work of the evil one, Jesus Christ obscures and defeats the schemes of the devil in his death and resurrection, and he has purchased you for himself.

—*Matthew McCormick*

January 10

And to Adam he said, "Because you have listened to the voice of your wife and have eaten of the tree of which I commanded you, 'You shall not eat of it,' cursed is the ground because of you; in pain you shall eat of it all the days of your life; thorns and thistles it shall bring forth for you; and you shall eat the plants of the field. By the sweat of your face you shall eat bread, till you return to the ground, for out of it you were taken; for you are dust, and to dust you shall return. (Genesis 3:17-19, ESV)

This passage deals heavily, I think, with the ideas of occupation and purpose. I remember struggling with these concepts and feeling incredible pressure after graduating. Entering the "real world," in need of something to do and somewhere to work, I have often wondered if the nine-to-five was God's intent when He made us. Is *this* where all my education and job training have lead me? What if I have a truer vocation, and that vocation is different? And what about all the people who have felt trapped in careers they don't enjoy—did they make a wrong turn somewhere? Were they just not listening closely enough for God's voice?

Earlier on in Genesis, God creates Adam and gives him a job: "The Lord took the man and put him in the Garden of Eden to work it and take care of it" (2:15-17). My own experience of garden tending, however, more closely aligns with this passage, where God describes his curse upon the man—"Cursed is the ground because of you; through painful toil you will eat of it all the days of your life."

It seems that God has now changed things. It's fair to assume that, before this point, Adam's occupation was a pleasure—he didn't know the shadowy stress of deadlines, the grinding fear of getting reamed by clients or bosses. He was nothing more or less than God's gardener, planting and tending exactly how God had designed. Adam's relationships to his occupation and to God were entirely free from condition or demand.

The curse forces Adam to eat through "painful toil," to work for his food in the midst of thistles and thorns. God has withdrawn His presence from Adam and Eve, their self-evident intimacy with their work cut off. The new system—the system we are still abiding in today—is a conditional system where "effort in" equals "reward out."

It's hard to understand how God could curse his own forever simply because they broke a rule. But it's important to remember God's chief purpose throughout all of Scripture—to reveal humankind's need for rescuing.

Though one day we may find that "perfect" job, one where our interests and talents combine in a harmony of purpose and drive, we are not—and will never be—good enough, smart enough, or talented enough to stand beyond conditions. Children of Adam, something will always be required from us. Only because of God's redeeming grace, paid for by Christ's death and resurrection, are all requirements and conditions annulled.

—Jeremy Coleman

36

January 11

> *And the LORD God made for Adam and for his wife garments of skins and clothed them. The LORD God said, "Behold, the man has become like one of us in knowing good and evil. Now, lest he reach out his hand and take also of the tree of life and eat, and live forever—" therefore the LORD God sent him out from the garden of Eden to work the ground from which he was taken. He drove out the man and at the east of the garden of Eden he placed the cherubim and a flaming sword that turned every way to guard the way to the tree of life. (Genesis 3:21-24, ESV)*

Could it get any worse? This had to have been the thought running through the minds of Adam and Eve as we find them at the end of Genesis 3. It must have seemed to them that it hadn't been that long ago that life had been wonderful. And now... well, now what? Here they were being told by God that, as a result of their disobedience towards Him when He gave them that one rule—"Do not eat of the fruit of the tree of the knowledge of good and evil"—they were about to have a host of hardships come their way.

Imagine for a moment the pain, the fear, the absolute sense of shame that Adam and Eve must feel. In the face of their angry, loving Maker, they must wonder if things can ever be the same. To make matters worse, they now stand before this God with the promise that pain and toil will mark the rest of their lives. Perhaps even worse than this, though, God promises them that they will die, that their lives will cease to exist; they will no longer enjoy the beauty of this garden. To top it all off, they stand naked and utterly exposed in their sin before God.

The more I reflect upon this story, the more I realize that I can easily relate to them. Every time I find myself in the place of having sinned against God—of having broken His divine Law (all too frequently, I must shamefully admit)—I, too, am racked by thoughts of fear and shame and find myself wanting to run away and try to hide from God. The reality is that I don't want to be seen by Him because I feel so naked in my sin before Him.

And yet this passage speaks a word of hope into these moments when we find ourselves naked in our sin before God. At the worst point of Adam and Eve's life, when God should rightfully have wiped them away for their sin, just done away with them and started over again, He does an amazing—albeit simple—thing: God clothes them! He doesn't leave them naked in sin and shame. In the midst of terrible judgment, a glimmer of God's grace comes shining through: He takes animal skins and makes garments for Adam and Eve to clothe their shameful nakedness. In a single, mundane act, God gives them a taste of the wonderful plan He has in store for dealing with our horrific, inherited blight of sin.

What is His plan? He will clothe us! He will not leave us alone in our sin and humiliation. And this is precisely what He has done through the crucifixion and resurrection of Jesus Christ; He has clothed us, not with garments of skin, but with the righteousness that belongs to His son. God has covered us with a garment so clean and so perfect that not even a speck of our sin remains seen by Him. So, in those terrible moments when we feel like Adam and Eve and wonder if we will be left exposed in the nakedness of our sin, see and hear the wonderful promise of God: "I clothed Adam and Eve with garments of skin, but you I have clothed in the righteousness of my son. Your sins are forgiven, my child, simply because I love you that much."

—*Kyle Tomlin*

January 12

If you do well, will you not be accepted? And if you do not do well, sin is lurking at the door; its desire is for you, but you must master it. (Genesis 4:7, NRSV)

If you're anything like me, you often think to yourself: if only I could get myself under control, then I would happy. If only I started working out, if only I started going to bed earlier, if only I started eating less or more or "better," if only I read more, if only I didn't watch so much television or play so many video games, if only I stopped being so obsessed with how I look all the time...

There is a great temptation to think that self-mastery, self-rule, self-control is the answer; that if we could somehow manage the sin in our lives, whatever form it may take, then everything would be better.

But the truth is that the more we try to control our lives, the more out-of-control we become, and God's demand for perfection—as seen in this verse—is no help in this endeavor. God commands Cain to get himself together, to simply "do well," and in the very next verse (4:8), enflamed with resentment and jealousy and anger, Cain kills his brother.

The impulse to self-mastery leads, ironically, to ever less control when filtered through the rebellious, untamable human heart.

The Apostle Paul knew this by experience, namely that his own "sinful passions" were "aroused by the law" (Rom 7:5), that the desire for control created rebellion, such that he was unable to do the thing he wanted to do and found himself doing the very things he loathed (Rom 7:15).

In our constant quest for peace, the answer is to be found not in the quest for control, but in the release of it. True peace only comes about when we receive the good news that in spite of our petty powerlessnesses and intractable addictions, however big or small they may be, we are loved and accepted; that we do not, in fact, control our own destiny, but rather our fate has been bought and our future secured by the cross of Christ. He is in control, even though we are not.

As we walk through life, constantly frustrated by our inability to be and do what we want, the answer is not self-mastery, but rather the love of the Master. We are not and will not be what we ought to be, yet God, through Jesus, says to us, over and over again, "You're not in control, but I am—and your future is secure in Me."

—R-J Heijmen

January 13

> They said, "Come, let us build ourselves a city and a tower with its top in the heavens, and let us make a name for ourselves, lest we be dispersed over the face of the whole earth." (Genesis 11:4, NIV)

This infamous "Tower of Babel" story in Genesis requires some theological unpacking, but it is worth the effort. The story has great relevance for us, for it reveals a significant and common error in religion.

At first glance, the Babel Project doesn't seem all that bad. I suppose one could even say that those constructing the great Tower are doing something noble: unifying diverse communities with a common mission; having an impressive religious structure that would inspire people for years to come—touching heaven itself!

Who would stand in the way of such a significant project? Why meddle with those who simply want to create something that will inspire others and lead them toward religion, toward God? Well, two things made this project doomed from the start. First, the builders wanted the tower to reach "the heavens." Second, the builders were using the Babel Project to "make a name for ourselves."

In the ancient world, many cultures would build ziggurats—tall, spiraled towers intended to reach up to the gods. The thought was if one could reach that high, the gods might be impressed, and the fates could be brought under human control. And this is the operative principle in most ancient—and modern—religious belief: if you can reach heaven, you control your destiny.

Human-oriented religion is by nature Babel-directed. That is, in the guise of religiosity, we naturally believe in our control over "upward mobility." We climb ladders and build tall towers to grab at what will make us noticed, respected and loved. Like the Babel Building Company, we do this in order to "make a name" for ourselves, in order to control what is beyond control. (Remember, Adam and Eve *fell* only so much as they reached—or *climbed*—for what was not theirs.) Raw ambition seems part and parcel to the human plight, even from the beginning, and ambition disguised in religious apparel is a very dangerous thing.

Interestingly, while our natural religious inclinations were moving up to the heights of glory, God was on His way down. Christianity believes in a God who "came down" in Jesus Christ to save His people. The Apostle Paul said that Jesus "did not count equality with God a thing to be grasped, but made himself nothing, taking the form of a servant, being born in the likeness of men. And being found in human form, he humbled himself by becoming obedient to the point of death, even death on a cross" (Phil 2:6-8). Christians believe that God lowered Himself to the limits of humanity, and made Himself known, not in the heights of human ambition, but in the depths of pain, sin and death.

The fact that God came down while we've struggled "up" shows us the futility of the Babel Project. Why? Because God's not there. If you want to climb upward for God, the only hill to climb is Calvary, where we find religious death—the end of our climbing ambition—and true, abiding rest.

—*Ethan Magness*

January 14

After these things the word of the LORD came to Abram in a vision, "Fear not, Abram, I am your shield; your reward shall be very great." But Abram said, "O Lord GOD, what wilt thou give me, for I continue childless, and the heir of my house is Eliezer of Damascus?" And Abram said, "Behold, thou hast given me no offspring; and a slave born in my house will be my heir." And behold, the word of the LORD came to him, "This man shall not be your heir; your own son shall be your heir." And he brought him outside and said, "Look toward heaven, and number the stars, if you are able to number them." Then he said to him, "So shall your descendants be." And he believed the LORD; and he reckoned it to him as righteousness. (Genesis 15:1-6, RSV)

When I look back on my life, it seems it is more often a story of the failures of my hopes and dreams rather than their realization. However, I have come to understand that fact very positively: all the good things important to me in my life right now would not be there had I "succeeded" more, whether in school or work or relationships. You would think that such a realization would strengthen my faith in God, but when things go wrong I still get angry at Him. I still doubt whether He is there, whether He cares; and then I feel guilty for getting mad, and worry that He will—or has already—abandoned me, as I have Him.

But there is tremendous comfort in this passage for a faith running on empty. It is not that Abram is some role model for us to emulate or compare traits with. He is not some superstar on faith steroids, batting 1.000 with record homeruns in the belief big leagues. No, he's really just a double-A dugout doubter like me. Time and again—in this passage, in telling Pharaoh his wife was his sister, in sleeping with Hagar—Abram doubts God's promise of provision. And yet, time and again, as God does with us, He takes Abram by the hand, reminds him of the promises that will never waver, however frail his faith in them may be—and that is enough for Abram to be reckoned righteous.

The point is that even our faith is not something we *do*; it is in our nature to resist it and take our lives into our own hands. "Many Christians," the late Paul Tillich noted, "feel anxiety, guilt and despair about what they call 'loss of faith.' But serious doubt is confirmation of faith." While a strong faith is a wonderful comfort when we feel it, even doubt is proof of God's love for us. The good news is that God never abandons us, and the proof is not in the stars, but rather comes to earth on the cross, where in the most monumental "failure" of all time, our plans, expectations, and fears meet their end. In that moment everything that ever needed to be done was done once and for all.

—Leonard Finn

January 15

And Sarah said, "God has made laughter for me; everyone who hears will laugh over me." And she said, "Who would have said to Abraham that Sarah would nurse children? Yet I have borne him a son in his old age." (Genesis 21:6-7, ESV)

God's promise to save humanity and restore creation is here riding on whether a husband and wife, both well over 90 years old, can have a child. It is a completely laughable scenario.

In fact, when God reveals to Sarah and Abraham His master plan of redemption, that the Messiah, the promised One, the Savior of the whole world would come through their family line, they literally laugh at him. This initial laugh is not one of joy, but of scoffing pain. Sarah is barren. They are both very old. This simply does not happen.

So they take matters in their own hands. They decide to try to do God's saving work themselves, in their way, at their time. Sarah tells Abram to go have a baby with her maidservant, Hagar. Soon Hagar gives birth to Ishmael. You can just hear Abram and Sarah saying, "We did it! Thanks to this plan *we* put together, the Son of Promise is here! Oh, and by the way, thanks for the help, God!"

And doesn't that tend to be our salvific default mode too? "I know the situation is grim, God! I'll keep my part of the bargain and be a good boy and follow through with a plan to fix it, and God, you'll keep your part of the bargain too, right?"

We flail and fail time after time, and after all our projects to fulfill God's promise have been exhausted, God steps in and does the impossible. It's no different here: "And Sarah conceived and bore Abraham a son in his old age at the time of which God had spoken to him. Abraham called the name of his son who was born to him, whom Sarah bore him, Isaac" (21:2).

God's salvation is not a transaction, where we keep our part of the deal and God keeps His. No! Salvation is the one-way movement of mercy from God to us. It's something God does in us and through us and to us, not something we do for God or for ourselves. Our salvation from our sin is not a partnership, and *that* is crazy good, laughable news.

Does God's promise to save you, to love you, to keep you seem laughable today? If you're honest, it probably should! The good news is that you can laugh that happy laugh right along with Sarah because our God keeps His promises—even the absurd ones.

—Curt Benham

January 16

Sometime later God tested Abraham... (Genesis 22:1-18, NIV)

"Majority of Americans Experience Profound Sense of Dread When Asked To Name Favorite Music" goes the classic headline from *The Onion.*[*] They are playing on the unspoken note of judgment contained in even the most asinine get-to-know-you questions. "What kind of music do you listen to?", for many people, is a test to be passed. The right answer unlocks approval and respect, the wrong one, a dismissal. "Where did you go to school?" strikes a similar chord, to name another common example. Life is unfortunately full of such tests.

Maybe you've been in a relationship where someone is constantly testing you. Every late night at the office becomes a potential (wrong) answer to the question, "Will you choose me over your career?" And when you're at work, the boss evaluates your every move through the rubric of "how committed to this company are you?" Or maybe there's a parent that you feel you are always failing. Or perhaps you're failing your own tests—the hardest of all. Whatever the case, it is an exhausting way to live, and we all know that an evaluative atmosphere produces self-consciousness at best and resentment at worst.

Things are rarely much different when it comes to the Almighty. In fact, life can often feel like one long test from above. We perceive problems and difficulties as opportunities to show our spiritual stuff, our chance to make it clear just how much faith we've got—with divine blessing doled out in direct proportion to our faith.

---

[*] http://www.theonion.com/articles/report-majority-of-americans-experience-profound-s,26676/

At first glance, the story of Abraham and Isaac confirms our fears in this regard. God *is* testing Abraham—and how! It's a horrifying passage, and not just because it involves a man putting a knife to his son's throat. It's horrifying because it paints a picture of test-passing faith that could not be more extreme. Indeed, if this is the "leap to faith" (S. Kierkegaard) that God requires of His children, then who could approach Him with confidence? Those of us whose lives are more marked by faithlessness and fear than courage and confidence know that this is a test we will fail every time. That is... unless someone else would be willing to take it for us.

There is in the Bible another son being "put on the wood," another Father who was willing to sacrifice a beloved child, in spite of having every reason not to. But unlike Isaac, this Son was not spared. This is the Son who passed every test, the one whose faith never faltered, the Lamb of God who took away the sin of the world. The world may test us, our colleagues may test us, our loved ones may test us, we may test ourselves. But God is not testing us. There is no test that He has not already passed on our behalf. He is well pleased. He even thinks we have good taste in music.

—David Zahl

January 17

> *After this, Abraham buried Sarah his wife in the cave of the field of Machpelah east of Mamre (that is, Hebron) in the land of Canaan. The field and the cave that is in it were made over to Abraham as property for a burying place by the Hittites. (Genesis 23:17-20, ESV)*

Making funeral arrangements is awful. So are real estate transactions. Poor Abraham had to do both at the same time.

Here is the situation: God has made a promise to Abraham years earlier. A promise that big things will be coming through his family line: a great nation, and enough land to house said nation.

God begins to fulfill the first part of the promise in the miraculous birth of Isaac, but the second part, the promise of land, has yet to be fulfilled because Abraham *owns no land*. He is a sojourner in the land God has promised to give him. Because of his alien status, therefore, his beloved wife Sarah dies, and he doesn't even have a plot of land on which to bury her.

So Abraham goes to the Hittites, the inhabitants of the land, and works out a deal to buy a small field and a cave so he can bury his wife. He has no idea, but something incredibly important is happening here— God is here pointing to His promise with a down payment. Even when the Israelites are exiled, they know they have a secure place because Abraham has this piece of land.

What seems like a common real estate transaction is actually the most important transaction in the history of an entire nation. With a little piece of land, God provides the foretaste of the *whole* Promised Land.

God seems to operate this way. Thousands of years later, what seems like the common execution of a rabble-rousing Galilean is actually the most monumental occurrence in human history—a full payment for the sins of the world.

A small piece of land as God's down payment—His way of promising that everything will be fulfilled. Likewise, when Jesus was raised from the dead, God made His down payment promise to us that death itself will someday be dead.

God keeps His promises, but those promises tend to move most profoundly through suffering. In fact, God's promises often come by way of death. That hasn't changed. But one day it will.

—Curt Benham

January 18

When the Lord saw that Leah was hated, he opened her womb (Genesis 29:31, ESV)

Am I really all that good at what I do? Do I measure up? Am I working hard enough? Am I thin enough? Smart enough? Am I really loved and accepted by my friends? My husband? My wife? My mother? My father?

Scary questions. And we ask them constantly, even on our best days. The pressure to perform and produce, to meet expectations, is ubiquitous. When we don't measure up—which when we're honest is much of the time—it crushes us.

Conan O'Brien said it best on Twitter: "Just reached 4 million Twitter followers. IS THIS GOOD ENOUGH FOR YOU, DAD?!?"

Leah asks similar questions her whole life. She isn't exactly what ancient Hebrew culture considers "physically attractive." And she knows it. It gets much worse: Leah's dad, Laban, decides it will be impossible to find a man willing to marry her, so he resorts to deception. Leah's cousin Jacob is engaged to marry her beautiful sister, Rachel. But Laban secretly arranges for Jacob to marry Leah instead. When Jacob wakes up the morning after his wedding and sees that he has in fact married Leah rather than Rachel, he is irate.

Jacob takes it out on Leah. This must be when "the questions" probably come to haunt Leah: Why must I suffer this humiliation? What do I have to *do* to make him love me?

These "on-the-ground" questions are almost always vertically oriented when you get down to it. We begin to ask the accusing questions the serpent whispered in the garden: "I know I can't measure up, so what does God think of me? Does *He* even love me? Can He really want what's best for me?"

When the Lord saw that Leah was hated, he opened her womb...

The love of God silences these accusations. Leah is given the comfort that, while she doesn't measure up, God knows her when no one else seems to. God lovingly tends to her in the midst of her failure. He chooses the ugly one, the abandoned one, and gives her a baby—the sign of rich blessing and compassion.

Just like Leah, God meets our isolation and despair in Christ. Through his life, death and resurrection, we have been given a reward that we never could have earned. Are we good enough? Nope. But our Creator loves us and has given Himself for us. And that's all we need.

—*Curt Benham*

January 19

Then Jacob was left alone, and a man wrestled with him until daybreak. And when he saw that he had not prevailed against him, he touched the socket of his thigh; so the socket of Jacob's thigh was dislocated while he wrestled with him. Then he said, "Let me go, for the dawn is breaking." But he said, "I will not let you go unless you bless me." So he said to him, "What is your name?" And he said, "Jacob." And

46

he said, "Your name shall no longer be Jacob, but Israel; for you have striven with God and with men and have prevailed." (Genesis 32:24-28, NRSV)

Although swooning on my part is a rarity, U2 is a band I like very much. In their song "Bullet in the Blue Sky," Bono sings, "Jacob wrestled the angel; and the angel was overcome." Bono then folds the famous story of Jacob wrestling the angel into the midst of a song about unjust violence and hypocrisy. Military force in El Salvador is mentioned, as is 1980s televangelism.

With all the flux and panic of humanity, what does it mean for Bono that Jacob overcomes the mysterious man with whom he is wrestling? As dour as Bono's prognosis is, Jacob's is no better. Jacob is sure that his sly chicanery has brought him a just and violent death, courtesy of his brother Esau. As you might remember, Jacob had stolen Esau's birthright by a despicable deception, and Esau is now on the way to meet him face-to-face. Jacob is backed into a corner, Beethoven's *Moonlight Sonata* playing in the background, with no one to blame but himself.

It is at this moment that God comes to Jacob. He does not come as a sweet and gentle person but as an adversary. As an adversary He breaks the remaining vestiges of Jacob's faith in himself. Wrestling with God, Jacob actually believes that he is prevailing, but all the mysterious "man of God" had to do was reach out and touch Jacob's leg to dislocate it. As dawn breaks, Jacob asks for God's blessing, and what a beautiful metaphor: Jacob's faith is transferred from himself to God as a new day dawns.

All the political and social unrest of the world adds to personal strife. Troubled relationships, broken dreams, and unexpected tragedies can be like a powerful Esau racing toward you with fires to start. "Bullet in the Blue Sky" plays as belief in your own ability to master your domain diminishes. It is then that God visits "under the guise of His opposite." A new day dawns as your faith is placed in One who does have control and dominion. It turns out that the One you have been fighting all night is totally in your corner.

—David Browder

January 20

Now Israel loved Joseph more than any of his children, because he was the son of his old age... Once Joseph had a dream, and when he told it to his brothers, they hated him even more. He said to them, "Listen to this dream that I dreamed. There we were, binding sheaves in the field. Suddenly my sheaf rose and stood upright; then your sheaves gathered around it, and bowed down to my sheaf." (Genesis 37:3-7, NRSV)

Who in the world talks like this? It's one thing to have a dream about everyone in your family bowing down to you, and quite another to tell all of them about it, especially when, in the all-important birthright system of Joseph's time, you're at the bottom. Joseph is clearly self-impressed, and obnoxiously so. What traits does he even have, to make his father favor him when he's clearly such an arrogant you-know-what?

According to the Genesis account, he has nothing—of course he has *some* positive traits, but there's a reason they are absent from this part of the story. Joseph's position of honor has everything to do with his father and nothing to do with himself. He does end up learning humility through imprisonment and slavery. But the story is so compelling because it is Joseph's weakness that God uses for him to end up in Egypt, and it is his suffering that produces virtue. Love, though, is independent of either, and it comes onto the scene here before suffering, before virtue, before accomplishment. Like much of the Bible, this story alights on weakness in order to dispel our persistent illusion that God's love and ability to use us derive from our strengths.

Israel's paternal preference for Joseph is arbitrary, gratuitous—foolish, even—and it's exactly how God loved Joseph, and loves us. Even when God, in His grace, gives Joseph this dream to assure him of God's love for him, Joseph is tactless, angering his brothers so much that they sell him off into slavery. But this merely "gets the ball rolling" on the whole rambling, thirteen-chapter, redemptive tale. At no point could any of the brothers have guessed that the foolish preference of their senile father would save Israel from famine, and yet Joseph does. God uses even Joseph's pride to save the family. He uses weak people, and He brings good from their weakness. God doesn't choose us *despite* our failures, but rather through them.

—Will McDavid

January 21

"For how can I go back to my father if the boy is not with me? I fear to see the suffering that would come upon my father." Joseph could no longer control himself before all those who stood by him, and he cried out, "Send everyone away from me." So no one stayed with him when Joseph made himself known to his brothers. (Genesis 44:34-45:1, NRSV)

A quick recap: after the hated and abandoned brother Joseph bizarrely finds favor with Pharaoh, and assumes charge of all Egypt's grain supply, his brothers are forced in hard times to go to Egypt and beg to buy grain from Joseph, whom they don't even recognize. In an act which can only seem vindictive, Joseph orders his brothers to bring back the family's youngest son, Joseph's brother Benjamin, before they get any grain. Joseph then frames Benjamin for a crime he doesn't commit (sound familiar?) and orders him held in slavery. It's like Joseph is testing them to see if they've learned their lesson.

Joseph's long-standing resentment against his brothers begins to fade when one of them stands in for Benjamin, offering enslavement in his place so that their father will not undergo so much grief. Seeing himself in his younger brother Benjamin, Joseph is touched by this act of mercy so much that he begins sobbing. He hugs his brothers in turn, simultaneously making himself known and forgiving each of them.

Reconciliation and forgiveness usually work this way. It's not a determination to forgive someone that heals longstanding grudges, nor is it an apology, in and of itself. The source of forgiveness is love, pure and simple, and once we feel we've received it, forgiveness happens naturally—like Joseph, we can no longer help ourselves.

Joseph feels love because he sees himself in his little brother—the youngest, the favorite, just as Joseph had once been. He sees the weakest of the family and loves him. Not only do the other brothers refuse to sell Benjamin, but also one of them goes so far as to give up his life to allow Benjamin to go unpunished for the "theft."

Loving us and seeing the sorrow of the Father, Jesus chooses in love to be the stand-in in every situation in our lives, willing to become a slave and take our punishment in every area where we are condemned. This substitution means forgiveness—all of the brothers, including their father, are reconciled and invited as Joseph's personal guests. The power of the stand-in for the condemned is the powerful agent of restoration in human relationships—and how much more in our standing with God!

—*Will McDavid*

January 22

> *When Joseph's brothers saw that their father was dead, they said, "It may be that Joseph will hate us and pay us back for all the evil we did to him"... But Joseph said to them, "Do not fear, for am I in the place of God? As for you, you meant evil against me, but God meant it for good, to bring it about that many people should be kept alive, as they are today. So do not fear; I will provide for you and your little ones." Thus he comforted them and spoke kindly to them. (Genesis 50:15-21, ESV)*

We live in an unforgiving world. We make decisions, and they have unforeseen consequences. It's been true in my life, and like it or not, all my actions, desires and dreams are informed by sin. Call it pride or envy or self-contempt; we cannot escape the inwardness of our motives.

In the book of Genesis, the major players are guilty in neither small nor insignificant ways. Abraham and Isaac lie about their relationships with their wives. Jacob's very name means "scoundrel," "supplanter," "deceiver." Judah dishonors his daughter-in-law, then sleeps with her, taking her to be a prostitute. Simeon and Levi invite a village to become part of their family and then slaughter them. And then this: the eldest sons of Jacob sell their youngest brother into slavery.

This is the conclusion of the book of Genesis. Joseph's brothers finally find themselves facing their comeuppance from Joseph. They have reason to fear: not only had Joseph been wronged, but he is also one of the most powerful people in all of Egypt—and now, with Jacob dead, there is no longer a father to mourn the deaths of his sons. The stage is set for revenge. But that is not how the story goes. Instead, Joseph, with tears in his eyes, looks upon his brothers and forgives them.

This forgiveness is a radical concept today, and I can't imagine it being any less scandalous in ancient Egypt. It is a scandal *we* know, too, on account of Jesus Christ. Like Joseph's brothers, the words of forgiveness stand powerfully true, all the more after we act against them.

Though we cannot escape the inwardness of our hearts, thanks be to God that we cannot escape the provision of His grace.

—Kris McInnes

January 23

> *And the angel of the Lord appeared to Moses in a flame of fire out of the midst of a bush; and he looked, and lo, the bush was burning, yet it was not consumed... And Moses hid his face, for he was afraid to look at God. (Exodus 3:2-6, RSV)*

The 1955 Hollywood epic entitled *The Prodigal* is now considered almost notorious, a "cult classic," the extreme end of the 50s religious lollapaloozas that people now like to make fun of. It's actually pretty bad, I am afraid to say; and the main reason people still see it is Lana Turner as Samarra, high priestess of the pagan goddess Astarte.

Yet this movie is hard not to like somehow, either because of its lurid sets or its apparent sincerity. An image that recurs throughout the movie is that of the sacrificial fire, both cleansing its victims and appeasing its god. The victims of the fire have to kind of dive into it, in order to receive the benefit of their gesture. Fire is that way in ancient times. It purifies and cleanses. Even in vampire movies, fire has the power to cleanse those "two little marks," on the hand or on the neck, from their cursed effects. Fire is really wonderful.

Here, in the encounter of Moses and the Lord on Mount Horeb, God is a fire that burns without consuming its object. It is fire without end. This means it is decontamination without end, the powerful visible sign of an urgently needed grace.

The Lord tells Moses, "Do not come near... for the place on which you are standing is holy ground" (3:5). It is then that Moses hides his face and is afraid.

You can't experience grace until you've experienced yourself. And "yourself" is a person that the truth *consumes*. Personal truth is a terrifying thing, and nobody likes it. You can administer a painful truth to someone other than yourself, and it doesn't sound like such a big thing from your point of view. But to the person concerned, to the person skewered by the truth, it is extremely unpleasant. It can make the recipient hate you and detest you. "Got to get you *out of* my life," to turn a Beatles lyric inside out.

Truth about yourself is not only unwelcome. It is also consumptive, meaning truth consumes your illusions and rationalizations. This is why, for example, few "interventions" in cases of addiction actually work. We're taught they are supposed to work, and they *should* work. After all, they're almost always motivated by love. But experience teaches that they more often fail. The "interventionee" does not want to buy what the intervening truth is selling.

God's message of historic love in Exodus 3, which is step one in His plan to extricate the Hebrews from their bondage, consists of a fire that does not consume and a voice that does not scold. "I have seen the affliction of my people in Egypt, and have heard their cry" (3:7). Moses the seer and hearer was not consumed, and he was also reassured.

It is a profound mystery: Sherlock Holmes's "The Case of the Burning Bush": not your everyday case of extortion or blackmail, but rather a case of fire that leaves the witness alive and sings, "God rest you merry, gentlemen, let nothing you dismay."

"Fear not, then," says the angel, "Let nothing you affright." How might Samarra, *The Prodigal*'s "pagan priestess of the flesh," have reacted to this fire?

—Paul Zahl

January 24

> When Pharaoh drew near, the people of Israel lifted up
> their eyes, and behold, the Egyptians were marching after
> them, and they feared greatly. And the people of Israel cried
> out to the LORD. They said to Moses, "Is it because there
> are no graves in Egypt that you have taken us away to die
> in the wilderness? What have you done to us in bringing us
> out of Egypt? Is not this what we said to you in Egypt:
> 'Leave us alone that we may serve the Egyptians? For it
> would have been better for us to serve the Egyptians than to
> die in the wilderness." And Moses said to the people, "Fear
> not, stand firm, and see the salvation of the LORD, which
> he will work for you today. For the Egyptians whom you see
> today, you shall never see again. (Exodus 14:10-13, ESV)

In a little town, a southern preacher, frustrated with his sermon preparations, plops mindlessly down on the couch to scan the TV stations. Providence brings a re-run of the 1956 classic, *The Ten Commandments*.

Setting Charlton Heston aside, close your eyes and imagine this southern preacher's hot, cramped, creaky-floored church and listen for that old pastorly cliché: "Friends, what Red Sea are *you* facing today?"

In reflecting on the temptations we've faced and the sufferings we've undergone, no doubt we've been faithless amidst life's domestic complexities. Juggling home, career and family; coming to terms with illness, debt, death—it hasn't gone too well. We've not laid our burdens down like we should have. And with this failure comes shame. Hold that thought.

Imagine helicoptering into this Red Sea situation, commando style, for a Barbara Walters cover story. These people—God's people—have known nothing but slavery for four hundred years. Suddenly the God they forgot comes to deal with Pharaoh. After the chilling plague narratives, Pharaoh relents, Israel packs up, and bonfires line the beach of the Red Sea. But of course it's not over there. In the throes of megalomania, Pharaoh changes his mind and chases after them. Now God's people stand hemmed in, at an impassable Red Sea and without water wings.

We often have similar experiences where we feel *this close*. We had great plans, and we almost got there, but now the hope of deliverance seems too good to be true—and now it's back to the old life.

In these moments of regress or failure, nothing quite pegs our identity like shame does. It becomes the way we self-describe. The "Who am I?" framework only shows us what we aren't: an ineffective employee. A failed father. A basket case. A pervert. Your shame has the power to terminally *name* you. Sure, Jesus-loves-me-this-I-know and all that—but what about here and now? What about this sea of shame?

In Christ, you are God's treasured possession. As part of His family, you are the beloved first-born son. Rather than receiving the wrath of Pharaoh, the chaos of the sea is the moment of His salvation. Naturally you've forgotten that and have placed an old shame back onto your shoulders again, but it was never yours to lug around in the first place. As Jesus says, "My yoke is easy and my burden is light." In Christ, you are clothed in righteousness and when God sees you, there's nothing more to be ashamed of. He sees the perfection of Jesus.

—*Matt Johnson*

January 25

"The Lord will fight for you; you need only to be still."
(Exodus 14:14, NLT)

This sentence is Moses' final instruction before he leads the Israelites through the Red Sea. The Israelites are being pursued by a large and powerful army, and their way forward is blocked. There is no apparent way out of their situation, so Moses tells them to "be still" and to watch for deliverance. Moses tells the Israelites that God will fight their battle.

The extent to which we believe that the LORD will fight our battles determines our ability to be still. Who among us, however, is inclined to be still when we are under attack? Whether under an emotional or physical assault, our natural response is either fight or flight. Our minds begin to race, and our bodies go taut.

With the Israelites, neither fight nor flight is a realistic option. Pharaoh's army is vastly superior to the Israelites, so any engagement would mean sure disaster. They cannot flee, as they are boxed in between the Red Sea and the oncoming army. It seems the Israelites will be still because there is no other choice. God has made them still by their circumstances.

Thankfully, God also makes *us* still. When we are boxed in, important realities are revealed. We see the magnitude of our battles and the limits of our ability to overcome them. We see that things are actually out of control—*our* control. Because we are so terribly human, it usually takes exhausting all our options to make us still and inactive.

Martin Luther addresses this stillness in Thesis 18 of the Heidelberg Disputation. "It is certain that man must utterly despair of his own ability before he is prepared to receive the grace of Christ." Stillness is the fruit of recognizing our inability. Stillness in a world of incessant human effort is unnatural, but it is God's good gift to His people. Stillness is what we find at the foot of the cross, where we admit our impotence and anticipate the revelation of God's power.

—Kemp Hill

January 26

Then Moses stretched out his hand over the sea, and all that
night the LORD drove the sea back with a strong east wind

and turned it into dry land. The waters were divided, and the Israelites went through the sea on dry ground, with a wall of water on their right and on their left. (Exodus 14:21-22, NIV)

This passage is about God showing up in the middle of insecurity and confusion. The Exodus and subsequent journey to the Promised Land are the great moments of deliverance in Jewish history. As it is written in the Psalms, "Come and see what God has done, how awesome his works in man's behalf! He turned the sea into dry land, they passed through the waters on foot—come, let us rejoice in him" (66:5-6). For thousands of years now, Jews remember and celebrate that God took them from slavery in Egypt to freedom in the Promised Land. At the last minute, on their way out of Egypt and to the Promised Land, God divided the Red Sea—had God not provided, they would have died.

To Christians, the Exodus foreshadows the ultimate story of deliverance. It points to the cross—the death and resurrection of Jesus Christ as "the work of God on our behalf." The Exodus and the ministry of Jesus both tell us that God provides for those in need, and that God causes life and flourishing where death and destruction try to reign. The Exodus and the cross tell us that God's operative principle is rescue. God comes near to us—down here in the thick of it—to rescue us.

There is no work we can do in exchange for this rescue: it is undeserved and unearned. As the psalmist highlights the mighty works of God on our behalf, so we see this fulfilled in Christ. Jesus, who came to "fulfill the law," did the work we couldn't do, on our behalf. We could never be good enough. We could never fulfill the righteousness required by the Law. God, in the person of Jesus, did the work we couldn't do for ourselves, and so God attributes Jesus' work as *our* work. God exchanges our sin for Jesus' righteousness. The work of God on our behalf is the best news possible to those in need of rescue.

—*Justin Holcomb*

January 27

And the whole congregation of the people of Israel murmured against Moses and Aaron in the wilderness, and said to them, "Would that we had died by the hand of the Lord in the land of Egypt... for you have brought us out into this wilderness to kill this whole assembly with hunger." (Exodus 16:2-3, RSV)

"How loooow can you goooo?" "The Limbo Rock" was a one-hit wonder in my long-ago high school days. It sums up the words of the people to Moses and Aaron reported in the sixteenth chapter of Exodus.

They have fallen so low. They have been delivered categorically from their real-world oppressors, and then have seen the Red Sea part, miraculously. Now they are afraid they won't have enough food to survive. They blame Moses, together with his reluctant pal, Aaron. Moses himself, by the way, has been reluctant right from day one. He knows the heart of a man, and he knows what he can expect in this thankless task of exodus: a reluctant, persecuted people following a reluctant leader. Wanting to blame somebody, the Israelites turn against Moses. Despairing and with nothing more to lose, they think, *Why don't we just kill him, and elect somebody else. If he fails, then we can kill that one, too.* How low can you go?

This pattern repeats throughout the Old Testament: the people beg for a leader, a deliverer—then they disobey, or revert to child-sacrifice, or form cults "under every green tree" (Isa 57:5). The people of the Old Testament are constantly rising, then falling, then rising, then falling. I don't see how one can read the recession-regression chronicles of the Old Testament kings without having an honest view of human nature. The people then were no different from us. Our problems, the internal ones, stay with us from birth to death. Some excellent psychological rearrangements are possible, such as when you hear the Word of Grace or feel it embodied within a graceful person or persons. But we never cure our sinful human nature.

I see recidivism in non-Christians as well as Christians. St. Paul recognizes it in Romans chapter seven, in his portrayal of the universal human being (as did Donovan—"The Universal Soldier"—*listen to it*), who slips back, within herself or himself, all the time.

The historical fact that Jesus was given to the world, given this personal and meta-history of us each and all, is the wonder of saving life. It is the only way out of this that I can see, for it is fully tuned in to the very high and deep frequency of universal stumbling. "How loooow can you goooo?"

—Paul Zahl

56

January 28

*Therefore the people found fault with Moses, and said,
"Give us water to drink." And Moses said to them, "Why
do you find fault with me? Why do you put the LORD to
the proof?" (Exodus 17:2, RSV)*

Anger: let's think about it for a minute. It's usually free floating, it can
get attached to anything, and it's often directed at the wrong object. In
other words, we're really angry at someone or something else, and we
just direct our big anger at a littler object. It never does anyone any good,
despite its rep for being a motivator. It gets the angry person in a most
uncomfortable frame of mind and simply hurts, like a bullet of molten
lead, the person to whom it is directed.

I, for one, do not think anger is a good thing. It is, however, a *real*
thing.

The Israelites' anger at Moses throughout the Book of Exodus is
classic. It keeps erupting out, the free-floating emotion that it is. It is
really anger at God, as Moses observes here. He means to say, "Don't get
angry at me. Get angry at God, who sent me, and who rescued you, to
your apparent dissatisfaction." And it does no one any good: the people
are clearly impossible. They sound unsatisfiable, carping, and accusatory.
And Moses cannot create water. Only God can do that, as God does
next, when he bids Moses strike the rock.

We used to say that anger is therapeutic. "Let it all hang out."
"Vent!" "Sick it up" (an English-ism), and so forth. But anger's really not
therapeutic. Anger is real, yes. But anger expressed at other human
beings is actually a "must" to avoid. If you've done it recently, you may
have found that the collateral damage of anger vented can be high.

I recommend we express our anger at God. He can take it. He is in
the "business" of absorbing it. "No one does it better." Jeremiah
expressed his anger at God. Paul expressed it in a plaint concerning his
"thorn in the flesh." Jesus almost did it—but not quite. Rather, Christ
expressed his dereliction to the Father. The psalmist seems often on the
verge of expressing anger at God. Oh, and Studdert-Kennedy did it, that
old "Woodbine Willie," in his immortal spiritual poems from World War
One.

Try it. For a second, stop blaming the "SOB" ruining your life, and
instead blame God, who, by definition, must be pulling the strings. It will

be for your good to have done so, though I don't expect anyone to pick up on that until... "Afterward" (Edith Wharton).

—*Paul Zahl*

January 29

"Behold, I will stand before you there on the rock at Horeb, and you shall strike the rock, and water shall come out of it, and the people will drink." And Moses did so, in the sight of the elders of Israel. (Exodus 17:6, ESV)

How good is your memory? Mine is extremely selective. There are certain things I don't think I will ever forget, like the entire script of *Dumb and Dumber*, or the model and year of every car I've ever owned. There are other things that it seems my mind cannot retain. No matter how many times I am reminded, I forget.

There is no greater example than how quickly I forget the faithfulness of God. I am like the Israelites in Exodus. God miraculously rescues them from slavery in Egypt, and no sooner does the Red Sea settle back into place than they begin complaining about their situation in the wilderness. They get thirsty and forget that God can move the ocean on their behalf. They get hungry and forget that God changed bitter water to sweet.

I am no different. When I come up against difficulty, my knee-jerk reaction is not faith in God, but faithlessness. When I have a bad day at work. When the market has record drops in one day. When I have to pay the bills. When I am stuck in traffic. When there's no more Miracle Whip for my sandwich. No matter what it is, I complain and grow fearful. I lose all hope. I forget all that He has already done on my behalf.

Thankfully, God continually proves faithful despite the faithlessness of His people, then and now. No matter what situation we face, and no matter how poorly we handle it, God is true to His promises every time. We probably won't see it until it has passed, but He will always stand before us.

—*Sean Norris*

January 30

> *"Take heed that you do not go up into the mountain or touch the border of it; whoever touches the mountain shall be put to death; no hand shall touch him, but he shall be stoned or shot; whether beast or man, he shall not live."*
> *(Exodus 19:12-13, RSV)*

The basic message of this word from God is, as the Marvelettes sang, "Don't mess with Bill." With God—as opposed to all other beings—things can become serious. They can become binding. We have absolutely no personal say-so in His department, unless He "gives us leave."

Yet there is no guarantee of that.

What took place at Sinai, when the Lord drew an absolute, unpassable boundary between Himself and the people, is that He made clear He holds all the cards. There is a complete distinction between Creator and creature, and this little piece of ancient history embodies that truth. If you were even to lay one finger for one second on the actual mountain of God, the large pile of created stone and hill where God was going to speak enduringly, you would die. And you would be so corrupted and tainted, through that little piece of terminal disobedience, that your body could not be touched by another. You would have to be shot with an arrow—killed without bodily contact from the executioner, in other words—or hit on the head with a stone, again without bodily contact. Disobedience and impurity: a "lethal cocktail."

What this says to me is that some things, a few things, are serious. I like to lighten things up with humor. Sometimes the humor is well received. Sometimes it is not. Sometimes my humor masks an element of aggression. Sarcasm does this.

But I have watched sometimes when something I think is funny is definitely not funny to someone else. My little joke falls flat. Why? Because the particular theme is so serious to the other person that it's almost sacred. No mocking, no deprecation, no sly aside. There are some serious things in life, even if we each define *serious* differently, based on our individual experience.

What is really serious for you? What is the non-jokeable subject? Whatever it is, it is something that someone else comes close to at his peril. And I'll tell you what the really serious element in life is: it's where you have been hurt. It's the wounded place, the open wounded place, predominantly from the past. That's the place you may have fenced around, which, when someone comes near, he or she is "stoned or shot."

Fortunately, God didn't stay this way. He broke down the border himself, and He "rent the veil of the Temple in twain" (Mark 15:38). But only after Jesus was, well, stoned and shot.

—Paul Zahl

January 31

"...Make us gods, who shall go before us..." (Exodus 32:1a, NKJV)

John Calvin famously said that the human heart is an idol factory. Although we may deny it, we are desperate for someone or something to tell us what to do, how to live. If you don't believe me, take a look at the books that people around you are reading the next time you're on a train or airplane. I guarantee that a majority will be of the self-help variety, instructions for the inner idol.

Yet, strangely, when we are told what to do, we either ignore the command, fulfill it begrudgingly (and fleetingly) or, perhaps most often, do the exact opposite. Instruction doesn't work, even when it's disguised as self-help or "life-coaching."

Such was the case with Israel, who, after receiving the Ten Commandments, the ultimate "to-do (or perhaps not-do) list" from the ultimate Source, almost immediately did the exact opposite, breaking the First and Greatest Commandment, "You shall have no other gods before me" (Ex. 20:3), by forging and worshipping a cow made of gold. Commandments don't work, whether they come from an idol, a therapeutic book, or God Himself.

The truth is that although we may think that we need some good teaching or some good instruction, what we actually need is a Savior. The search for a better teaching, a better idol, a better self-help method is actually a defense mechanism. A defense against the truth about our sinful, rebellious selves and a defense against the God who did not come to instruct us, but to save us. Approaching Jesus as Teacher, rather than Savior, is the wrong course, as the so-called "rich young ruler" discovered (Matt 19:16-23). We simply can't follow the instructions and thus, like him, we end up walking away, moving on to the next idol, the next teaching, the next strategy.

Jesus comes to silence the idols, to debunk the myth that we can help ourselves, to cancel the commandments. He does not tell us what to do but rather bids us to trust that he has done and will do it all. "This is the work of God," he says, "to believe in the One whom He has sent" (John 6:29).

—*R-J Heijmen*

February 1

"...as for this fellow Moses who brought us up out of Egypt, we don't know what has happened to him." (Exodus 32:1b, NIV)

No sooner has Moses has been called away to Mount Sinai by God than his people begin to "move on." This happens despite a number of explicit warnings to the contrary, direct from the mouth of God, backed by thunder and lightning and smoking mountains (21:18).

Perhaps the Israelites have grown impatient, perhaps they are dissatisfied, or perhaps they've just given up. Whatever the case, they decide to take matters into their own hands and fashion an idol that can serve them according to their own schedule, the infamous golden calf.

Can you relate? There may have been a time in your life when the hand of God seemed easy to detect. A turning point, a time when you were brought out of the proverbial desert and delivered from an unhealthy relationship, sickness, or job. But then something happened. The new job didn't pan out. Another relationship fell apart. The sickness returned. Suddenly, you "don't know what has happened to him." You feel abandoned and confused, and you find yourself asking, *where did God go?!*

These moments are much more common than most of us would care to admit. And like the Israelites, our patience is embarrassingly short and our faithfulness profoundly lacking. We move on. We regress. We focus our devotion somewhere more convenient and easier to control. We are constantly in the business of creating newer, shinier golden calves.

Where are you feeling God's absence this week? Where are you feeling like a victim? Where is the idol factory at work, and what is it producing? Probably not what was intended.

The good news is that we may move on, but God does not. He did not abandon the Israelites to self-destruction, and He has not abandoned us either. Instead, He gave us His son, that we might be forgiven of our impatience and loved despite our faithlessness. The cross reminds us that God is present, especially when it looks like He is not. This is the Rock from which we can't move on, however hard we might try.

—David Zahl

February 2

...Then they said, "These are your gods, Israel, who brought you up out of Egypt." (Exodus 32:1-4, NIV)

The word *idolatry* sounds archaic to our modern ears. I mean, besides the iPhone, why would *anyone* bow down to an inanimate object? It's so savage, so *pagan*.

But flip toward the end of the Bible, and the early church martyr Stephen puts the idolatry thing into perspective. Here's the scene: Jesus has already ascended to heaven, and Stephen is giving the Pharisees a tongue-lashing for their hardness of heart, and he uses this golden calf narrative. What does he say? "But our fathers refused to obey [Moses]. Instead, they rejected him and in their hearts turned back to Egypt." After Moses disappeared for a while, "That was the time they made an idol in the form of a calf" (Acts 7:41).

It's no different today. The heart kindles our minds and motivates our actions. Our actions have a tendency to mirror back to us the motivation of our hearts, exposing our idolatries. The Apostle Paul says, "They exchanged the truth about God for a lie and worshiped and served the creature rather than the Creator..." (Rom 1:25).

The things to which we assign savior status cannot, for very long, carry God freight. The tricky thing is, contemporary idols can be good things, too, not just the *Skid Row* variety. Whether it's whole food diets or urban mission work or foreign film snobbery, on the whole, our idol-worship, like the golden calf, is our pursuit of a means to control what is uncontrollable, to pigeonhole and barter with a God whose "ways are not our ways" (Isa 55).

If you put all your hopes into your kids or spouse, they'll buckle under the pressure and resent you. If you live for success on the job, the deadlines won't stop, and you'll run yourself into the ground. You can even throw orthodox Christian belief onto the pile. Because life disaster will come, and that kind of trouble isn't some kind of theological riddle to be cracked. Our idols will always break our hearts.

As Saint Augustine wisely said, "You have made us for yourself, O Lord, and our hearts are restless until they find their rest in you." Thank God that God doesn't let us find our ultimate satisfaction in created things.

—Matt Johnson

February 3

> *I will remember my covenant with Jacob and my covenant with Isaac and my covenant with Abraham, and I will remember the land. For the land will be deserted by them and will enjoy its Sabbaths while it lies desolate without them. They will pay for their sins because they rejected my laws and abhorred my decrees. Yet in spite of this, when they are in the land of their enemies, I will not reject them or abhor them so as to destroy them completely, breaking my covenant with them. I am the Lord their God. But for their sake I will remember the covenant with their ancestors whom I brought out of Egypt in the sight of the nations to be their God. I am the Lord. (Leviticus 26:42-45, NIV)*

When God makes a covenant with His people, He creates an event to be remembered. The covenant is this: for all generations to come, He will be their God, and they will be His people, and never will God destroy them (completely). Despite having an event to remember, the people forget about God. They rebel and disobey time and time again—forgetting and dishonoring the covenant that God, in His mercy, has established for them.

"Yet in spite of this... I am the Lord their God." Though the people continually break their covenant with God, He grants mercy through remembering His covenant with them. Though they forget, He does not. When God overlooks our offense and instead remembers the covenant He made with us, it is an act of mercy without reservation. Instead of judging us, He recalls a time in the past, a promise to be our God who would never forsake us.

Though we do not remember as God remembers, memories are important to human beings. We take photographs, make scrapbooks, and celebrate birthdays and anniversaries because we want to remember important times. Memories tell us who we are and where we come from. They give us a sense of connection with people who have been there with us. Memories keep relationships alive, for better or for worse. When we do remember God, we look past our worries and concerns of the day and bring to the foreground of our minds the times when God met us. When God remembers us, as He always does, He is lovingly and mercifully keeping our relationship with Him alive for our sake.

—*Bonnie Poon Zahl*

February 4

> *Then Caleb silenced the people before Moses and said, "We should go up and take possession of the land, for we can certainly do it." But the men who had gone up with him said, "We can't attack those people; they are stronger than we are." And they spread among the Israelites a bad report about the land they had explored... All the Israelites grumbled against Moses and Aaron, and the whole assembly said to them, "If only we had died in Egypt! Or in this desert! Why is the LORD bringing us to this land only to let us fall by the sword? Our wives and children will be taken as plunder. Wouldn't it be better for us to go back to Egypt?" And they said to each other, "We should choose a leader and go back to Egypt." (Numbers 13:30-14:4, NIV)*

Someone once said to me, "We are a Numbers people," and it couldn't be truer. Before diving into Numbers, God's promises to Abraham are becoming a reality in the history of Israel. From the barren womb of Sarah, God brings and preserves His people through bondage and exile. His faithfulness unwavering and creative, He displays his love and trustworthiness by commissioning Moses to free the Israelites from slavery. Despite the Red Sea rescue and all the wondrous signs, the Israelites grumble and complain: they don't like the food God provides in the desert and so they demand quail; they reminisce about the wonderful days of slavery in Egypt with a twisted sort of nostalgia; they try to impeach Moses. All the while, God patiently continues carrying out His plan. He sends spies to scope out the Promised Land and, instead of trusting God's provision, the spies insist it is impossible and plot a plan B.

We are still a Numbers people to the very core. We seem to know only how to *forget* God's provision. We lambast His promises and shake our fists, having our own idea of how we think it ought to go. We cannot bear a sustenance that does not fit our neat little pictures of sustenance. To put it simply, we trust ourselves more than we trust God. Although "the righteous shall live by faith," God's promises always seem laughable to us; our eyes blind us and our ears deafen us to the gracious absurdity of it all.

Although we writhe and wail with our Numbers disease, He stands true to His promises. He sent us Jesus Christ, providing the all-encompassing *Yes* to His wayward people. As with Abraham, our faith is all the righteousness we need. God did not condition His rescue promise on the proper conduct of His people, but ordained His rescue before we even misbehaved. Take comfort, then, if you are worried because you seem to have forgotten God, if you think your mistakes will exclude you from the promise. God is greater than your memory, and His patient promise endures above and beyond your hesitations and reservations. Be consoled when you don't understand what is going on in your life or how God can be sovereign over it: spies spitting in the face of God's promises do not stop God from doing what He will.

Look to Christ the babe. Look to his cross. The Lord provides solace, perhaps in the most surprising of ways. He is the guarantor of your life now and forever. Nothing can stop Christ and his faithfulness to his promise—not even you.

—*Javier Garcia*

February 5

While the people of Israel were in the wilderness, they found a man gathering sticks on the Sabbath day. And those who found him gathering sticks brought him to Moses and Aaron and to all the congregation. They put him in custody, because it had not been made clear what should be done to him. And the Lord said to Moses, "The man shall be put to death; all the congregation shall stone him with stones outside the camp." And all the congregation brought him outside the camp and stoned him to death with stones, as the LORD commanded Moses. (Numbers 15:32-36, ESV)

This story from Numbers reminds me of the dojo scene in the 1984 movie *The Karate Kid*, when the evil karate teacher asks his students what they are learning. "The way of the fist sir," they shout, "Strike first, strike hard, no mercy sir. Strike first, strike hard, no mercy sir!"

This passage has absolutely no mercy. A man is stoned to death for breaking the Sabbath. He is struck down for breaking the Law of God.

Numbers and many other sections of the Law remind us that God has impassable standards. One deliberate wrongdoing, and you are dragged out and stoned to death. There is no time for explanation, defense, or justification. God's exacting perfection demands death for a man who gathered sticks on the day of rest.

Jesus knew the Law of God better than anyone. He knew it better than the teachers of the Law. And yet Jesus forgave the woman caught in adultery in chapter eight of John's Gospel. He stepped in and saved her when she should have been stoned to death for her wrongdoing. He saved her even though she failed to meet God's rules and standards.

Jesus also stepped in for us deliberate sinners. He steps in for our extramarital affairs, our lies when we should be faithful to our spouse. He steps in for our wasteful spending when we should give our money to those in need. He steps in for our self-centeredness when we should be listening instead of talking. He steps in for the lies and cover-ups at work when we should be honest. He steps in for our tongues when we say something hurtful to our brothers and sisters.

Jesus steps in for our continual failure to do what we are supposed to do. We, too, deserve and Old Covenant stoning.

You will not survive the Law of Numbers. Flee any teaching that seeks judgment over grace, discipline over forgiveness, or condemnation over freedom.

Jesus is the reprieve from an accusing past into a new life of forgiveness. Do not return now to an agreement with God that you cannot keep. Do not return to an agreement based on tablets of stone consequences. Instead, put on that "helmet of salvation" that will protect you from yourself. Jesus grants you freedom and protection from the penalty you cannot handle. He gives you this to wear: a safety and assurance in an accusing and unsure world.

—Alex Large

February 6

"...Behold, I have come out to oppose you because your way is perverse before me." (Numbers 22:9-32, ESV)

In college I played on an intramural co-ed flag football team. One of the suggestions floated for a funny team name was "Balaam's Asses" referring to this passage in Numbers with Balaam and his donkey on their way from Moab.

However much mileage we get out of talking donkeys these days, this passage in Numbers is *heavy*. Balaam is a soothsayer (think palm reader) who charged people for his skills in divination. The King of Moab tries to hire him to curse the Israelites because he is afraid they will invade his land. So here is a pagan king hiring a pagan professional curse-dispenser to strike the people of God.

This account shows God in a strange light. God tells Balaam to go with the King's servants, but when Balaam goes, God gets angry with him. However, if that's as far as you go "into" the story, you've only caught the second most important part, and you'll miss the most important part. The second most important part is the problem of choice, i.e. Balaam's choice as a sinner. The most important part of the story is... the donkey. Yes, the donkey.

God gives Balaam the option to go, but just prior to that had told Balaam that he shouldn't go, because the Moabites want him to curse Israel. Balaam's choice leads him right into God's judgment. That's the problem with sinners like us: a sinner making good choices is still a sinner. God tells Balaam in verse 32 that the reason He has opposed him is because Balaam's "way was perverse before me." Strangely enough, that's the very distinction between a theology of glory and a theology of the cross. A theology of glory tells us our choices can (and *do!*) sync up with God's will. A theology of the cross tells us our choices never can. Heavy? Well, yes, but that's why we need intervention.

In Balaam's case, intervention comes through the donkey. The donkey sees the angel in the road, but Balaam can't. Why would this be? Only because God arranged it so. When the donkey actually changes course and saves Balaam from this "holy ambush," he gets upset and beats the donkey. God opens the donkey's mouth and it talks to Balaam, and only then does he see the angel and realize the peril he was in.

God's ways are not our ways, and even when we think we are doing the right thing, very often it is the wrong thing. It happens all the time in our lives. If it happens all the time, what does this mean? What hope do we have?! We can never be "saved" by our choice(s). We always need someone between us and our penalties. In Balaam-the-pagan-curse-dispenser's case it was a donkey, ordained by God to keep him from judgment, but what about you and me?

We have been given a message that God can and has provided better than a donkey. God has intervened with Himself. God the Son was offered as a sacrifice to turn aside God's holy and righteous judgment against a sinful and disobedient people—a disobedient people who chose to beat and kill him, much like Balaam with his beast of burden. To trust in the intervening cross, to believe in that "precious flow that makes me white as snow," is the product of grace indeed.

—Ben Phillips

February 7

> *But you were unwilling to go up; you rebelled against the command of the LORD your God. You grumbled in your tents and said, "The LORD hates us; so he brought us out of Egypt to deliver us into the hands of the Amorites to destroy us." (Deuteronomy 1:26-27, NIV)*

What we believe about God matters. If we believe that God is some cosmic Santa, perpetually weighing out our good and bad deeds, then we will most likely respond with either uncertain fear or righteous anger. If we think God is uninvolved in the world, then we will mirror God's indifference with a dismissive yawn. Israel, having been delivered from 400 years of slavery, is promised by God to be given a "land flowing with milk and honey" (Ex. 3:8). Upon arrival to the land, Moses reiterates God's promise to Israel, but the people want scouts to explore the land and "bring back report about the route [they] are to take" (Deuteronomy 1:22). The report of the land given by the spies is overwhelmingly good!

But the people do not believe the report and rebel, saying, "The Lord hates us." Moses reassures them that God will come through and deliver them yet again from their enemies and give them the land. Twice Moses assures the people of God's goodness and faithfulness, and both times the people refuse to listen. They believe God hates them and claim that God has determined to annihilate them by the hand of an enemy army. The Israelites assume that God hates them, and so they rebel against God and reject His covenant.

The same is true for us: if we think that God hates us—is out to get us—then His promises will seem empty. It's a matter of trustworthiness. I have a friend who is known to be constantly late to everything he is invited to. Because I think of him as a procrastinator in desperate need of a watch, when I invite him to something, I routinely tell him an earlier time. If you don't trust a friend to keep a secret, you aren't going to tell them anything personal.

But when it comes to God, we know that He *is* trustworthy. Because of Jesus we know that God has chosen to steadfastly love us in the midst of our unworthiness. Jesus did not come to condemn us, but rather came to save us from ourselves. God can be trusted. In light of such love, we can have the confidence that God will protect and support us in our despair and protect us from our enemies.

—Todd Brewer

February 8

> *For you are a people holy to the LORD your God. The LORD your God has chosen you to be a people for his treasured possession, out of all the peoples who are on the face of the earth. It was not because you were more in number than any other people that the LORD set his love on you and chose you, for you were the fewest of all peoples, but it is because the LORD loves you and is keeping the oath that he swore to your fathers, that the LORD has brought you out with a mighty hand and redeemed you from the house of slavery, from the hand of Pharaoh king of Egypt. (Deuteronomy 7:6-8, NIV)*

Many Christians will say that they've made a decision for Christ, that they have chosen him as their savior. It's a true sentiment, but not in the way we normally think—Christians *have*, like all sinners, certainly made a decision for Christ, the decision to crucify him. We did it in self-righteousness, or jealousy, or because of the creeping sense of injustice or fear we feel when God loves sinners as indiscriminately as He has us. How can we develop a moral fiber, a religious identity, if God simply wastes His grace on those folks? Despite the fact that it is also *our* only admission ticket, we often don't want that kind of God.

The decision that really matters is God's. And God has made up His mind about us, His decisive crucifiers. His decision is irrevocable and categorical: "You are my treasured possession." With blood on our hands, God has changed it for good, so that we might have the assurance that we are claimed as God's own.

It is not because of your looks, wit, or wealth that God claims you. Far from it. God wants you for Himself because *God actually enjoys you.* He doesn't enjoy your sin—no one enjoys those entitled and discriminating tendencies any more than influenza—but He chooses to love you in spite of it.

God's eternal choice to love sinners is nothing like a business transaction, where one wants to get the best for the least. God's economy of salvation is inverse: He reaches out to the least to give of His best— that those least and lowly might celebrate new life.

This new life is the empowerment to live freely in a world claimed by the love of God. No longer slaves to sin or death or devil—or even to God's own Law—we are irremediably free. We are a "treasured possession" to God. Keeping you close to Him and guarding you with love and might, God's heart is supporting you with love and favor.

Gracious Father, you give us your best, your very self. May we, this day, share your love with others and glorify you.

—*Mark Mattes*

February 9

...Circumcise, then, the foreskin of your heart, and do not be stubborn any longer... (Deuteronomy 10:14-19, NRSV)

God is always and ever interested in your heart. This is not because your actions don't matter. They do. God is interested in your heart because your actions spring from your heart. There is a well-worn beeline from who you are to what you do. If you are stubborn, it is because your heart is stubborn. If you insist on your own way, if you draw line after line in the sand, if you are inflexible in relation to others, it is because your heart is stubborn.

Most people can pretend for a while; you can grin and bear it in public for a period of time. But the real conversation erupts on the way home after the dinner party, doesn't it? The man seated at your left, with whom you maintained "polite conversation" is now the "obnoxious egocentric bore" of your complaints.

Facades help make society function, but they can't last. The non-integration between what you actually are and what you do will wear you down. Non-integration always leads to the disintegration of a person. The heart always wins. A stubborn heart must finally lead to a stubborn face, a set jaw, and a furrowed brow. As U2 sings, "You were pretty as a picture, it was all there to see, but your face caught up to your psychology." If you believe that you can "fake it 'til you make it," you will only be fooling yourself. You probably won't fool others, and you certainly won't fool God, who is always and ever interested in your heart.

A stubborn heart, finally, is a heart that says "no" to God and is the essence of sin. It is a heart that says, "I will rule *as* I please, *when* I please." If there is to be any hope for who we are and what we do, the help must be administered to the heart.

The Lord knows this, obviously. This is why God says to His people, "Circumcise the foreskins of your hearts." Physical circumcision isn't enough; it might get you through the dinner party, but not the ride home. The heart must be circumcised. Yet circumcision of the heart is a physical impossibility! What can be done?

What can be done is what the Lord has already done. The Lord has already "set his heart in love" on you. Yes, it's true that "to the Lord your God belong heaven and the heavens of heaven, the earth and all that is in it." But it is also true that you belong to the Lord, and that even in your stubbornness God has set His heart of love on you. And it is the heart of His prior love for you that circumcises your heart.

What you cannot do for your own heart, God does for you through the power of His heart of love. A heart that knows that it is perfectly loved by God is a heart that is circumcised. It is a heart that gives way to God and gives itself away to others. It is a heart that integrates who you are and what you do. The heart always wins.

—*Paul Walker*

February 10

At the end of every seven years you must cancel debts. This is how it is to be done: Every creditor shall cancel the loan he made to his fellow Israelites. He shall not require payment, because the Lord's time for canceling debts has been proclaimed. (Deuteronomy 15:1-2, NIV)

In 2008, many Americans decided that they would no longer pay their mortgages. Some tried to renegotiate their debts for lower rates and extended schedules and others simply ran from their creditors because the debts had grown too big and beyond their ability to repay.

I can relate. In the summer of 2007, I moved and was unable to sell or rent the condo that I owned in the former city. I could barely afford to keep making payments and was not able to sell the property at a price that would repay the loan. I feared that one month I would not be able to make the required payment and that the bank would take everything that I owned. In my financial indebtedness, which always seems to carry its own emotional components of insufficiency and bankruptcy, the proclamation of the Lord's time for cancelling debt became good news to me in a fresh, new way.

Jesus' death on Calvary proclaims that our debts before Him have been cancelled and forgiven. My indebtedness before God far exceeds what I owe to my bank, and yet Jesus pays my debt and does not replace it with another heavy requirement. It is to those who are in debt that Jesus says, "Come to me all who are weary and burdened, and I will give you rest. Take my yoke upon you and you will find rest for your souls. For my yoke is easy and my burden is light" (Matt 11:28-30).

—Drake Richey

February 11

Surely, this commandment that I am commanding you today is not too hard for you, nor is it too far away... See, I have set before you today life and prosperity, death and adversity. If you obey the commandments of the Lord your God that I am commanding you today, by loving the Lord your God, walking in his ways, and observing his commandments, decrees, and ordinances, then you shall live and become numerous, and the Lord your God will bless you in the land that you are entering to possess. (Deuteronomy 30:11-16, NRSV)

This is the sort of passage that at first sounds kind-of-nice but when it sinks in "kind-of-scary." God reveals His perfect standard and requires my obedience to approach Him. It's like a visitor at the zoo who, having just watched a lion roar and spring into action, is then invited to stick her hand through the gate to pet his mane. Upon first reading this passage I wonder, *What is God talking about—'not too hard?"* Are we here talking about what Jesus summed up in Matthew 5:48, being *perfect* as our heavenly Father is perfect? Is God offering to accept these, my paltry attempts? Is this an offer to have me go 30% and He the rest? That doesn't seem to jive with Jesus' standard in Matthew, or God's throughout the first 30 chapters of Deuteronomy.

And the trying's not everything. To make matters worse, even when I *am* trying to do the good, I fail. As Robert Farrar Capon wrote in *The Parables of Grace,*

> The world's deepest problem is not badness as opposed to goodness; it is sin, the incurable human tendency to put self first, to trust number one and no one else... when I crippled my children emotionally (or when my parents crippled me) it was not done out of meanness or spite, it was done out of love: genuine, deeply felt, endlessly pondered human love—flawed, alas, by a self-regard so profound that none of us ever noticed it (102).

Does this ring true?

In truth, this speech from God is riddled with conditions: *if* you love, *if* you walk, *if* you keep his ways, *then* you will live, *then* you will succeed, *then* you will be blessed. This is the way this writer thinks, and it is the way the world operates. If I work 90 hours per week, I will make more money; conversely, if I speed, then I pay the fine. This is the way we operate, but in reality there's still discontinuity: hard workers still get laid off, and some speeders never get pulled over. If we are honest, our *quid pro quo* attempts at justice are riddled with the sin Capon describes.

And yet here God encourages. Why? It is encouraging because the whole of this demand, the whole of Scripture, points to one man for all. In the midst of the blinding standard of perfection, the imminent death if you fail, God is proclaiming throughout history the fact that there is one who has fulfilled every possible permutation of righteous, holy, perfect love. *He* is God's word to us, God's own son Jesus, the final word of forgiveness and mercy. Nothing that God has called us to be is too hard for Jesus, who has given himself for that very purpose. We live in the freedom of God's final word: *I forgive you, I am with you. Whatever it might be today, it is too hard for you. It is not too hard for me.*

—Kate Norris

February 12

> *Be strong and courageous. Do not be afraid or terrified because of them, for the LORD your God goes with you; he will never leave you nor forsake you. (Deuteronomy 31:6, NIV)*

The Israelites are stranded in the middle of a wasteland, with their leader on death's doorstep and a young, inexperienced Joshua waiting in the wings. Regardless of their place in world history, their predicament is not dissimilar to ours: no matter who you are, the future is always opaque and forbidding. After all, what comfort comes from the unknown? The best filmmakers know that nothing is more frightening to an audience than not knowing what comes next. Merely living life presumes an acquaintance with this kind of fear—we often ask ourselves questions that reveal this future-oriented anxiety: *Where will I work? Will mom beat the cancer? What will become of our teenager? Where is God now?*

This very concept is captured brilliantly by T.S. Eliot's "Love Song of J. Alfred Prufrock":

> I have seen the moment of my greatness flicker,
> And I have seen the eternal Footman hold my coat,
> and snicker,
> And in short, I was afraid."

Unlike Eliot's Prufrock, it strikes me that we are often afraid even to acknowledge the simple truth that we are afraid. We resist this admission of weakness because we prefer the illusion of strength. Fear is a primeval motivator, but fear typically masquerades as strength: in an aggressive power hunger, an expensive sports car, excessive hours in the gym. We are basically afraid that by not asserting ourselves, we would need to depend upon God's promise instead—we would need to believe that He is greater than whatever unknown we are currently facing.

Thinking on a larger scale, it is even possible to see the insidious traces of fear in the way consumers shop-till-they-drop, the way nations use a rhetoric of fear, the way churches insulate themselves from anything and anyone who might upset the proverbial apple cart. Yet Jesus routinely ventured into these fear-based motivations: what these people met in Jesus was a person who was simply neither afraid nor ashamed of his utter dependence upon God. "The son can do nothing by himself," he said (John 5:19). Neither can we. The only way we can experience this kind of surrender is to recognize God has been doing quite a good job at leading people through the void long before we were born, and will continue to do so even as we, like Moses, are swept up into His eternity.

What are you afraid of today? And what uncertainties are causing these fears? Christianity says that these fears are both entirely understandable and entirely unnecessary. They are understandable in the sense that life is daunting: dogs will bite, waistlines will grow, and winter always comes. These things are all legitimate. But despite the fact that you will fear, you fear unnecessarily: "Do not be afraid or terrified because of them!" Moses booms during his last moments on earth, "God goes with you!" What ultimately and objectively matters in life is God's word of promise in the face of your particular fears. This promise Jesus continues to echo to you today: "I am with you always. I will never leave you nor forsake you."

—Dylan Potter

February 13

Moses was a hundred and twenty years old when he died, yet his eyes were not weak nor his strength gone. The Israelites grieved for Moses in the plains of Moab thirty days, until the time of weeping and mourning was over. (Deuteronomy 34:7-8, NIV)

My great-grandfather died when he was 101 years old. He didn't live to be quite as old as Moses, but had an impressive lifespan nonetheless; one marked by a healthy mind and body. During his 101st year, he bragged that an entire empire—the Soviet Union—had risen and fallen during his lifetime. Shortly before his death, my grandfather commented that he wished he could live for ten more years, to be there for my wedding and my ordination. He had a profound perspective and a lifetime of humble wisdom, and he shared with anyone who'd listen. When he died, my family experienced deep pain and uncertainty. What did the loss of our sage patriarch mean? Would anything be the same now that he was gone? What would happen to our family?

The last chapter of Deuteronomy is the end of an era, and what an era Moses has led: specially chosen to lead several thousand people out of slavery, he shows the triumph of God over the most powerful nation on earth. Moses gives God's Law to the Jewish people. And while the era of Moses is marked by certain unpleasant realities, Moses oversees the most significant period of Jewish history, and his name becomes inseparable from Jewish identity and religion.

In today's text, we read that Moses has died, which creates for Israel an uncertain future. What is to become of them? Will God still bless a nation that had so frequently rebelled against its leader? Does the end of Moses mean the end of God's people?

We read, of course, that Israel neither fails nor fades after the death of Moses. In fact, his legacy helps to form and sustain God's people for thousands of years to come. The story of Moses frames the future of his nation (and all nations) in two significant ways: First, Moses stands as Israel's Law-giver. By reading further into the Israelites' biblical history, the hand-delivered commandments do not necessarily *perfect* God's people, but instead act as a kind of standard for their shortcomings (and, subsequently, the shortcomings of the entire human race).

Second, Moses leading God's people out of Egyptian slavery is a legacy foreshadowing what Jesus Christ fulfills for *all* people on the cross. Jesus leads the fundamental exodus from the slavery of sin into the freedom of God's grace. Moses, therefore, stands in history as both accuser and liberator. He provides for us a foretaste of God's Law and Gospel—two great and constant themes of the Scriptures.

The end of Moses is not the end of God's plan, nor the end of God's dealings with His people. And Moses knew this: before his death, he foreshadows the coming Messiah, the one who would outshine his own ministry: "The Lord your God will raise up for you a prophet like me from among you, from your brothers—it is to him you shall listen" (Deut. 17). Moses realizes that the center stage belongs to another, and that this One to come would bring salvation not only to Israel, but to the whole world.

Times of transition bring a great deal of uncertainty to our lives— we do not know what life will look like after a loss, a miscarriage, a new job, a new town. But we can rest assured that the same God who inspired Moses, and ultimately gave us His Son, is good. His providence always extends far beyond what we can now see.

—*Ethan Magness*

February 14

Be strong and courageous, for you shall cause this people to inherit the land that I swore to their fathers to give them. Only be strong and very courageous, being very careful to do according to all the law that Moses my servant commanded you. Do not turn from it to the right hand or to the left, that you may have good success wherever you go. This Book of the Law shall not depart from your mouth, but you shall meditate on it day and night, so that you may be careful to do according to all that is written in it. For then you will make your way prosperous, and then you will have good success. Have I not commanded you? Be strong and courageous. Do not be frightened, and do not be dismayed, for the LORD your God is with you wherever you go. (Joshua 1:6-9, ESV)

I have been taught much of my life that this passage's intent, and others like it, is to provide motivation and encouragement for Bible memorization. Quite evidently, God tells Joshua that he shall be successful in all that he does by following the path of the Law: prosperity and success await all who "do everything written in it."

But is there more going on here? If someone were to read the entire account of Joshua's life, it would quickly become clear that that neither he nor the people of Israel are careful to do everything written in the "Book of the Law." And, consequently, God's promise to place Israel's enemies beneath their feet is never completely carried out. What, then, is God saying in this passage? Why would He command Joshua to carry out a command we never see fulfilled?

The key to this quandary is in our interpretation. We assume that because God told Joshua not to let "this Book of the Law depart from your mouth," both he and we are capable of doing such a thing. It is logical to think that because God commands us to do something, we *can* do it. But real life experience shows that we fall short of this interpretation. Even the disciples, on the eve of Jesus' arrest and crucifixion, can't stay awake to wait and watch. I think, instead, God wants to communicate a much deeper truth to Joshua.

God repeatedly commands Joshua to be "strong and courageous"—three times in this short passage. Right after telling Joshua that he can only be prosperous and successful by following the Law, it's as if we see Joshua's face become horror-stricken because God immediately says for the third time, "Have I not commanded you? Be strong and courageous." God bolsters (rather than threatens) Joshua with these words because He, God, understands the gravity of His command, the weighty and incredible responsibility for Joshua filling Moses' shoes.

The fact that God repeats His command of encouragement three times is significant—it's like a crescendo, a swelling promise to Joshua that "the Lord your God will be with you wherever you go." God speaks relief into the wound revealed by the Law. God doesn't say, "So, yeah, stick to those rules and you should be good," or "Now get out there and make me proud!" God instead promises Joshua relationship above all else, in spite of Joshua's achievement. God moves first—He comes down to Joshua because Joshua cannot meet Him. God's promise in this passage points to His own fulfillment of the command. He answers His own requirements with a word of comfort.

—*Jeremy Coleman*

February 15

"...Behold, when we come into the land, you shall tie this scarlet cord in the window through which you let us down, and you shall gather into your house your father and mother, your brothers, and all your father's household. Then if anyone goes out of the doors of your house into the street, his blood shall be on his own head, and shall be guiltless. But if a hand is laid on anyone who is with you in the house, his blood shall be on our head. But if you tell this business of ours, then we shall be guiltless with respect to your oath that you have made us swear." And she said, "According to your words, so be it." Then she sent them away, and they departed. And she tied the scarlet cord in the window. (Joshua 2:1-21, ESV)

Before the Lord brings the walls of Jericho tumbling down, an expedition force is sent to scope out the city. There the Lord uses Rahab, a prostitute, to protect the two spies from harm. In addition, Rahab pleads for her family to be spared from death when the Israelites take the city. The spies agree and ask her to hang a scarlet cord from her window so that the Israelites will know to spare her household.

It's an obscure story from the Old Testament, but it was near and dear to the heart of the martyred 16th century Archbishop of Canterbury, Thomas Cranmer. He saw in this story an image of the unmerited love of God for those who might be considered the worst of sinners. Ashley Null writes that Cranmer

> intended his well-known reputation for giving grace to the unworthy to be a cardinal signal, a scarlet cord hung openly from the window of Canterbury, so that in the midst of the battles of his times and since, those with eyes to see should spot where the wall of the old order was first breached in England and recognize as comrades those in the household where the gospel conspiracy was first forged.

This scarlet cord has a double meaning—one to those who hang it from their window and another to those who see it. For Rahab it is an assurance of deliverance and protection. It is a reminder of the promise made to her and her family that they would be delivered from death.

For those who see the cord from the outside, it is much like the blood of the lamb smeared upon the doorposts at the first Passover (Ex. 12:1-14), a tangible sign of the non-negotiable mercy of God. No matter the character of the person within, God has covered those transgressions and held out His mercy. The blood makes the place a refuge, a place of safety to all who enter.

We, like Rahab, have been covered in the blood of the Lamb, Jesus Christ. Though we have no standing to escape the coming judgment, we know that God's mercy is a seal of protection over us. And to those who see that scarlet cord know that in Him, there is infinite mercy, grace, and forgiveness for the sinner.

—Andrew Pearson

February 16

Now Jericho was shut up inside and outside because of the people of Israel. None went out and none came in. And the LORD said to Joshua, "See, I have given Jericho into your hand, with its king and mighty men of valor. And when they make a long blast with the ram's horn, when you hear the sound of the trumpet, then all the people shall shout with a great shout, and the wall of the city will fall down flat, and the people shall go up, everyone straight before him." (Joshua 6:1-5, ESV)

In my high school days, I had developed a reputation for being a bit of a tough guy. I didn't care one bit what other people thought of me. Back then I would describe myself as "confident, not cocky." I drove a big blue Ford pick-up truck, I was a jock, and I swore a lot. I had a pretty hard exterior, and this was completely intentional.

I was just like Jericho; I needed a strong defense because on the inside I was weak, and weak was vulnerable. I built up walls to prevent any kind of infiltration: nothing got in, nothing got out. The fact of the matter was that I really just wanted to have someone infiltrate, but I wanted them to stick around after seeing what was on the inside of the wall. But I didn't think that someone existed. The potential for being completely routed was too great, so the wall remained.

Times have changed. I don't drive a big pick-up anymore, and I am embarrassed by my old mantra, but I still have that old desire in my life to build up that wall. It may *look* a little different, but it's really the same, and I think it's a common tendency.

It's certainly true of our relationship with God. For centuries humanity has developed intricate belief systems to defend ourselves *against* God's invasive grace. We don't believe that it is possible for Him to actually love us as we truly are. All we know is conditionality, and we're often sure God is no different. Religion generally helps us here: we can maintain some notions of responsibility and control in relation to God, and we like that, because that way it's up to us as to how much God is allowed in. If we are "co-laborers with God," we can forget that we are trapped in a game of self-preservation. How can we be free when we are too scared to actually face whom we really are?

Thankfully, God has "given Jericho into your hand." He breaks through your walls and claims you for His own. He takes your sin.

Through the cross He unlocks your self-fashioned prison and calls you into the freedom of His unconditional grace.

—*Sean Norris*

February 17

Then they burned the whole city and everything in it, but they put the silver and gold and the articles of bronze and iron into the treasury of the Lord's house. But Joshua spared Rahab the prostitute, with her family and all who belonged to her, because she hid the men Joshua had sent as spies to Jericho—and she lives among the Israelites to this day. (Joshua 6:15-25, NIV)

Joshua 6 tells the story of the fall of Jericho, one of the most spectacular and disturbing stories in the Old Testament. You know the shtick: big walls, a seven-day parade around the walls, a few trumpet blasts, and the walls come "a tumblin" down." If you were in children's Sunday school, though, this is where story-time would end, because the next few verses are actually pretty disturbing: the walls come down, and the Israelites proceed to destroy every living thing in Jericho—men, women, and children; even the animals are slaughtered and burned. These are the foul words of genocide more than the words of a children's tale.

This entire section of Scripture, often called "the Conquest of Canaan," tells two stories. On a most basic level, it is the story of God giving the land He had promised Abraham. On a more literarily complex level, it is the foreshadowing of the judgment that we read about in the book of Revelation: when John writes Revelation, he uses the imagery of seven trumpet judgments so we'll think back to this book and chapter. In both cases, nobody escapes. The virtuous are burned with the guilty. The beautiful along with the ugly. The old and young, male and female, all have come under God's holy judgment. This is true in the land of Canaan, and this is true in the book of Revelation. And once God's judgment is pronounced, there is no mercy or leniency for anybody.

"But wait!", you quizzically interject, "what about this Rahab person? Doesn't Rahab and her family escape judgment?" And I am happy, of course, to concede this truth. But the fact that Rahab and her family are spared from God's judgment proves difficult for us, doesn't it? It completely turns our notions of justice and punishment upside down.

Rahab is a prostitute. If anybody goes down, we expect her to be among the first to go. We read that her entire household was saved that day, and while we don't know anybody in her household, we can surmise that none of them were particularly important people if they still associated with a prostitute. The people saved in this story are not saved because they are remarkable or saintly. They are saved even though they are unremarkable and sinful. This one family becomes, in turn, part of the people of God. As Hebrews 11 reminds us, it is by faith that Rahab fears God and the invading Israelites, and it is by that faith she is saved.

Fyodor Dostoevsky, the renowned Russian writer, picks up on this theme throughout *Crime and Punishment*. Raskolnikov, the insane murdering protagonist, meets his alcoholic friend Marmeladov at a local bar. After discussing religion over drinks, some of the bar's patrons ask the drunken Marmeladov if he thinks he will get into heaven. In drunken anger and frustration, he rises to the occasion and (ironically) preaches on this very subject. He and Rahab have a lot in common, and Marmeladov's words powerfully echo the grace of God to his (and our) kind:

> "He will say, 'come forth ye drunkards, come forth, ye weak ones, come forth, ye children of shame!' and we shall all come forth, without shame and stand before him. And He will say unto us, 'Ye are swine, and made in the Image of the Beast and with his mark; but come [into my kingdom] ye also!' And the wise ones and those of understanding will say, 'Oh Lord, why dost Thou receive these men?' And He will say, 'this is why I receive them... that not one of them believed himself to be worthy of this.' And He will hold out his hands to us and we shall fall down before him... and we shall weep... and we shall understand all things..."

> —*T. Bryan Jarrell*

February 18

And if you be unwilling to serve the LORD, choose this day whom you will serve, whether the gods your fathers served in the region beyond the River, or the gods of the Amorites in whose land you dwell; but as for me and my house, we will serve the LORD. (Joshua 24:15, RSV)

You ever get the feeling you're being watched? I do. But not in a bad way. I remember having dinner with two friends in New York City a few years ago. We were talking about our Christian friends and what was going on in their lives; some of the guys were behaving like (gasp) *non*-Christians. I was indignant. I couldn't understand how that was possible. My friend patiently reminded me that there's no real difference between the "Christian" and the "non-Christian," meaning that there's not a different standard for the two, and there's certainly not a sudden ability to perform, to do, or to be better once one is converted. The *only* difference is the cross. I thought that was ridiculous. Absurd. I was offended.

I kid you not, within hours I found myself in the exact situation of non-Christian misbehavior I had argued against—I mean *exactly*! And in that moment, I felt God's presence, lovingly observing me. In a flash, I realized that the only reason I hadn't found myself in that sort of conundrum more frequently was God's grace, plain and simple.

"Choose this day whom you will serve." Left to my own devices, I will *never* choose God, always me. Thank God that He chose me through the cross. Because of that, and only that, once in a blue moon, the "right" thing curiously happens in my life. Amazing.

—*Nate Michaux*

February 19

> But Joshua said to the people, "You are not able to serve the LORD, for he is a holy God. He is a jealous God; he will not forgive your transgressions or your sins." (Joshua 24:19, ESV)

Imagine you are at a wedding. Sitting comfortably in the pew, the couple and the minister finally get to the vows. The groom turns to his bride and says, "I will love you and cherish you whenever it is convenient for me." There is a pause and the bride smiles and, wiping a tear from her eye, says, "And I will be faithful to you as long as I feel you deserve it, and I will care for and comfort you only when I am in a good mood."

Now there's a realistic profession! Imagine that kind of honesty in any public ceremony. This is what happens at the end of the book of Joshua during the covenant renewal ceremony. Joshua asks the people of Israel to choose whether they will serve false gods and idols or if they will serve the Lord and his Law. The answer seems obvious, and it is for the Israelites, too. They tell Joshua that they "will serve the Lord, for he is our God," and Joshua then goes off script: "You are not able to serve the Lord" (24:18-19).

Joshua understands, correctly, that people are not *able* to do what they promise. Despite all the best intentions and desires, we will fail to live up to the standards we publicly or privately affirm and reaffirm. A brief look at the behavior of the Hebrews in the book of Judges proves that Joshua was completely right.

Whether it is with God, your spouse, or your family, you—and everyone else—probably fail to consistently love and cherish people as you should. Rather than denying that we are unfaithful and inconsistent, we have another option: the good news is that when we are honest before God regarding our faithlessness, our merciful Savior forgives and restores us. We no longer need to make promises we cannot keep. And we no longer need to live under half-truths and dishonestly earnest desires. We can live instead in the rest of our faithful Lord.

—Alex Large

February 20

> *The Israelites did evil in the eyes of the Lord; they forgot the Lord their God... But when they cried out to the Lord, he raised up for them a deliverer... So the land had peace for forty years...*
> *Again the Israelites did evil in the eyes of the Lord, and... again the Israelites cried out to the Lord, and he gave them a deliverer... and the land had peace for eighty years...*
> *Again the Israelites did evil in the eyes of the Lord. So the Lord sold them into the hands of Jabin... They cried to the Lord for help... Then the land had peace for forty years.*
> *(Judges 3:7-5:31, NIV)*

There is an unmistakable pattern present in these passages. The Israelites are quick to lose their trust in God. They abandon Him over and over again, only to then return in each instance (and in wake of the subsequent hardship that followed) with their spiritual tails between their legs. And He receives them each time without hesitation.

It's a three-thousand-year-old problem, not unique to the Ancient Near East. We do it, too. We forget about God until times get tough. Then we pray again, seeking His guidance and clinging anew to the unfailing mercy of our loving heavenly Father. The hymn "Come Thou Fount" describes this predicament famously: "Prone to wander, Lord, I feel it, prone to leave the God I love." Have you ever forgotten about God ("again")?

Just as there was good news for the Israelites, there is good news for us. "If we are faithless, he remains faithful" (2 Tim 2:13). God desires to help the sinner, not to punish.

A powerful example of this dynamic comes from the 1980 film *My Bodyguard*. The story focuses on a high school student named Linderman. Linderman is a depressed teenage boy who exudes a reclusive, don't-mess-with-me temperament. There are rumors that he once "killed a kid" floating about the hallways of the school. The truth is that he witnessed the death of his younger brother and has come to blame himself for the incident. The film makes clear that Linderman is in full-scale shut-down mode, and he's headed for trouble.

But one day, a new student named Carl (who himself is a bit of an outcast) befriends the reclusive Linderman. Carl invites him over to his house to meet his family, including Carl's grandmother, the inimitable Ruth Gordon, with a warning: "My grandmother is a little crazy."

When they enter the dining room, Ruth Gordon immediately gravitates toward the new guest. She insists on showing the boys a parlor trick, imposing upon Linderman to allow her to read his palm. She takes his open hand in hers, and after a minute points to a pronounced scar on the boy's wrist: "What's this?" she asks. "It's nothing," he responds, pulling his sleeve down and retracting his hand in a closed fist.

But Ruth Gordon persists. She grabs his fist back and opens his hand, saying, *"I'm not through with you yet, kid. Give me your hand; you're among friends."* He relents. Then she looks down at his hand, and looks back at him, making eye contact. "Let's see... I see a long life... and good things... lots of good things." The boy's whole countenance suddenly does a 180, and it is the beginning of a hugely redemptive plot line.

And so it is with the grace of God, even when the "again" side of life creeps back in. "Come unto me, all ye that travail and are heavy-laden, and I will refresh you" (Matt 11:28). Or to quote Ruth Gordon: "I'm not through with you yet, kid."

—John Zahl

February 21

"Please, Lord, how can I save Israel? Behold, my clan is the weakest in Manasseh, and I am the least in my father's house." (Judges 6:15-16, ESV)

"Little ones to Him belong, they are weak but He is strong." Many have sung this line from the children's song "Jesus Loves Me," and perhaps a few have even believed it. And yet, given the choice, who would ever choose his or her own weakness over strength? That is not the way of the world, nor is it the way of the self-oriented heart. Weakness is embarrassing; weakness is to be hidden away.

When faced with a challenge, it makes so much more sense to marshal your resources, summon your strength, and put your best foot forward. In a world where we are taught to play to our strengths, who would choose the weak to do the job of the strong?

God would, apparently. After the strong and oppressive Midianites have "overpowered Israel" for seven years, the Lord is on the move to save His people. As His instrument, He chooses Gideon, whose clan is the "weakest in Manasseh." And if that isn't bad enough, the appointed deliverer is the "least in [his] father's house." God deliberately chooses the least of the least.

There is only one reason to trust in this way of madness, this counter-intuitive preference for weakness over strength. And this is the reason God gives the bewildered Gideon: "I will be with you." God does not offer a detailed explanation of His rationale, nor does He outline a plan for how He intends to accomplish the task at hand.

Instead, God simply offers Himself: "I will be with you." And it is enough. God is actually much, much more than enough, for He fills up our weakness with His strength. "His power is made perfect in our weakness" (2 Cor 12:9).

"I will be with you." Simply put, it is our weakness that allows us to be with God. It is weakness that allows the little ones to belong to God. Little ones who know that though it is not the way of the world, God chooses what is foolish to shame the wise. And little ones like Gideon, whom the angel renames to be a "mighty man of valor."

—Paul Walker

86

February 22

The Lord said to Gideon, "You have too many men for me to deliver Midian into their hands. In order that Israel may not boast against me that her own strength has saved her, announce now to the people, 'Anyone who trembles with fear may turn back and leave Mount Gilead.'" (Judges 7:2-3, NIV)

In this passage we see God preparing Gideon and the Israelites for battle in the oddest way. The Lord tells Gideon that his army is too large, and that he will need to get rid of some of the men if they are going to be victorious. He then proceeds to whittle Gideon's army down from 32,000 troops to a meager band of 300.

Why would anyone employ such a terrible strategy? God answers, "In order that Israel may not boast against me that her own strength has saved her..." We find this message repeated over and over again in the Bible, that our strength is not very strong, and that at our most impressive, we are still not very impressive. But here in Judges the point is taken further. The problem lies not just in a miscalculation about the reliability of our own strength, but also it lies in the fact that assuming such a posture blocks out our need for God's help.

From God's perspective, the prospect of having too much strength is a far more serious problem than not having enough of it. In fact, being weak is a crucial ingredient in true spirituality; it is actually one of life's most important *virtues*. As it is said in the New Testament, "The weakness of God is stronger than man's strength" (1 Cor 1:25).

Do you have any pressing weaknesses? We all do. Where are you stuck? Where do you need help? Today, you might try praying to God by reaching up from the point of impasse, your place of helplessness. It will not take many words.

—John Zahl

February 23

...But he did not tell his father or his mother what he had done. (Judges 14:5-6, ESV)

I am sure you've heard it before. If you didn't hear it in a Sunday school class, then maybe you did on the lips of a preacher: "Be a *Samson* for God! Be a strong man for the Lord!" In my own case, this is the only lesson about Samson I remember from childhood. I couldn't put the pieces together then, and I still cannot now. I always wondered if I'm supposed to be like Samson, does that mean I'm supposed to screw up? Because it sure seems to me that he makes a mess of his life. No one addressed that problem, so I left Samson's story on the back shelf.

Several years ago, as I was reflecting on this passage to prepare a sermon, it came to me anew: Samson demands that his father and mother give him what he wants, namely, a Philistine woman, even when it is perfectly clear that as a Nazarite he is not to be with a pagan, Gentile woman (14:1-3). Then, knowing full well that he shouldn't touch dead things, Samson does it anyway. He scoops some honey out of a lion's carcass and takes some to his parents. Hmmm... acting with rebellious motives, out of selfish pride... it sounds, well, *uncomfortably* familiar! In truth, I *am* Samson! I don't need to try and be like him because I already am compelled and motivated by my own self-centered persuasions.

Whenever I read this passage, it strikes me as a word of judgment. At the core of who I am as a human being, I am a sinner. I will do anything in order to get my way and make myself feel good. This passage leads me to first acknowledge my position among those who have made and continue to make a mess of their lives. And then it makes me want to say, "Thank you, Lord, for Samson, because he not only shows me to myself, but he also shows me the depth of my need for the cross and the resurrection." That depth just makes the grace of God all the more amazing.

—*Kyle Tomlin*

February 24

> ..."*Entreat me not to leave thee, or to return from following after thee: for whither thou goest, I will go, and where thou lodgest, I will lodge; thy people shall be my people, and thy God, my God.*" (Ruth 1:15-18, KJV)

I have a memory. I don't recall exactly where or when it happened. I simply remember my father reciting these words from the Book of Ruth. The memory is firm, because there were tears in my father's eyes, as he was deeply moved by Ruth's words to her mother-in-law, Naomi: "for whither thou goest, I will go..."

These enduring words of love and commitment that so touched my father are uttered by an outcast. All of the power and passion of Ruth's love for Naomi are set in the context of Ruth being an outcast in a hostile, alien land—and of her choosing to move into that land, in order to be with Naomi.

What is your understanding of being an outcast? There are refugees in war torn lands. There are homeless folk on the streets of our prosperous nation—a recent survey noted that 150,000 Vietnam veterans are homeless in America, thirty-five years after that war. There are patients in hospitals and nursing homes who know that even with all the love in the world, you feel different and set apart when you're sick, when you've got cancer, when you use a walker, when you've contracted Alzheimer's.

Some of us have tasted outcast experience when we've been out of work, when our marriages have failed, or when our bodies haven't measured up to standards set by Jane Fonda workouts and Lance Armstrong posters. And even for those of us who show no outward hint of being an outcast—even for those of us with a secure home and a loving spouse and a good job—even then, there comes that 3 A.M. moment when the dreams are still unfulfilled and the pressure to "make it" mounts—that secret, solitary moment when being an outcast defines us all.

I asked a friend about when he feels like an outcast, and he said, "The question is, when *don't* I?"

We are children of Ruth. We are heirs of this woman for all seasons—and this is good news. Because Ruth marries a terrific fellow named Boaz. They have a son named Obed. Obed has a son named Jesse. And Jesse has a son named David—King David, whom God calls, "A man after my own heart." (Acts 13:22)

But that's not all. David also has a son, and his son has a son, and on and on, until generations later, in the same little town of Bethlehem where Ruth had married Boaz, another child in the house and lineage of David is born—a child whose ancestor is an outcast.

It's the heart of the Gospel—that God took on flesh and chose to be an outcast, chose to take on His shoulders all the pain and the consequences of our 3 A.M. moments, so that we may hear Him say to us, "Welcome home."

—*Jim Munroe*

February 25

But Naomi said, "Turn back, my daughters; why will you go with me? Have I yet sons in my womb that they may become your husbands? Turn back, my daughters; go your way, for I am too old to have a husband. If I should say I have hope, even if I should have a husband this night and should bear sons, would you therefore wait till they were grown? Would you therefore refrain from marrying? No, my daughters, for it is exceedingly bitter to me for your sake that the hand of the LORD has gone out against me." Then they lifted up their voices and wept again. And Orpah kissed her mother-in-law, but Ruth clung to her. (Ruth 3:11-14, ESV)

In 1923, Jimmy Cox wrote the timeless "Nobody Knows You When You're Down and Out." It has been covered now for almost a century, by the likes of artists from Count Basie to Otis Redding to Derek and the Dominoes. Quite good staying power, needless to say, and this is unsurprising, given the universal message it expressed. We have all been here:

> 'Cause no, no, nobody knows you
> When you're down and out
> In your pocket, not one penny,
> And as for friends, you don't have any.

Human existence is driven by advantage. "Associate yourself with those who will help you advance." "Make allies of the strong and you will be strong." But the singer of the Jimmy Cox song is not strong. He isn't of any use to anyone. He used to be, but he isn't anymore: any associations now offer no advantage.

It is much the same with Naomi—she's certainly down and out. Widowed with dead sons, left alone with her daughters-in-law: it is far more than loneliness that awaits these Naomi and what's left of her family. Naomi is no longer of any use to her two daughters-in-law. She has no husband to provide for them and no sons to protect them. If you wanted to make allies with the strong, you would stay far away from Naomi.

A very interesting and unexpected thing takes place, though. While Orpah leaves her mother-in-law to pursue better prospects (and, honestly, who can blame her?), Ruth clings to her. In the original language it is exactly the same word used to describe a husband clinging to his wife in Genesis 2: "and they will be one flesh." Ruth becomes as one with Naomi as she suffers. In her love for her mother-in-law, Ruth makes Naomi's fate her own.

This would just be a nice and inspiring story if it were self-contained, but it is not. If you go to the first chapter of Matthew, you will see the only mention of Ruth in the New Testament. It is in the genealogy of our Lord, Jesus Christ. The woman who forsakes her own prerogatives in order to fasten herself to a tragic widow gives us a glimpse into who Jesus is. It helps us understand that in his life as "a man of sorrows" and his death on a cross, he fastens himself to us in our suffering so that we also share in the hope of his resurrection.

—David Browder

February 26

> *But Hannah answered, "No, my lord, I am a woman troubled in spirit. I have drunk neither wine nor strong drink, but I have been pouring out my soul before the Lord. Do not regard your servant as a worthless woman, for all along I have been speaking out of my great anxiety and vexation." Then Eli answered, "Go in peace, and the God of Israel grant your petition that you have made to him." And she said, "Let your servant find favor in your eyes." Then the woman went her way and ate, and her face was no longer sad. (1 Samuel 1:15-18, ESV)*

We don't like feeling helpless, but we *really* don't like feeling helpless while trying to make something good happen. This happens a lot: it could be finding the right job, the right spouse, the time to get it all accomplished. It could also be interior, like wanting to get over your self-esteem problems, like wanting to stop sounding so depressed all the time. We feel so uncomfortable with the helplessness, mostly because we think there might be some karmic payoff for our good intentions. In Hannah's case, she just wants to have a child.

To make matters worse for us, we humans aren't too good at helping each other out, either. It's not that we necessarily want to ostracize other sufferers; it's more that we, sometimes unwittingly, do whatever we can to minimize the reminders of our own suffering. We can make fun of it, offer a "fix it," suggest steps to self-improvement—anything but sit helplessly together. Ultimately, perhaps it is a faithless fear that if we can't control the circumstances, then there is no help anywhere. It is a fear that God can't or won't act. In the yawning gap between where we are and where we want to be, we often do not think that God could potentially be able to work—and even work *especially*—through that place of helplessness.

Usually we hide these feelings because they seem unseemly, needy, or weak. Like Hannah, we can repress these feelings for a long, long time, but they always seem to find their way out.

Like many of us, Hannah has been hiding these feelings until they finally find their release at the altar, and it seems that her comfort does not come until this admission that she is anxious and vexed. It is as if God's presence persistently provokes her to the point of honesty, and at least to me, this seems to be how we always come to Him. He always moves first.

Eli mentions the "God of Israel" as if to say this is the God of history. God has always and will always be this way; He knows each one of our particular places of hidden woe and meets us there with the kind of forgiveness that Jesus died to give. Notice how Hannah leaves in peace, "her face no longer sad," her appetite returned. Moments in our life like this one remind us of our helpless state, and isn't it encouraging to know that God—throughout history—meets us there? Even if, in the face of helplessness, this is the only truth we have to go on, it is all the truth we need.

—*Kate Norris*

February 27

The Lord kills and makes alive; he brings down to the grave and raises up. (1 Samuel 2:6, ESV)

The problem of pain, of suffering and death, is perhaps the greatest and most enduring challenge to the Christian idea of a loving, gracious God. Yet over and over again, the Bible declares that God is present—and actually *active*—in suffering and death, from the plagues poured out on the Egyptians, to the many exiles of Israel, to the cross of Christ, and beyond.

As we encounter suffering in our own lives, perhaps the best question to ask is not "How could God let this happen?", but "How could God not?" That is to say, would we rather believe in a God who is present and active in our sufferings, or absent and powerless? Furthermore, if God *is* absent in our sufferings, where exactly is He? What portion of our life could we honestly say is without difficulty? If we excuse or exclude God from our pain, we practically cut him out of our lives altogether.

Killing is part of God's work, but it is not the end, for on the other side of every death, every suffering, both great and small, is resurrection. "The Lord kills and makes alive; he brings down to the grave and raises up." Indeed, all of life could be understood as a series of deaths and resurrections culminating in the final, physical death and resurrection, when God will "wipe away every tear from their eyes, and death shall be no more" (Rev 21:4).

The idea that God "kills" and "brings down," which at first strikes us as quite troubling, actually ends up being a great comfort, affirmation that "in all things God is working for the good of those who love him" (Rom 8:28). God's killing work is always the prologue to His saving redemption.

—*R-J Heijmen*

February 28

> But the people refused to listen to the voice of Samuel; and they said, "No! but we will have a king over us, that we also may be like all the nations, and that our king may govern us and go out before us and fight our battles." And when Samuel had heard all the words of the people, he repeated them in the ears of the LORD. And the LORD said to Samuel, "Hearken to their voice, and make them a king." Samuel then said to the men of Israel, "Go every man to his city." (1 Samuel 8:19-22, NRSV)

"There's a time and place for everything," Chef on *South Park* once explained, "and it's called 'College.'" A time that seems to sanction rebellion, college can be one of the most challenging moments in the relationship of parents and their children. The child is far away, out of sight, and (from the background ruckus on the other end of the phone) completely out of control. However, one of the most powerful forms of grace is when a parent releases that control and allows their son or daughter to make a mistake—or two or three—in unconditional love.

When we talk about my college years now, my father tells me that he has no idea what he was doing or how he managed to survive that time himself. The bottom fell out when I arrived home for winter break sophomore year: I had done miserably in my classes; I was worn out and thoroughly depressed. I told my father that I had had enough of college and planned to drop out.

My father was hurt, and also concerned about the education I was giving up. Of course, he wanted to fix everything, but instead he just asked me, "Are you sure?" When I said yes, he let the matter drop. We talked about other things over winter break—my part-time job, politics, the Patriots—anything except dropping out. However, a few days before the semester was to begin, I strangely felt capable of returning. I didn't know why.

It took me years to understand that moment: that the space allowed for mistakes—and love despite them—is utterly and beautifully superhuman. This space is a total game-changer when it touches you. In the passage above, God acquiesces to the Israelites' request for a king, so that they can "go to college" with the other nations. He lets them make the mistake, even though it not only means rejecting Him, but also *more* mistakes. However, what we see is that God's love never abandons us, even when we abandon Him. His love is always there: it is always bigger than the mistakes we make, and nothing—not even our own foolish desires and decisions—can ever separate us from it.

—*Leonard Finn*

February 29

And Samuel said to the people, "Do not be afraid; you have done all this evil. Yet do not turn aside from following the LORD, but serve the LORD with all your heart. And do not turn aside after empty things that cannot profit or deliver, for they are empty. For the Lord will not forsake his people, for his great name's sake, because it has pleased the

Lord to make you a people for himself. (1 Samuel 12:20-24, ESV)

"You have done all this evil..." These are the dread words of judgment, of being found out. We might be good at hiding our sins from others, but we have no way of hiding them from God. We all stand before objective goodness, even the most pious of us, and know that, though we claim to be followers of God, we could never justify ourselves on account of our own goodness.

Yet these words of judgment to God's people come joined with words of love: "Do not be afraid... for the Lord will not forsake his people... because it has pleased the Lord to make you a people for himself." This is perfect love, the kind that drives out fear (1 John 4:18).

Though you have everything to fear as you stand before God's judgment, you also have *nothing* to fear—because there is no fear in love. God's love compels Him to forget judgment in order to make you His own. As you stand before the righteous God, He will see every part of you, and in spite of it all, He will not forsake you. He sees you through perfect *Love*—Jesus Christ.

—Bonnie Poon Zahl

March 1

> *Goliath stood and shouted, "Why do you come out and line up for battle? Choose a man and have him come down to me. If he is able to fight and kill me, we will become your subjects; but if I overcome and kill him, you will become our subjects and serve us." (1 Samuel 17:8-9, NIV)*

Goliath proposes a one-on-one, winner-take-all battle between himself and anyone of Israel's choosing. No one steps forward initially, and when David finally accepts the challenge from Goliath, he is met with mocking from his brothers. At David's defeat of Goliath, all of Israel—his brothers included—charge up in victory.

In the same way, Christ's death at Calvary brings victory to all, even the mockers. Our victory does not consist of running up the mountain after the Philistines, but rather a righteousness that has been bestowed upon us that we did not earn. The message of the Gospel is that victory has been won. The battle was one-on-one, winner-take-all, and the outcome has been decided. It is with this confidence that St. Paul writes, "Death has been swallowed up in victory. The sting of death is sin and the power of sin is the law. But thanks be to God! He gives us the victory through our Lord Christ Jesus" (1 Cor 15:54, 56).

—*Drake Richey*

March 2

And Mephibosheth lived in Jerusalem, because he always ate at the king's table, and he was crippled in both feet. (2 Samuel 9:13, NIV)

Try saying "Mephibosheth" five times in row—it's a mouthful! But it's also a name that should conjure up only the most positive associations. To set the scene: After David becomes king of Israel (following Saul's defeat and suicide), his first order of business is to find any surviving relations of his late, beloved friend Jonathan, Saul's son, so that he might show them kindness.

David soon finds out that Jonathan's sole living heir, Mephibosheth, is "crippled in both feet" and not exactly regal material. Mephibosheth seems to have internalized his disabilities, referring to himself in front of David as "a dead dog" (9:8). Yet without any hesitation, David restores to him all of his family land and issues the command that Mephibosheth is to dine at the king's table at every meal, henceforth.

This is a touching example of grace in the Old Testament. An unworthy person receives love and favor on account of something that someone else has done. Even more, there is a deep security to the new situation—Mephibosheth will always eat at David's table, like one of his sons. What is the result of this radical decree? We are told that Mephibosheth himself has a son. That is, hope springs where there was once desperation and life where there once was death. (Of course, the feet remain crippled...)

Sometimes we get to witness grace like this, and occasionally we even get to experience it. Even though acts of grace astound us, it is only a shadow of the real thing: the grace given by God on account of the death of Jesus.

Have you ever felt like a dead dog? Or perhaps there is something in your life that feels (or looks) like a dead dog? That's where the voice of the King is to be heard, the voice of unconditional love that makes dead things alive and brings hope to the hopeless. The voice that says, "Because of My beloved son, you will always eat at my table."

—*David Zahl*

March 3

Nathan said to David, "You are the man!" (2 Samuel 12:7, NIV)

Life is a game of denial. In fact, I would argue that most of the things we fill our day with are, or at least can be, tools for denial. Work, play, shopping, television, relationships, hobbies, philosophies—*anything* can be used to manipulate the reality of things gone wrong. It would not be too far to say that Christianity itself has often been used as a tool of reality-rejection.

People often have a sober view of themselves around the time of their conversion. They are confronted with the reality of their need for help, and like Saul on the road to Damascus, they fall off their horse and cry out for mercy from the Lord. This sobriety, however, proves fleeting. Old habits die hard, and we return to striving against reality faster than you can say *pickle*. Almost as soon as we become Christians, we start the business of working Jesus out of a job.

Consider David. We often look at him as an example of humility and dependence upon God. He suffered greatly while being persecuted under King Saul, and he was keenly aware of his need for God's grace. But when Nathan comes to him, he is now the king of Israel, the chosen one of God, the "man after God's own heart." Nathan comes to him and tells him a story of betrayal, deceit, and murder and asks David to judge the fate of the perpetrator in the tale. An amazing thing happens: David is so disconnected from himself that he promptly and indignantly dispenses a harsh judgment upon the guy in Nathan's story. Then the anvil falls. David has taken the bait, as it were, and Nathan delivers the crushing reality to which David is blind: "*You* are the man!"

There is no wiggle room here. There is no compromise due to his kingship. There is simply the pointing of the finger; the definitive, indisputable reality that David is the guilty man. This "man after God's own heart" is the adulterer, murderer, betrayer, liar, and denier. (Aside:

97

Isn't it interesting that often, like David, the qualities you react to most harshly in someone else are also true of you?)

We are just like David. We are okay with the fact that we are the guilty ones until we are the chosen ones, but no one wants to face the fact that we *continue* to be the guilty ones afterward. In becoming Christians we often think our deceit and pride have (or should have) been arrested. But just like David, our denial cannot last. No matter how hard we resist it, we will always be brought face-to-face with the mirror. God's Law, which demands absolute perfection, will always catch up to us. After all, it is written on our hearts that Nathan's words are true.

—*Sean Norris*

March 4

> But [Elijah] went a day's journey into the wilderness and came and sat down under a broom tree. And he asked that he might die, saying, "It is enough; now, O LORD, take away my life, for I am no better than my fathers." And he lay down and slept under a broom tree. And behold, an angel touched him and said to him, "Arise and eat." And he looked, and behold, there was at his head a cake baked on hot stones and a jar of water. And he ate and drank and lay down again. And the angel of the LORD came again a second time and touched him and said, "Arise and eat, for the journey is too great for you." (1 Kings 19:4-7, ESV)

The grace of God is not always grand. Elijah here is trying very hard to see the big picture, to understand what is happening to him in epic scope. He wants to die; he is overcome by guilt and the legacy of his past; he wants to believe this is the end of his great and noble prophetic mission. He is doing his very best to have a *Thelma & Louise* moment.

God has compassion on Elijah anyways, despite the melodrama: "The journey is too great for you." But instead of reminding him of his mighty task, or of the limitlessness of divine mercy, or of the importance of life and the beauty of Creation, God just gives him cake. And lets him sleep. And then gives him cake again.

God knows what we need far better than we do, and often our true needs are embarrassingly mundane. It is humiliating to hear that sometimes, when we think we are wrestling with angels, we are mainly just tired and hungry, or that the sensation of drowning in oceans of guilt is mostly just a hangover. The worst attack of anxiety we can experience is, in the end, mainly the product of a couple of temporary chemical reactions in the chest and stomach.

At the end of John's Gospel, Jesus meets with Simon Peter, absolves him of guilt for his three denials, sets his life task ahead of him, and predicts his painful death. But before any of this, he says, "Come and have breakfast" (John 21:12).

—Simeon Zahl

March 5

> *He said, "Go out and stand on the mountain before the Lord, for the Lord is about to pass by." Now there was a great wind, so strong that it was splitting mountains and breaking rocks in pieces before the Lord, but the Lord was not in the wind; and after the wind an earthquake, but the Lord was not in the earthquake; and after the earthquake a fire, but the Lord was not in the fire; and after the fire a sound of sheer silence. When Elijah heard it, he wrapped his face in his mantle and went out and stood at the entrance of the cave. (1 Kings 19:11-13, NRSV)*

Elijah is frustrated because his faithfulness has not produced the result he had been expecting. After serving as the main character in one of the most exciting spectacles of the Old Testament, Elijah becomes so miserable that he prays that God would take his life. How does this happen?

Elijah has boldly challenged Israel's unbelief by proposing a duel, a test of powers between the false gods they are worshiping and the true God of Israel. God answers this prayer, triumphantly bringing down fire from heaven on Elijah's sacrifice before all of Israel, proving that He alone is God.

Rather than admitting Elijah's success and God's supremacy, Jezebel, the queen of Israel, threatens to kill Elijah. After a great victory, Elijah is running for his life again, now so sick and tired of it all that he sits under a tree and just prays to die. God answers his prayer by feeding him. Frustrated, Elijah presses on and finally finds a cave to crawl into. When God asks him what he's doing there, Elijah vents his disappointment, saying that despite his zeal, despite his faithfulness to the Lord, the Israelites have "forsaken your covenant, thrown down your altars, and killed your prophets with the sword" (19:14). Elijah had prayed, and *fire* had come down from heaven—what's it going to take to change people's hearts?

God responds by dismantling Elijah's expectations. He tells Elijah to stand because he's about to pass by. The spectacle starts big and gets bigger. A terrible wind passes, an earthquake rumbles and fire comes down from heaven, but God is in none of these. Finally, "a sound of sheer silence" causes Elijah to cover his face with his mantle.

This reminds us, as God says, that it is "not by might, nor by power, but by my spirit," that it is always God's faithfulness that turns hearts to Him, in the quietness of God's time. And God's time often works *against* our expectations. Signs and wonders, faithfulness, miracles, community, social justice, discipleship are all good things, but they are not the mark of Christianity. The mark of Christianity is the faithful love of God, the good news that Jesus died in our place and, by his Spirit, helps us believe.

—*Dusty Brown*

March 6

So [Naaman] went down and dipped himself seven times in the Jordan, according to the word of the man of God, and his flesh was restored like the flesh of a little child, and he was clean. (2 Kings 5:14, ESV)

Again and again in the Bible, we are told of the relationship between being restored and becoming like a child. To be "clean" is to be like a little child. Forgiveness relieves us from the burden of world-weariness. So-called "experience" is too often a euphemism for resignation to "the ways of the world." To be like a child is not to put your head in the sand or to be naïve about the world. It is rather to remember, once more, that with God all things are possible (Matt 19:26). At home, at work, or with family, it is freedom to love again instead of just manipulating those we once loved.

To be like a little child is also to be relieved of the illusion of self-sufficiency and control. One of the great abiding images of our relationship to God is the helplessness of the crying, struggling newborn, full of need and utterly powerless to do anything about it. Babies are some of the most purely self-absorbed creatures on the planet, but at least they have no illusion of autonomy. To be an adult, on the other hand, is to be just as self-absorbed and powerless as a baby, and then to lie to yourself about the fact.

Lord, forgive us that we may be like little children once again.

—Simeon Zahl

March 7

And when they came to the threshing floor of Chidon, Uzzah put out his hand to take hold of the ark, for the oxen stumbled. And the anger of the LORD was kindled against Uzzah, and he struck him down because he put out his hand to the ark, and he died there before God. And David was angry because the LORD had broken out against Uzzah. And that place is called Perez-uzza to this day. And David was afraid of God that day, and he said, "How can I bring the ark of God home to me?" (1 Chronicles 13:9-12, ESV)

I remember hearing this passage when I was a child and thinking it was the most unfair in the Bible. Why on earth would God do such a thing to someone, especially someone trying to help? Poor Uzzah! Shouldn't he be rewarded for trying to prevent the Ark of the Covenant from falling to the ground? Doesn't God, shouldn't God appreciate good intentions?

It seems Scripture is clear here that humans cannot control God's terms for how we relate to Him—even when it seems like He needs our intervention. This not only includes salvation, but also the way we live our lives. In other words, our lives before God are not established by the plans we make, but by the plans that God has made.

In the Old Testament, God's Law requires people to carry the Ark of the Covenant with wooden poles attached through rings (Ex 25). In this passage, though, the Ark is not carried by people, but pulled by oxen on a cart. Still, we think, *Big deal, why smite a man because of that?*

What was his offense? Though King David is the one calling the shots, Uzzah does not revere God's holiness. What would have happened had Uzzah allowed the Ark to fall into the dirt, truthfully is... nothing. It was worse for an unclean human hand to touch the Ark, the symbol of

God's holiness, than for dirt to touch the Ark. *How archaic*, you might think—*people, more unclean than dirt?*

Dirt never determines right from wrong on its own terms. This passage is a stinging reminder that even in the face of God's blessing—for David wins the day and brings the Ark into the new capital—we are still sinners before a holy God. We cannot help God out. We are unfit to handle His business.

This is also a warning against thinking that our own efforts, even with the best intentions, are righteous to God. God's holiness quickly strips us of that pretension; our best is simply not enough. We need something better than our best: we need God's mercy. What Uzzah needs, and what you and I need, is not our best intentions under God's Law, but God's grace in our failings.

—Ben Phillips

March 8

> *"O our God, will you not execute judgment on them? For we are powerless against this great horde that is coming against us. We do not know what to do, but our eyes are on You." (2 Chronicles 20:12, ESV)*

To admit powerlessness is to invoke the power of the Holy Spirit. It is "to start a train of events/ Beyond your control" (T.S. Eliot, *The Cocktail Party*). It is the deepest mystery in the Christian arsenal. Sometimes it comes upon you like a fit—a jarring, sudden, forcefully attractive revelation of the truth. It can seem fleeting, like a trick of the light, but when the Spirit is unleashed, the Almighty Himself is involved.

In this passage, the whole of Judah has fallen prey to a fit of powerlessness. "Our eyes are on you." The consequence is their salvation—and the decimation of the opposing army: "they looked toward the horde, and behold, there were dead bodies lying on the ground; none had escaped" (20:24).

Sometimes, of course, the revelation is that the "great horde coming against us" is none other than God Himself. The thing we are trying to avoid turns out to be our own salvation rising to meet us. For these reasons, prayers of this sort may seem dangerous. Once we let the genie out of the bottle, we are committed to the help of the Spirit summoned, the same One who was incarnated because God so loved the world—who understood better than any the power of powerlessness.

—Simeon Zahl

March 9

"...Behold, we are before you in our guilt, for none can stand before you because of this." (Ezra 9:15, ESV)

Martin Luther wrote a hymn that captures the essence of the human situation before God:

> From the depths of woe I raise to Thee the voice of lamentation.
> Lord, turn a gracious ear to me and hear my supplication.
> If Thou iniquities dost mark, our secret sins and misdeeds dark,
> O who shall stand before Thee, O who shall stand before Thee?

He is referring to Psalm 130, but he could have been commenting on the Israelites who, during the time of the prophet Ezra, have "forsaken God's commandments."

Many people are able to camouflage their more obvious sins beneath a veneer of manners or propriety or religiosity. Trusting in your own basic goodness—at least in comparison to others—allows you to think that all is right with God. It allows you to think of yourself as an upright citizen.

But enter your "secret sins and misdeeds dark" into the equation and everyone is on equal footing. Actually, according to the Law of God, everyone has lost his or her footing completely. Given the subliminal lives we lead, we are forced to conclude with Ezra: "for none can stand before you because of this." The "because of this" can be your fill-in-the-blank: all that you have done or left undone, in the light of day or the dark of night.

The good news about our common bad news is that it blows out the knees of our self-righteousness. I love the story of the two guys who spend a wild Saturday night on the town, getting into all kinds of obvious and embarrassing trouble. They get arrested for their rowdy and lawless behavior and end up in jail. Fortunately a kind friend bails them out early on Sunday morning.

Stumbling home, they pass an old Episcopal church and decide to go to the somber early service. They slip in the door and fall into the back pew, arousing the sneering condescension of the prim and well-dressed congregation. The two men are late, but they arrive just in time for the confession of sin. As the congregation says, "Almighty God... we acknowledge and bewail our manifold sins and wickedness," one guy looks at the other and says, "Wow! They are just like us!"

When you are on your knees, it's hard to look down on anyone else, isn't it? From the depth of woe there is only one place for everyone together to look—to Jesus Christ, who stands before God for our sake.

—Paul Walker

March 10

> *Then I sent to him, saying, "No such things as you say have been done, for you are inventing them out of your own mind." For they all wanted to frighten us, thinking, "Their hands will drop from the work, and it will not be done." But now, O God, strengthen my hands. (Nehemiah 6:8-9, ESV)*

The mind is a master illusionist. It is possible to spend our whole lives shadowboxing with unrealities we have "invented out of our own minds." Nothing seems more real than the rejection we perceive in an oddly raised eyebrow, an inopportune yawn, the scowl of a stranger. The mind can spin an epic tale of misunderstanding and betrayal out of the smallest and most meaningless experience. In that sense it is immensely creative. But it is a dull sort of creativity, because it so often manufactures the same boring story of our fears, our aspirations, and our anxieties. There is no reality here. "No such things as you say have been done." Our heart races—"Did she look at me? Or is she avoiding me?"—but only because our minds have fooled our bodies into thinking something real is happening.

True work of our hands is an antidote to such projection. There is freedom in performing the task that has been given each day. The picture of Nehemiah building a very un-illusory wall is a picture of freedom. It is a freedom that can only be granted from without, but it is a true freedom.

Lord, strengthen our hands, and save us from our unrealities.

—Simeon Zahl

March 11

Then Nehemiah said to the people, "Go, eat of the fat, drink of the sweet, and send portions to him who has nothing prepared; for this day is holy to our Lord. Do not be grieved, for the joy of the LORD is your strength."
(Nehemiah 8:10, NASB)

Human experience involves pain. There is no way around this difficult fact. Painful memories of poor decisions made and noble hopes unrealized can gnaw away at us like termites to wood. I have found little consolation, however, in merely wallowing in my crises. If I insist upon trying to satisfy myself by drinking exclusively from the trough of my own predicament, I taste nothing but the bitter tones of wormwood. The good news is that God is simultaneously speaking two words to you and me—Law and Gospel—and one is louder than the other. It is the louder word of the Gospel, His love in the presence of my grief, which never fails to pull me from the trough again.

The people in Nehemiah's day have just returned to Jerusalem from their captivity in Babylon. What they come back to is a pale remnant of its former glory: all that remains is a crumbling city wall, with no temple to speak of.

The Israelites are to blame for the calamity: they were the ones who had turned on God, and as a result God sent them into captivity for 70 years. It seems to me that God is good to serve these pints of sorrow, but that this serving is never meant to be the last call. He is too wise a bartender to withhold the sweet cordial.

The narrator tells us that Nehemiah has gathered the people together after the wall had been built and a new, smaller temple was standing once again. Just then, the Levites begin to read the Law to the people, and the Israelites fall apart. The entire community begins to weep tears of contrition, the memories of what had been and what *could* have been becoming too much to bear.

This seems natural. It may even seem like what God desires from us even after we have repented. I recall times in my life when I felt the need to confess the same sin over and over again. This compulsion seemed right to me until I heard my pastor preach one Sunday about God's abundant forgiveness and goodness in Christ, which is essentially what Nehemiah says once he sees Israel reaching for the bottle of wormwood: "Go, eat of the fat, drink of the sweet," he implores them, "for this day is holy to our Lord. Do not be grieved, for the joy of the LORD is your strength."

You do not have the ability to grieve over all of your sins all the time. You do not even know them all! As the Israelites demonstrate, there is a time for our grief, but those of us who stand in the shadow of Christ's cross are invited into the Lord's joy as well. We read about the congregation's response to Nehemiah's gracious message later, that "all the people went away to eat and drink, to send portions of food and to celebrate with great joy, because they now understood the words that had been made known to them" (8:12). May we celebrate God's goodness and mercy along with them today.

—*Dylan Potter*

March 12

> *"Therefore I will not keep silent; I will speak out in the anguish of my spirit, I will complain in the bitterness of my soul." (Job 7:11, NIV)*

There is no greater comfort in our daily lives than the steadfast assurance that God *wants* to hear our prayers because of His love for us. We are often silent or inarticulate with Him, pridefully nervous about praying the wrong thing or too faithless to think prayer worthwhile. Yet the Bible insists that God delights in meager voices. From Genesis to Revelation, and in the whole history of the Church, the voices of God's people resound with this hope, perhaps the most basic of them all: God hears you.

In this passage from the most tortured sufferer we know, Job, we hear the true voice of prayer. It is not one that speaks the right words. It is not one that spends time trying to "create space" for God, to "posture your attitude" before God. Job yells at God, completely freaks out at Him. His tears can't find their end. It's a Robert Duvall kind of prayer in *The Apostle*, the kind that wakes the neighbors at night. Job cannot silence his affliction—he has no idea why God was allowing these horrible things to happen in his life—so he clings to the hope that God hears him. In the innermost recesses of all of his bereavement, Job cannot help but continue depending on the one certitude he has left—that God, at the very least, hears him.

My life would not look the same without this assurance. After college I decided that I wanted to do ministry, and I was dating a girl overseas. Distance was hurting the relationship, and my dad was not particularly thrilled about my career choice. Thankfully, I was accepted into a ministry training program in a church in London, but the visa process was taking way too long, and my girlfriend couldn't find a job in London. I tried to pray, but kept feeling like God was completely absent from the entire situation. Towards the end of August I was just praying out of sheer desperation and was practically cursing at God, and soon after my visa fell through.

Back to square one, out of the blue, my father offered to pay for a Master of Theology degree in England. I was floored by the generosity and support, and it seemed like everything was working out. I got to England, however, and my girlfriend and I couldn't stop fighting. Again, angry prayers were dispatched, this time from my dorm room in England. The answer came the next Sunday when my girlfriend began crying and couldn't stop because she felt so unhappy. The breakup made it seem as if everything that had passed was futile—all that effort for nothing.

When I think about that time in my life, which was actually quite recently, I can remember most vividly my time spent in prayer. I didn't know what God was doing, but it looked like He was doing the opposite of what I thought He should be doing. I still don't understand *why*. But I grew closer to God because I learned even more that God hears me.

It is this promise that brings us to "bend the knees of our hearts," as the French Reformer Guillaume Farel once put it. God hears us. Although we don't understand so much of our lives, let us be bold to lift up our hearts, for God is good and hears our prayer.

—*Javier Garcia*

March 13

Who among all these does not know that the hand of the LORD has done this? In his hand is the life of every living thing and the breath of all mankind. (Job 12:9-10, ESV)

My wife was stretched out on the table as the doctor passed the transducer back and forth on her stomach. We sat silently watching the screen and listening for the sound of hope, listening for that little fast-paced heartbeat. But there was nothing. No blip on the screen and no evidence of life. Just silence.

For the past eight weeks or so we had been elated. Finally, after over a year of trying, there were *two* lines on the pregnancy test instead of one! We went to the doctor's office, and it was confirmed—we were pregnant. Prior to that news, we had reached the point of facing the very painful reality that we may not be able to have children. It was a scary thought, but with that pregnancy test it was gone. We praised God for this answer to prayer, for this baby. It was a renewal of hope. But these moments of silence during the ultrasound that day seized our joy. The doctor told us that it was very likely that we would miscarry.

So what this time? What did we do wrong? What caused this? Who has answers? Heartbroken and furious, the hardest part was that there was nothing to do. There were no answers to our questions. There was just the shadowy revelation that, like Job when faced with catastrophe, the Lord had done this when His hand was supposed to preserve the life of all things, the breath of all mankind. "He's got the whole world in His hands." Really?

This is enough to crush the faith in you and leave nothing left but resentment. It is a death, and there is no coping mechanism for it. When you're faced with the shadow side of the reality that life is *not* yours to give or to hold onto, there is only one question left to helplessly ask, and that is, "But is God giving life? And is He trustworthy?"

Nothing you're going through tells you He is. There's no evidence that you can point to in the physical world around you that will satisfy. There is only one thing that can stand up to your real suffering— to loss, to cancer, to miscarriages. That is His own final death for us. His suffering for ours. His pain speaking into our pain and the promise in His resurrection that death does not and will not have the final word.

—*Sean Norris*

March 14

> *"Worthless physicians are you all. Oh that you would keep silent, and it would be your wisdom... Shall windy words have an end? What provokes you that you answer?... How long will you torment me, and break me in pieces with words?"* (Job 13:4-5, 16:3, 19:2, ESV)

We know the story of Job. Caught in a wager between God and Satan, Job loses everything: children, servants, cattle, crops, even his health. When three friends come to comfort and console Job, they are so shocked by his appearance that they merely sit in silence with him for seven days, "for they saw that his suffering was very great" (2:13).

After this impressive week of silent empathy, Job lets loose with what is on his mind. He says he wishes he had never been born, that he prefers death to his present state, that he continually wonders why life is given to "a man whom God has hedged in." His anger and frustration, while understandable, make his friends uneasy. They respond to Job's lament with words that they hope will help Job, that will comfort him by making some sense of what has happened.

Are they helpful? Do they have wisdom and understanding? As we read later in the book, much—but not all—of what they say does ring true. But how does Job *receive* their words?

Two thoughts come to mind: First, Job is not helped by their words. Again and again, he complains of their wordy responses, sort of like Eliza Doolittle in *My Fair Lady*: "Words, words, words. All I hear is words!" He begs his friends to be silent. He calls them "worthless physicians" and tells them that "to keep silent would be wise" (13:5). That is to say, there is *nothing* we can say in the face of suffering that is going to be helpful. To be silent, to be present but silent, is the wise response rather than any attempt to comfort or explain with words.

Secondly, I wonder whether Job's time of suffering might not have been shortened, had his friends remained quiet. Why? Because Job ultimately has to deal with God Himself, directly, regarding His injustice. This is only speculation, but do not his well-intentioned friends actually *prolong* his suffering and *postpone* his coming to peace with God with their wordy explanations? Would their continued silence have given Job the space in which to hear his own voice and listen to God's? One thing is for sure: Job did not *receive* his friends' words as either helpful or comforting.

"Oh, that you would keep silent, and it would be your wisdom."

—*Mary Zahl*

March 15

> *"For I know that my Redeemer lives, and at the last he will stand upon the earth. And after my skin has been thus destroyed, yet in my flesh I shall see God, whom I shall see for myself, and my eyes shall behold, and not another. My heart faints within me! If you say, 'How we will pursue him!' and, 'The root of the matter is found in him,' be afraid of the sword, for wrath brings the punishment of the sword, that you may know there is a judgment."* (Job 19:25-29, ESV)

I recently was at a bookstore (one of the big ones that begins with a "B") looking to rid myself of a gift card that was burning a hole in my pocket. Most trips to any bookstore for me involve a quick stroll through the "Christian Inspiration" section, and interestingly enough, I routinely find that almost all the books there have the same motifs of self-improvement or new techniques for spiritual disciplines. I think the idea of self-improvement is what really inspires us these days.

The God of the Book of Job doesn't seem to inspire Americans these days. After all, if self-discovery and happiness are the "alpha and omega" of our existence, how on earth could the themes of failure, judgment, and authority possibly make waves?

This is greatest problem about a lot of the books I see in these shelves: a person's greatest need is not to be inspired, but to experience grace. The fundamental view of people as OK, and maybe just needing a little inspiration, falls short of the reality of lost people in dire need of intervention.

Now enter the Book of Job.

There's no doubt about it; Job is a tough book. It's a really long journey into one man's misery, but few other scriptural books fly in the face of "Christian Inspiration" like Job. After being cosmically dumped, Job is visited by three friends trying to pry out the reason for his suffering. His friends think, much like we do today, that because we are generally OK people, doing good brings health and wealth, and doing wrong brings plagues and famines.

No matter how common it is, life based on this kind of performance-ism eventually falls either into denial of our weaknesses or denial of God. People burdened under this law of karma find themselves buying inspirational books or burned out with church, tired of their lives not changing. These burnouts usually happen when tragedy strikes.

The passage in Job today works against our inspiration-minded, performance-based persuasions. In verse 29 Job reminds himself that he is a sinner—unable to control of please God with obedience. If a person could do such a thing, then Job would not be in the mess he's in. But there *is* hope, not in our fulfillment of God's Law, as good as it is, but in God's grace. Hope that God will be a redeemer of sinners (19:25), that He will resurrect dead sinners to new life, both in body and spirit (19:26).

This is the promise of resurrection in Jesus Christ, that he is the Resurrection and the Life (John 11:25), and those who believe in him will be raised up with him (John 6:40). On that day, when God's saving work is finished, we are promised, "yet in our flesh we shall see God."

—*Ben Phillips*

March 16

Salvation belongs to the Lord... (Psalm 3:8, ESV)

This line is repeated throughout the entire Bible: "Salvation belongs to the Lord." In the Old Testament, God is always saving His people from encroaching danger—there are stories about it, songs about it in Psalms, and prophecies of it in books from Isaiah to Malachi. Later, when the angel comes to Mary in the New Testament, he says, "Name him Jesus, because he will save his people." During his ministry Jesus says, "I have come to seek and save the lost." When the Bible talks about salvation, it is proclaiming the central concept of the Christian faith and Scriptures.

You may have been asked before by someone, "Are you saved?" It is a great question, but what does it mean? Saved from what? We say, "saved from our sins," but why?

The Christian belief is that we are saved *from* God *by* God. This sounds odd at first hearing, and we may even protest. Often times we prefer to "bail God out of actually being God." We are more or less comfortable with a God who saves, but we don't often like to think of God as Judge. But in order to be the saving God, God must also be a judging God. If He is sovereign enough to save His people, God must have sovereignty not to. It cannot be me, or the devil, or the world; it is His call either to leave us condemned and dead, or to raise us to life.

Salvation belongs to the Lord. In other words, as Dr. Mark Mattes, theology professor at Grandview College, has said, "God is so for you as your defender that he is against himself as your accuser." This is the message of the cross, God saving you from God's wrath by diverting it onto Jesus. You are saved from God's wrath by God's mercy.

—*Justin Holcomb*

March 17

The fool has said in his heart, "There is no God." They are corrupt, they have committed abominable deeds; There is no one who does good. The Lord has looked down from heaven upon the sons of men to see if there are any who understand, who seek after God. They have all turned aside, together they have become corrupt; There is no one who does good, not even one. (Psalm 14:1-3, ESV)

Modernity's demand for political correctness has created a culture in which we thirst for and command equality. Whether it comes in the form of open-mindedness towards race, criminal history, gender, religious belief or sexual orientation, we operate under the expectations to accept our neighbor as our equal or become the black sheep ourselves. In order to accomplish this, we're asked to dig deep within ourselves and learn to tolerate each other's differences so that we may live together harmoniously. Not only does this commandment create yet another mindset for us to rebel against; it merely accomplishes a facade of tolerance towards those around us and does little to move our hearts towards truly loving one another.

I met a homeless man a few months ago with a history of unspeakable offenses and addictions that he still struggles with to this day. Our friendship began under the framework of my feeble attempt to "dutifully" love my neighbor, but thankfully developed into something much more sincere. At the same time of our encounter, I happened to be reading through Martin Luther's *Bondage of the Will* and had thus been thinking of our inabilities to will ourselves away from evil towards good. This was remarkable. In the context of my newly forged friendship, the darkness of the human condition proved to be mankind's only true source of equality. This man, at first glance appearing to be from an entirely different level of despair, was no more or less broken than myself.

No more deserving of the grace of God, no more capable of fulfilling what the law requires, my friend and I have been forgiven just the same. I no longer viewed him as someone I should merely tolerate, but rather a brother I could love. The beauty of the Gospel is that it shows us to be the moral equivalent of everyone other than Christ, which enables genuine friendships and true love for our neighbor. We are all equally fallen and equally forgiven.

—Josh Bascom

March 18

> *The LORD is my shepherd; I shall not want. He makes me lie down in green pastures. He leads me beside still waters. He restores my soul. He leads me in paths of righteousness for his name's sake. Even though I walk through the valley of the shadow of death, I will fear no evil, for you are with me; your rod and your staff, they comfort me. You prepare a table before me in the presence of my enemies; you anoint my head with oil; my cup overflows. Surely goodness and mercy shall follow me all the days of my life, and I shall dwell in the house of the LORD forever. (Psalm 23, ESV)*

Consider the following version of this prayer of comfort written by a recovering drug addict who fell back into the habit once again:

> Heroin is my shepherd
> I shall always want.
> It maketh me to lie down in gutters
> It leadeth me beside still madness
> It destroyeth my soul.
> It leadeth me in the paths of hell for its name's sake.
> Yea, though I walk through the valley of the shadow of death,
> I will fear no evil,
> For heroin art with me.
> My syringe and spike shall comfort me.
> Thou puttest me to shame in the presence of my enemies.
> Thou anointest my head with madness.
> My cup runneth over with sorrow.
> Surely hate and evil shall follow me all the days of my life,

And I will dwell in the house of misery and disgrace
forever.

Addiction, posits Gerald May in *Addiction and Grace*, is anything to
which we are drawn that keeps us from loving God with all our hearts,
minds, souls and strength, and our neighbors as ourselves. These habits,
attitudes, activities can be relatively innocent to an outside observer, but
they grip us and ineluctably pull us down and away from our true home.

David finds that in the middle of his own "shadow of death" there
is somewhere to go, or—as he would put it—Someone with him. He
pours out his soul to one he knows will hear and understand.

What darkness dims your spirit today? What keeps keeping you
from love, what continues to draw you down into despair? May we lift
these things to God, and be thankful He is there, that He hears and
understands.

—Peter Moore

March 19

*Even though I walk through the valley of the shadow of
death, I fear no evil, for thou are with me; thy rod and thy
staff, they comfort me. (Psalm 23:4, KJV)*

Which of us would ever willingly enter a place road-marked: "Now
Entering the Valley of the Shadow of Death?" My instinct is to run in
the opposite direction. Why not try to find another route on my
journey—anything to avoid a place whose description includes valley or
shadow or death? Do we not instinctively prefer mountaintops, grand
views, triumphs, *life*?

What if, instead, that directing sign said, "Now Entering the Place
of No Fear?" This, apparently, is how the psalmist sees this valley,
where the great enemy Death makes its home. It is a place where the
psalmist can confidently "fear no evil" surprising him from the shadows;
where those immovable, shadow-casting mountains are no longer seen as
a challenge to be scaled.

How is this possible, though? What is this secret formula that
equals no fear? The psalmist answers, "Because thou art with me." I am
not alone. In fact, the good shepherd, the one who provides all I need
(23:1-3), is the one who is not just guiding me, but is as close as the air I

breathe. Nothing can separate me from Him, not even Death itself. He is my friend, my companion, my guide. He does not condemn me for my fear. Instead of merely cheering me from the mountain, He comes alongside me to help, to protect me and give me someone to lean on.

The German theologian Jürgen Moltmann wrote years ago that what we see in Jesus could be summarized as, "God is for us and God is with us." This is the expressed message of Psalm 23.

As I meditate on this verse, I think: Yes, I am in a valley right now. This place is dark, and full of dread. Thank you, Lord, that I can *acknowledge* I am in a valley. I cannot see whatever might be around the corner in the shadows. My imagination is starting to run wild—but thou art with me. I am not alone.

There are mountains in my life, huge situations or relationships that do not change. They often make my life seem truly dark. Sure, some of these may just be projections of my imagination, but they are real to me and they make me edgy, anxious, guarded. They loom—I cannot get any distance on them in this valley. But, thou art with me. You do not condemn me for my anxiety. You will not leave me to find the way through these mountains. You know the way, and together we will keep walking.

—Mary Zahl

March 20

> *Remember not the sins of my youth or my transgressions;*
> *according to your steadfast love remember me, for the sake*
> *of your goodness, O Lord! (Psalm 25:7, ESV)*

One of the reasons the Psalms have been so cherished for so long is because they echo our own hearts. The psalmist's prayers come out of desperation and real need in times when absolutely nothing else matters.

When we suffer, the rubber hits the road in terms of our understanding of the Gospel. As opposed to our sparse moments in the limelight, it is when the chips are down and hope is dim that the Gospel actually makes the most sense. When you are struggling with regret or the scars of life's disappointments, absolutely nothing but the Gospel will speak to you. Looking to ourselves for resolve can only add to the unease and worry. Will we ever do enough, we ask?

From this place of suffering, David knows he cannot, and he cries out to God for just this kind of mercy. He bases that request for mercy not upon his actions or his inherent goodness, but rather upon the goodness of the Lord. The great King David specifically asks God *not* to look at his past or present.

We are able to cry out to God no matter what, not because we have built up enough credit with God, but because God regards us as if we were each His own beloved Son. May we always remember that while God knows every inch of our hearts, He will not hold it against us.

—Alex Large

March 21

> *Give me not up to the will of my adversaries; for false witnesses have risen against me, and they breathe out violence. I believe that I shall look upon the goodness of the LORD in the land of the living! Wait for the LORD; be strong, and let your heart take courage; wait for the LORD! (Psalm 27:12-14, ESV)*

When under pressure, human beings go into fight or flight mode. Adrenaline pumps, and we assess the situation to determine whether fighting or fleeing is the best course of action. When under attack, we survey our surroundings and are poised to move—and these defenses are equated with strength. We do not often equate strength and courage with the passivity of waiting.

Yet the psalmist writes: "Be strong, and let your heart take courage; wait for the Lord!" Passive waiting is a sign of strength and courage, not of weakness or cowardice. When we wait, we give up control over the situation, and giving up control is no easy task. We can wait because we believe that we shall "look upon the goodness of the Lord," and it is this goodness in which we can always and ultimately trust. It is God's goodness that gives us the strength to wait for Him in the difficult times.

Where are you being asked, or forced, to wait? Where in life do you feel the impulse to fight or flee? Whether it is a crisis at work, some long-awaited news, or the endless freeway traffic, the passive place of waiting is the surprisingly fertile space for the patient power of God.

—Bonnie Poon Zahl

March 22

Save me in your steadfast love! (Psalm 31:16, ESV)

The Bible tells of God's uncaused and generous love: God is under no obligation to rescue us, but He willingly chooses to do it. The vocabulary for this uncaused and generous love is varied throughout the Scriptures, but the main one is *hesed*. The entire history of God's relationship with Israel and Jesus' message can be summarized in terms of *hesed*.

Hesed is the Hebrew word for God's steadfast love—the consistent, relentless, lavish, extravagant, unrestrained, one-way love of God. It turns up regularly in the Old Testament, particularly in the Psalms, but it is not just an Old Testament concept; rather, it points to this love's fulfillment in the gift of God's Son.

Through Jesus, God has and is actively reaching into our chaos, our sin, our pain, and our confusion. God initiates this relationship, and when we are grasped through His *hesed*, we are secure, not driven away or lost. This great love has the strange capacity to lift up and bring to new life. We have been given life now—"all who believe in the Son will have life"—and will be given eternal new life at the end—"I will raise you up on the last day" (John 6:37-40). This is our God-initiated security in Christ Jesus.

—Justin Holcomb

March 23

Blessed is the one whose transgression is forgiven, whose sin is covered. Blessed is the man against whom the LORD counts no iniquity, and in whose spirit there is no deceit... I acknowledged my sin to you and I did not cover my iniquity; I said, "I will confess my transgressions to the LORD," and you forgave the iniquity of my sin... Many are the sorrows of the wicked, but steadfast love surrounds the one who trusts in the Lord. Be glad in the LORD, and rejoice, O righteous, and shout for joy, all you upright in heart! (Psalm 32:1-2, 5, 10-11, ESV)

Forgiveness really doesn't make any sense. Retribution does. Retribution is the most natural and effective impulse that arises when someone has wronged us. This vengeance takes different forms but I, for one, have perfected the grudge. I withhold forgiveness until there's groveling, and *then* I acquiesce, just so long as the offender shows enough remorse not to repeat the transgression. Passive aggression is key: cold shoulder, silent treatment, condescending eyes. When you finally relent, you store the episode for future reference; a type of collateral, if you will. You don't even have to say it, but the other person knows you have a storehouse of past faults to keep them in your hand—it's the only way to win.

Surely enough, family life is where retribution explodes. This summer I have been crashing at my parents' apartment in New York City. Almost every day a new grudge match surfaces. It has been exhausting, but not nearly as exhausting as if we actually *forgave* one another. If we forgave one another, which is out of the question, we would have to *continue* forgiving each other, because it would never stop, and I know they'd take my forgiveness as license to keep getting under my skin! And God forbid me actually receiving *their* forgiveness...

There is an old joke that a man, after getting drunk on vodka and tonic, rum and tonic, and gin and tonic, figures it all out and says, "It must be the tonic!" I've come to think this is a description of our stance towards forgiveness.

Behind the evasion tactics and blame shifting; behind the ploys at self-justification and self-promoting; behind all of it, there is a poor sufferer that thirsts for respite. This respite can only be found in the nonsensical forgiveness of God. It is the alien work of the cross, the only solution to our pluses and minuses within the merit-demerit system. For both the occasional colossal mistakes and the routinely subconscious ones, cosmic forgiveness is the only escape.

This passage tells us of the unconditional promise that God's forgiveness is assured beyond measure. According to the psalmist, God's forgiveness *surrounds* us. There are no gaps to this assurance; God doesn't play games with us and doesn't hold grudges or toy with our standing—God's favor does not fluctuate like ours.

When we dwell on this steadfast love of God and how it surrounds us, gratitude swells naturally within us. Let us rejoice, because we are utterly forgiven, accepted and covered by our Father, His Son and the Holy Spirit!

—Javier Garcia

March 24

This poor man cried, and the LORD heard him and saved him out of all his troubles. (Psalm 34:6, ESV)

My wife and I often joke about our different responses in difficult times. I tend to want to be more of an optimist when life throws a curveball, priding myself on "looking on the bright side of life" *(Monty Python)*. She, on the other hand, tends to lean pessimist, at least in my opinion. She usually counters the label by saying, "I'm not a pessimist. I'm a *realist.*" Truthfully, she's right. She usually looks at the troubles in life with a more sober view than me.

I tend to prefer denial. I don't like admitting disappointment or dissatisfaction with how things turn out. I tend to prefer an un-fazed exterior to an emotive one. I do these things, I think, because I hope that in doing this I might not feel—and others won't see—what feels out of control under the surface.

But hiding can't last, and as a professor used to say, "The boys in the basement always come up." Suppression is a losing game and the "boys" (anger, fear, loneliness, jealousy, grief) only get louder until they come upstairs unexpectedly. It might be road rage, an unexpected panic attack, or a breakdown after bumping your head.

It is God who stops the denial. He does not leave us to our fantasies; He exposes the truth of our troubled lives so that we might look to Him as the answer. He allows life to become unbearable. He allows a no-choice impasse, so that we cry out for help, and then we find that God hears us and saves us from all our troubles.

—Sean Norris

March 25

The Lord is close to the brokenhearted and saves those who are crushed in spirit. (Psalm 34:18, NIV)

There are many, many great songs about broken hearts. One of the greatest has to be Jimmy Ruffin's 1966 hit, "What Becomes of the Broken Hearted?" The record is as close to perfection as pop music can get: a powerful lyric married to an irresistible melody, delivered with feeling in just under three minutes. Pure Motown gold.

The song captures something powerful in its vivid description of brokenheartedness: "I walk in shadows, searching for light, cold and alone, no comfort in sight, hoping and praying for someone to care, always moving and going nowhere". Most of us can point to a time when these words felt true for us, when we were hurt so badly that we thought we would never heal. The end of a romantic relationship is the most common culprit, but there are plenty of others. The death of a loved one, the disappointment of a dream, even the wrong candidate winning an election—and the list goes on.

Sadly, heartbreaking experiences tend to be definitive. They leave their mark whether we like it or not. I am reminded of a friend who broke up with his college sweetheart almost ten years ago. He confessed to me recently that he still thinks about it every day and wonders if the majority of his subsequent relationships have been an attempt to mitigate that pain. He can't seem to "get over it" because he cannot mend his own heart.

A broken heart is characterized by need. The psalmist reminds us here that God meets us in that place of need. He does not shun people who have been hurt. He does not reject those who have been rejected or disappoint those who have been disappointed. Thanks be to God, He is close to them and saves them.

—*David Zahl*

March 26

How long, O LORD, wilt thou look on? Rescue me from their ravages, my life from the lions! (Psalm 35:17, RSV)

Can you relate? Heavy duty. For me, nothing feels more impossible than the notion that "This is how I feel and it's never going to change." I've had periods in my life where depression has hit me hard. At one point, I barely shaved for about 2 years. I recently came across an old (but not that old) notebook entry of mine:

> I have a hard time believing in a God who would allow a world like this to exist. I have a hard time believing in a Father who hears his child cry 'Help' and does nothing. I am anguished. My depression hounds me.

Clearly, the psalmist had similar thoughts run through his mind. But it doesn't have to be depression. We all have things in our life that simply seem intractable. The good news is that God did come and rescue me. The bad news is that it took a lot longer than I had hoped. More pain followed that entry.

But it did pass. And it will pass. God's answer to the child who cries out, "How long?" is invariably, "Not much longer." I wish that the answer were "Never again!" One day it will be, but for now, just knowing that it passed for other people... that the feeling *won't* last forever, is enough to get me through. Little by little.

—Nate Michaux

March 27

Because of your wrath there is no health in my body; my bones have no soundness because of my sin. My guilt has overwhelmed me like a burden too heavy to bear... O Lord, do not forsake me; be not far from me, O my God. (Psalm 38:3-4, 21, NIV)

While there may be "varieties of religious experience" (W. James), I often wonder if they aren't more accurately distilled into a single substance of *need*. As the fermenting of life happens—if indeed there is anything or anyone outside of ourselves fermenting us—the substance that results is 180-proof need.

This is why my prayers most often resemble the end of this psalm: "Do not forsake me; be not far from me; come quickly to help me." I *need*!

Allowing these verses the opportunity to do their work is a fearful thing. The image of "my bones having no soundness" is an assault, growing so that one is afraid even to stand, for fear of a compound fracture. The old prayer book got it, as we declared in the confession that there is "no health in us"—as miserable offenders, we can only plead mercy, as those who were already crushed.

This psalm depicts perfectly the paradox of the work of God, leaving it plain to me why it is offensive to so many. "Because of *your* wrath"—there's no fancy maneuvering here, no attempt to dodge the source of bonebreaking. The Law of God has made my bones brittle. In the strongest possible sense, the psalmist knows—deep-seated, bone-shaking knowledge—that the Lord is behind all possible phenomena: there is nothing in all creation that happens outside of His sight.

Thankfully, the promise of the Lord's provision is even more sound; it is the "deeper magic." "The Lord brings death and makes alive; he brings down to the grave and raises up" (1 Sam 2). There is indeed nothing in all creation that shall separate us from the love of God that is in Christ Jesus our Lord. He is the answer to our plea to be remembered and spared. Thanks be to God, he is nearer the deepest part of me than my own bones.

—*Gil Kracke*

March 28

O Lord, make me know my end and what is the measure of my days; let me know how fleeting I am! (Psalm 39:1-6, ESV)

I worry about everything. If it's possible to worry about it, I worry about it. If I'm appeased, and someone tells me it's not a big deal, I still worry about it—I just stop telling that person my worries. I'm starting to learn that this worry about everything really stems from an insecurity more deeply and discreetly rooted in a tragic self-centeredness. I tend to think that my problems are bigger than anything else, the biggest of all time.

Back when I was a classroom teacher, there were these moments in staff meetings at work when this became glaringly clear, glaringly sad, and somehow comforting, because I could see this tendency of mine play itself out in just about everyone else around the room. During these meetings, we were supposed to go around and share our opinions on a new policy. Looking around the room at that point was really interesting—*no one* would actually listen to the speaker, and *everyone* would be planning what they were going to say. It was sad, but also kind of funny: everyone would gush out these well-phrased opinions, nervously skirting the judgment of their audience, and there really was no audience. We would leave the room having made "progress" towards this new policy, having "built staff community"—and then would all rush to punch out in the lounge to quickly get in our cars and onto our real lives.

I think our days are so exhausting sometimes because it's actually not supposed to be like this. I exhaust myself thinking about myself. The psalmist here seems to know the feeling: he is actually begging to be saved from it, in the knowledge of his own finitude. Somehow, if he knows that he and his problems are "fleeting," he can have rest. Why is this? Is it because he can then understand that he was being ridiculous after all, making his molehill a mountain, and can then attack the problem and rise victorious? No, he's not saying this. This passage isn't a snapping reproof to "keep small things small." It's not an encouragement for me to let it go, relax, chill out, stop thinking your problems are such a big deal—this passage is about *control*, and who has it. And the good news is that it's not the psalmist, and it's not me, and it's not you. The psalmist is praying to remember that the God of grace, the God who loves you, is in control absolutely, without your "fleeting" help, without your inevitable worries, forever. *Always.* And in that we find provision and rest.

Lord, make me know my end, and what is the measure of my days; let me know how fleeting I am.

—*Ethan Richardson*

March 29

Why are you cast down, O my soul, and why are you in turmoil within me? (Psalm 42:5, ESV)

Ernest Hemingway, the brilliant and depressed writer who finally ended his own life, said, "that terrible mood of depression of whether it's any good or not is what is known as the Artist's Reward." Hemingway was referring to whatever his latest creative work was, but he could have been describing everyone's reality. The pressure to produce in life, and then to be judged as "any good or not," is enough to cast down the most buoyant soul.

The terrible mood of depression is larger, of course, than any one cause or definition. Psychological, genetic, and physiological forces are all at play. But there is something else going on—a factor rarely discussed by the American Medical Association, but ever-present throughout Scripture: sin.

By sin, we don't mean, "I lied and cheated, therefore I am depressed." (Although it is true that sin does create "turmoil" in one's soul.) By sin we mean that because of the Fall, our hearts are wired to see life in terms of *production,* followed inevitably by the awful *judgment* of that production. By sin, we mean the terrible human burden of wondering whether we're any good or not. By rejecting the judgment-free life of the Garden of Eden, we have all reaped the Sinner's Reward.

The psalmist wrestles with God as he wrestles with his own soul. The outward factors that attend his despair, the multiple causes that create the "tears that have been (his) food day and night" (42:3), may or may not be similar to the disparate demons and devils that cast a pall over our lives. But we can be sure that the root of the psalmist's "deadly wound" is the root of all our deadly wounds: the sin that says I must earn my way in order to be accepted and happy and satisfied.

And there is only one place of help for this fundamental "oppression of the enemy." The psalmist says it concisely: "Hope in God." For God has given us His Son who has loved us in our sin. Jesus took the deadly wound of judgment on himself so that we could be delivered into the judgment-free world of grace. We have been given the reward of Life that Jesus earned for our sake.

To hope in God is to know that the categories of "any good or not" no longer apply to those who trust in Jesus' goodness. "Hope in God; for I shall again praise him, my salvation and my God."

—*Paul Walker*

March 30

Deep calls to deep at the roar of your waterfalls; all your breakers and your waves have gone over me. (Psalm 42:7, ESV)

This psalm comes from a person at the bottom of the ocean. He has been deafened by the roar of a waterfall and crushed under the pounding surf of the sea. There is darkness all around and profoundly honest confession. Death.

I had a friend say to me the other day that he used to pray for clarity and direction, but now his life feels so out of control that it's become a simple "*save me.*" This is the thing of which we're most afraid. The car has crashed. The divorce paper is signed. The child is lost. The depression has kept us in bed. It might be happening to us, be true about us; it's what we can't stop, try as we might. It is defeat.

It's the dark place. It's where we could not be more scared, more angry, more despairing, more unattractive, more selfish. Many of us live with this every day in some way, and sometimes it all comes crashing in.

The psalm says that God is at the bottom with us, speaking to this deep, dark, repressed place. Shockingly, He uses whatever thing it happens to be today to address us there. That is how we are first introduced to Him—in some area of our failure and His unending forgiveness. Despite however good a day we might be having, we come to Him no other way but at the bottom of the cross, under the waterfall of blood Jesus shed for us. I actually need Jesus; I need his grace. Christ has stirred whatever wave has crashed over me, and he is the one able to pull me up and give me breath. His deep love calls to my deep pain.

In fact, even as I write this, I feel so low and uncertain about the future that I doubt these very words of faith and comfort. May He prove true.

—*Kate Norris*

March 31

Restore to me the joy of your salvation, and sustain in me a willing spirit. (Psalm 51:12, NRSV)

The psalmist brings two things to bear here:

First, it is okay to ask God for joy. Joy is good. The reality of sin and of human limitations, and the truth of the cost of atonement, are no excuse for being grim and boring. Quite the reverse! Secure in God and His salvation, the true and natural way is to laugh at ourselves and at this world, and to seek and find the joy in it. God's world is brimming with joy if you are willing to look. All joy is from God and is a fruit of the Spirit (Gal. 5:22). The joy of our salvation means, not least, that I have received God's help and love in my life, really and concretely; now it's time to play.

But O for a willing spirit! How do I become "willing?" The will is God's specialty. We try so hard to change our wills and our desires, and we are so bad at it. God is good at it though. He knows how to change desires deep down, where it counts; He tinkers far below in the dark, in the foundations, the "archaeology" beyond our reach that drives our actions. And, inscrutably and frustratingly, God also knows when not to tinker.

This means that the way to engage the will, the path to a willing spirit, is not effort but prayer. "God, go down there, down where I cannot reach, down into the dark mess where the secret engines are. Make the changes I cannot make. Grant me a willing spirit each morning."

—Simeon Zahl

April 1

Save me, O God! For the waters have come up to my neck. I sink in deep mire, where there is no foothold; I have come into deep waters, and the flood sweeps over me... (Psalm 69:1-18, ESV)

The feeling of drowning is unlike any other. When I was a child, I was waterskiing in the Chesapeake Bay and wiped out, and I was not wearing a life jacket. Normally the skis act as a buoy, but both had come off of my feet, and as I tried to reach my foot down to find a foothold, no skis were there.

A wave of panic came over me. My only hope was to cry out for help. My uncle, who was driving the boat, heard the cry and quickly circled around, reached down to pull me out of the water, and lifted me back onto the deck of the boat.

The feeling of helplessness and desperation is certainly not confined to drowning—as my life goes on, there are other circumstances where I feel like I did in that murky bay, hopeless even with my feet on dry land.

In college, I found myself in a situation in which I could not rescue myself. I wept night after night. There was nowhere to turn: my family had a hand in the difficulties, my friends were no help, and I was certainly no help to myself. I was alone in a very scary place.

We all seek footholds in these places, but when the situation is hopeless, or the bottom falls out of what foothold you had, then what? We find ourselves in a situation *beyond* self-help, and as the waves begin to overwhelm us, we can only call out for help.

Someone once said that God's office is at the end of our ropes. Just when He seems furthest away, God is, in fact, unimaginably close to those in distress. Even in the darkness of Jesus' death, when God seemed to have turned His face from the world, God was most powerfully demonstrating His love for us.

When we cry out in these places, His arms are the only ones able to reach us and save us. In these moments where we are completely overwhelmed, the Lord Jesus is there as our sure foundation.

—*Andrew Pearson*

April 2

We are consumed by your anger and terrified by your indignation. You have set our iniquities before you, our secret sins in the light of your presence. (Psalm 90:7-8, NIV)

This psalm is subtitled "A prayer of Moses, the man of God." Whenever I read the Ten Commandments, I can't help but imagine the expression Moses wore when getting to number six: "You shall not murder." Of course, being face-to-face with God, he was probably in a completely maniacal state, but I like to think that hearing this sixth commandment could have sent an extra shiver down his spine.

I only think so because it may have resurrected a ghost long buried in Moses' mind. After killing an Egyptian slave driver in Exodus 2, Moses flees the country in fear and doesn't return until a new Pharaoh is appointed. Upon his return, everyone has clearly moved on, and we don't hear of Moses' crime again.

Yet who has ever done something wrong and successfully buried the deed? As William Faulkner said, "The past is never dead. It's not even past" (*Requiem for a Nun*). Even if society does not find fault with you, the conscience can be powerful enough to sentence your spirit for life. Every time I'm reminded of a regrettable decision or a slip of the tongue, my past becomes my present all over again. Despite our fleeing and keeping our sins secret, we cannot escape the light of God's presence.

Against our will, God continually reveals our secrets to set us free from them. As terrifying as that sounds, so often the things that keep me from living in the present are the mistakes of my past, and the only freedom I will ever have from them rests in God's revealing light.

What comes least expected is that when we are fully exposed, Jesus is there to cover us in his mercy and love. Moses' prayer ends with, "May the favor of the Lord our God rest upon us; establish the work of our hands for us—yes, establish the work of our hands." Indeed, when we are naked and ashamed, God's favor is there, resting on our shoulders.

—*Sam Bush*

April 3

He has not dealt with us according to our sins, nor rewarded us according to our iniquities... As far as the east is from the west, so far has He removed our transgressions from us. (Psalm 103:10-12, NASB)

For me, it's easy to get bored with the Christianity thing at this point. Seminary, pastoral ministry, post-graduate theology work—I've reached a point where I feel more like a producer than a consumer. I generally have difficulty listening to sermons because I am filtering them through my own approval. I know where the liturgy is going on Sunday. I can strike up conversations with all sorts of people in the congregation, and I can usually make them laugh. I resent handing out bulletins at church because, truth be told, I would rather be up front disseminating my knowledge.

It's not all a bowl of lemons, though; don't get me wrong. I still enjoy worship and love people. I still pray and read the Bible. I just feel different than I did during the more exuberant days as a fresh-faced believer. Like a child grown weary with his toys, I long for something else, something more real, perhaps. I wonder at times, *Is this all there is to it? Do I have to spend the rest of my days on a Christian safari, hunting for that rare and elusive contentment?* Even the Law-Gospel idea wearies me. I know what I am supposed to think, and I know what so-and-so said about this-and-that—I just feel indifferent to them at times. Some people struggle with the allure of gambling or alcohol; I struggle with Christianity. Do you?

What to do? Left to myself, I will continue evaluating until there's no tomorrow. However, what the psalmist tells me here is that despite my recalcitrance, God does not expect me to play-act my way through life. He refuses to deal with you and me according to our sins, and He actively separates our sins from us. The yawning chasm of His forgiveness is as wide as east is from west, and it is perpetually fixed there. For those of us whose feet are shuffling toward Sunday, think on the psalmist's words as they apply to faith-resistant hearts: I may get tired of church, but this is probably why I never get bored with the fact that God loves me, even when we I lose sight of the bigger picture. Though I may tire of theologizing, God's cross-shaped mercy does not weary me because it is the one thing I cannot master—*it masters me.* This is the filament that brings God's stubborn light where I am dark.

—Dylan Potter

April 4

When you send forth your spirit, they are created; and you renew the face of the ground. (Psalm 104:30, NRSV)

Here we have one of the great verses on the Holy Spirit in the Old Testament.

The world on its own terms is full of repeating the same old thing. The actors and the scene shuffle around, but the scripts have not changed: the same argument with our spouses about money, the same frustrations at work, the same patterns of procrastination and self-sabotage, the same frustrations with stubborn parents and siblings and children, the same worries about what lies ahead. Year after year for a lifetime, we live for a future that never arrives. "When we finally have an income like that, we'll be able to do all the things we want." "Once this stressful period in my job ends, I'll finally be able to relax and spend more time with the kids." "Once I finally meet the right person, my real life can begin." But the moment never comes. The goalposts shift quietly back, and we're returned again to the futurizing storyline, the same longing for a golden age ever delayed.

God's Spirit is sent forth: a glorious whirlwind of creation, smashing old patterns and systems, opening up strange and wonderful new possibilities, infusing dead ground with life again. When God is involved, creativity and renewal come to marriages, to callings, to churches, to writer's block, to broken hearts. God's Spirit brings hope and life and the unexpected. "Behold, I am doing a new thing; now it springs forth, do you not perceive it?" (Isa 43:19).

Come Holy Spirit: create a way forward where we are blocked, renew love and passion where they have faded, and inspire us as we build and create.

—Simeon Zahl

April 5

Let those who fear the Lord say, "His steadfast love endures forever." (Psalm 118:4, ESV)

What next? What next in the responsibilities of life? What next with the people I love, with my career? Sorrow is always lurking nearby, and trouble is a phone call away. I am in awe of the Lord's power and majesty, but in fear, too, because He brings both weal and woe. And I know I deserve woe. With trouble comes the accusation that I failed to plan well, or that I cut corners, or I forgot something. What about the deeper woe? At the death of a loved one, the memories and the what-ifs are horrible to endure. And when someone I love suffers, I strain with helplessness and awkward words.

I believe I am describing a burden we all share. As much as woe itself, we fear the judgment that comes with it. This includes the judgment of faithlessness: knowing that we *shouldn't* fear because we can trust the Lord to work good in everything. We shouldn't fear the burdens of life, but we do.

It is good to hear that the Lord knows all this. Just hearing that is a reprieve from pretending bravery. But then we also hear the promise that God's steadfast love and mercy endure forever. This promise, for now and always, frees us from our constant striving to prevent bad times, and it rebukes our anxious what-if thoughts. Though our fear may remain, His steadfast love is specifically given to those who suffer.

Once, I was fretting terribly, and then I saw on the floor a tiny heart-shaped leaf, miles away from where it grew. I saw it as a little note from the Lord, a reminder of the promise. Tribulation is the word for the spoiled plans, the wrong choices, the world's upper hand. It awaits us daily, but the more threatening the tribulation, the deeper the knowledge of the love of God. It is a marvelous alchemy, grief into love, which started on Easter Sunday and will not end until sorrow and pain are no more.

—Robin Anderson

April 6

A Song of Ascents. Of David. If it had not been the LORD who was on our side, let Israel now say—if it had not been the LORD who was on our side, when men rose up against us, then they would have swallowed us up alive, when their anger was kindled against us; then the flood would have swept us away, the torrent would have gone over us; then over us would have gone the raging waters. Blessed be the LORD, who has not given us as prey to their teeth! We have escaped as a bird from the snare of the fowlers; the snare is broken, and we have escaped! Our help is in the name of the LORD, who made heaven and earth. (Psalm 124, RSV)

I love road trips. I love getting in my truck with a cup of coffee and music for the road, knowing that I have a long drive in front of me. Choosing albums for the drive is one of the best parts about getting ready for a road trip—some U2, Neil Young, Elton John, some Brian Regan for laughs and Mozart for sophistication. For me, no road trip is complete without the proper tunes. One of my favorite movies, *Elizabethtown* (2005), culminates with a classic road trip sequence, replete with a moving soundtrack.

Songs for the road are nothing new. Psalm 124 is a "Psalm of Ascent" or "Gradual Psalm," one of the fifteen psalms that were recited or sung by the Israelites while walking to Jerusalem for one of the major annual feasts. Psalms 120 through 134 were their songs for the road. Psalm 124 is a road song reminding us of something we often forget: God is on your side. It begins by reminding you twice that God is on your side: "If it had not been the Lord who was on our side, let Israel now say—if it had not been the Lord who was on our side…"

As you know, it's easier to believe God is on your side when life's going well, when you're feeling blessed by God. But it doesn't stop there, because the good news is that God is on your side when things are *not* going well. God is on your side *especially* when things are not going well.

Sometimes people in our lives—including ourselves—rise up like enemies. And there are other times when we are overwhelmed by circumstances that simply happen. As Psalm 124 demonstrates, there are times in our lives when we feel swallowed up by other people, or by our own mistakes, times in our lives when we feel like we're drowning—in sorrow or sickness or despair or debt or any number of things. At times we find ourselves utterly overwhelmed, in situations that are bigger than us, situations in which only God can help.

In these situations, God "has not given us as prey" because God the Son, Jesus Christ, was given for us. Jesus gave himself over to death on the cross because God is on our side, and because God is on our side, even death is not the end of the story. Psalm 124 tells us, "If it had not been the Lord who was on our side... [our enemies] "would have swallowed us up alive." But God *is* on our side, and as Paul wrote to the Corinthians, even death, the last and greatest enemy, "has been *swallowed up* in victory... thanks be to God, who gives us the victory through our Lord, Jesus Christ" (1 Cor 15:54b, 57).

—Dave Johnson

April 7

It is in vain that you rise up early and go late to rest, eating the bread of anxious toil; for he gives to his beloved sleep. (Psalm 127:2, ESV)

In 1965, the U.S. Senate appointed a subcommittee to plan for the 20-hour work week that advances in technology would be making a reality by the year 2000. Summer camps held emergency board meetings to decide how they would stay open year-round, to accommodate all the free time that the American public would soon have on their hands. The frenzy displayed an astonishing lack of insight on the part of our forebears. Technological advances have not increased rest. Just the opposite!

An editorial in *The New York Times* went so far as to describe us as a society that has gotten caught in "The Busy Trap":

> If you live in America in the 21st century you've probably had to listen to a lot of people tell you how busy they are. It's become the default response when you ask anyone how they're doing: "Busy!" "*So* busy." "*Crazy* busy... obviously your life cannot possibly be silly or trivial or meaningless if you are so busy, completely booked, in demand every hour of the day.[*]

It's true: for a great many of us, busyness has come to serve as a barometer of identity and, therefore, self-worth. We use non-stop effort as a means of

---

[*] http://opinionator.blogs.nytimes.com/2012/06/30/the-busy-trap/

comforting ourselves, in other words, and placating the voices of condemnation in our lives. Does this ring any bells? How busy are you?

What would it say about you if you weren't busy? Clearly nothing good. Yet our inability to rest has consequences. Reports of migraine headaches increased by nearly 60% over the last twenty years.[*]

The psalmist tells us that God is a God of rest. "He gives to his beloved sleep." What a beautiful image! The verdict that we are so afraid of, the one that drives so much of our compulsive activity and "anxious toil"—that we are not enough somehow—has been dealt with, once for all. It is secure. When God looks at us, He does not see anything that needs to be done. He is not waiting for us to do more or to be more. And no amount of scurrying around can change that.

So where are you caught in the busy trap? Where do you believe that if you don't do it, no one will? Where are you growing weary? Perhaps today is the day to slow down and take a break. "You can close your eyes" (J. Taylor). You can sleep because He doesn't. In fact, He's staying up all night tonight, and tomorrow night, and the night after that, and the night after that...

—David Zahl

April 8

How shall we sing the Lord's song in a strange land? If I forget thee, O Jerusalem, let my right hand forget her cunning. (Psalm 137:4-5, KJV)

We all feel homesickness in one way or another. The Beach Boys famously sing, "I feel so broke up, I wanna go home." I certainly have felt it. As a boy I would go two hours from home, to my aunt's house for a long weekend, and by the second day my father would be meeting us halfway back at an off-road Arby's, just because I couldn't handle being away. I'm not much better now; I'm maybe just better at shushing the initial impulse to call home every time I need an oil change. Whether you know homesickness, or know instead the jet-set alternative, I believe there is something to be said of home-hunger in the deeper sense, a feeling of homesickness or pariah-hood that is elemental and biblical, as we see in the psalmist's cry from the shores of Babylon.

---

[*] http://www.sciencedaily.com/releases/1999/10/991025075957.htm

"Lord, how can we go on like this?" he says in the fourth verse. Where is my comfort? Where is my home in this new place? Where can I hide? Where is my familiarity, my comfort in this land of desolation? This rootlessness is everywhere: whether it's a new job in a new city, whether it's the death of a friend, the betrayal of a spouse, losing standing at work, losing money at work, or a season of unexplainable depression, we remember intimately our places of desolation. The walls of the familiar temple are gone, and we are left without shelter. So what can be done?

He continues his prayer in the fifth verse: "If I forget who has made me, let what I've made crumble before me!" It is a common yearning: help me to remember home, what's most important, where I come from, in whose hands I rest. Now that the temple is miles away, now that my walls have crumbled, remind me that I'm not alone. The psalmist's prayer is rooted in the solid ground of the Gospel, the message that when the temples of comfort fall, when suffering brings forth a new and strange land, the hope of the Lord's loving provision remains. Hard times remain hard times, and yet they are intimately shared with Him who loves us. We are not forgotten. In a foreign land, the Lord's song of unremitting love abides.

—*Ethan Richardson*

April 9

Where shall I go from your Spirit? Or where shall I flee from your presence? If I ascend to heaven, you are there! If I make my bed in Sheol, you are there! If I take the wings of the morning and dwell in the uttermost parts of the sea, even there your hand shall lead me, and your right hand shall hold me. If I say, "Surely the darkness shall cover me, and the light about me be night," even the darkness is not dark to you; the night is bright as the day, for darkness is as light with you. (Psalm 139:7-12, ESV)

In England in the year 1215, King John signed the Magna Charta in a field called Runnymede. It's a beautiful spot, with a stream running through it and wildflowers blanketing it in the spring.

There are gently sloping hills on each side of the field. On the top of one hill, the English people have constructed a memorial to the flyers of the Royal Air Force who died in World War Two, the thousands of pilots who lost their lives defending their country in the Battle of Britain.

The memorial consists of two marble walls, ten feet high, on which are inscribed the names of those who died. As the walls move toward the brow of the hill, they also move closer together. Where the walls converge, they are joined by clear glass.

You look through the glass down onto the field of Runnymede. As you do, you realize that there are words etched into the glass. They come from Psalm 139:

> If I take the wings of the morning,
> And dwell in the uttermost parts of the sea,
> Even there thy hand shall lead me,
> And thy right hand shall hold me.

Those RAF pilots took the wings of the morning, and many of their bodies now dwell in the uttermost parts of the North Sea and the English Channel.

And the promise of God through the psalmist is that this separation is not the last word. The promise is that the reach of the hand of God is even to the uttermost parts of the English Channel. The last word for those pilots is that as they fell from the sky, they were caught and held and led forth in love by God's hand.

For you who are in some uttermost place right now as you're reading this—that hand has the scar of a nail hole.

—Jim Munroe

April 10

Search me, O God, and know my heart! Try me and know my thoughts! And see if there be any grievous way in me, and lead me in the way everlasting! (Psalm 139:23-24, ESV)

Years ago my wife and I were embroiled in a controversy about some friends that had each of us pretty torn up. Truth be told, I was the one embroiled and torn up, not her.

And since I tend to beat dead horses with my words, I was nit-picking on and on about these friends' bad-mannered behavior, how they were just so selfish, illogical even. *Surely she's seeing this*, I thought at my wife, as I continued to rant on about the hypocrisy–the hypocrisy!–impressing myself with my smooth argument, my own nimble dismantling of my imaginary opponent's point of view.

To be honest, she didn't even have to say a word. All it took was that glazed-over look, and suddenly it struck me: These people I was talking about (no longer *friends*) and their crude logic had ceased to be people at all and had merely become ideas. Ideas upon which I could easily do my intellectual judo from a safe but no-less-poisonous distance. In a short, one-sided conversation, I was alone in my own sad empire.

Later that week, while standing in the shower, I remembered an interesting quote that I'd heard that week. It went something like, "What you think about in your free time reveals your true religion." *Very insightful, I'll have to use that sometime*, I thought as I lathered up and got back to my "very insightful" critique of my new frenemies. I froze mid-armpit scrub. In an instant, my circulatory system went to ice water. There, in the shower, I'd just found my true religion, and it was ugly.

These days, shower time serves as a kind of barometer for where I'm really at. I call it "The Shower Test." Wretched man that I am, most mornings I cannot help myself. I'm back to the make-believe-opponent-conquering the moment the hot water hits me. This is where Psalm 139 comes in. The moment the Spirit kindly reminds me of my dark religious proclivities, I can automatically pray this psalm. Some days it is a joyful repentance; other days it's merely verse memorization exercises.

Either way, in finding me out, I find He is faithful to lead me back to the way everlasting.

—*Matt Johnson*

April 11

> *Praise the LORD from the earth, you great sea creatures and all deeps, fire and hail, snow and mist, stormy wind fulfilling his word! Mountains and all hills, fruit trees and all cedars! Beasts and all livestock, creeping things and flying birds!... (Psalm 148, ESV)*

Perhaps, as a kid, you also experienced the absolute *downer* of being told by some adult that in heaven "we just praise God for all eternity." Great. So all visions of surfing perfect waves, jumping waterfalls, finally dunking a basketball, and recording with Billy Joel are out the window, because instead we're just going to "praise God" in a never-ending church service. And who is this God who has designed eternity around Himself receiving praise from His creatures? Who is this God who even now *commands* us to praise him? Does he really need the boost?

Of course I knew there had to be more to it, but it wasn't until a couple of years ago that I read something that turned all my thoughts upside down about the whole thing and made me want heaven (and God) more than I ever had.

It was an essay on "praising" in C. S. Lewis' *Reflections on the Psalms*. He had apparently been asking some of the same questions, including this one: why does it seem that the psalmist's favorite way to praise God is simply to tell other people to praise Him? And not only people, but as we see in the above passage, stars and sea monsters and snowstorms! What is this all about? Lewis gives two simple observations:

First, that God Himself actually "demands praise" inherently. In other words, even if He did not command it, to praise God is simply to be awake, to be healthy, to be sane, to have "entered the real world." And consequently, not to praise Him is to have missed everything and lost all.

Second, he writes of our everyday lives, "I had never noticed that all enjoyment spontaneously overflows into praise." Whether wine, music, books, sunsets, artists, sports, or children, we cannot fully enjoy a thing *unless* we praise it. Lewis continues, "and just as men spontaneously praise what they value, so they spontaneously urge us to join them in praising it: '*Isn't she lovely?*'"

In the same way, the psalmists praise God, the true and ultimate object of praise, by telling us (and *everything!*) to praise Him. And so I picture heaven as being kind of like the moment after a last-second championship win for the home team where you're just grabbing your friends, shaking them, and saying, "Can you believe this? Are you seeing this?" And there our praise, which is our happiness being fully directed toward the thing it was always meant for, will never end.

In the meantime, we may find ourselves more often resonating with the psalms of complaint (or revenge!) rather than the psalms of praise. But even then, we may find true comfort in the fact that we have a God who loves us enough to make His glory and our happiness ultimately the same thing.

—Ross Byrd

April 12

There is a way that seems right to a man, but its end is the way to death. (Proverbs 16:25, ESV)

We do so many things in life to try to justify ourselves before others in order to get them to love us or accept us. We take on false personas, we put on masks, to try and cover up the person we know ourselves to be, and yet still the person we fear everyone will hate and reject. We try to align ourselves with certain social cliques that we think will boost our status in the world around us. We labor to get into the best schools that we can, thinking that having our name linked with the name of that particular institution will give us clout and make people look at us in a different light. We even try to keep abreast of the latest fashion trends and the newest devices that the marketing machine has to offer us in the hope that people will see us wearing the right clothes or carrying the latest and best technology and, therefore, think that we'll be somehow "cool," somehow worthy.

Funnily enough, all these attempts at self-justification feel so right! When we are successful in our efforts to earn the love and acceptance that we so long for, it seems like we're doing the right thing. In a word of judgment, though, this proverb rebukes: "There is a way that seems right to a man, but in the end it leads to death." It certainly feels right, and yet the author of Proverbs says with confidence that these paths that feel right in the end lead "to death." In other words, those paths that offer us comfort, love, and peace in this life will ultimately lead us in the wrong direction because they only attend to the "now." You may feel justified now, you may even feel loved and accepted now, but ultimately, in the face of death, these feelings will only be a series of passing feelings.

Where do you find these self-justifying attempts in life? May we come to see that it is only the justification of Jesus Christ that really matters. His justification, his love and acceptance, ultimately mean everything in this world and in the world to come, and there is nothing that you can do to earn any of it. He gives it to you as an absolutely free gift. He gives it to you because in His love He wills to give it to you. And He gives it to you by the words, "I forgive you." This, and this alone, is the path to life.

—Kyle Tomlin

April 13

Faithful are the wounds of a friend. (Proverbs 27:6, KJV)

We, of course, expect wounds from our enemies. And the person without enemies is the person without convictions, without conscience, without passion. "Beware when all men speak well of you," said Jesus, a man who, as we know from the Gospels, knew an enemy when he saw one.

But it is wounds from those who are our friends that surprise us and hurt us the most. We expect our friends to be trustworthy, kind, understanding, and forgiving. When they are not, we are often undone. The hurt we feel goes deeper the closer that friend was to us, because the magnitude of the hurt is always measured by the magnitude of the loyalty that it breached. It's what made Jesus' death so utterly painful. "He came to his own, and his own received him not" (John 1:11).

In Proverbs 27:17, the writer hails the virtues of friendship: "As iron sharpens iron, so sharpens a man the countenance of his friend" (KJV). We know, therefore, that the writer is no cynic, looking at relationships as unimportant and expendable. No, he knows that, difficult though they are, they are critical to our well-being and growth.

So maybe the writer here is talking about those wounds that are aimed at our betterment, and not at our destruction. Occasionally someone "cares enough to confront," and we are given the grace to change. Not often. Most of the time we react, and we take those hurts far too personally.

But what if God is our great wound-er? As the writer of the Hebrews puts it, quoting a Psalm (94:12), "the Lord disciplines him whom he loves" (12:6). As misguided as our friends' judgments often are, even they can be used by God to help us.

I recall a time when I got a verbal thrashing from someone of another race whom I had treated less than respectfully. The person was doing something stupid, but that didn't excuse my abrasiveness, which very likely had an unhealthy dose of racism built into it. The reason why honesty hurts so much is because we believe something else about ourselves. We do not think that we are capable of the offense we have caused. I certainly don't think of myself as a racist, but I clearly came across as one to my friend.

What if we had a different view of ourselves? What if we agreed with the Bible's low, low anthropology? We would see ourselves as capable of anything and, by default, guilty. When confronted with the truth by another we would not respond with defensiveness but rather with humility and repentance. The forgiveness found at the cross sets us free to do exactly that.

—Peter Moore

April 14

...Charm is deceitful, and beauty is vain, but a woman who fears the LORD is to be praised... (Proverbs 31:10-31, ESV)

So often this Proverbs 31 woman is used as the benchmark for what a "Christian woman" is supposed to look like. She has a clean and beautifully decorated house: obedient children taught, gardens tilled, fruits gathered, meals made, clothes washed and pressed; she is tirelessly put-together, diligent, well-versed, resourceful. She is a servant to all, both privately and publicly. For all intents and purposes, she is upstanding in her thoughts, words, and deeds. In Christ, it is thought by many, we are given the power and the ability to actually *become* this Proverbs 31 woman; she is woman's prototype, who we are (and, of course, *want* to be).

This certainly is a tall order. I am exhausted just thinking about it. The first question we should ask about this poem when we hear such literal application is: "Are we really to take this poem literally, as a check-list for what we, women, are to look like?" And the answer is: No. This poem needs to be understood as poetry; it is an alphabetized list from A to Z (in the Hebrew), defining a woman metaphorically. As with metaphors in English poetry, one looks to what is being conveyed. To take this poem literally is to lose the beauty of the author's message of restoration.

The Proverbs woman is the epitome of what it means to be in Christ, thus restored to God, thus restored to her neighbor. The author conveys to his audience that this is not just Eve, but Eve restored.

The very end says it all: restoration falls not on works but faith. After all that has been said of this woman, only one thing matters: "a woman who fears the LORD is to be praised." As in Proverbs 1:7, it is the fear of the Lord that is "the beginning of all wisdom."

Fear of the Lord is not from our own works or abilities—the entire Old Testament demonstrates that *our* faith is fleeting. Fear of the Lord is demonstrated instead in Jesus Christ, the "True Israelite" who fulfills God's Law for us. It is only by Jesus that we are able to see, for real, our true place in relation to God, which is restoration.

We should not be over-laden with guilt because we don't have obedient children or tilled gardens or Scripture memorized. Rather, we are this woman because Jesus Christ has made it so. It is by the fear of the Lord, by faith and not by works, that we are saved.

—Lauren R.E. Larkin

April 15

> *I thought in my heart, "Come now, I will test you with pleasure to find out what is good." But that also proved to be meaningless... when I surveyed all that my hands had done and what I had toiled to achieve, everything was meaningless, a chasing after the wind; nothing was gained under the sun. (Ecclesiastes 2:1-3, 11, NIV)*

1965 brought "(I Can't Get No) Satisfaction," and it seems that the Stones were merely echoing the sentiments of the writer of Ecclesiastes over 2000 years later. Thinking pleasure might escape meaninglessness, the writer of Ecclesiastes came to the same conclusion. But I often think the same way: life would be so much better if I could sleep in late, have a nice breakfast, spend the morning playing *Halo*, spend my afternoons walking my dogs in the park, and enjoy an endless romantic evening with my wife and a bottle of wine. My life then, without any extraneous demands, would be fulfilled.

This belief system means I live my life always looking forward to my next vacation, where I can finally live life as it's meant to be lived.

The trouble that the writer of Ecclesiastes finds is that the pursuit of pleasure fails to give any lasting meaning. Pleasure is unable to alleviate the pain of life. At the end of the day, he says, pleasure of its own is "chasing after the wind." Despite the fact that we all look forward to the next big thing on the calendar—whether it's the next episode of a favorite TV program, the coming weekend, the car classifieds, that new book in the mail—the enjoyment of its arrival is fleeting, and we look forward again, disappointed.

The love of God is the only salve for the vanity of life. True satisfaction is found not in pleasure but at the foot of the cross of Christ. It is the place where *our* pursuit of meaning and purpose finds its death, and where true meaning is born and freely given.

—Todd Brewer

April 16

So I turned about and gave my heart up to despair over all the toil of my labors under the sun, because sometimes a person who has toiled with wisdom and knowledge and skill must leave everything to be enjoyed by someone who did not toil for it. This also is vanity and a great evil. What has a man from all the toil and striving of heart with which he toils beneath the sun? For all his days are full of sorrow, and his work is a vexation. Even in the night his heart does not rest. This also is vanity. (Ecclesiastes 2:20-23, ESV)

In a former life, I worked extensively in banking, in the nonprofit sector where there are all sorts of worthy causes that do a great deal of good. In this one instance, I worked on a nonprofit entity that was struggling financially, and one of the executive managers of the bank was on its board of directors. This manager had a long record of service in the bank and was highly respected for his contributions and financial shrewdness.

The financial condition of the nonprofit began to deteriorate and the executive tried with all his might to help. He was personally tied to it and genuinely wanted to see it succeed. Well, the financial deterioration increased in severity and, finally, action had to be taken to protect the bank's interest. This was done, but there was an additional caveat. A head had to roll. It turned out that this executive manager who had given so many years of dedicated and competent service was fired. To add insult to injury, there were certain ambitious young managers who gleefully and smugly approved of this "justice."

Perhaps you have seen this happen in whatever part of the world you live and work in. Maybe it was a coach who gave years of successful service, impacted many young lives, had a bad season, and then was fired immediately. Maybe it was a pastor who had a public moral failure and was subjected to a self-righteous feeding frenzy.

The givens of life very quickly destroy two naive notions: *cause-and-effect* and *self-created identity*. Cause-and-effect basically says that you will get out of a thing what you put into it. For instance, if you read your Bible, good things will happen (commonly called "magic"). If you succeed academically, you will be accepted into Stanford Law, work on Wall Street, marry the man of your dreams, and have a fulfilled life. This is a terrible myth, as the former bank executive will be quick to tell you. The empirical fact is that life will, eventually, crush cause-and-effect thinking.

Another thing that dies is the idea of a self-created identity. This is baldly prevalent in the United States, but it is the same in Africa or anywhere else. It is Aristotle's idea that "you are the sum of your actions." If this is true (and it is if there is no Christ) then life is "vexation" and "striving after wind" because you have to re-create your identity every day for your entire life. Even if you were to theoretically succeed, the end of your life comes and you are quickly forgotten. Your gains are distributed among others, and the whole process begins anew.

I invite you to despair of cause-and-effect thinking and self-creation. Receive, instead, the perfect and unconditional gift of eternal love through our Savior Jesus Christ.

—David Browder

April 17

> *I perceived that whatever God does endures forever; nothing can be added to it, nor anything taken from it. God has done it, so that people fear before him. That which is, already has been; that which is to be, already has been; and God seeks what has been driven away. (Ecclesiastes 3:14-15, ESV)*

Ecclesiastes is a heavy book. Solomon essentially takes a good hard look at life and all we think it is and says, "All is vanity." Everything we build up in an attempt to find purpose, all that we acquire in an attempt to satisfy, never delivers. It all ends in vain. It is a hopeless picture Solomon describes, and he is describing life itself.

It is offensive. Solomon leaves no rock unturned. He says that wisdom is vanity, self-indulgence is vanity, work is vanity, wealth is vanity, honor is vanity. Everything that we stand on, that we use to justify ourselves before God, is pointless. We balk—"Surely all of my effort at work to make a better life for my family is worth something!" Or, "What about the fact that I gave up my Thanksgiving to serve the poor?" Or, "How about the fact that I work as a minister full-time?" It is all vanity. All of it will come under judgment, and none of it will prevent death. Death is the lowest common denominator for Solomon.

So what *does* matter for Solomon? What is not vanity? Nothing we do, but everything God does. God's work endures forever, and it is complete. There is nothing for us to do that is of any value that God has not already done. His work, and more specifically His work through His Son's death and resurrection, has accomplished all that matters to us in life. There is nothing we can do to add to it or to take away from it. He has conquered death.

We can rest in this knowledge that God's work on our behalf is complete. Though our relentless faith in our own vain works continues to drive us away, our hope is His constant pursuit. He comes for us, and what He does is never in vain.

—*Sean Norris*

April 18

> *My beloved speaks and says to me: "Arise, my love, my beautiful one, and come away, for behold the winter is past; the rain is over and gone. The flowers appear on the earth, the time of singing has come, and the voice of the turtledove is heard in our land." (Song of Songs 2:10-12, ESV)*

What we take to be "good news" is all about starting points.

I think too often we tend to think humans start in a place of goodness and health, and then we fall into evil or sickness. Good news, then, becomes a matter of life being restored to former glory, to what we once knew. It doesn't take much to see this is not where we live but that, instead, we are born dying in a dead world. We are born subject to sin, and so our starting point is not purity but sickness.

We don't believe this in practice, though. We tend to con ourselves by calling one other to higher moral ground, by appealing to one another's good will and natural ability. We buy into the advertisements that say, "It's up to you to make a change." There's a satisfaction that comes from believing that we are the primary actors and that our fate is in our hands. Purpose comes from the myth that if we improve, eventually we'll figure out how "to form a more perfect union."

The Bible doesn't have such a generous starting point. Instead, we are born into the winters of sickness, hatred, adultery, theft, fear, war. It is in this starting point, not despite it, that any real hope is recognizable. It is here, in the real presence of an absence, that good news is any good at all. Like a slave being freed, a refugee being brought home, a lost child being found in a crowd, this is the starting point from which comes real redemption. It is also why Jesus said, "Those who are well have no need of a physician, but those who are sick. I came not to call the righteous, but sinners" (Mark 2:17). Those who do not think they are sick do not recognize the doctor or the health he offers.

This is why Jesus taught God's Law to its highest degree; he knew it would perpetually show everyone his or her starting point. Without this, we would not recognize the winter around us, which means we would never understand the spring.

Where is your starting point today? The Lord moves into your winter and calls you out in love: "Arise, my love, my beautiful one, and come away, for behold, the winter is past; the rain is over and gone. The flowers appear on the earth, the time of singing has come..."

—*Sean Norris*

April 19

> *"O my dove, in the clefts of the rock, in the crannies of the cliff, let me see your face, let me hear your voice, for your voice is sweet, and your face is lovely. Catch the foxes for us, the little foxes that spoil the vineyards, for our vineyards are in blossom." My beloved is mine, and I am his. (Song of Songs 2:14-16a, ESV)*

It was 8 a.m., and I was in my pajamas finishing my final paper for my study abroad program in Paris. The doorbell rang and my French host-woman answered the door and said it was for me. My boyfriend was waiting in the hallway—my boyfriend who had secretly traveled from Pittsburgh to Paris that night to surprise me—and got down on one knee. I said yes. I absolutely loved him and wanted to be with him, but in the back of my mind I was very disappointed.

I had struggled with anorexia ever since we met during high school—it was my secret life behind all the Christian leadership roles and academic achievements. I had had a very powerful recovery experience through the help of some wise therapists, but during my semester abroad I had gone back to the old friend—or enemy, I should say—to cope.

Sean proposed to me in a period of real failing—failing as a devout Christian who had been in therapy and had a supportive family. I wanted to be a lot more "figured out" by the time I got engaged. I wanted to be engaged in strength, not weakness. I wanted to hide my flaws, my "foxes" as the passage says. Subconsciously, in "the cleft of the rock" so to speak—I expected judgment and rejection; I sort of even sought it out, because it had been the voice in my head for so long. Shouldn't he wait? But he didn't.

Our default modus operandi is repression. We stuff away all the fears and failings because we don't know what to do with them, and we try to carry on. A line in one of the songs by The Killers reads, "I offer you survival, it's hard enough to live." Honestly, that's where most of us are, I think, merely surviving something: our marriage, our job, our isolating habit. We survive and then cope.

So the big question becomes: who can save us—from egocentric, self-destructive repression? Nothing but love. Not the way we do it but unremitting, unconditional, biblical love. This love refuses to deny our issues. It stays with us there and won't ever let us go. This love, too, compels us to love: "I am my beloved's, and he is mine."

I take comfort that this love was not deterred by whatever it is that I got myself into on my semester abroad, or what you may be into at 8 a.m. in your pajamas. You haven't been expecting this kind of love. It is alien to your whole way of operating. And yet it's true. He has decided to put an end to all the judgment and condemnation that drives you into hiding. He has forgiven all. He has overcome your attempts to sabotage His love and isolate yourself. May God continue that work of love in your life today.

"O my dove, in the clefts of the rock, in the crannies of the cliff, let me see your face, let me hear your voice, for your voice is sweet, and your face is lovely."

—*Kate Norris*

146

April 20

"Woe to me!" I cried. "I am ruined! For I am a man of
unclean lips, and I live among a people of unclean lips, and
my eyes have seen the King, the LORD Almighty." (Isaiah
6:5, NIV)

C.S. Lewis once pointed out that "the closer you get to the sun, the bigger the shadows." This is surprisingly true of the Christian life. The knowledge of sin in one's own life can only grow as we get to know God better.

Along the same lines, Bishop Fitz Allison speaks of a psychologist in South Carolina who worked with a death row serial murderer, of the most nasty and violent variety; she said she never met a man with "such high self-esteem!" Saints know their sin better than do criminals. It is for this reason that Christians who understand grace are much more readily able to cry when something sad happens, to apologize when they make a mistake, and to laugh at themselves when they do something stupid.

Christian people cannot be defensive because, in encountering God's grace, they have come to understand themselves to be people of "unclean lips." What about yourself would you defend? Are you so sure of your own merit?

—John Zahl

April 21

And in that day his burden will depart from your shoulder,
and his yoke from your neck; and the yoke will be broken
because of the fat. (Isaiah 10:27, ESV)

When it comes to yokes and shoulders, two movie scenes spring to mind. One is from *The Mission* (1986), and the second is in Jet Li's *Twin Warriors* (1993). In the first film there is a powerful scene of a man who is part of a Spanish expedition in the New World—as penance for a murder he has committed, he is dragging a net filled with armor, swords, and metal up a waterlogged cliff. One of the "natives" sees his struggle, climbs down, and cuts the cords.

The second film is a fantastic kung fu flick: Jet Li's character, Junbao, is wounded by a friend's betrayal. One day in a field he sees two peasants running back to their village—they have just found out one of their wives is about to be sold into labor camps. However, the husband can't keep up due to the huge load of wood he's carrying, and his friend has to convince him to drop the load; otherwise, he'll never make it in time. Witnessing this simple event is cathartic for Junbao, who goes on to learn Tai Chi and defeat his enemies. Per usual.

Our passage today is about burdens. Isaiah is foretelling a time when Israel will go into exile for their continued disobedience towards God. This exile is not without hope, and Isaiah sees a time when "his burden will depart from your shoulder." While most of us have never had our homeland destroyed and been shipped off to a foreign land as slaves (although that sadly still does happen in our world), we are no strangers to burdens. Christianity's understanding of relief is much more in keeping with *The Mission* than with *Twin Warriors*: our relief is not something we are able to do for ourselves. It must be something done for us, or better yet, to us.

The answer to lugging burdens is not getting to the top of the hill with them, or even dropping them, but being cut free from them. We often try to release them ourselves—a futile task. Someone must come and act for us. That was Isaiah's message to Israel, that God must come and deliver them from their own disobedience and evil. That is our message for Christianity, too: not the newest issue for better tips on burden-lugging, but freedom from it in the presence of a deliverer.

"It is for freedom that Christ has set us free, stand firm therefore and do not submit again to the yolk of slavery" (Gal 5:1). This is the good news, that God Himself came down and said, "Come to me all you who are weary, and I will give you rest, for my burden is easy and my yolk is light" (Matt 11:30). Thanks be to God.

—*Ben Phillips*

April 22

On this mountain the Lord of hosts will make for all peoples a feast of rich food, a feast of well-aged wine, of rich food full of marrow, of aged wine well refined. And he will swallow up on this mountain the covering that is cast over all peoples, the veil that is spread over all nations. He will swallow up death forever; and the Lord God will wipe away tears from all faces, and the reproach of his people he will take away from all the earth, for the Lord has spoken. It will be said on that day, "Behold, this is our God; we have waited for him, that he might save us. This is the Lord; we have waited for him; let us be glad and rejoice in his salvation." (Isaiah 25:6-9, ESV)

You and I have a problem. Sure, we have tons, but there's one biggie, and there's absolutely nothing we can do about it. No amount of money can solve it. No amount of "moral living" or "positive thinking" or "healthy lifestyles" or "trips to the gym" will fix it. "Hard work" will not answer it.

As Axl said, "You're gonna die!"

But why do people die? Why will you die one day? Why is this the insurmountable problem of humanity? The Bible says we die because of sin. Adam and Eve sinned and died, and we, their progeny, die too. Our deepest-rooted condition, like theirs, is rebellion against God, so we die—*"the wages of sin is death"*—forever.

An answer came to this unfixable problem from afar, as it only could. Paul talks about this answer in his letter to the Corinthian church. "For as by a man came death, by a man has come also the resurrection of the dead. For as in Adam all die, so also in Christ shall all be made alive" (1 Cor 15:21). Isaiah talks about him here, thousands of years before he was born: "He will swallow up death forever."

Both physical and spiritual death were swallowed up at the cross of Christ. There Christ proclaimed, "It is finished," and this was certified by his resurrection three days later. While the physical expressions of death will one day be destroyed, the spiritual reversal is already here.

The answer to our problem is not self-help gurus or motivational speakers or life coaches. We don't need a little help to tip us over the edge. We need an elixir of life, a death-destroyer, if you will. We have it in Jesus: because of Jesus death is dead.

—*Curt Benham*

April 23

The wilderness and the dry land shall be glad; the desert shall rejoice and blossom like the crocus; it shall blossom abundantly and rejoice with joy and singing. The glory of Lebanon shall be given to it, the majesty of Carmel and

Sharon. They shall see the glory of the Lord, the majesty of our God. Strengthen the weak hands, and make firm the feeble knees. Say to those have an anxious heart, "Be strong; fear not! Behold, your God will come with vengeance, with the recompense of God. He will come and save you." (Isaiah 35:1-4, ESV)

I think that French hitman was onto something!

One of my favorite scenes in Luc Besson's 1994 film, *The Professional*, is when a young (her first role) Natalie Portman, after witnessing a tragedy, asks Jean Reno, "Is life always this hard, or is it just when you're a kid?" He responds in a thick accent, "Always like this." It's very touching, beautifully acted, and right on the money.

You ever feel like God just isn't up there? Or if He is, He's not listening? I've been in the wilderness for over three years now. No end in sight. Puzzled, frazzled, wounded, and spent. Lost faith and found it over and over (and over).

What's the wilderness? Why do we have to experience it? More importantly, how can we avoid it? We always need someone or something to either stridently blame (the *Super 8* space alien that lives down that dark hole) or shallowly believe in (take your pick).

The desperate need to make sense of, or give order to, a world that resists both at every turn is hardwired into us. Because if there's order, there's potential for control: diets, books, steps, denominations, political parties, etc. And if there's control, our ego tells us everything's going to be okay—because we collectively say so. Failure? Fear? Insomnia? Depression? That's the other guy's problem.

As I see it, the only, and I mean only, answer is death and resurrection. I have little use for action-consequence. Thankfully, mercifully, that's been decided for us. Like the American saint Johnny Cash once sang: "the old account was settled long ago."

Is it possible that it's less important what I believe in and far more important that something believes in me? Sometimes, in the wilderness and the dry land, that's all I can grasp hold of.

—*Nate Michaux*

April 24

Even youths grow tired and weary, and young men stumble and fall; but those who hope in the Lord will renew their strength. They will soar on wings like eagles; they will run and not grow weary, they will walk and not be faint. (Isaiah 40:30-31, NIV)

Isaiah gives comforting words to Israel, which here suffers from the mistakes of yesterday. Carried away from their jobs and the only homes they ever knew, they are moving to a foreign land. It seems hopeless, as though they will always bear this as the consequence of their past mistakes.

I don't know about you, but often it's hard to get out of bed in the morning. It's not that I don't get enough sleep, and it's definitely not that I don't drink enough coffee. I wake up tired because the sleep hasn't unburdened the cumulative weight of yesterday. I have heard that every day is a fresh start; it doesn't always feel true to me.

It's not just yesterday. In general, we have a hard time shaking free of our shadows, and this makes us weary. We wake up and think of the strained relationships, all the work waiting in the wings, the consequential missing substance with our families, our spouses. The failures weary us, and regret surfaces as we wonder if there was something else we could have done differently.

But Isaiah speaks of a God who renews the strength of the weak. The chains of the past are taken away by God's renewing forgiveness. In God, "morning by morning new mercies I see." All the regrets, all the waiting work, find their end in God's forgiveness, where we may truly run and not grow weary.

—Todd Brewer

April 25

"...a bruised reed he will not break, and a faintly burning wick he will not quench; he will faithfully bring forth justice. (Isaiah 42:2-3, ESV)

The disciple Matthew references this prophecy to describe Jesus: "many followed him, and he healed them all and ordered them not to make him

known. This was to fulfill what was spoken by the prophet Isaiah..."
(Matt 12). There's not much weaker than a bruised reed or a faintly
burning wick: a stepped-on branch cannot right itself, a smoldering flame
cannot reignite; they are both in danger of being crushed forever by a
careless foot or a single well-placed breath, and yet this is the
forethought of the gentle and compassionate Jesus.

I used to think this passage applied to those who were *truly*
weak—you know, "the least of these"—the poor, the disabled, people
suffering under terminal illnesses. And this didn't apply to me: I was
strong, I led a youth group, I ran Bible studies. And then came a time
when I doubted, my life grew dark, and I couldn't pull myself out of it or
rekindle my faith, and I was scared.

But how many of us really are bruised reeds and smoldering wicks?
Maybe at times we stand straight and tall, burning brightly, but life itself
does the damage, until we worry that one more mishap, one more failure,
one more harsh word could crush us. And here, having become "the least
of these," we see Jesus who says, "I will not condemn you, I will not cast
you out. I will heal you; come to me." It is the gentle and no-less-
powerful love of Jesus, who himself was subjected to weakness, that
restores the weak at heart.

—Sarah Richey

April 26

*I, even I, am the one who wipes out your transgressions for
My own sake, and I will not remember your sins. (Isaiah
43:25, NASB)*

The people of God pause to see if a qualifier is attached to this promise, a
bait-and-switch that might consign them to spiritual servitude. After all,
who hasn't suspected that God has something up His sleeve? Perhaps
your faith is no longer as fresh as the day when Christianity "clicked."
Since then, like Israel here, many of us have experienced years of faith
where God's covenant felt like legal clauses and insurance disclaimers.
Rather than that first-heard Gospel "Yes!", we have begun to think that
Christianity is more about saying "Yes!" to Someone who prefers saying
"No!" It's sad, but we long for legalism. This "Christianity of the fine
print" is nothing more than an echo of Israel's hollow-chested service
here.

Where's the zeal gone? Gone are the days when the most mundane events feel like pregnant opportunities for gospel-sharing, and in exchange comes the play-acting of the seasoned churchgoer. Hands in pockets, head bowed low, my spiritual maturity is a mumbled prayer, a way of saying "Yes" to God while really saying, "You've disregarded me—look at the sacrifices I've bestowed!" It goes without saying that this self-imposed martyrdom is a million miles from God's "Yes!" My lifeless "Yes" to Him only adds to the trail of my empty sacrifices.

I have been made aware that after two years in the church, the most difficult thing to believe is that God loves me. Being taken up into that kind of love means my reluctant sacrifices will pale in comparison—and my sacrifices are certainly easier to control.

"Look," says God, to Israel and to us, "I am not petty. Let's simply start again, with this: I am the Forgiving One." Like Israel, we strain our ears for the "however," but it never comes. He reiterates for emphasis: "I, even I, am the one!" How reluctant is the human heart!

God repeats this "Yes!" over and over throughout Scripture, because that is simply who He is: God is for us, on our side. The persistence of His "Yes!" is offensive, but take that away and we have the cold comfort of religious procedure. Though we may not feel zealous today, the Ancient of Days is not putting us on: He knows we can't carry the load of religious requirement for long, so He continually shoulders it for us.

—*Dylan Potter*

April 27

How beautiful on the mountains are the feet of those who bring good news, who proclaim peace, who bring good tidings, who proclaim salvation, who say to Zion, "Your God reigns!" (Isaiah 52:7, NIV)

At mile twenty in a marathon, most runners start to falter: one man grabs his hamstring and hobbles to the curb, another mutters about a toenail, and a young woman sits down right in the middle of the road. When my wife saw me at mile twenty-two, neither she nor I knew if I would survive the rest of the race. For the last few miles, I followed right behind another runner and tried to block out the pain. With three hundred yards to go, I finally saw the finish line with thousands of people cheering, including my wife screaming at the top of her lungs, rejoicing that I was nearly there.

And though there can be glory in a marathon, its origin is a story of sacrifice—the first Marathon runner needing to get news to Athens, sacrificing his own body in the process, the story goes, dying immediately after delivering the news of victory (where the word "Nike" comes from).

Isaiah, too, tells of a watchmen's joy when he sees the messenger who has run from the battle to proclaim the news of their army's victory. "We are free," the messenger proclaims, "Your God reigns!" The messenger's feet cannot hold him another minute, but how lovely are his feet, which bring the good news. Good news comes to those of us who need it most, at a supreme cost to its messenger.

In Jesus, the fundamental messenger of Good News, the message of deliverance is conclusive. In him, we are delivered not from foreign political powers, but from sin and death—and what good news this is! St. Paul quotes this passage in Romans 10:15, referring to the messengers who preach this good news of Jesus. How beautiful are the feet of the weary messenger who has run the race to bring the news of salvation to those who are in need.

—*Drake Richey*

April 28

He was despised and rejected by men; a man of sorrows, and acquainted with grief; and as one from whom men hide their faces he was despised, and we esteemed him not. Surely he has borne our griefs and carried our sorrows; yet we esteemed him stricken, smitten by God, and afflicted. But he was pierced for our transgressions; he was crushed for our iniquities; upon him was the chastisement that brought us peace, and with his wounds we are healed. (Isaiah 53:3-5, ESV)

I love stories, you love stories, we all love stories. We like to read them, watch them, hear them, tell them, experience them. We always have and we always will. In fact, sociologist Christian Smith claims that our ability and propensity for storytelling is a big part of what makes us human. He calls us "animals who make stories but also animals who are *made by* our stories."[*]

Listen closely the next time someone tells you their life story—or the next time you tell someone yours—and you will inevitably hear some kind of over-arching narrative. It may have to do with overcoming adversity; it may have to do with tragedy and victimhood; it may have to do with overriding social or political forces, or with success, failure, beauty, money, power, etc. It could be as simple as "I was worse, but now I am better," or as arbitrary as "I used to have a difficult relationship with my mother, but now it's much easier." And there are the stories we tell ourselves, and the stories about ourselves that we buy into. As soon as we identify with these stories—i.e. who we have to be or want to be or should be—we set ourselves up to rationalize or straight-up deny any experiences or feelings that don't fit. We all do it, but that doesn't make it any less a recipe for loneliness and resentment.

The story we read here about God is a surprising one. It is not a story of triumph or glory. It is not a story of retribution or blessing or even joy. It is a story about those things that we tend leave out of the narratives we project onto God—namely, suffering, loss, and grief. That is because this is the story about Jesus. Which means it is a story of comfort for those whose lives haven't followed a neat or consistent trajectory and sometimes don't seem to make any sense at all. Tullian Tchividjian puts it this way:

> God is not interested in what you think you *should* be or feel. He is not interested in the narrative you construct for yourself, or that others construct for you... Rather, He is interested in you, the you who suffers, the you who inflicts suffering on others, the you who hides, the you who has bad days (and good ones). And He meets you where you are. Jesus is not the man at the top of the stairs; He is the man at the bottom, the friend of sinners, the savior of those in need of one. Which is all of us, all of the time, praise be to God![†]

So what stories are you telling about yourself today? What stories are you telling yourself about God? Perhaps we might pray that we would

---

[*] Smith, Christian. *Moral, Believing Animals: Human Personhood and Culture.* p. 64.

[†] Tchividjian, Tullian. *Glorious Ruin: How Suffering Sets You Free,* David C Cook: 2012, p. 90

be given fresh ears to listen to a new story: the story of a suffering servant who loves us as we are, not as we should be. The story that no one in their right mind would make up, especially not if they wanted anyone else to believe it. Unless, of course, it were true.

—*David Zahl*

April 29

For my thoughts are not your thoughts, nor are your ways my ways, says the Lord. For as the heavens are higher than the earth, so are my ways higher than your ways and my thoughts than your thoughts. (Isaiah 55:8-9, NRSV)

In his book *The Shallows*, Nicholas Carr talks extensively about a scientist named Michael Merzenich and something called "neuroplasticity," which basically means our brain will morph its circuitry in tandem with our circumstances and habits. Just in the last 50 years, we've learned all this complicated stuff about the brain that seems to put all the puzzle pieces together. It's funny, though, because in that same chapter, Carr says that Aristotle thought the brain was a big blood refrigerator that "tempers the heat of the seething heart."[*] It's funny to laugh at how wrong he was, but Aristotle is one of the fathers of Western thought, and no one's ever heard of Merzenich.

Whether those reputations change in the next decade, or the next millennium, or they never do, one thing is safe to say: no matter how right we think we are today, we're almost always going to look back with a little chagrin tomorrow. Says psychologist Jordi Quoidbach in the *New York Times*, we tend to have an "end of history illusion," the idea that the "*I wish that I knew then what I know now* experience might give us a sense of satisfaction and meaning, whereas realizing how transient our preferences and values are (currently) might lead us to doubt every decision and generate anxiety."[†] In other words, we are good at laughing at our past selves, but we still tend to feel an earnest sense of propriety when it comes to the here-and-now.

---

[*] Carr, Nicholas. *The Shallows: What the Internet Is Doing to Our Brains*. NY: W.W. Norton & Company. 2011. p. 36.

[†] Tierney, John. "Why You Won't Be the Person You Expect to Be." *The New York Times*. January 3, 2013. http://www.nytimes.com/2013/01/04/science/study-in-science-shows-end-of-history-illusion.html

This passage mirrors this sentiment, that we humans, despite thinking ourselves in circles for the right answers, will not find any fewer muddles and mazes along the line for our efforts. Isaiah says this is because "our ways" are not "God's ways."

Though God is omnipotent and we are not, part of "our way" certainly includes a misplaced sense of omnipotence. We are by nature strivers and fortune-seekers; for centuries we've used idioms with bullhorns and bootstraps; we will always tell stories of those destiny makers and dream chasers and do-it-yourselfers. We have promoted the narrative that our lives are for the taking, and we will continue to do so. And yet how hard it is *not* to think of Jesus coming upon a crowd of five thousand people and merely seeing "sheep without a shepherd" (Mark 6).

This is the paradoxical wisdom of "God's ways" —not just that we humans are indeed *not* omnipotent, but that God subverts His own omnipotence for our sake. In Jesus, and most deliberately on the cross, we see "God's way" as *impotence*-unto-death, a way in which strength is weakness and weakness is strength.

While laughing or crying at who you were ten years ago, and while facing your circumstances today, remember Aristotle's brain fridge, and the lasting comfort that has made its home amidst all these transient tempers.

—*Ethan Richardson*

April 30

Arise, shine; for your light has come, and the glory of the Lord has risen upon you. For behold, darkness shall cover the earth, and thick darkness the peoples; but the Lord will arise upon you, and his glory will be seen upon you. (Isaiah 60:1-2, RSV)

Rise and shine! On first impression, this passage simply seems to be an exhortation to get up, make the best of it, and put on a good attitude. But how can such an exhortation take away the thick darkness described? If we rise, it is to a huge pile of responsibilities, and the way through is littered with things left undone, promises not kept. How can one shine when there is so much darkness *within*, interior closets of bad thoughts and faithless worry?

It is exhausting, really, this hiding in the dark, and deep down we wish to be known. We do want light. But on the other hand, light would show what we *are* hiding, and how poorly we use our time, and how often we worry needlessly—it is safer to keep that hidden, though the cry of despondency often comes: "Who cares what I do? Does anybody?"

In this passage we hear that "your light has come," and we brace ourselves for exposure. Yet when the light of the glory of the Lord shines on us, we receive not condemnation but comfort; the Lord, who knows us no less because of His mercy, comforts His people and has compassion on them. His glory is revealed through forgiveness, perfect understanding, and the hope before us. This gift of light is Jesus Christ, who sees into us with the eyes of love and says, "Child, arise."

—Robin Anderson

May 1

He has sent me... to proclaim freedom for the captives and release from darkness to the prisoners. (Isaiah 61:1, NIV)

Freedom. It is not a word often associated with Christians. Not remotely. Yet freedom is an integral aspect of what Jesus was "all about." He caused quite the uproar when he applied this passage to himself (Luke 4), and we should take it at least as seriously as he did. After all, the German theologian Ernst Käsemann did not pull the title of his book *Jesus Means Freedom* out of thin air. Nor did Martin Luther when he wrote his historic treatise, *The Freedom of a Christian.*

There are many ways to define freedom in Jesus' terms, but here's one for today: it is the freedom from being responsible for your own value. This often then bestows the freedom to love other people.

Take, for example, the coarse yet charming 2006 film *Little Miss Sunshine*, which portrays the collective nervous breakdown of the dysfunctional Hoover family. The son, who has spent a year in silence preparing to be an Air Force pilot, finds out that he is color-blind and unfit for training. The father, who has put his life savings into launching a self-help empire, receives the final rejection of his program. Their goals, which in themselves were noble and good, ultimately imprisoned them in tunnels of self-determination wherein they became completely unable to love (or even see) the other members of their family. But as their hopes are frustrated, something remarkable happens—they begin to care about each other. For the Hoovers, the breakdowns function as "break-free" moments.

The cross of Christ both exposes the futility of our efforts at establishing ourselves and answers them. It ushers in the real freedom that we are loved and valued, not according to what we do, but what Jesus has done. That is, we are good because God is good, not because we are good. The shackles are off, once and for all! Perhaps today we can pray that it won't take a Hoover-sized breakdown for us to see it.

—David Zahl

May 2

> *For Zion's sake I will not keep silent, and for Jerusalem's sake I will not be quiet, until her righteousness goes forth as brightness, and her salvation as a burning torch. The nations shall see your righteousness, and all the kings your glory, and you shall be called by a new name that the mouth of the Lord will give. You shall be a crown of beauty in the hand of the Lord, and a royal diadem in the hand of your God. You shall no more be termed Forsaken, and your land shall no more be termed Desolate, but you shall be called My Delight Is in Her, and your land Married; for the LORD delights in you, and your land shall be married. (Isaiah 62:1-4, ESV)*

There's the old Shakespeare line, "What's in a name? / That which we call a rose / By any other name would smell as sweet." (*Romeo and Juliet*). Juliet may not have made much of names, but our names have the tendency to transcend us. In the Bible, significant changes in a person's life were accompanied by a change in their name: Abram was re-named Abraham—"Father of Nations"—after God declared him to be so (Gen 17:5). Jacob was re-named Israel—"God contended"—after wrestling with God until morning (Gen 32:28). Simon became Peter, the "rock" on which God would build his Church (Mark 3:16). When God re-names people, He creates a new hope, something stretching much further beyond who they've known themselves to be. By changing their names, He changes their lives.

Although names seem to possess less inherent meaning today, we still wish to be known as people whose lives *mean* something. We strive to maximize the positive traits by which we are known and minimize the jeopardizing ones, and sometimes we wish we were someone else altogether. We are not usually completely happy with who we are: we know well what we lack, yet we also lack the means to really change it. It is hard for us to render a new name in any sustainable or significant way.

And yet the old story of a new hope is true for us: "you shall be called a new name that the mouth of the Lord will give." God promises that we will be known by a new name—a name that, in renaming, transforms us. No longer shall we be called "Forsaken," but "Righteous;" no longer shall we be called "Desolate," but "Delight of God." The Lord has and will continue to transform us, and the first step is to call us by something different than what we are; He will name our righteousness into existence.

—Bonnie Poon Zahl

May 3

You meet him who joyfully works righteousness, those who remember you in your ways. Behold, you were angry, and we sinned; in our sins we have been a long time, and shall we be saved? We have all become like one who is unclean, and all our righteous deeds are like a polluted garment. We all fade like a leaf, and our iniquities, like the wind, take us away... I delight greatly in the LORD; my soul rejoices in my God. For he has clothed me with garments of salvation and arrayed me in a robe of righteousness. (Isaiah 64:5-6, 61:10, ESV)

Moralism, one of the great swindlers of the age, has come off so well because it's successful in appealing to our pride. With moral righteousness, we can wear royal robes for doing great and "selfless" deeds. The picture offered here in Isaiah 64, though, is that we are parading in our own soiled clothes. All your righteous acts—think about the charity drive, the listening good-friend moment, the dinner table prayer—God calls filthy rags.

There is a reason we do not boast in our morality or spirituality. Faith in Christ means we are not draped in our own rags but in the righteous robe of Christ. Isaiah writes, "I delight greatly in the Lord, my soul rejoices in my God. For he has clothed me with garments of salvation and arrayed me in a robe of righteousness" (61:10). Jesus has made the exchange, taking on ours and giving us his. This is what we call justification: the declaration of your righteous status before God.

Justification is the polar antithesis of condemnation. While a condemned man is declared guilty and sentenced to death, a justified man is declared innocent and set free to live. In the Christian faith we flip the poles: born guilty, we stand condemned; yet with Christ for your righteousness, we are made righteous before God. His righteousness becomes our righteousness.

This is the wonderful doctrine of *imputation*. The righteousness of Christ is presently placed upon us, credited to our account, covering over "the sins of the world." And what a comforting and liberating doctrine! You may be strong today and weak tomorrow—life will always provide its peaks and valleys. "Old sins" may re-emerge, or God may deliver you from them. You may make spiritual progress or spiritual regress. But there is no waxing and waning of the imputed righteousness of God. You are clothed in a love to which you can never add and from which you can never detract.

—Justin Holcomb

May 4

For behold, I create new heavens and a new earth; and the former things shall not be remembered or come into mind. (Isaiah 65:17, RSV)

Despite being on Facebook along with most of my friends, I've not yet figured out whether I think it is really a good thing or a bad thing. There's definitely something to be said for keeping in touch with current friends and reconnecting with old ones. Just the other week, because of Facebook, I reconnected with my high school best friend after almost 15 years. On the other hand, I often dread what new old face is going to show up next in the "People You Might Know" column off to the side— someone who hurt me, or whom I hurt, or who just frankly annoyed me.

The problem is that I like to imagine that certain memories and people in my past can somehow be left behind. The truth is that no matter how hard we might wish otherwise, our past remains with us and affects us today. We certainly don't need Facebook to remind us of past hurt and guilt. The scars of previous relationships—with parents, siblings, friends, or spouses—affect our current ones. They can dramatically hinder our ability to love and to be loved. Our pasts have the potential to create something of a veil between us and the world around us.

True healing is not about being fixed—about clearing up the veil—but it is about being *remade*, given new sight. It is about being loved when we are unlovable, seen as beautiful when ugly, and valued as perfect when we are anything but. It is that feeling we get when we meet someone who "really understands me." Unconditional acceptance—in spite of pasts, problems, and shortcomings—has tremendously transformative power. It has the potential to tear the veil "from top to bottom."

The Gospel is that no one understands us better or accepts us more than God. It is truly a mercy that we don't remember everything we've thought, said or done; however, God does. In that darkness, He understands us as broken, desperate sinners more deeply than we could ever imagine, and He still loves us. The Gospel is that in that love He didn't come into the world to tweak the Ten Commandments, or to help us live a little better. Instead, He came into the world to demonstrate that love, to save us from ourselves even though it meant death on the cross, a death bringing all "things old" to death as well. "Behold, I make all things new," says Christ from the throne (Rev 21:5). The good news is that even if we can't quite see that for ourselves right now, Jesus did and still does, and the cross is our assurance. We are given the vision of hope in a past unremembered and, thus, a present that is permanently "unveiled."

—*Leonard Finn*

May 5

...Now the word of the LORD came to me, saying, "Before I formed you in the womb I knew you, and before you were born I consecrated you; I appointed you a prophet to the nations." Then I said, "Ah, Lord GOD! Behold, I do not know how to speak, for I am only a youth." But the LORD said to me, "Do not say, 'I am only a youth'; for to all to whom I send you, you shall go, and whatever I command you, you shall speak. Do not be afraid of them, for I am

with you to deliver you, declares the LORD." Then the LORD put out his hand and touched my mouth. And the LORD said to me, "Behold, I have put my words in your mouth." (Jeremiah 1:1-9, ESV)

God really knows His people in the Bible. This is one of the constant themes—He not only knows the number of hairs on their heads, but even knows them before they were in their mothers' wombs, and He knows them better than they know themselves. And this is true of life today, too. Even though we almost always "look within" for the resources to accomplish everything, we don't really know as much about ourselves as we think.

On one hand, this inadequacy leads us to despair, both of ourselves and our so-called abilities to do what the Lord asks of us. On the other hand, with the self-realization we so long for yawning beyond us, we are strangely brought to a place of freedom.

Jeremiah, coming to this impasse, is able to go out in strength because this power came from outside of him. Jeremiah is called by God, as they say, but Jeremiah's ability to fulfill the calling was not contingent upon the depth of his résumé, but instead his complete reliance on the Lord to stand in for him and walk with him. Armed with only this, Jeremiah does the impossible because it was actually *not* Jeremiah doing anything, but the Lord doing it all.

This kind of supernatural strength is necessary for all of life, from birth to grave—it doesn't just apply to Jeremiah or the Patriarchs. Life is a challenge that leaves all of us muttering, like Jeremiah, "I do not know how to..." Are you in a job in which you feel way over your head? Struggling with a frigid marriage? A hapless child? Life confronts all of us with issues with which we feel woefully inept to deal. And God uses these things to show us the need for complete reliance. Just like Jeremiah, God is in the midst of it all, doing it all, while you do nothing.

Whatever it is you are faced with in your life today, God has called you to this place, but He is not leaving you there. He will use your weakness to His glory.

—Andrew Pearson

May 6

"The heart is deceitful above all things, and desperately sick; who can understand it?" (Jeremiah 17:9, ESV)

C. S. Lewis said, "Christ takes it for granted that men are bad." Most of the world operates on the opposite assumption—that people are intrinsically good. The world takes it for granted that we are "born free, as free as the wind blows, as free as the grass grows, born free to follow our hearts." Jeremiah expresses a different view of our hearts—they are deceitful and desperately sick. Given that reality, who would actually want to follow his or her heart?

A quick inventory of your own anger, lust, jealousy, greed, or self-preoccupation confirms Jeremiah's diagnosis, not to mention Jesus'. Or maybe it's your need to shop, or your miserly grip on your money, or your non-stop critical commentary of others. Or perhaps it is the malaise or boredom that has sealed you into the margins of life.

It could be that your unforgiving attitude or your chronic defensiveness is the culprit. And we haven't even touched on your dependence on sex, drugs, work, thrill, or entertainment to get you through another year, another month, another day, another hour. Whatever the outward and visible expression of your sickness, we know the origin: the heart is deceitful above all things.

The good news about this bad news is that Christ takes it for granted that you are this way. There's no need to pretend to be something you are not. That is gracious of him, isn't it? And wise too. After all he is the One to whom "all hearts are open, all desires known, and from whom no secrets are hid." Adam and Eve tried to hide from God in the Garden after their own hearts were corrupted. But to no avail; God found them out just as He has found us out.

The other good news about casting your lot in with Jeremiah's assessment is that you are now in a position to be found out, and thus saved by God. Lewis continues, "Until we really feel this assumption of His to be true, though we are part of the world He came to save, we are not part of the audience to whom His words are addressed." Once we agree with the diagnosis, there is the hope of healing.

The Gospel is always bad news before good; bad news about ourselves followed by the good news about God. In Christ, God comes to the slums of your heart to find and save you. As Jeremiah, the diagnostician of the heart, concludes, "Heal me, Lord, and I shall be healed; save me and I shall be saved, for you are my praise."

—Paul Walker

May 7

> *...If I say, "I will not mention him, or speak any more in his name," there is in my heart as it were a burning fire shut up in my bones, and I am weary with holding it in, and I cannot. (Jeremiah 20:7-9, ESV)*

Some time ago, a friend of mine went through an especially difficult period in her life. There were times when she felt that her prayers to God were falling on deaf ears. This period finally ended, and my friend emerged with a new sense of life and purpose.

She was praying one day when a vivid scene came to her mind. She saw herself standing on the banks of a lovely river running through a beautiful forest. Suddenly, she saw a man. He was walking on top of the water in the river. As he drew closer, she realized that it was Jesus. He stepped off the water and onto the bank and stood beside her. She looked at him for a minute.

Then she said in a firm voice, "Where the hell have you been?"

Do you see how healthy and full of love those words from my friend were? And do you sense the fire that my friend has within her? It's a fire born of God and of such strength that she cannot hold it in.

My friend is a vivid picture of the prophet Jeremiah. God gives Jeremiah a message to proclaim. But every time he speaks, he bombs. However, he is so overwhelmed by his experience of God that he can't shut up. He cries out, "There is within me something like a burning fire shut up in my bones, and I am weary with holding it in, and I cannot."

In a movie called *Stars in My Crown*, an African-American man has been a wonderful grandfather figure to several generations of children in the town. But a valuable mineral deposit is discovered on his property. Some white business leaders in town offer to buy his land, but he simply wants to live out his days there. When he refuses to sell, things get ugly. The people whom he had counted as friends turn on him. It comes to a head when the former friends say, "If you're not off the property by sundown tomorrow, we'll hang you."

At the appointed hour the next day, the townsmen appear, hiding behind white hoods. A friend comes out onto the porch with the old man and says, "John knows that he is going to die. He asked me to come out today and write his last will and testimony. He wants me to read it to you. He wants to give his fishing rod to Pete, because he remembers the first bass he caught with it. He wants to give his rifle to James, because he remembers using it to teach him to shoot."

Item by item, the old man gives away his possessions to the very people who have come to take his life. And one by one, the townsmen turn their horses around and leave. A little grandson has been watching this scene from a distance. When it's all over, he runs to the porch and says to the old man, "What kind of a will was that?"

The old man answers gently, "The will of God, son—the will of God."

May it be the will of God that you be granted a fire in your heart that cannot be contained. Most of all, may it be the will of God that all your fire be sustained by the same fire of that old gentleman—which is to say, by the love of Christ.

—*Jim Munroe*

May 8

"Is not my word like fire," declares the Lord, "and like a hammer that breaks a rock in pieces?" (Jeremiah 23:29, NIV)

U2 opens their 1997 PopMart Tour with each member of the band approaching the massive, gaudy stage in full costume, each an outward shell of someone else. There is a pulsing extended intro—"Pop Musik"—and Bono enters from the back of the stadium, on ground level, surrounded by bodyguards, in a boxer's get-up. He plays the part as he approaches the stage-slash-ring, walking through the crowd with showtime heavyweight bravado, set on convincing the world (and himself) that he is larger-than-life. After nearly eight minutes, the entire stadium is frenetic with this masquerade; as the intro fades into the first electronic loops of the opening song, Bono's swagger matches his alter ego point for point. The song is "Mofo," the title itself trying to convince everyone of a supposed grandeur: "Looking for to save my, save my soul."

"Is not my word like a hammer that breaks a rock in pieces?" We carry our personas no differently, grandstanding like a title fighter, doing anything we can to posture invincibility and sufficiency. The human heart yearns to believe it is an immovable force. But then our song starts and, like "Mofo," we fissure and crack. Life happens, and the Word of God speaks as a hammer. Behind the boxer's robe we are revealed for what we really are. The life we live is a facade, surpassing even the ironic extravagance of the ten-story arch of PopMart.

We need a miracle; we need someone to save us from the lie. Thanks be to God, our posturing is crushed with the swift blow of a hammer, the truth already declared and provided in the One who is the Truth. Bono closes the song by crooning, "move me a mountain." It is a clear cry to the One who has done so on our behalf.

—Gil Kracke

May 9

Thus says the LORD of hosts, the God of Israel, to all the exiles whom I have sent into exile from Jerusalem to Babylon: Build houses and live in them; plant gardens and eat their produce. Take wives and have sons and daughters; take wives for your sons, and give your daughters in marriage, that they may bear sons and daughters; multiply there, and do not decrease. But seek the welfare of the city where I have sent you into exile, and pray to the LORD on its behalf, for in its welfare you will find your welfare. (Jeremiah 29:4-7, ESV)

To be in exile is to be far from home. Anywhere you go that is not home is a place of exile. This does not just mean the home you grew up in—for example, you might find by your fourth year, surrounded by friends with whom you have shared so much, that your college feels more like "home" than your parents' house. Whenever leaving a place or situation is painful, scary, uncomfortable, or sad, that is the sign that you are going into exile. Sometimes home leaves you—you stay in the same place, but the people who made it so special move away.

The passage tells us something very important: that it is the Lord who is the author of exile. He is the one who sent you to the lonely place, the alien place, the difficult place, just as He was the one who made the old place home. To feel cut off from family, friends, and fellowship is in part to understand more truly the reality that we are "strangers and exiles on the earth." (Heb 11:13)

The second point here is that the way to deal with exile is to be open to it becoming a new home. The most difficult part is letting go of the idea that it is temporary—what if you are to stay there until your children have children, as in the passage? The reason any place can be home is that the Lord is the one who will always go with you, wherever you go. The one who animates friendships and creates fellowship, who fosters feelings of belonging and belovedness, is neither your family, nor your friends, in the end. It is the Lord. "For in its welfare you will find your welfare." The Lord has gone ahead to the new place; He has not lingered behind. Your welfare lies with Him, ahead, in the unknown future.

There is a further consolation, however, for Christians. It is that there is indeed a final Home, of which the safest, happiest place here is but a forerunner and a shadow. "They desire a better country, that is, a heavenly one. Therefore God is not ashamed to be called their God, for he has prepared for them a city." (Heb 11:16)

—Simeon Zahl

May 10

The days are surely coming, says the Lord, when I will make a new covenant with the house of Israel and the house of Judah. It will not be like the covenant that I made with their ancestors when I took them by the hand to bring them out of the land of Egypt—a covenant that they broke, though I was their husband, says the Lord. But this is the covenant that I will make with the house of Israel after those days, says the Lord: I will put my law within them, and I will write it on their hearts; and I will be their God, and they shall be my people. No longer shall they teach one another, or say to each other, "Know the Lord," for they shall all know me, from the least of them to the greatest, says the Lord; for I will forgive their iniquity, and remember their sin no more. (Jeremiah 31:31-34, NRSV)

A few months ago, I was in a local grocery store where a clerk had neatly stacked this large pyramid of mac-&-cheese boxes. All of a sudden, a revved-up, red-haired three-year-old tackled the pyramid, scattering them across the floor. His clearly exasperated and embarrassed mother grabbed her child by the shoulders and said, "Sam, I love you, but you can't be a part of our family if you act that way."

This passage from Jeremiah 31 highlights the chilling distinction between what theologians call the Old Covenant and the New Covenant. And it's all to do with what's acceptable and what gets you kicked out of God's family. This Old Covenant, often known as the Law, is an elementally conditional relationship: blessing is promised for those who obey, but cursing for those who don't. Jeremiah says that this covenant was broken by the people with whom it was made.

Like the macaroni fiasco, it is easy to break up a conditional relationship, and Israel's biblical history demonstrates this fact. But what is it? Is the moral *content* of the Law deficient? Does it point people in the wrong direction? No—it just demands more than humans can give; it expects a dead tree to bear fruit. There is thus a need for more.

The New Covenant is un-conditional. Here in Jeremiah, God promises not to break up with us; He's simply going to "forgive our iniquity and remember our sins no more." This new relationship comes from the heart rather than command, and, therefore, love and all the other fruits of God spring from there. Whereas the old relationship showed a God of justice, the new one shows the foolish wisdom of God's grace.

We learn in the New Testament that this new relationship is enacted by the forgiveness of God in Christ. He doesn't ask our permission to forgive us, nor does He ask us to do anything to earn it or keep it. He simply forgives everyone.

While the Old Covenant teaches that you will be accepted once you become acceptable, the New Covenant proclaims that you are accepted already. The forgiveness offered in the New Covenant flies in the face of justice and fairness—and this is wonderful news! Right here and now, you stand forgiven of everything you've ever done and will ever continue to do. This is what it means to be a Christian: to learn to cope with the audacious nonsense of this New Covenant.

—*Ethan Magness*

May 11

I have become the laughingstock of all peoples, the object of their taunts all day long. He has filled me with bitterness; he has sated me with wormwood. He has made my teeth grind on gravel, and made me cower in ashes; my soul is bereft of peace; I have forgotten what happiness is; so I say, "My endurance has perished; so has my hope from the LORD."...But this I call to mind, and therefore I have hope: The steadfast love of the LORD never ceases; his mercies never come to an end; they are new every morning; great is your faithfulness. (Lamentations 3:14-18, 21-23, ESV)

"It's time to get over it and move on." This is one of the worst things to say to someone who is grieving or suffering. Not only does the suggestion ignore the fact that suffering is real and, therefore, impossible to manage, but also we cannot *decide* to feel better. Suffering itself is the ground upon which the slow work of "moving on" happens. This slow work is God's work, and it cannot be rushed or abandoned.

In Lamentations we have an entire book demonstrating God's acknowledgement of and commiseration with human grief. Written after the siege and destruction of Jerusalem, the book communicates the sadness of an utterly defeated people.

There is no smoothing over in Lamentations, no positive spin or bright side, just this "soul... bereft of peace" that has "forgotten what happiness is."

There is space given for anger, sadness, and even loss of hope in God. It is only after this honest confrontation with anguish that the author can then write, "The steadfast love of the Lord never ceases." *Because there is space to suffer, there is space for God's healing work.* There is no divine accusation or advice, but time and listening, which allow the sorrowful to finally return to the hope of God.

God not only understands our suffering; He personally suffered for our sake. Inherent in the cross is God's answer to suffering: Jesus, the suffering servant, who was inclined not to the healthy but to the sick, endured the cross to be with us forever in our grief.

Only in God's good timing are our hearts mended and our hope restored. This is not accomplished by willpower or by friendly advice.

Instead, it is completely accomplished by the Man of Sorrows who allows us to say, "Great is your faithfulness."

—*Alex Large*

May 12

I called on your name, O Lord, from the depths of the pit. You heard my plea: "Do not close your ears to my cry for help!" You came near when I called you and you said, "Do not fear!" (Lamentations 3:55-57, NIV)

Prayer can be confusing. Jesus teaches us to pray, "Thy will be done" (Matt 6:10). But he also tells us, "Ask and it will be given to you" (Matt 7:7). Should we be correct or should we be honest? Those two things often seem diametrically opposed.

When we are honest, our prayers frequently devolve into wishes. The great doo-wop singer Dion gave us a powerful example of this phenomenon in 1975, when he and legendary producer Phil Spector recorded "Make The Woman Love Me":

> Lord, I know I haven't asked for much
> In such a long, long time
> Not since that brand new pair of Levi's
> Back when I was eight or nine
> And I know, the world's in such a state
> And you've got a lot to do
> But if you ever find yourself with a minute or two
> Won't you please make the woman love me?

Both the childhood prayer for jeans and the adulthood prayer for romance are sincere. Yet they sound more like a job for Santa Claus than God. *I want, I want, I want!*

Then there are the "correct" prayers, typified by the Lord's prayer of "Thy will be done." Or even more daunting, "Father, if you are willing, take this cup from me"—when you consider the outcome of that particular prayer, it becomes difficult to follow suit. These may be the right words, but they rarely come from the heart. At the least, the motives behind them are often mixed: "If I just pray the right way, God will do my bidding." "If I can just figure out the right formula..." In other words, *I want, I want, I want!*

In this passage from Lamentations, these two types of prayer meet. We hear the cry of a person in despair, begging for relief from the only place it can come from: on High. It is a prayer that says, "My will has failed me—your will is my only hope, please let it be done." It is honest, and it is right. It says, *I need, I need, I need!* The answer comes back: "Do not fear." This is not only the answer we want; it is the answer we need and the answer we have been given.

—David Zahl

May 13

"I will give them one heart, and put a new spirit within them; I will remove the heart of stone from their flesh and give them a heart of flesh, so that they may follow my statutes and keep my ordinances and obey them. Then they shall be my people, and I will be their God." (Ezekiel 11:19-20, NRSV)

It is miserable to have a heart of stone. Most Christians can remember some time when they knew what it was like to have a new heart and spirit—to be filled with joy and delight and mighty purpose for God, to wake up knowing that with God the world is new each morning, pregnant with possibility and meaning. As this fades and the heart fills again with dullness and weight, we like to tell ourselves that this is a consequence of growing up—that this is what Paul meant about being ready for solid food instead of milk. We hide our disappointment, sometimes by throwing ourselves into Christian activities, sometimes by taking up theology or some cause, sometimes by just drifting slowly away. We feel heavy, dull, rattling back and forth in the same old groove, the lustre faded.

The first thing is to know that the rationalizations are lies: the stone in the chest and the constriction in the lungs is not what we were made for, it is not what is being given in Ezekiel 11, and it really is miserable. We must first lodge our protest about the weight we have been given, not explain it away. Protest like this is a form of prayer.

The second thing is to push it, prod it, feel it, live with it, learn what we can about it. Come to accept the weight in the heart, the way kids have to accept the fact that the new sibling is not going anywhere. Everything is God-given. So give the weight the space to be turned into flesh again. God acts, desiccated veins fill again with Blood, the heap of bones reassembles, Spirit fills the lungs again.

And whether it happens or not, you are still one of His own, and He will always be your God.

—Simeon Zahl

May 14

(I said to them, What is the high place to which you go? So its name is called Bamah to this day.) (Ezekiel 20:29, ESV)

At first glance this verse seems like a throwaway; it is better that I go ahead and explain why it is not. In the state of Alabama, Crimson Tide football is quite the spectacle. At a time when the whole southeastern part of the country was under derision for everything from civil rights abuses to educational standards, the Crimson Tide was winning championships.

This created a powerful attachment to the team and a transference of identity. What I mean by that is "the team" became "us." Fans' identities became direct correlations of the successes or failures of the football team. As I write this, "we" are in the height of recruiting season (the "second season," we call it), and "our" collective state of mind can actually be determined by the college decision of a 17-year-old. Let that sink in for a moment.

This brings us to the Scripture reading. Ezekiel 20:29 has been ballyhooed as the pro-Alabama portion of the Bible. Get it? "Bama" has a place in the "high places." The only problem is that as much as people in Alabama go to church, they often don't understand what the high places were. The high places were the places where idolatry ran rampant. They were obviously places that irritated God immensely.

This really fits, ironically—it really does. Idolatry, from what I make of it, is man's attempt to control his fate. You carve out a wooden idol, infer a god, and try to appease it. Really, you do unto a god rather than have it do unto you.

In the same way, when you attach yourself to Alabama football, you are historically attaching yourself to a winner. When a game or championship is won, you win. In a way, you falsely impute your own identity by attaching yourself to a winner. And you get to let all the fans of Tennessee and Auburn know about it. Isn't that the definition of what the Bible calls idolatry? Using the things that reinforce the enthronement of the self, you create your own identity rather than receiving the identity God has given us.

God, in grace, gives us more. God imputes on us a true and eternal identity—one that does not wax and wane with each neck-and-neck quarter, but one that stands guiltless and free, even in the offseason.

—*David Browder*

May 15

> *Therefore, you shepherds, hear the word of the LORD: As I live, declares the Lord GOD, surely because my sheep have become a prey, and my sheep have become food for all the wild beasts, since there was no shepherd, and because my shepherds have not searched for my sheep, but the shepherds have fed themselves, and have not fed my sheep, therefore, you shepherds, hear the word of the LORD: Thus says the Lord GOD, Behold, I am against the shepherds, and I will require my sheep at their hand and put a stop to their feeding the sheep. No longer shall the shepherds feed themselves. I will rescue my sheep from their mouths, that they may not be food for them. (Ezekiel 34:7-10, ESV)*

Who we admire says a lot about us, but often we put too much hope in flawed people like ourselves. The examples are myriad and the consequence is two-fold: we are let down, and then we inherit their techniques. The cycle is then perpetuated as we bestow our abuse and brokenness onto others.

God obviously does not want us to carry these patterns of abuse onto ourselves or onto others. He intrudes into these habitual tendencies and gives us a transformative and forgiving word: "It will not return to me empty, but will accomplish what I desire and achieve the purpose for which I sent it" (Isa 55:11). God takes us out of our own corrupted hands to put us in the arms of a shepherd. He seeks to deliver us from our false shepherds, some of whom may be the "most Christian" of all—our mentors, our leaders; even they will fail us.

Jesus Christ came to be the only shepherd: the shepherd who "lays down his life for his sheep" (John 10:10-11). He shepherds the lost sheep, and he stands in before all the false shepherds we helplessly graze toward. He does not work for his benefit, but for ours, so that we may belong to his fold. No one can snatch us away, for Jesus, unlike the false shepherds, knows us. He guides his sheep with a light hand and removes their burdens with his tender word (John 1:29).

—*Matthew McCormick*

May 16

Then he said to me, "Prophesy to these bones and say to them, 'Dry bones, hear the word of the Lord! This is what the Sovereign Lord says to these bones: I will make breath enter you, and you will come to life. I will attach tendons to you and make flesh come upon you and cover you with skin; I will put breath in you, and you will come to life. Then you will know that I am the Lord"
(Ezekiel 37:4-6, NIV)

This is one of the most famous passages in Ezekiel, and what a wild scene! The throwback King James English calls this passage "The Valley of the Dry Bones." Ezekiel prophesies over this valley of dead, picked over, sun-bleached bones, and "behold, a rattling..."—there are muscles and tendons and skin and hair and eyes, and life is breathed into them.

It almost reminds you of a Tim Burton film, doesn't it? Burton is the master of the macabre: maybe you've seen one of his more recent movies, *Corpse Bride* (2005). In *Corpse Bride,* the art directors worked to create two different worlds where the movie would take place—Victorian England and the Afterlife. Ironically, the world of the living, Victorian England, was painted almost exclusively with grey tones: the people, the buildings, and the church are all greyscale, and the world of the dead has jazz music, vibrant colors, beer-guzzling skeletons and reanimated dancing corpses. The film's mood seems to ask its viewer in simple terms: what if the world after this one is *better* than the world we're in? What if life, love, and happiness come after we kick the bucket here on earth?

Ezekiel's prophecy here promises what Tim Burton's colorful underworld can only vaguely gesture. He speaks these words to Israel, who by this time is exiled from home. Israel pleads for help, with nowhere else to turn, to the God who has left them: "Our bones are dried up, our hope is lost, we are indeed cut off." This prophecy is the message of hope to them: *you* are *dead, but you will be made alive.* From dry bones in a valley, God will make you whole again—He will breathe you back into existence, just like He made you back in Genesis 2.

Our situations may sound familiar. When the world hits us hardest, we start to see things in shades of grey. The realities of our own personal strife, of death itself, and the inability to escape either, all show through in Tim Burton's ghoulish universe and in the universe of Ezekiel's prophecy. And yet, God promises that He will not leave us here. He will raise us from the dead, filling us with His Spirit and, in doing so, will make certain we never forget we are His people. He has not just created us, proclaims Ezekiel, but will one day re-create us, breathing resurrection into these dead bones.

—T. Bryan Jarrell

May 17

"...for there is no other god who is able to rescue in this way." (Daniel 3:29, ESV)

There is much to say about these three men of faith, thrown into the fiery furnace because of a valiant stand-off with the ruling king, Nebuchadnezzar. However, this story really ought to be read as a stand-off between Nebuchadnezzar and God.

Daniel records that Nebuchadnezzar has built an idol and is commanding that everyone "fall down and worship the image I have made." If they refuse, as Shadrach, Meshach, and Abednego do, they are to be thrown into the fiery furnace. The three conquered Judeans trusted God *could* deliver them, but they did not know whether or not He *would*. Living in exile under this tyrant, with new Chaldean names, there is no reason why these three men should *not* have died. Even in their moment of faith, they must have wondered, what is God going to do?

God could have justified His men of faith *and* destroyed Nebuchadnezzar, who was an egomaniacal dictator, after all. God could also have just let the boys die—He would have been justified to do so. God could have done it; we most certainly *would* have, and the truth is that we often do. We are the idol-maker Nebuchadnezzar, fascinated with our own perverse deities and insidious judgments. Ironically, though, God is the only one who has the right to condemn, and He is the only one who doesn't.

God does *not* destroy Nebuchadnezzar. Shadrach, Meshach, and Abednego do not burn in the fire of death. Instead, there in the fire, a man who does not deserve to die stands with them. "Did we not cast three men bound into the fire?... But I see four men unbound, walking in the midst of the fire, and they are not hurt; and the appearance of the fourth is like a son of the gods." They are neither burned nor killed; the "son of the gods" dances in the fire and undoes their ropes. As Nebuchadnezzar proclaims, "There is no other god who rescues in this way."

—Kate Norris

May 18

...The same hour was the thing fulfilled upon Nebuchadnezzar: and he was driven from men, and did eat grass as oxen, and his body was wet with the dew of heaven, till his hairs were grown like eagles' feathers, and his nails like birds' claws... (Daniel 4:28-37, KJV)

Sometimes the blows just keep coming. If you're down, you're *down.* After the prophetic words of Daniel are spoken regarding his dream, Nebuchadnezzar is chopped down; he plummets in one foul swoop from the pinnacle of comfort and opulence into the desolate wilderness, becoming an animal of the wild. Nebuchadnezzar has lost it all. All remnants of the life he once had are stripped. It leaves him (and us) with a question: Why? And how is it ever going to be okay again?

Like Nebuchadnezzar, we're often pulled "Undone," as Robert Earl Keen sings:

> Now the storm's comin' and the sky's turned black
> It's too late now you can't turn back
> Lightnin' strikes on the telephone wire
> You're drunk as a skunk your shack's on fire
> The wife took the baby and the other two kids
> The dogs are a-howlin' and the chickens are dead
> It's your last night out and you're gonna have fun
> They'll read it in the papers when you come undone.

I was having a conversation with a new coworker during a professional development *ice-breaker* activity, about "something no one knows about you at work." I kept my cards close, telling her I used to be an occasional runner. In exchange, she told me that her boyfriend of four years was killed in a car accident three months ago. This happened to be the same coworker who, since her hire at work, had been forced to switch jobs three times, including a new position that, honestly, would kill anyone. She was sleepless, strung out, overcommitted, overwhelmed. I sort of gawked, asked her how she was even functioning, why she hadn't quit by now. She shrugged, half-smiled, and said she was keeping herself busy. I couldn't imagine, but then I kind of could.

We know our own places of desolation and wilderness, places where the familiar is exchanged for the foreign—and not in the good way—where suffering seems to be the milk you're pouring on your cereal in the morning and there's nowhere to go, no one to lean on. Lonely, strung out, beat up, in over your head, wishing you were anywhere else but here. Why is this a part of life?

It seems that Nebuchadnezzar's hope in telling his story is to show that the Lord's undoing is the doing of something *new*. The king's humiliation ends in restoration, and this seems to be the answer. Everything is taken from him so that he might know, as he says himself, "The Lord's kingdom is an everlasting kingdom, / and his dominion endures from generation to generation." His riches, his comfort are restored to him in excess—and "greatness was added to him" in a way he couldn't have known or expected. In losing everything, he is restored to that which gave him all he had to begin with.

It doesn't make the hard times go away in any sense, and it may not even make them any easier at all—but it certainly founds them in the solid hope that, as Paul says in Romans 8, "all things work together for good, for those who are called according to his purpose." So in these places of despair and hopelessness, we have the hope that we have not escaped His good purpose and great love for us, and that an unexpected, invisible thing is springing forth new life.

—*Ethan Richardson*

May 19

...O Lord, according to all your righteous acts, let your anger and your wrath turn away from your city Jerusalem,

your holy hill, because for our sins, and for the iniquities of our fathers, Jerusalem and your people have become a byword among all who are around us. Now therefore, O our God, listen to the prayer of your servant and to his pleas for mercy, and for your own sake, O Lord, make your face to shine upon your sanctuary, which is desolate... For we do not present our pleas before you because of our righteousness, but because of your great mercy. O Lord, hear; O Lord, forgive... (Daniel 9:1-19, ESV)

Daniel, living in exile when he prayed this prayer, is suffering under God's judgment for breaking his—and all of Israel's—end of the bargain with God, which was to obey the commandments. The Law requires that God's people live an upright life and have a pure heart; Daniel's prayer demonstrates that this is impossible. We are in the same boat: we live in exile for our disobedience.

If God had known adherence to the Law would be impossible for us, why did He give it in the first place? Doesn't He know all things? We find the answer in Daniel's prayer: before the Law we reach an impasse, and this impasse brings us to our need for mercy—in our failure, we are driven to the grace given at the cross. Because of God's sacrifice in Jesus, the Law's temple curtain has been torn, and the impossible is forever possible; we stand in the midst of the presence of God.

Daniel's prayer illuminates one thing in particular: that God's upside-down justice transcends our human understanding. Daniel's hope is based on God forgiving the guilty and redeeming those who do not deserve to be redeemed, but this goes against everything we believe is rational or ethical. Why die for the thankless? Why forgive a person with a past?

Though it is the basis of Christian doctrine—Daniel's prayer has been answered, and we undeservedly receive the blessings of God—it is no less difficult to understand. Only in faith are we assured that we cannot get there on our own. Only in faith are we able to see it is in Jesus, who confesses this to us: "I am the way, and the truth, and the life..." (John 14:6).

This is what Daniel's prayer is all about: it is about Jesus. From the very beginning it's been about him. Every breath out is a response to the first initial breath that went in (Gen 2:7). The Israelites were sent into exile because they failed to keep the Law; this was the failure promised in the covenant, and a failure that led them to hope. Jesus fulfilled this hope, and, thus, the blessings of a new covenant are realized: it may transcend our understand, but the exile is over.

—Lauren R.E. Larkin

May 20

> *When the Lord first spoke through Hosea, the Lord said to Hosea, "Go, take to yourself a wife of whoredom and have children of whoredom, for the land commits great whoredom by forsaking the Lord." So he went and took Gomer, the daughter of Diblaim, and she conceived and bore him a son... And the LORD said to me, "Go again, love a woman who is loved by another man and is an adulteress, even as the LORD loves the children of Israel, though they turn to other gods and love cakes of raisins... For the children of Israel shall dwell many days without king or prince, without sacrifice or pillar, without ephod or household gods. Afterward the children of Israel shall return and seek the LORD their God, and David their kin, and they shall come in fear to the LORD and to his goodness in the latter days. (Hosea 1:2-3, 3:1-5, ESV)*

Hosea the prophet was called to marry a prostitute named Gomer. Though you might be willing to understand your lover's love for "cakes of raisins," no one really plans or wishes to marry someone who has proven to be unfaithful, and certainly no one would want to marry someone who had once been unfaithful and continued to be so.

Hosea's marriage to Gomer illustrates God's relationship to an unfaithful Israel. In spite of the fact that Gomer is an adulteress, she is ransomed by Hosea, showing God's love for His people in the face of their unfaithfulness. The Lord's love for Israel remains untethered to any sinful behavior—breaking its bonds. God is faithful despite the ongoing reality that they are still unfaithful.

This message is often lost in churches today. Often we hear, "If you behave yourself, then God, who loves you, will bless you. He chose you because He sees great potential in who you could be." And why shouldn't we believe this? This is how many of our relationships work. We often say to our spouses or family members, "If you loved me, then you would..."

But this is not how God operates. God knows you are a conditionally bought-and-sold human being, and still Jesus' death on the cross is the final declarative statement that God's love for you is unconditional. As it is said, "There is nothing that can separate us from the love of God" (Rom 8). It is not a love that forgives once or any number of times, but is timeless and unremitting. This is the love that brings redemption, even to those of us who often feel like Gomer.

—Andrew Pearson

May 21

"And in that day, declares the Lord, you will call me 'My Husband,' and no longer will you call me 'My Baal' [or 'master']... And I will betroth you to me forever. I will betroth you to me in righteousness and in justice, in steadfast love and in mercy. I will betroth you to me in faithfulness. And you shall know the LORD. I will have mercy on [the one I called] No Mercy, and I will say to [those called] Not My People, 'You are my people'; and he shall say, 'You are my God.'" (Hosea 2:16-23, ESV)

At the time of the writing of Hosea, Israel had been worshipping other gods—a thoughtless rejection deserving God's own rejection: exile, death, damnation. That is why this passage is so shocking: rather than seething anger, God's response to rejection is this impractical, frustratingly persistent affection.

A resulting theme in this book is the issue of identity, of Gomer's shift from slave to spouse. The last lines of Dietrich Bonhoeffer's poem, "Whom Am I?" are relevant here: "Who am I? / They mock me, these lonely questions of mine. / Whoever I am, thou knowest, O God, I am thine."

Though much of who we are will change, one thing that will not is the abiding acceptance of God—God will never let you go, even when you're sure He's unimpressed with you. Martin Luther gave us a helpful phrase to understand this phenomenon: *simul justus et peccator*— "simultaneously justified and sinful." This is a realistic identity: according to your desires and actions, you are a sinner deserving judgment; however, because of God's mercy on the cross, you are covered. God's grace changes our identity problem.

If you've seen *Fight Club* you'll remember Tyler Durden's powerful diatribe against the false identities we assume: "You're not how much money you've got in the bank. You're not your job. You're not the car you drive. You're not the contents of your wallet. You're not your family. You're not your problems. You're not your age. You are not your hopes. You're not your khakis."

In the spirit of Durden (and Luther), you are not your real or perceived set of identifiers. You are not your divorce. You're not your parents' divorce. You are not your addiction or disorder or STD. You aren't your pattern of dealing with relationships, your adultery, your anger. You are not your wallet or your wit.

Isaiah tells us that our righteousness is as filthy rags, but it is Jesus' robe of righteousness draped over us that God sees. We need a God before whom we can put aside the disguise—trusting that when He sees us He won't turn away or smite us in anger. With this possible, for just a moment, the vicious habits of identity maintenance can stop, and we can step down onto the firm ground of acceptance.

—*Justin Holcomb*

May 22

They do not cry out to me from their hearts, but wail upon their beds. (Hosea 7:14, NIV)

Many of us spend a lot of time wailing upon our beds rather than talking to God about whatever keeps us from sleeping. Some of us even spend a lifetime huddled up in complaint or victimhood rather than reaching out to God or others for help. Why do we consign ourselves to despair?

One reason is that we believe our problem is too big or too hopeless for anyone to be able to help. We lack faith of any kind. We are like the invalid who had sat by the pool of Bethesda for thirty-eight years: we cannot get into the water because there is no one to help us, no one who can help us (John 5). Jesus asked the invalid, "Do you want to be healed?" This is the first question we ought to ask ourselves when stuck with an intractable problem.

Another reason is that we do not want to examine our pain because we think it will destroy rather than heal us. We fear facing our need, and we fear feeling our dereliction; crying out to God from our heart is simply too painful. It feels like death. What if there is no answer? What if God has abandoned us?

We prefer murmuring over going to the doctor. We know in our heads that anger and resentment hurt us more than the people at whom we direct them, but we cannot bring ourselves to face the source. Meanwhile, we slowly erode, by sleepless nights, in an effort to avoid what feels like death. But death can lead to resurrection.

Lord, give us the courage we need to face our pain and bring it to you, the Great Physician, the one who brought Easter out of Good Friday.

—*Mary Zahl*

May 23

> *I will restore to you the years that the swarming locust has eaten, the hopper, the destroyer and the cutter, my great army which I sent among you. (Joel 2:25-27, ESV)*

Everything, ultimately, comes from the hand of God: the good, the bad, and the ugly. God is sovereign, which means that He is in control of everything. The bad things in your life have not escaped God's notice, nor do they fall outside of His sphere of influence. This means that hurt and disease and disaster and death are all under His command and authority.

Most of us want to shy away from this biblical view of God. We are loath to attribute anything bad to our good God. We are more likely to say that bad things happen because of sin and the devil. God then swoops into the mess to make things right. It is true that the devil is real and threatens to undo us. It is also true that we reap our own misery because of our sin.

God, however, is not a God on the sidelines, watching our lives unfold and rushing in to help fix what is broken. If God is omnipotent, as we say He is, then He could stop our hands from sinning and save us from our own misery. Satan, like everything and everyone else, is subject to His command. Affirming God's sovereignty means concluding that God wields both healing and woe for His own good, yet often inscrutable, purpose.

God's sovereignty is clear to Joel. God refers to the devastating plague of locusts as His "great army which I sent among you." The destroyers did real and severe damage in Israel, His chosen people; they brought years of loss built on more years of sorrow. Perhaps you have experienced what feels like years wasted in loss or sickness or suffering, or years spent idly or in vain—years you wish you could have back. The good and comforting news is that those years, and all years, come from the hand of God. And the better news is that God does not waste time—neither His time nor yours.

He doesn't always provide an explanation of why He does what He does. The bad in the world will remain a mystery until the end of the world as we know it. But He does give us a promise we can trust: "I will restore to you the years that the swarming locust has eaten... You shall eat in plenty and be satisfied." It is His goodness and love that allows us to say in both the triumphs and trials of our lives that God "has dealt wondrously with me" and to thank Him for everything that comes from His hand.

—*Paul Walker*

May 24

And in that day the mountains shall drip sweet wine, and the hills shall flow with milk, and all the streambeds of Judah shall flow with water; and a fountain shall come forth from the house of the LORD and water the Valley of Shittim. (Joel 3:18, ESV)

We all long for "that day" and the good that it will bring: a job promotion, the arrival of a baby, some long-awaited significant change in our life circumstances. We are always looking ahead, hoping that someday we might be happier, be free from our current issues, have more time with our families, or finally have our dream job. We long for that day to arrive. We do not know when that day will come, nor are we certain what that day will bring.

When we wait on and hope in the Lord, we are no less subjected to this process being a mystery. In waiting, there are times when we do not think that day could ever come. No matter what, waiting is difficult; we cannot tell with each passing moment how much closer we are getting. We can only sigh and tell ourselves that, sometime, that day will come.

But one thing is certain: new life *will* arrive. It may come after several "false alarms," and it most likely will come by way of its opposite, like a dream-deterring failure or more gridlock traffic. It probably will not look how you envisioned, and it may not come this side of the River Jordan, but it will, in time, arrive. "And in that day the mountains shall drip sweet wine, and the hills shall flow with milk," writes the prophet. As with anything, we may not know when, and we may often grow weary and discouraged, but we can be sure that "that day" overflows with the goodness of the Lord. We can take heart in trusting that in "that day," our streams shall flow with fresh water from the living God.

—Bonnie Poon Zahl

May 25

> *Woe to you who desire the day of the LORD! Why would you have the day of the LORD? It is darkness, and not light... But let justice roll down like waters, and righteousness like an ever-flowing stream. (Amos 5:18-24, ESV)*

Amos is speaking at a time when all of Israel is looking forward to an event called "The Day of the Lord," a time in which God will come to the aid of the Hebrew people. But when Amos appears on the scene, he says, "Yes, there'll be a Day of the Lord. But it will be an occasion for the Lord to purge everyone, not just the enemies of Israel. What God is going to purge," says Amos, "is pseudo-morality, wherever it's found. God is going to say, *I hate, I despise your feasts. Let justice roll down like waters, and righteousness like an ever-flowing stream.*"

God grant that you and I encounter some women and men like Amos in our culture today. Because the "abomination," as Amos called it, of pseudo-morality and half-truth doesn't seem to have been eradicated since the time of ancient Israel. There is so much pain all around us that's not getting relieved by just saying the right words.

So let's bring on the Day of the Lord. Let's bring it on all the way up to—but stop just short of—the point where God says, "I hate, I despise your feasts—Jim." Because the Day of the Lord seems great, *until it gets to me.*

I eagerly look forward to the day of truth-telling—until it's truth-telling time about me. Then I start feeling like the five maidens who weren't ready when the bridegroom appeared, who were shut out of the feast. Then I don't want justice to roll down like waters, because I'd be washed away.

But the Day of the Lord has already arrived. Justice has already rolled down like waters. The wrath of God toward the pseudo-morality in me, and the judgment of God on the compromises I make—all of that wrath has already fallen. As another prophet put it, "He was pierced for our transgressions... and with his wounds we are healed" (Isa 53:5).

Here is how the Day of the Lord came to St. Nicholas Church in the city of Leipzig in what used to be East Germany. In the spring of 1989, Christian Führer, the pastor of St. Nicholas, decided one Monday evening to hold a prayer service for peace in the world. A few people attended. Pastor Führer held another prayer service the next Monday. More people attended. Into the summer, the Monday evening prayer service continued—and the numbers grew. The sanctuary of St. Nicholas can hold 1,000 people. By the end of the summer, the people were spilling out the doors. Every Monday night—no sermons, no political references—just prayers for peace.

On Monday, October 9, 1,000 people were in the sanctuary, and 70,000 more were in the streets, holding candles and singing hymns. The next Monday, October 16, there were 120,000 people praying for peace. The following Monday, there were 320,000—two thirds of the city's population. On the following Monday, 500,000 people prayed and sang for peace. Ten days later, on November 9, the Berlin Wall came down.

So what justice do you *long* to see uncovered—at work, at home, abroad? What judgments do you fear might wash you away? And what peace might the Day of the Lord have in store for you?

—*Jim Munroe*

May 26

...Jonah rose to flee to Tarshish from the presence of the Lord... (Jonah 1:1-10, ESV)

Suffering comes in many forms, but we usually do not recognize this until disaster hits.

Jonah was an impetuous man given a very difficult task: travel hundreds of miles to the great city of Nineveh, denounce it, and tell the people that they must repent. Try to imagine this one: you must go to Baghdad today and do the same, alone.

Tarshish is conveniently about as far from Nineveh as a man could go, and Jonah, thinking understandably that he might wriggle out from under an unpleasant assignment, goes in the opposite direction. His decision is costly, as most runaway decisions are; as a non-seafaring Jew, he has to make the journey by ship; and the waters of the Mediterranean are perilous. (He also has to fork over a significant amount of cash for the trip. This was no free ride.)

When you are running away—from people, your past, your habits—things rarely go right. The storm hits, and you slip into denial as Jonah did, sneaking off into the hold for a little nap.

But God, the great Pursuer, rarely lets you off the hook. In Jonah's case He sends a group of pagan sailors to ask him some uncomfortable questions. "Who caused this storm to happen? What business are you in? Where are you from? Who are your people?" In other words, who are you? Jonah here is forced to confront his denial, and he sees that he is running away from God.

Recently, in a dark and discouraging time in my life when I was running, I found myself walking by a marina, and glanced over to read the name written on the stern of a sailboat: "Paracletos," Greek for "helper." Jesus used this word for the Holy Spirit. Like Jonah, it was a wake-up call: *Peter, do you get the message? I'm here, alongside you, even in your efforts to run from me.*

—*Peter Moore*

May 27

I called to the Lord, out of my distress, and he answered me... (Jonah 2:2, ESV)

There are no atheists in foxholes, as the saying goes. We turn to God when things get desperate, and we often *wait* until things get desperate before we do.

And just how desperate is Jonah's condition when he calls to the Lord? Interpretations vary. On the optimistic reading, Jonah is merely in a tough spot, but things are basically OK. Like Geppetto and his wooden toy Pinocchio, he is sitting there on a tranquil raft inside the belly of the great whale, merely awaiting rescue. Others might grant Jonah is in great danger, but deliverance is only a prayer away. "Call on the Lord, Jonah, and things will be fine." This is the hopeful point of view that life is good and most distress is overstated.

But it's quite different when you realize that Jonah is experiencing a kind of death. He is lost, utterly helpless, and beyond any possibility of rescue. Look at the cumulative images in this chapter. Water is the perpetual symbol of death in the Bible (think baptism); the whale, or "fish" is that great monster of the deep, Leviathan (Job 41:1; Ps 104:26), a symbol of disorder and chaos. Jonah is wrapped in the undersea weeds, drowning; the bars of the land have been "closed" to him forever; he is in the "Pit," "cast out from God's presence." These are not symbols of "difficulty"—these are symbols of death and dereliction. Jonah has died there in the depths, and his prayer reflects a belief that even in extremis, so to speak, God has not abandoned and will not abandon him.

So, what of you and me? Do we feel completely abandoned at times, "dead" to all relationships, including God; caught in the web of encircling problems that are completely beyond us?

Since Jonah's story is meant to be a sign to us, take heart. God is still watching, waiting, listening. Your awareness of this truth may be clouded by the sheer magnitude of our problems. But as the hymn writer William Cowper put it, "behind a frowning providence, He hides a smiling face."

—Peter Moore

May 28

...I knew that you are a gracious God and merciful, slow to anger and abounding in steadfast love, and relenting from disaster. (Jonah 4:2, ESV)

You've got to read the whole book of Jonah to see why this last chapter is a shocker. God repents of His plan to destroy Nineveh because they respond to Jonah's preaching. But Jonah is not only *not* pleased; he is actually angry. All along Jonah has held on to an exclusive view of God's love. Like the old Wessex Prayer, Jonah would have prayed: "God bless me, my wife, my two children, us four, no more!"

Jonah stands for all of us who believe that God's special care and concern should be restricted to those who are demonstrably good. In this view, God has no business forgiving those who have spurned Him, pursued other things, lived on the wild side. Yet what Jonah most fears is exactly what happens.

Jonah is so depressed that he sees absolutely no point in living. Wouldn't you, too, if the good guys actually *don't* win in the end? So the Lord gives him a little lesson in ecology. The plant that shades his little makeshift gazebo looks great in the morning, but then wilts and dies under the hot midday sun. Filled with misplaced compassion for the plant, Jonah again lets loose with his all-too-ready anger (4:4,9).

The point of this parable—for that is one thing the book of Jonah is—boils down to one simple truth: God loves everyone, especially the unlovable. The irony of Jonah's disappointment in God's mercy toward the Ninevites is that he is also unlovable. Unwittingly, he is on the same level as those who he thinks are beyond God's love.

We'd be better off to get with God's love for the unlovable, or we'll end up like Jonah—one of those self-righteous grouches who couldn't, for their own sake, recognize the love of God staring them in the face. You and I are fully loved, even though we deserve His wrath. Fortunately, as with the Ninevites and Jonah, God has another plan.

—Peter Moore

May 29

Then God said to Jonah, "Do you have good reason to be angry about the plant?" And he said, "I have good reason to be angry, even to death." (Jonah 4:9, NASB)

I laugh a little bit every time I come across this verse. Jonah is the Eddie Haskell of the biblical world—what our grandparents would have called a "wiseacre." Childishly stubborn and smug, it is no wonder that he always seemed to get upstaged by the whale on the flannelgraph reenactment in Sunday school. It's hard to make "life application" segues, such as *Have faith like Jonah*, because Jonah doesn't even seem to *like* God all that much. I was repeatedly told to be like Noah, Abraham and Moses, but the three-inch cutout of Jonah was never the icon to emulate.

To a fidgety fourth grade boy, the bearded biblical figures all looked surprisingly austere despite the fact that they were so, well, adhesive. When the teacher was not looking, it was just too easy for us to turn her Bible morals into a fabric *Clash of the Titans* death-match: Moses spins his ninja staff against the switchblade-wielding Abraham, while Jonah surfs the whale's back. Noah, stuck upside down, nervously watches for cops from the sidelines.

Behind this gladiatorial scene sits God, peeking over the shoulders of mischievous boys who have no idea why dead guys with Bible beards ought to matter. God smiles because He knows that boys and girls like this will one day sing the hymns, and they will also long for the days when life was as easy and fun as this ad hoc flannelgraph throwdown.

Most importantly, God knows that one day they will look less like the austere heroes and more like the jaded, flesh-and-blood Jonah. One day these boys may become reluctant prophets in the middle of a tempest, in the belly of a whale, on a beach so far from the safe room of their silly childhood. God knows this about the Jonahs, too: "What's your problem?" God asks. "You!" we answer, "This whole plan of yours... the way you have taken me to this absurd place and withered this little shade tree, the thing which most reminded me of that childhood place." Words seem to fail both parties for different reasons, but one thing is certain: there is hope that we, like Jonah, reluctant and maybe even bitter, will live to tell the story.

—Dylan Potter

May 30

Woe is me! For I have become as when the summer fruit has been gathered, as when the grapes have been gleaned: there is no cluster to eat, no first-ripe fig that my soul desires. The godly has perished from the earth, and there is no one upright among mankind; they all lie in wait for blood, and each hunts the other with a net. Their hands are on what is evil, to do it well; the prince and the judge ask for a bribe, and the great man utters the evil desire of his soul; thus they weave it together. The best of them is like a brier, the most upright of them a thorn hedge. The day of your watchmen, of your punishment, has come... But as for me, I will look to the LORD; I will wait for the God of my salvation; my God will hear me. (Micah 7:1-7, ESV)

What hope is there in a world of corruption? Micah's society, overcome by greed and perversion, wasn't looking good: crooked leaders, overt oppression, and neglect of the poor. It sounds post-apocalyptic: there are no neighbors to trust, locked doors, no confidence given—the "godly have perished from the earth." When nothing good remains, what hope is there?

Micah's lament turns into a hopeful proclamation, "I will look to the Lord, I will wait for the God who saves me; my God will hear me." Micah forsakes his own strength and the strength of his society, and he expresses—with nothing left—his reliance on God. David Prior writes that the people and the leaders in this passage "trust in their own resources and devices; [Micah] trusts in God."* As the leaders and their people turn from dependence, chaos ensues and self-interest wreaks havoc upon the people and the land.

We are no different from Micah's audience. Quick to neglect the poor, easily swayed by bribes or smooth words, consumed with worry about finances or status or family matters, we like to solve our problems before waiting on God to solve them. We, too, are inwardly focused; we constitute this degenerate society, and we wreak the same kinds of havoc. We not only fall woefully short of the mark we expect of ourselves, but also we stand dead in our transgressions before God (Eph 2:1-3).

Micah's hope is our hope: Christ is the promise Micah waits for. Christ fulfills the Old Testament's cry and its need for redemption, restoration, and rest for the destitute. In a time where there is "no cluster to eat" from the vine, we look to the hope of Christ, who "nourishes a vine that brings forth good fruit" (John 15). The root of that fruit is the wellspring of love. Micah 7:7 is a promise fulfilled in Christ, where God hears the destitute and provides rest.

—*Lauren R.E. Larkin*

May 31

The Lord is good, a refuge in times of trouble. He cares for those who trust in him. (Nahum 1:7, NIV)

As I child, I was taken by a few books, and by "taken" I mean something close to an abduction. I would fall asleep reading them, awaking the next morning actually dreaming that I was still reading them. To my delight, when I realized that I wasn't, it was all the sweeter when I rolled over, grabbed the book, and read on.

---

* Prior, David. *The Message of Joel, Micah, and Habakkuk: Listening to the Voice of God.* Downers Grove, IL; InterVarsity Press, 1999, pp. 191-92.

One of those books was *Mrs. Frisby and the Rats of NIMH*. There is a time when the mouse's home is in danger of being turned over by a tractor tilling the field. Frantically and methodically, the rats of NIMH work to move the dwelling "to the lee of the stone! Move it to the lee of the stone!" If the dwelling place could be on the lee side of the stone—the side of the stone in the field where the tractor would have to pass it by—then protection for the mouse and her house would be assured.

The prophet knows of the Lord's anger against Nineveh, and though He is slow to anger, He is great in power: "His way is in the whirlwind and the storm, and clouds are the dust of his feet" (1:3).

Fearsome, indeed. Fearsome, but good. At one and the same time, the Lord shatters the rocks before Him, while He is himself the rock. He is our refuge, our very present help in times of trouble. Even as the wrath of God is poured out on himself on the cross, and even as that wrath shatters the rocks before Him and the rocky parts of our hearts, we stand in "the lee of the stone," in the good refuge of His protection.

As a hen gathers her chicks under her wings, so are we gathered beneath the protection of our defender Jesus. Indeed, as the gathered people of God—the church—our dwelling is prepared for us on the lee side of the stone, in the trustworthy and secure refuge of our mighty fortress.

—Gil Kracke

June 1

Now I will break their yoke from your neck and tear your shackles away. (Nahum 1:13, NIV)

At first glance, a linguistic barrier seems to cloud this passage. More than just the cultural inexperience we have with yokes and shackles, it seems our modern sensibility affirms our personal and bodily freedom. The seeds of autonomy are sown deeply into our nature, and those seeds are nurtured carefully by our surroundings. We are oriented to narratives that make us the "master and commander" of our soul, of our decisions, and of our lives.

If we don't come to terms with the reality of the bondage the Bible so often illustrates, we'll be forced to do some creative interpreting, always thinking about "that other poor guy" it must refer to, who must not be as spiritually endowed as ourselves. *Thank God we have advanced*, we think, *and have the wherewithal needed to escape this kind of bondage.* How we've deluded ourselves!

We are yoked and shackled by someone. If the Bible says anything, it says that we are bonded unto another, that we are not free to ourselves. This begs the question: to whom am I bonded? Inasmuch as I am selfish and sinful, my yokefellow can go by many names: the world, the flesh, the devil. Call it what you will, but they all lead to the same end.

What news, then, that Nahum delivers! As the King James puts it: "For now I will break his yoke from off thee, and I will burst thy bonds in sunder!" Our hearts are broken, to be sure; but we are granted new life and real freedom, as the shackles are broken and we walk free to our savior, Christ Jesus. We come to a new master, whose burden is easy and whose yoke is light. What good news—what delicious, wonderful, life-changing news!

Where in life are you "nurtured" in autonomous thinking? Where in life has autonomy become a burden? Here's to praying God undoes the chains that bind us to our false senses of imagined freedom, and that He gives us the real thing!

—Gil Kracke

June 2

I will rejoice in the LORD, I will be joyful in God my Savior. (Habakkuk 3:18, NIV)

Habakkuk's prayer is a profound testimony to the crucial role of weakness in the life of the believer. Frustrated by the wickedness around him, he cries out to God. God assures him that those who have acted wickedly will reap their fruit by the hands of the Babylonians. This does not exactly "scratch the itch" for Habakkuk because the Babylonians, he objects, are just as corrupt as the Israelites, if not more so. God eventually convinces Habakkuk that He will reveal just how short anyone's arms are when they step into the ring against the Almighty. In response to this declaration of God's justice, Habakkuk raises his voice in spontaneous praise: "I will rejoice in the LORD, I will be joyful in God my Savior."

What I find helpful about Habakkuk's prayer is that it does not undermine the cruciform pattern of the power of weakness in the world: "Though the fig tree should not blossom, nor fruit be on the vines, the produce of the olive fail and the fields yield no food, the flock be cut off from the fold and there be no herd in the stalls, yet I will rejoice..." In other words, Habakkuk calls it as he sees it: wars and injustice, economic instability, and rising divorce rates all suggest the apparent absence of a loving Creator. But God reminds the prophet that it is precisely in the midst of such decay that God chooses to show His strength. Because of this message, in the midst of all else failing, Habakkuk clings to Him.

William Cowper, the 18th century poet and hymnist, echoes Habakkuk's sentiment in his hymn "Sometimes a Light Surprises":

> The vine, nor fig–tree neither,
> Their wonted fruit should hear,
> Though all the fields should wither,
> Nor flocks, nor herds, be there:
> Yet God the same abiding,
> His praise shall tune my voice;
> For while in him confiding,
> I cannot but rejoice.

Cowper's attitude here is even more astounding, knowing that he suffered from periods of such intense depression that he attempted to commit suicide on at least three occasions. He actually saw the world through the keyhole of the cross: this recognition of the weakness that God will resurrect into new life.

You are not the strong one. You are in the company of weak prophets with wrinkled brows and hymnists writing out of the depths. This is good company, however, because only the weak ever find the priceless power of clinging to God the Savior.

—*Dylan Potter*

June 3

Sing aloud, O daughter of Zion; shout, O Israel! Rejoice and exult with all your heart, O daughter of Jerusalem! The LORD has taken away the judgments against you; he has cleared away your enemies. The King of Israel, the LORD, is in your midst; you shall never again fear evil. On

194

that day it shall be said to Jerusalem, "Fear not, O Zion; let not your hands grow weak. The LORD your God is in your midst, a mighty one who will save; he will rejoice over you with gladness; he will quiet you by his love; he will exult over you with loud singing. (Zephaniah 3:14-17, ESV)

Warnings don't work with my daughter. Granted, she's less than two years old, and I tend to expect more mature behavior during mealtime, but every meal it's the same. My wife reminds me that this is what kids her age do—throw food rather than eat it—and so I grimace forgiveness, but it doesn't come easy. Despite wanting to put limits on how often I can let her bad behavior slide, I am forced to relent.

Zephaniah, and really most of the prophets, do a pretty good job relaying God the Angry Father. And it's generally for the right reasons: Israel is behaving badly, and God tells them this with specific examples. The warnings, however justified, never seem to work, though; God's children continue to disobey, and God throws His hands up, passing over their sin once again.

Nothing has changed: we, too, are repeat offenders. We've done it enough times to know full well right from wrong, and yet knowing this doesn't change our intent. After yet another repeated inner-judgment, another passive-aggressive comment at your spouse, another ignored call, we hear from God that "The Lord has taken away the judgments against you" (3:15). He could judge, but He doesn't. There's no "Shape up or ship out;" there's no thin ice. It's counterintuitive, but strangely, "God did not send his Son into the world to condemn the world, but in order that the world might be saved through him" (John 3:17). God in Jesus brings instant forgiveness to the repeat offenders—may this perpetual Passover comfort us today and renew our hearts.

—Alex Large

June 4

You have planted much, but have harvested little. You eat, but never have enough. You drink, but never have your fill. You put on clothes, but are not warm. You earn wages, only to put them in a purse with holes in it. (Haggai 1:6, NIV)

Did you know there's a book in the Bible called Haggai? Immediately before speaking these words, the Lord—through Haggai—instructs His people to "give careful thought to your ways" and, in a not-so-subtle way, hands us a searing description of our life's natural inclinations.

It is a picture of fret-filled impotence. Like George Jetson, there is a sense of "running, running, running," for no purpose except to *not* fall flat: "Get me off this crazy thing!"

I wonder if Jesus had these Haggai verses in mind when he met the woman at the well (John 4). "You will drink that water," he said, "but you will never have your fill. You will eat again, but you will only be hungry a few hours later"—you'll never have enough. You will work, you will get paid, you will spend your money, and you will need to keep on working. Is this really all there is? Surely, if it is, we may as well eat, drink, and be merry, for tomorrow we die!

There's a memorable scene towards the end of Joseph Heller's *Catch-22*. The main character, Yossarian, recalls a time when he was on a mission, inside a bomber in WWII; someone had called over the intercom to go help the gunner who'd been shot. The plane had taken heavy fire, and the gunner was hit in the leg, not too bad as wounds go. Even as the gunner listlessly complained that he was cold, dutifully and carefully, Yossarian had tended the wound, proud of himself for handling the situation, confidently reassuring the gunner: "there, there; there, there."

As he finished, he sat back to admire himself and his work. To his horror, Yossarian saw a trickle of blood coming from beneath the other's flak jacket: upon opening it, his blood and guts—the gunner's actual life—spilled onto the floor. He had been caring for the wrong wound; this wound was inoperable.

All Yossarian could do was hold his friend, saying again and again, "There, there." "I'm cold." "There, there." All Yossarian could do was run to stand still.

Who among us hasn't dealt with this impotence with the fatal wounds? And who can't feel hope and expectancy well up from deep within when we hear that one day we will "run and not grow weary, walk and not grow faint" (Isa 40)? Or that "living water will one day be given, so that we will never again thirst" (John 4)? The good news of God's invasion on our life will mean that there will be "no more death or mourning or crying or pain" (Rev 22).

—*Gil Kracke*

June 5

Who is left among you that saw this house in its former glory? How do you see it now? Is it not in your sight as nothing? Yet now take courage, O Zerub babel, says the LORD; take courage, O Joshua, son of Jehoz adak, the high priest; take courage, all you people of the land, says the LORD; work, for I am with you, says the LORD of hosts, according to the promise that I made you when you came out of Egypt. My Spirit abides among you; fear not. (Haggai 2:3-5, ESV)

I was with a considerably younger friend when we spotted an old poster for *Ocean's Eleven*—the original 1960 version with Frank Sinatra and the Rat Pack. She pointed, asking, "What is that?" I had to explain that the Brad Pitt and George Clooney version was a remake. Well, that floored her. "Are there any more of my favorite movies that are also remakes?" I started listing them. "And don't even get me started on music," I added.

It's sometimes easy to focus on whether things were better in the past, how things may have been smarter, simpler, or just plain happier "back then." Gil Scott Heron, one of the forerunners of hip-hop in 1970s and 1980s, once said something to the effect that we all want nostalgia— we want to go as far back as we can "even if it's only as far as last week." However, so often this nostalgia is rooted in personal pain. When we think about our careers or our troubled relationships, it's easy to reminisce about being happier when we were single, or in high school, or before the kids came. Yet none of this gets to the heart of the real problem, because I know I wasn't happy when I was single, and let's not even talk about high school.

Now, there was a time when things definitely were better (roughly two chapters in Genesis), and understanding this, namely who we are as creatures after "the Fall," really gets to the heart of things. It's not about how I might have been happier at some other time in my life, but rather about who I am and have been since my conception—namely a hurt, frightened, fallen being, who hides from God in my solutions to my hurt.

But I thank God that He comes to me, and to all of us, then and now and always, where we are, in our bad jobs and confusing relationships, in the days of fear and weakness. We don't need the original temples of nostalgia (or even the original *Ocean's Eleven*); while our memories deceive us, what is fundamentally true now was true then. Instead, we can take courage in this truth: God's promise to us demonstrated on the cross of His son, Jesus Christ, who is the real temple, who has made known God's steadfast Spirit among us.

—Leonard Finn

June 6

And I will pour out on the house of David and the inhabitants of Jerusalem a spirit of grace and pleas for mercy, so that, when they look on me, on him whom they have pierced, they shall mourn for him, as one mourns for an only child, and weep bitterly over him, as one weeps over a firstborn (Zechariah 12:10, NIV)

On the heels of a previous declaration that the Lord alone will be the source of a fearsome and awesome salvation, the prophet continues with this thunderbolt about the "one whom they have pierced."

"And I will pour out a spirit of grace; And I will pour out pleas of mercy." The Lord is speaking here: the spirit of grace and supplication is *given* to us—it is never natural to who we are. This givenness always prevails: the work of the Lord within me continues hour-by-hour, moment-by-moment, as I relate to Him in a fundamental position of reception. Without this grace *given*, my heart is hardened; my judgment remains clouded; my sense of perspective stays skewed. In short, I remain self-interested and self-absorbed.

"When they look on me, on the one whom they have pierced, they shall mourn for him, as one mourns for an only child, and weep bitterly over him, as one weeps over a firstborn." This is the remarkable fruit of being given a spirit of grace and pleas for mercy. As I look on the one whom *I* have pierced, I am also given the right portions of gut-churning remorse and despair.

Why is this important? Because if the spirit of grace is not first given, if the Lord is not this "first mover," if I am not given the eyes to see—then I look on this "one who was pierced" in an entirely different light. Naturally, I move to blame-shifting and disassociation: *It wasn't me, I had nothing to do with it.* Naturally, self-justification reigns: *Well, he deserved it; she got what was coming to her; they didn't leave me any other options—I had to take care of myself and my family.*

198

The Lord has none of this—He squares each of these directly, and directly God transfers the justice upon Himself. Pouring out grace and mercy, the Lord draws us to see *our* hands driving the nails of our transgressions, gives us the sobriety to deal with *our* part in the death. In a flood of guilt, we are yet loved, even by the one we have crucified, resulting in "true repentance, amendment of life, and the grace and consolation of the Holy Spirit." We can then join in declaring with fearful wonder, "Surely this man was the Son of God!"

—Gil Kracke

June 7

See, I will send my messenger, who will prepare the way before me. Then suddenly the Lord you are seeking will come to his temple; the messenger of the covenant, whom you desire, will come," says the Lord Almighty. (Malachi 3:1-4, NIV)

God says a messenger will come to purify and to judge, like a refiner's fire or a launderer's soap, all to reconcile people to Him. But the purification process does not quite come as expected.

In summers during college, I worked at youth camps: for a couple of years, a song called "Refiner's Fire" captured me. I loved that song. I imagined being purified, allowing the dross and deep-buried dirt within me to rise to the surface and be skimmed off the top, like a cauldron heated by the love of God. This idea resonated deeply within my newly formed faith.

But the idea of purification I had has a fatal flaw. Though there is clearly an element of truth in this process, it is not the way we are prepared for the Lord's coming. No amount of preparation brings us to a satisfactory point. Part and parcel with my "refiner's fire" metaphor was the idea that elements of impurity are resting alongside the elements of silver and gold; one needs only to go through the—albeit painful and tedious—heat to distill the original elements. Implicit here is the idea that we only need the "sins and impurities" in our life exposed, and then rooted out.

But the reality is quite different. There's no silver and gold here: it's all dross. As I am, there's nothing worthy of a listing on the Periodic Table. Instead, this dross—these dregs of sin—are part of me; they are who I am (and not just what I do). To be purified means total substitution—what's in there must die and be replaced by something entirely new.

And here we find that same old story: it requires a death. More specifically, the death "by whose stripes we are healed;" by Christ's death, I am prepared for his coming. By his death, I can stand and I can endure, for by his death I am given life.

How we are prepared and purified, to be "righteousness" acceptable to the Lord? Simply and only because there is a new cauldron thrown on the fire; God made the One who knew no sin—pure gold, nothing to be refined—to be the filth distilled, that we might be the gold instead, the righteousness of God.

—Gil Kracke

NEW
TESTAMENT

June 8

She will give birth to a son, and you are to give him the
name Jesus, because he will save his people from their sins.
(Matthew 1:21, NIV)

The poet W.H. Auden once wrote, "Nothing that is possible can save us / We who must die demand a miracle." This is a bold statement, and one whose truth might not be self-evident in everyday life. Many of the daily problems we face can be fixed, or at least addressed: if our car breaks down, we can take it to the garage. If we get a headache, we can take some aspirin. If we say something mean, we can apologize, and so on.

Auden's meaning becomes clearer when we consider problems of a less everyday nature, the kind that keep us up at night. I was speaking with a friend recently who just separated from his wife. He told me, "I've done everything I can think of. Even couples' counseling hasn't helped. She just doesn't want me. It's going to take a miracle to save our marriage." He had pursued all the right options, and nothing had worked. The problem was simply beyond him. So it is with us. Our condition is not fixable. That is, we can empirically say that the solution to human nature has not been found in the realm of "what's possible." Instead, we need a miracle to save us—from ourselves, from our sin, and, ultimately, from death.

It should come as no surprise that the birth of the one "who will save his people from their sins" was full of the impossible. Mary's pregnancy is merely the first part. Equally miraculous is the fact that Joseph actually believes what the angel tells him here. And he not only believes—he obeys. These are miracles! To explain them away or downplay their importance is to deny the extent of the Good News.

Is there a situation in your life where nothing short of a miracle will help? An impossible problem or person that just won't go away? This passage gives us permission to acknowledge that some problems are indeed too big for us. You are not imagining things—"we who must die demand a miracle." Yet the "glad tidings" are that Jesus *is* the miracle we have been waiting for, the one who saves us. The impossible problems of this life have found their impossible answer in him.

—*David Zahl*

June 9

And when Jesus was baptized, immediately he went up from the water, and behold, the heavens were opened to him, and he saw the Spirit of God descending like a dove and coming to rest on him; and behold, a voice from heaven said, "This is my beloved Son, with whom I am well pleased." (Matthew 3:16-17, ESV)

There's a classic New Yorker cartoon of a woman sitting in a therapist's office, and the caption reads, "First, I did things for my parents' approval, then I did things for my parents' disapproval, and now I don't know why I do things." No matter what your relationship is like with your mother and father, you can probably relate. Parents loom large in our lives and in our minds, even after they are long gone.

You don't have to be a child psychologist to know that from the moment children are born they look to their parents not only for protection and sustenance, but love as well. They look to their mother and father to answer the fundamental questions, "Do you love me?" and "Am I enough?" When these questions are left unanswered, or are answered with ambivalence, people can spend the rest of their lives looking elsewhere for answers, casting for substitute fathers and mothers wherever they go. Our work, our friendships, our marriages—every project and every person become a potential oracle, or place where we might find the answer we have been looking for. Maybe you know someone who is always overreacting to perceived slights, someone with whom you walk on eggshells, knowing that even a hint of disapproval will set them off. Someone to whom every interaction feels like a test. Maybe you've noticed that tendency in yourself. It's exhausting!

The passage we have here, of Jesus' baptism, contains an unequivocal affirmation of a Son by a Father. This blessing inaugurates rather than eulogizes Jesus' ministry. It is an approval that comes first, in other words, before the temptations in the desert, before the miracles in Galilee, before the trials in Jerusalem. Approval precedes them all. Christ did not spend his ministry trying to earn his Father's approval. It was his from the beginning, and this is no coincidence. He was free to love others, independent of the answers they might give him.

Perhaps you had wonderful parents, and if so, praise God! But even those who have grown up in supportive, loving households will find themselves asking these questions from time to time. No one's parents are God, after all. (The Onion once produced a hilarious article entitled, "Study Finds Every Style of Parenting Produces Disturbed, Miserable Adults.") But if your upbringing was not what you would have asked for, if the answers you received were tentative, know that God's response to you is not. He responds to you the way He did to His own son: "You are my beloved child, with whom I am well pleased." His approval comes before our strivings and successes and failures, not after them. It is not contingent on performance. This is the kind of Father he is. Regardless of how you feel about yourself, and regardless of what your accomplishments say or don't say, your Father is well pleased with you.

So where are you asking the question today? Is anyone asking you the question? Where are you looking for your answers? Today you've found one.

—David Zahl

June 10

> *Then the devil took him to the holy city and placed him on the pinnacle of the temple, saying to him, "If you are the Son of God, throw yourself down; for it is written, 'He will command his angels concerning you,' and 'On their hands they will bear you up, so that you will not dash your foot against a stone.'" Jesus said to him, "Again it is written, 'Do not put the Lord your God to the test.'" (Matthew 4:5-7, NRSV)*

In her short story "Revelation," Flannery O'Connor tells the story of an arrogant woman named Ruby, who is enamored of her racist, classist view of the world and her place in it—better than some types of people, inferior to others. It gives her a way of thinking that allows her to have self-esteem. Along comes a girl named Mary Grace, who insults her straight-on, telling her she's a "dirty warthog from hell," and this immediately disrupts her vision of the world. Suddenly she sees a vision of heaven with all the "freaks and lunatics" leading the procession, the last being first, the least being greatest, and herself—a "good" woman with a grateful disposition—at the rear of the parade.

We all have a worldview that helps us to feel good about ourselves, whether we view ourselves as resting at the top of the career ladder, leading in the church, or raising high-achieving, well-behaved children. This hierarchy-love has been called a "theology of glory," a term that describes our attraction to believing things—about ourselves and the world—that elevate our position and give us clear criteria for self-justification. Paradoxically, in O'Connor's story, it is only when Ruby is insulted and brought low that she has any true religious experience at all.

In the devil's temptation of Jesus, we see two worldviews at work, competing for Christ's affections. The first is the world of glory—where Christ can produce food, power, faith, and rulership—and the second is the world of the weak, where he will experience hunger, captivity, powerlessness, and death. Throughout the Bible God chooses the weak and lowly to be His vessels, and here we see God himself choosing the way of weakness, suffering, rejection, and condemnation, not only to favor the weak, but to *be* the weak.

Essayist John Jeremiah Sullivan says that Christ's "breakthrough was the aestheticization of weakness. Not in what conquers, not in glory, but in what's fragile and what suffers."[*] It's impossible, as inveterate achievers, to find this paradoxical beauty of weakness for ourselves. But we can say that the beautiful aspect of Christ's love for weakness is simply the weakness itself. Pain and suffering are not beautiful, except for the potential, unique to weakness, to be loved *undeservedly*. Jesus chooses weakness and becomes weakness, going so far as to "become sin," because it is in this poverty that grace arrives (2 Cor 5:21). It is only in Christ's choice of weakness that weakness itself is made lovely.

—*Will McDavid*

June 11

> *Blessed are the poor in spirit, for theirs is the kingdom of heaven... Blessed are those who are persecuted for righteousness' sake, for theirs is the kingdom of heaven. (Matthew 5:3-10, ESV)*

One way to read the Beatitudes is to see them as a description of how the grace of God takes hold in someone's life. Any genuine conversion experience, indeed any movement of the Spirit, begins with a breakdown.

---

[*] Sullivan, John Jeremiah, *Pulphead*. New York: Farrar, Straus, and Giroux, 2011, p 33.

Generally we have done something or said something or experienced something that has brought us to our knees. This *something* has created a poverty of spirit which is both the hallmark of, and the necessary condition for, the work of the Spirit in our lives.

Next comes the mourning—mourning ourselves and the world—then humility (Jesus calls it meekness), born of God's undeserved goodness; hunger for the righteousness which only God can give; mercifulness born of God's mercy on us; then purity, then peace and, finally, the willingness to suffer like God suffered.

In reading through the Beatitudes, one notices that the "reward" of the first is the same as the last: "for theirs is the kingdom of heaven." What this tells us is that there is really no such thing as a "law of progression" in the Christian life, and that sinners and martyrs are really the same, because our reward is the same. It has been secured not on the basis of what we have done or will do, but on the merits of Jesus' death and resurrection.

Christianity is a faith in which we do nothing and God does everything. He is the one who humbles, who restores, and who brings forth fruit, often in the same breath. He brings us to our knees and gives us the strength to withstand persecution. Through it all, our need for a savior never wanes, nor does his readiness and willingness to save.

—*R-J Heijmen*

June 12

Blessed are they that mourn: for they shall be comforted.
(Matthew 5:4, ASV)

Again and again, I have been struck by Christians using the language of faith to ward off the presence of pain. It's understandable—pain is painful. All of us want to avoid it as much as possible, and when we can't avoid it, we try what we can to minimize its side effects. As Christians, we get nervous admitting the depth of our pain, because what if it is a sign of a lack of trust in the goodness of God, a lack of faith?

I was listening to a friend tell me about her life in recent months. She had moved across the country after living happily in the South for many years. As I listened to her, it was clear to me that she was on the verge of tears from the change, but every time the tears came to the surface, she would say, "but I know I have so much to be thankful for, and I know God loves me, and that is all that matters." No tears allowed.

I don't believe in telling people what to do, but if I did, I would have said to my sad, exhausted friend, "What you need is a good cry. You have lost so much. Of course, there are also good things about your move, but you will not be able to see those clearly until you mourn the losses. Cry until you cannot cry any more. And, for God's sake, don't think your tears are a sign of faithlessness or ingratitude. Did not Jesus himself say, 'Blessed are they that mourn?'"

When pain is denied or kept at bay, the sufferer misses out on the opportunity that comes with facing pain honestly, which is feeling the weight and powerlessness of it. Counterintuitively, the experience of going *into* the pain generally brings out compassion, peace, and even joy on the other side.

Like the day we call Good Friday, our deaths (no matter how small) can be transformed—resurrected—such that we might even call them good. Conversely, when we hold onto words of "Christian hope" almost as if they were magic, we miss out on the joy and hope that come when the resurrection power is *given* rather than *grasped*.

—*Mary Zahl*

June 13

Blessed are the merciful, for they will be shown mercy.
(Matthew 5:7, NIV)

Let us consider what "mercy" may or may not look like in interpersonal relationships. Let us say that someone you love has a habit that you find irritating, something that they continue to do, even when you've asked them not to. For example, maybe they chew their food with their mouths open. The non-lenient response, of course, would be to make them aware of this fact, each and every time they do it. The lenient, merciful response would be to let it go.

But as any of us who have been in a relationship know, mercy is easier said than done. We find ourselves bringing the bothersome behavior up, even when we know that doing so has never helped in the past, that it has only ever produced conflict and hurt. This may be a trivial example, but the feelings at work are not. It is not surprising that so many relationships that are born in love end in bitterness, where one or both parties feel scrutinized and trapped.

Brian Wilson of The Beach Boys sings, "Love and mercy is what you need tonight." That is, we don't need to be made more aware of our alienating traits—that just produces more alienation. We need to be shown mercy. Think about it: Have you ever been given "space" when it comes to your personality? How did it make you feel? Odds are, you felt loved, and you wanted to spend more time, not less, with the one who showed you mercy. You loved them in return. "Blessed are the merciful."

What then for those of us who can't seem to keep our mouths shut? Those of us who have acted mercilessly towards the ones we love? While the *quid pro quo* mercy exchange may be true of our relational lives, fortunately God doesn't operate on this continuum. On the cross, Jesus suffered the full mercilessness of God (and humanity) that we deserve, so that we might be shown the opposite. We can trust in the power of "lenient and compassionate treatment" because it worked on Calvary, once and for all. In other words, blessed are the merciless, for they have been shown mercy.

—*David Zahl*

June 14

> *Do not think that I have come to abolish the Law or the Prophets; I have not come to abolish them but to fulfill them. For truly, I say to you, until heaven and earth pass away not an iota, not a dot, will pass away from the Law until all is accomplished. Therefore whoever relaxes one of the least of these commandments and teaches others to do the same will be called least in the kingdom of heaven, but whoever does them and teaches them will be called great in the kingdom of heaven. For I tell you, unless your righteousness exceeds that of the scribes and Pharisees, you will never enter the kingdom of heaven. (Matthew 5:17-20, ESV)*

All of us are confronted with the next new thing. If you're a parent, maybe it's the latest toys or clothes for your kids. If you're into software, maybe it's the latest technological gadget or social media platform. During this economic crunch maybe it's the newest way to invest your money. As a pastor I am constantly confronted with the newest "ministry tools" to get my parishioners to *be better disciples* or, even bigger and better, *transform the world.*

Many of these ministry tools and programs—maybe you are currently victim to them—are designed to help us fulfill some sort of religious lifestyle requirement and make us more "mature Christians." Now, it is true Jesus did not come to abolish the Law and the Prophets, but he came to *fulfill* them. The Law does not disappear in our lives, but rather it hangs over our heads. It continues to demonstrate that we are not better disciples than the first ones, that we still haven't transformed the world, that the world is still spinning madly on. These new ministry tools may help in certain areas of our lives, but they cannot undo the comprehensive severity of the Law.

Spiritually speaking, the last thing we need is the latest new thing. God's Law is not the stuff for "Christian Inspiration" books, but repentance. The Law brings us to a better understanding of our need; even on our best days, our righteousness cannot exceed that of the Pharisees and the scribes.

The righteousness we need but don't have comes in Jesus Christ. In Jesus, we are set free from "next new things," because he is the newness we seek. There's no need for more programs or tools—the world has already been transformed!

—Jacob Smith

June 15

> *So when you are offering your gift at the altar, if you remember that your brother or sister has something against you, leave your gift there before the altar and go; first be reconciled to your brother or sister, and then come and offer your gift. (Matthew 5:23-24, NRSV)*

In the multiple Oscar-winning 1979 film *Kramer vs. Kramer*, Meryl Streep and Dustin Hoffman portray a couple whose marriage ends in divorce and a bitter custody battle over their son, Billy.

There are a lot of elevator scenes in *Kramer vs. Kramer*. Near the beginning of the film, Joanna leaves Ted, and while she is on an elevator he begs her not to go, to which she replies, "I don't love you anymore," and the door closes. Later in the film, after a brutal day in court, as Ted boards an elevator Joanna tries to apologize to him for her lawyer raking him over the coals during the custody hearings, but he looks at her and says nothing, and the door closes. Although Joanna wins the custody battle, she decides Billy would be better off with Ted, and, in the final scene of the film, Joanna boards an elevator as she goes to tell Billy goodbye. She has been crying, and her makeup is running, and she asks Ted, "How do I look?" Ted smiles and replies, "Terrific." The elevator door closes and the credits roll. The film never shows Ted and Joanna riding an elevator together. There is no reconciliation.

Often our relationships lack reconciliation, and this lack creates feelings that ricochet between hidden resentment and open hostility. It's not the way it's supposed to be but it's the way it is. We live in a world where marriages end in divorce, grown children refuse to see their aging parents, and best friends become inexplicably estranged. This lack of reconciliation feels to a relationship like a looming cloud hanging overhead, a potential storm held in suspension. Sometimes all it takes is an apology or a statement of guilt, but this is all but impossible to rouse. As Philip Roth says it in *American Pastoral*,

> You fight your superficiality, your shallowness, so as to try
> to come at people without unreal expectations, without an
> overload of bias or hope or arrogance, as untanklike as you
> can be, sans cannon and machine guns and steel plating half
> a foot thick... and yet you never fail to get them wrong.*

Apparently Jesus considers reconciliation more important than worship: "leave your gift there at the altar and go," he says, "first be reconciled to your brother or sister, and then come and offer your gift." The good news is that we have been reconciled to God, and therefore we can be reconciled with others. Our reconciliation to others seems to come in response to *being* reconciled to God through the death of Jesus on the cross. As Paul writes, "(God has) reconciled us to himself through Christ, and has given us the ministry of reconciliation" (2 Cor 5:18).

What about you today? Perhaps there are people in your life with whom God is calling you to be reconciled, or perhaps you've already tried to be reconciled but it just won't happen. The good news is that it's not up to you; in Jesus' death on the cross, you have already *been* reconciled

---

* Roth, Philip. *American Pastoral*. New York: Random House, First Vintage
International Ed, 1998, p 35.

to God, fully. The burden has been lifted and the black cloud has vanished.

—*David Johnson*

June 16

You have heard that it was said, "You shall not commit adultery." But I say to you that everyone who looks at a woman with lustful intent has already committed adultery with her in his heart. If your right eye causes you to sin, tear it out and throw it away. For it is better that you lose one of your members than that your whole body be thrown into hell. And if your right hand causes you to sin, cut it off and throw it away. For it is better that you lose one of your members than that your whole body go into hell. (Matthew 5:27-30, NASB)

With the current state of sexuality in the West, there is no way to avoid the issues raised by Jesus in this passage. Sex is everywhere, and yet most of the Church is unwilling to talk about it honestly. Instead, we have found it easier to close our eyes and point our fingers, making sure "pure Christians" don't stray from the path.

We have chosen to deal with modern sexuality in a misleading way, with abstinence programs peddling "save yourself for marriage" slogans, while not having a sure scope of what "saving yourself" entails. We hold rallies for kids in their sexual prime and promote purity, as if kids had ever been "pure." Alienating those we perceive to be sexual deviants, we have made scapegoats of cohabitating 20-somethings, all the while conveniently overlooking the married or single churchgoers with less apparent sexual backgrounds and hang-ups.

What Jesus says in this passage condemns us all. While we finger point and blame shift, Jesus says the only direction a finger rightly points is toward the self. *I am the lustful one, I am an adulterer, I have sinned and fallen short of the glory of God.*

I remember youth functions that talked about sex and the inevitable question was, "How far is too far?" Every single leader had a different right answer, as did I. "Am I still a virgin?" It seems like that depends on whom you ask. Whatever the answer is, the point is this: the boundary becomes a misleading badge of honor when you toe the line, and a self-destructive shame when you cross it.

God loves you. Jesus gave his life that you might live. There is no such thing as a "pure" Christian. There are only Christians. By calling ourselves this, we identify with a crucified outcast who has given all that we might not have shame. Human sexuality is broadly broken, but it is also beautiful and God-given. It is difficult to reconcile these two realities, except to say this: you are forgiven for everything you've ever done or thought or believed. Go and live your life trusting that the Spirit will guide and protect you, for on account of Jesus it is holy and acceptable to God.

—*Kris McInnes*

June 17

You therefore must be perfect, as your heavenly Father is perfect. (Matthew 5:48, ESV)

One of the Biblical words translated "sin" is actually an archery term meaning "to have missed the mark or target." It reminds me of the Disney cartoon version of *Robin Hood*, with Robin as the cunning fox and the Sheriff of Nottingham as a big ugly wolf. In the movie there is an archery contest in which the winner would get a chance to meet the lovely maiden Marion. The Sheriff wants to win so badly that he has one of his vulture goons hide inside the target so that, if his shot should be off, if he should *sin*, the goon can move the target so that the arrow hits the bulls-eye.

We of course play the same game as the Sheriff, trying to move the target closer to have a greater chance of hitting it. This happens when we make excuses, when we pity ourselves or blame others. This is foolish thinking: it assumes that we are the target setters, the game changers. Jesus, not you or I, sets the target very plainly here, and it is no game. The target is to "be perfect, as our heavenly Father is perfect."

We may try casuistry, as the Pharisees in the Bible often do, to maneuver this goal. We may say it's all about being a good steward with our money, or not swearing, or not physically killing anyone, or not binge drinking, or paying our taxes, or helping out at the shelter on Thanksgiving, or not looking at pornography, or not starving ourselves, or calling mom and dad on weekends, or whatever. We may say it's about something else, but it's really this: life is about being perfect.

With this impossibly high target, sin becomes the *lingua franca*. We miss this mark on all counts; there is no matter of manipulation or posturing that will alter it or make it more attainable. Rather, it is a state of being. We have no way to change our state, our being, but that is exactly what must happen. You therefore must be perfect.

Where do you stand hopeless today? Where do you most often feel the pressure to hit the mark? Or maybe more appropriately, where *don't* you? There is no hope for sinners like us when the stakes are this high, at least not from within.

—*Sean Norris*

June 18

> *Beware of practicing your righteousness before other people in order to be seen by them, for then you will have no reward from your Father who is in heaven. Thus, when you give to the needy, sound no trumpet before you, as the hypocrites do in the synagogues and in the streets, that they may be praised by others. Truly, I say to you, they have received their reward. (Matthew 6:1-2, ESV)*

In giving of all kinds—money, time, energy—Jesus here is basically saying, "It must be so pure that even your hands are ignorant of your actions. When you achieve this, when you un-self-consciously live out a life of giving, then God will surely reward you."

I haven't always read it this way. For years during my youth, I thought this passage referred to some strange tithing ritual, where you planned to somehow forget which hand had actually deposited cash in the offering plate. If you did this correctly, then God, seeing fulfillment of His tithing prescription, would make the money expand. Understanding this, I believed I was topping off my heavenly 401K every week, and God was matching my righteousness with His heavenly bonuses.

Still, the absurdity of "right" giving is no less absurd to me now. Christ is describing an impossible act, one in which I fail miserably. The only way I can truly give to the needy and *not* announce my offering with acclamation is if I am completely taken out of the equation. This is a gift, to be able to give away something because I don't believe it is mine, because I don't feel entitled to it. It is a gift of the Holy Spirit to believe I am merely the vessel of the gifts God's given.

The good news of Jesus Christ is this gift from without, in which I am taken out of the equation. No longer must I fret upon "right" giving in hopes of gaining God's favor—God has already rewarded me through the justifying gift of his Son. Oddly enough, this one gift of grace has a peculiar way of inspiring giving of its own.

—Jeremy Coleman

June 19

> *Do not lay up treasures on earth, where moths and rust destroy and where thieves break in and steal, but lay up for yourselves treasures in heaven, where neither moth nor rust destroys and where thieves do not break in and steal. For where your treasure is, there your heart will be also. (Matthew 6:19-24, ESV)*

I have this friend who calls himself "a nomad with a penchant for idealism." Whether it's deciding the right microbrew or just the right record to "make the moment," or the right next-step-two-year-career towards intentional living, this friend has a tendency to construct illustrious plans for a life in total congruence with what he envisions will "complete a picture." Of course, it's not surprising that these plans tend to bounce back a bit, to pick up and move on at almost predictable intervals. It's extremely easy to mock this perspective from an objective standpoint, but it also sounds really, really good when the things envisioned seem so perfect.

And yet they're not. Nothing's perfect, and I should have guessed this as I rode in the car with this friend, newly returned a bearded locavore from his latest overseas, return-to-simplicity, slow-food, socially just excursion. I should have guessed, but at the time I was just as enamored of his narrative as he had been before he left. And yet he told me it was actually pretty miserable, and he wondered if he wholly regretted having gone. He said it didn't add up. The image he had created had no room for the imperfections that eventually rotted it away. The ideal just ended up feeling hollow.

I could relate. I had recently been looking forward to a trip to London for months, to finally have *that time* to write *those poems* I had been longing to write, in that coffee shop with that perfect cup, of course. And there I sat, in that coffee shop with that latte and that perfect pen and paper, and my back sweating and somewhere it smelled like gas. And I realized I had no poem, but merely a shell, and I began to feel really sad.

Who doesn't look back ten years and think to themselves, "I was a complete idiot! Why did I ever think calling her back was a good idea?", or "Why did I take that job? I was so much happier before." And yet we somehow believe that the idealistic constructions within the mind we have *now* are safe from anything similar happening ten years down the road. Somehow we still believe that we know what we need best.

Thankfully, the Gospel message here bluntly says we're wrong. The good news here is that we actually don't know what's best, and that this ignorance is actually right and good and peace-giving. It's best not to put a lot of stock in our own ideas for what will fulfill us, because all our treasures will eventually be eaten up in the moths and rust of human reality. What we can bank on, though, is the gracious supply of our loving Lord, who meets our silly plans where we are and moves us beyond them in ways we cannot see or hope for, and yet strangely, unknowingly long for. Laying up our treasures in heaven means depending upon a loving God who, by the cross, will not leave us. This allows our hearts to rest in what's always been in control anyways—and therein find peace.

—*Ethan Richardson*

June 20

Why do you look at the speck of sawdust in your brother's eye and pay no attention to the plank in your own eye? (Matthew 7:3, NIV)

Jesus reveals an unsettling truth here: our desire "to help" a brother or sister says more about us than about them. And what it says about us is not something we want to hear, which is quite a shock, given that we thought we were trying to help someone else.

Jesus reads this desire to help as revealing a three-fold problem. First, we have a plank—a much, much bigger item than a speck of sawdust—in our own eye; second, that we are unable to see clearly *because* of this plank; and, third, we are hypocrites.

218

Jesus turns it back on the help-giver, making it clear that the help-giver is the one who needs help. Have you ever pictured this scene and wondered how one is able to see clearly enough to remove a plank in their own eye? Is he not saying, "You are the one who really needs help. There is no way you can ever see clearly enough to remove your own plank without help from someone else." Jesus even calls the help-giver a hypocrite, which is a serious accusation.

It is interesting that Jesus does not qualify this scenario with a "sometimes' or "perhaps." He is saying that if people want to be helpful, they must first understand that they are hypocrites, self-righteous do-gooders who do not even know themselves.

Where does this leave us? First, confessing that our spotting the speck in our brother's eye is a clue that we are not seeing ourselves as the self-righteous people we are. Second, we are the ones needing help. We need help seeing and removing these huge planks, and we cannot do that on our own. We need help knowing ourselves truly. We need help from outside ourselves, and we need it now.

—*Mary Zahl*

June 21

If you then, though you are evil, know how to give good gifts to your children, how much more will your Father in heaven give good gifts to those who ask him? (Matthew 7:11, NIV)

How often we think our role in prayer is to convince God to do something that we think is a good idea. We approach him as an insistent teenager: "Please, please, please!"

There are two problems with this scenario. First, we somehow believe we have the ability to influence the Almighty God if we want something badly enough. Not exactly humility on our part.

But the second problem is much more serious, and the main misconception here is that we deep down believe that God is miserly, not willing or desiring to give us the good gifts Jesus refers to in this verse. We do not believe He is for us, but rather wants only to "teach us a lesson" through some sort of tough love. We honestly believe He will give us a serpent if we ask for a fish.

Asking according to the will of the Father requires stepping back from this scene whenever we hear ourselves saying or implying "please, please, please." In stepping back, we ask God to give us His view of the situation we are praying about. Often, our prayer changes immediately to "Thank you, Father. Thank you that you desire to heal, to provide, to give good gifts."

Sometimes a strong "theology of the cross" leads us to think that God can only work through the bad times and the suffering. True, he is at work in the *sub contrario*, the places of suffering where we don't expect Him to be. But just like parents at a clumsy dance recital, He is also proudly cheering his beloved children on. As much as God suffers with us, God also delights in our delight.

Heavenly Father, give us your eyes to see ourselves with the compassion of a loving parent.

—*Mary Zahl*

June 22

You will know them by their fruits. Are grapes gathered from thorns, or figs from thistles? So, every sound tree bears good fruit, but the bad tree bears evil fruit. A sound tree cannot bear evil fruit, nor can a bad tree bear good fruit. Every tree that does not bear good fruit is cut down and thrown into the fire. (Matthew 7:16-19, NASB)

I grew up in the South, where this was an often-quoted verse. And people said things like, "We're not *judging*, we're just being fruit inspectors." I'm not kidding. I've actually heard people say that, and they believed it. Conversely, I recently came across this quote from good ol' Honest Abe: "A man watches his pear tree day after day, impatient for the ripening of the fruit. Let him attempt to force the process, and he may spoil both fruit and tree. But let him patiently wait, and the ripe pear falls at length into his lap."

Quaint as it may be, I feel like this relates much more to what Jesus is really talking about. If the standard is perfection, and we all fail equally, then how can anyone be a "fruit inspector"?

I once listened to a preacher talk about how profoundly passive a metaphor the fruit tree was. Think about it: a tree has no input on where it's planted, where it grows, or even what kind of fruit it produces. It's completely at the mercy of external forces as to whether it even produces fruit to begin with. A tree has no say in the matter. It simply must be what it is.

This is oddly comforting. God is working out His plan in, through, and all around us. It's often difficult, but I know I can trust that. Passivity is the key to activity. Seems counterintuitive, but if we take Abe for his word, it actually works.

—Nate Michaux

June 23

Whoever loses his life for my sake will find it. (Matthew 10:39, NIV)

Life is full of the unexpected. When unanticipated events occur, we are forced to re-evaluate our plans and our hopes.

It is important to realize this. The Christian message will always bring human beings to a place where they must confront a thing that they are deeply afraid of: the limits of their own ability to shape life into that which they desire. Despite the fact that people tend to treat God a bit like Santa Claus, it is the unexpected events of life that drive us into a deeper relationship with God, one in which we are no longer trying to hold onto the reigns.

This is both offensive and freeing. It is offensive because, in God, our myopic and meager plans for our lives are thwarted; but it is freeing because in Him, we find a much better biography than anything we could come up with for ourselves. If you are tired of playing God, then you can instead step into the good works that God has prepared for you.

Of course, there are some things that we cannot relinquish, even if we know better. They are the kinds of things that we worry will get in the way of our spiritual life. Sometimes those particular fascinations become, for us, a bit too non-negotiable. You might consider praying about those things, even starting briefly right now. Don't worry about getting past them; just start the conversation.

—John Zahl

June 24

Now when John heard in prison about the deeds of the Christ, he sent word by his disciples and said to him, "Are you the one who is to come, or shall we look for another?" And Jesus answered them, 'Go and tell John what you hear and see: the blind receive their sight and the lame walk, lepers are cleansed and the deaf hear, and the dead are raised up, and the poor have good news preached to them. And blessed is the one who is not offended by me."
(Matthew 11:2-6, ESV)

The Crystal Skull movie notwithstanding, *Indiana Jones* movies have made me glad to be alive. Honestly, what makes you happier than coming home at night to watch someone else dodge poison darts? Anyway, *Indiana Jones and the Last Crusade* has a very poignant illustration for us as we consider this reading from Matthew.

Jones and a bunch of other people (Nazis included) are searching for the Holy Grail. They end up in a cave with a lot of different chalices to choose from. The Nazi guy chooses first and he chooses the beautiful, ornate chalice meant for a king. All of the sudden, you see him melt like rubber, and an ancient knight says, "He chose... poorly." Indiana Jones is up next, and he gives it a lot of thought. He chooses the most earthen and common cup he could find, and he chooses wisely.

The first idea—the Nazi's choosing of a kingly cup—is the idea of straight-line power. This is a portrayal of Jesus the Regal, who brings historic deliverance for his people and deals wrath to his foes. This is what all Jews in Jesus' day were looking for, perhaps including John the Baptist. Not that you can blame them at all—but here sits John, in prison-cell squalor, alone and at the total mercy of a captor who hates him. And as the rodents scurry beneath the bars of his cell, you can surely imagine his own certainty about who Jesus is scurrying, too. So, he sends some of his disciples to ask Jesus if he is the one John thinks he is. If not, should they expect another?

The second idea—the common cup of Indiana's choosing—is the hidden God, who reveals himself in suffering. You can see it in verse 25 of this chapter, too: Jesus thanks the Father that He has hidden himself from the typical halls of power, and has instead chosen to reveal himself in the places power ignores. In other words, God is not revealing himself in glorious revolution or social upheaval, or any other demonstrative form of power. God is revealing himself as the suffering servant; as the one *everyone* turns away from. He is hiding himself so well, in fact, that it even eludes the prophet.

This hiddenness is where we meet Him. It is the lostness and lastness in all of us that meets God, without having to hide or run. Strangely enough, God in this place is much more powerful than power ever could be.

—David Browder

June 25

"All things have been handed over to me by my Father, and no one knows the Son except the Father, and no one knows the Father except the Son and anyone to whom the Son chooses to reveal him. Come to me, all who labor and are heavy laden, and I will give you rest. Take my yoke upon you, and learn from me, for I am gentle and lowly in heart, and you will find rest for your souls. For my yoke is easy, and my burden is light." (Matthew 11:27-30, ESV)

The sobering (and, frankly, nauseating) story of *The Metamorphosis* by Franz Kafka tells of a normal workingman who happens to wake up one morning as a giant beetle. He has been supporting his parents and sister but is obviously unable to go to work as long as he remains a beetle. At first, the entire family cares for him; then, it's just his sister; finally no one's around and he dies of starvation. It is a tragic story, but Kafka's observation is important: as long as we are productive, we are valuable. As soon as we are unable to produce, however, we lose our value. We die, so to speak. Kafka, in my opinion, is lamenting this.

Some questions that may arise: Am I just a pawn in society? Am I loved apart from what I produce? Am I replaceable or not? Am I valuable apart from creating my own value?

Speaking with a psychologist friend of mine, I learned that children of alcoholics have an uncanny ability to self-destruct throughout their lives. I guess I had seen it, but never made the connection. Addicts themselves tend to self-destruct, too. I have known divorced people who have slept round-the-clock for two years straight from grief. Have these sufferers lost their *value*? To the outside world, to their families and friends, maybe they have.

I personally remember a conversation with a past boss of mine that was along these lines. I had made a mistake, and he came into my office. He said to me, "I want you to know that I totally support you..." (sigh of relief) "... as long as you produce." I felt like my chest was caving in. It occurred to me that this is life; life is *quid pro quo*. All the time. Your worth is directly correlated to the quality of your output.

But, for all the production and its costs, we see in this passage a Man making home among the impotent. Jesus addresses the ones contributing nearly nothing of value. "Come to me, all who labor and are heavy laden, and I will give you rest." This Man is God Himself. And that turns everything on its ear.

—David Browder

June 26

> *"...while you are pulling the weeds, you might root up the wheat with them. Let both grow together until the harvest. At that time I will tell the harvesters: 'First collect the weeds and tie them in bundles to be burned; then gather the wheat and bring it into my barn.'" (Matthew 13:29-30, NIV)*

In this brilliant parable called "The Wheat and the Tares," a group of people approach a crop owner about a "growing" problem. There are weeds growing with the wheat. The good stuff is being threatened by some bad stuff. Isn't this true to life? I bet that right now, you can see some good stuff on the horizon of your life, some developments that get you excited, things worth hoping for. But then there is apprehension, too. Are there not possible "mitigating factors," things to be avoided, possibilities that could cause the whole plan to go pear-shaped?

The people in the parable come to the master with the intention of doing the thing that people always want to do in these situations. They want permission to try to weed out the bad in order to protect the good. They want to enlist caller ID, alternate routes, good strategies, careful seating charts, pest control, and the like—all in an attempt to disentangle the good from the bad. They want the good without any bad, and they're pretty sure they can make it happen if they're given the chance.

Jesus is quick to point out the fallacy in this train of thought: "While you are pulling the weeds, you might uproot the wheat with them." In other words, we're not all that great at distinguishing between the good and the bad. We get it wrong all the time. Like a friend of mine who had a crush on a girl who wasn't interested in him: while he was preoccupied with trying to get things rolling romantically, another girl entered the scene. He could barely see her. That is, until Girl #1 made it clear that she was not interested in him. When that happened, to his good fortune, Girl #2 turned out to be great for him, and today they are happily married.

God is the only one who knows what is *actually* good and what is *actually* bad. We do not. Given this insight, His word for us, while still a bit odd, makes sense: "Let both grow together until the harvest."

Today we are reminded that God knows best, and that we do not and cannot have full access to that information. He will separate the wheat from the chaff in his own way and at just the right moment. Doesn't that simplify things a bit?

—John Zahl

June 27

> *"The kingdom of heaven is like a treasure hidden in the field, which a man found and hid; and from joy over it he goes and sells all that he has, and buys that field. Again, the kingdom of heaven is like a merchant seeking fine pearls, and upon finding one pearl of great value, he went and sold all that he had, and bought it." (Matthew 13:44-46, NASB)*

Here we have two very distinct parables with two very distinct messages: the "Treasure in the Field" and the "Pearl of Great Price." Let's start by getting our actors straight. In the first parable, the kingdom of heaven is like a treasure, and you and I are the man. In the second parable the kingdom of heaven is like the merchant, and you and I are the pearl. The simple observation that the kingdom of heaven is said to be like the merchant, not like the pearl, ends up being very significant, as you will see.

After years of thinking and writing about it, I am more convinced than ever that the message of the parable of the treasure hidden in the field is critical for us. It is because there was a treasure that the man sacrifices all. It is from joy that he sells all that he has. It is from a great and a true desire that he acts. The Gospel is not simply doctrinal correctness or sound theology—it is a great treasure, and once we perceive its surpassing value hidden in the scrubby field of the church, it engages our desire powerfully. We drop our self-justification projects with joy, because we have found a treasure of much greater worth. We are released from all care and worry, and we have become impossibly and eternally rich and taken care of. Of all the people on earth, we have found our way and have obtained our fortune—we are spiritual gazillionaires.

I am even more convinced that the message of the Pearl of Great Value is critical for us. The heart of the message of the Gospel is that God truly *wants* us. He is greedy and jealous for us. He has sold all that He had, to obtain us:

> In this is love, not that we loved God, but that He loved us and sent His Son to be the propitiation for our sins. Beloved, if God so loved us, we also ought to love one another. (1 John 4:10-11, NASB)

Why do we call Christ's death on the cross the "*Passion?*" I haven't researched it at all and I have no idea why we call it that. But I know what passion means—it means extreme desire, reckless love, fierce devotion to the point of obsession. It means laser-like focus born of strong wanting. How does this word relate to Jesus' death on the cross? His love for us is an absolutely reckless and dangerous love. It is abandon-everything-else desire. It is the pearl merchant selling all he had to get that one perfect pearl. It is passion for us that led to such sacrifice. He wanted us. Badly. Enough to do this.

God is love. Not just any love. Not just idle affection. Not the gentle, detached love of a grandmother. That is a wonderful kind of love, but it is not this love. His is a passionate, reckless, die-for-you love. His is a throw-away-every-other-option love. We are His obsession. We are not His obligation, we are His joy (Heb 12:2). This is the God who is love—the God who would go to such shocking lengths on our behalf.

Beloved, if God so loved us, we also ought to love one another. Amen.

—*Jim McNeely III*

June 28

> *Now when Jesus heard this, he withdrew from there in a boat to a deserted place by himself. But when the crowds heard it, they followed him on foot from the towns. When he went ashore, he saw a great crowd; and he had compassion for them and cured their sick... (Matthew 14:13-21, NRSV)*

In 2010, The Rolling Stones reissued what is often proclaimed to be the best rock 'n' roll album ever made—*Exile on Main Street*. Like all reissues, its relevance has stood the test of time, and so it gets to be officially celebrated all over again (with some key editing on the sound mix). Similarly, the "Feeding of the Five Thousand," easily considered to be one of Jesus' greatest hits, is the only passage to be reissued in all four gospels, which suggests it deserves to be read again and again.

Among many things, the story shows the power of God as well as the abundance of His loving provision for people. What has recently caught my attention about this passage, however, lies at the beginning of the story when Jesus first encounters the crowd.

After hearing that his friend John the Baptist has been beheaded, Jesus withdraws by boat to a solitary place. Whether they understand Jesus' state of mourning or not, a growing crowd of people can't help but follow him from the shore. He's probably in no state to answer to an assembly of sick and needy—and hungry—people. What is equally surprising is that Jesus doesn't soak in his celebrity. As an aspiring musician, this kind of crowd would seem to me like an *opportunity*. Yet attention never seems to be on Jesus' wish list.

It would have been reasonable for Jesus to avoid the crowd to lament alone, and it would have also been reasonable for a man of Jesus' popularity to wave to the crowd, toss along a few catchphrases, kiss some babies and *then* retire to solitude. But Jesus seeks neither. Instead, he has compassion on these people and heals their sick, his "compassion" working to show that Jesus isn't acting out of piety or moral duty, but out of a true desire to alleviate suffering.

I am convinced that based on the power within them, no one else would act in such a way. In times of great vulnerability, our human nature compels us to seek comfort; Jesus, instead, refuses to play the victim. Ultimately, this story points ahead to the crucifixion—where

Christ, who deserved to be let alone, gave himself up, and died on the cross that we could be fed and healed.

—Sam Bush

June 29

> *...For out of the heart come evil thoughts, murder, adultery, fornication, theft, false witness, slander. These are what defile a man; but to eat with unwashed hands does not defile a man... (Matthew 15:10-20, NRSV)*

The Pharisees have faulted Jesus and his disciples for being too lax with ritual purity. Jesus and his friends ate with unwashed hands. Strike one. And they ate with lawbreakers. Strike two. In response, Jesus points out two things.

First, sin is an *internal* problem. The things that make us unclean, Jesus says, are hard-wired into us. Sin bursts forth from our hearts, fully grown like Athena from Zeus' head. We see the evidence of this everywhere: parents know they never had to teach their children to lie. You know you never faced a moment in your young adulthood where you had to decide whether to be a self-interested person or not. It seemed you just were.

The second thing Jesus points out is that outside-in approaches to sin management don't work. You see, the Pharisees tried to establish moral purity by method, by focusing on external actions. The modern-day analogy is to Christians who try to maintain purity by monitoring their intake (or their children's intake) of cultural matter: "Don't watch this type of movie. Don't listen to that kind of music."

The mistaken assumption with this approach is that there is some pre-existent *pure* state of being, that can then be corrupted by watching *Wedding Crashers* or listening to deathcore metal. Certainly what we read, watch, or hear has some influence, but only so far as it stirs up everything that was already there. Indeed, one might say that we seek out "bad influences" based on our built-in sin. Human violence, aggression, and self-destructive impulses did not begin with the advent of Hollywood or video games. Since Eden, people have hungered after evil. As Article IX of the Anglican Church's Articles of Religion says, "...man is very far gone from original righteousness, and is of his own nature inclined to evil, so that the flesh lusteth always contrary to the Spirit."

This leaves us in a bad way. I wish the Pharisees were right, that all we had to do was wash our hands the right way, or just listen to Christian music, or only watch ABC Family. But as good as these things are, we find we don't even scratch the surface of our deep predisposition to seek our own good over others, to "follow the devices and desires of our own hearts," as the Anglican confessional prayer goes.

What, then, should we do? The Apostle Paul knew the answer. We are helpless. We can do nothing. But God has done everything. Paul says it twice in Romans 5: "while we were still sinners..." In the midst of our broken lives and corrupted hearts, Jesus comes to us. And he knows our problem is not unclean hands, but unclean hearts, hearts we cannot change. So he removes the stain, and he washes us clean.

—Aaron Zimmerman

June 30

For whoever would save his life will lose it, but whoever loses his life for my sake will find it. (Matthew 16:24-25, ESV)

Jesus describes the two realities of human existence (and ultimately there are only two): trust in yourself and suffer eternal loss, or trust in God and gain eternal life. In these potent, descriptive verses, Jesus calls a thing what it is. "For whoever would save his life will lose it." Trusting in yourself, worshipping yourself, saving and securing your own life may very well gain you the trappings of success in this world. But in all cases, without exception, it will lead to your own destruction.

The inevitable end of trusting yourself is illustrated in the Roman version of the Narcissus myth. One day while hunting, the handsome and thirsty Narcissus bends down to drink from a stream. He sees his own reflection and falls in love with it. As he bends down to kiss the image in the water, it seems to run away. Narcissus is heartbroken; he grows thirstier and thirstier, but he will not drink for fear of damaging his own beautiful image. He eventually dies of thirst and self-love, staring at his own reflection.

Bob Dylan, commenting on Narcissus, sings, "Now he worships at an altar of a stagnant pool /And when he sees his reflection, he's fulfilled." Narcissus may be thrilled and fulfilled as he gazes into his ephemeral reflection, but in the end, he dies because he loves his image at the expense of himself.

"But whoever loses his life for my sake will find it." Trusting in Jesus may very well lead to physical death in this world and will always lead to death of your own petty and narcissistic hopes and dreams and ambitions. This is what Jesus means when he tells us to take up our cross and follow him. Following him can mean nothing else but death to self.

But death to self is a good thing, isn't it? Death to all that is greedy and addicted and lustful and jealous and sardonic. Do you really want to go on living with those hateful monkeys on your back? Do you really like the incessant chatter in your ear and their pointed nails in your back?

There is pain involved in the removal of the monkeys, because there is always pain in death. And yet, there is also your new life. Trusting in Jesus means trusting in the one who has taken the monkeys with their teeth and claws off your back and placed them on his own. He has taken them to the cross to die with him.

When the day is finally done, trusting in Jesus, in the words of Flannery O'Connor, means, "the life you save may be your own."

—*Paul Walker*

July 1

...Peter came and said to Jesus, "Lord, if another member of the church sins against me, how often should I forgive? As many as seven times?" Jesus said to him, "Not seven times, but, I tell you, seventy-seven times." (Matthew 18:21-35, NRSV)

Forgiveness is hard, and the forgiveness God demands is impossible. Jesus tells a story of a man who was forgiven much and then refused to forgive one who owed him little. This unforgiving man was tortured until he paid back all he owed, an amount so staggering that it would have been impossible for him to recover.

We often assume the point of the parable is simple, that we should forgive others and not hold grudges, but that end is impossible to attain. If we walk away from the parable thinking that this is something we can live up to, or worse, something we *are* living up to, then we are lost. The parable can only help us if through it we hear what we are supposed to do and realize that we are *not* doing it. And this should come naturally—it won't take long to think about how unforgiving we are: think about the last time you heard someone sing the national anthem, the last time you watched Access Hollywood, the last time you sized someone up in the grocery store, the latest gossip you heard.

These are our shortcomings before the Law of Forgiveness. We may like that Jesus forgives, we may even like the *idea* of forgiving others, but we cannot do it ourselves. Like any other, this law can only assist us in illuminating our death before it and our need for an external forgiver. Thankfully, on the other side of this death is the new life in a forgiving and loving God, who sent his son Jesus to show us how it's done.

From the cross Jesus says, "Father, forgive them, for they know not what they do," and that is exactly what God does. He doesn't even wait for us to ask. Before we go looking for it or even realize we need help, we are forgiven. Before our mouths can even form the words "I'm sorry," we are forgiven.

—*Kris McInnes*

July 2

> "...Am I not allowed to do what I choose with what belongs to me? Or are you envious because I am generous? So the last will be first and the first will be last." (Matthew 20:1-16, NRSV)

We humans are in love with justice. It is probably one of the most recurring themes in cultural expression since the Stone Age. Today, it's not just that we have our *Judge Judy* and *Law & Order* courtroom obsessions—we also just love the narrative of justice *served*. This is Quentin Tarantino's shtick (*Kill Bill* and, more recently, *Django Unchained*), and this is why his movies are so critically successful. They playfully enter into a long line of comeuppances and vengeance stories that people have loved since their dawn-of-time inception.

More than just the retributive brand of justice—of bad guys getting what's coming to them—we are also fascinated with the *restorative* form. Politicians, policy-makers, and administrators all use words like "social justice" and "the common good" and "equality" to talk about defending the defenseless and bringing up the lowly. This is a very good and true thing—the Bible itself speaks highly of advocacy for the poor.

But it seems that we only want this kind of advocacy for others so long as it is expressed in terms of "deserving." One of the most glaring examples of this is the feel-good era of reality television, like *Extreme Makeover: Home Edition*. We've all seen it: Ty Pennington yells aloud, "Move that bus!" and a disadvantaged family is captured, mouths agape, before their brand new house, their excessively nice cars, their new full-size basketball court. For a moment, it feels like the cosmos has been generously righted, but in truth, this kind of generosity is only warranted for the "right" kind of poor. These programs—and people in general—are comfortable with generosity only as a leg up for the hardworking, stand-up variety of unfortunates. Generosity for us does not mean blind "handouts," but trustworthy "investments" with reimbursements. (I wonder how long these shows would last if the same generosity landed upon chronic gamblers, crooks, and sexual deviants?)

This is what Jesus is saying about the human brand of justice in relation to God's. As Feist sang, "There's A Limit to Your Love." The kind of deep generosity we may accept for ourselves runs counter to the deep judgment we hope others get. This parable gives a new—and too-often revolting—take on equality: everyone gets this generosity, without repayment plans, starting with those who deserve it least.

—*Ethan Richardson*

July 3

This took place to fulfill what was spoken by the prophet, saying, "Tell the daughter of Zion, 'Behold, your king is coming to you, humble, and mounted on an ass, and on a colt, the foal of an ass.'" (Matthew 21:4-5, RSV)

Palm Sunday is a day in the Christian Calendar, and a day in history, that could define the word "irony."

It depicts the advance on Jerusalem of the city's "King," but in the form of a man seated on a donkey. It begins a week of "triumphal entry" that only ends in complete disaster. It marks the enthusiastic reception by a large crowd of pilgrims who will, in five days, completely melt away, with the remaining "welcomers" shouting "Crucify him!" In short, it depicts a symbolic action that is both true and false: he is the King, and he is also the "Quasimodo" King of Carnival. He is past and present—the prophets foretold this but not in the way it was going to go. Mighty and frail—he doesn't look like the only person who could ever get to Easter, yet he is definitely thermonuclear!

The inward and the outward senses of this ironic situation are captured perfectly in the old hymn for Palm Sunday that is called "Ride on! Ride on in majesty!" It was written in 1827 by Henry Hart Milman. The stunning words of Milman's hymn reach their climax in the four lines of verse five:

> Ride on! ride on in majesty!
> In lowly pomp ride on to die;
> Bow thy meek head to mortal pain,
> Then take, O God, thy power and reign.

An odd and curious truth of Christianity is that in the places of anguish within the human drama—within our individual dramas of intense pain—that is where God almost always does His "best work." How strange to say! And how strange still, after 40 years of seeing it and thinking about it, it *still* seems. It is true to experience, though.

At the same time, whenever something painful comes up, I still want to look elsewhere for my hope. "I haven't got time for the pain," as Carly Simon sang, and that's not a joke. I absolutely do not wish to make time for the pain.

I naturally want anything but God in the pain. But then I sing again—*ugh!*—my Palm Sunday hymn, and hear that connection between "majesty" and "lowly pomp" and "mortal pain." Say it isn't so! Or, rather, tell me again that it is.

—Paul Zahl

July 4

"... Then (the king) said to his slaves, 'The wedding feast is ready, but those invited were not worthy. Go therefore into the main roads and invite to the wedding feast as many as you find.' And those servants went out into the roads and gathered all whom they found, both bad and good. So the wedding hall was filled with guests. But when the king came in to look at the guests, he saw there a man who had no wedding garment. And he said to him, 'Friend, how did

*you get in here without a wedding garment?' And he was
speechless. Then the king said to the attendants, 'Bind him
hand and foot and cast him into the outer darkness. In that
place there will be weeping and gnashing of teeth.' For
many are called, but few are chosen." (Matthew 22:1-14,
ESV)*

The king's original wedding guests in this story are the sort of people
who go to real Hollywood power weddings. It's as if no one on the guest
list accepted the invitation to a royal wedding because they had other
things to do, so instead, hundreds of Joe Schmoes are brought in off the
street, to eat their veal and drink their 1978 Montrachet.

Stories like this give us a chance, because suddenly invitations
aren't addressed to the "haves" and withheld from the "have-nots." Jesus
works this way on principle, not just rubbing elbows with the fancy
people who sleep well at night with a lot of money and a clean
conscience. Jesus heads for the streets, where people fear being found
out, or don't know how it's going to turn out, or wonder if they'd even
recognize success if it ever came their way. In short, the Gospel is for
us—we're the ones who end up attending the wedding feast.

The next thing Jesus says is a little harder to understand: What's
all this about wearing a wedding robe, and the outer darkness?

Robes are significant symbols in the Bible. Today, robes go with
slippers. Then, robes went with sacrifice. Samuel wore a robe when an
animal was slaughtered during the annual sacrifice to God. Priests wore
robes when making sacrifices on behalf of their people. Even Joseph's robe
of many colors ends up drenched in blood as his brothers pretend that he's
been murdered. This imagery is most poignant in Revelation, when Jesus'
robe is dipped in his own blood (Rev 19). This association of robes with
blood would have been well known to those listening to Jesus, and to the
readers of Matthew's Gospel, who would then surmise Jesus' point: The
wedding robe in this parable carries the blood of his own sacrifice.

Jesus seems to be saying that in order to attend *this* Hollywood
wedding, you need the right get-up, and it can't be just any Italian Brioni
from Clooney's closet. For this party you must be clothed in the blood of
Christ, which is really just a redundancy, because there's no party
without it. And there's no purchase necessary– it's right there in front of
you, freely given out in the "main roads."

—*Nick Lannon*

July 5

Then the Pharisees went and plotted how to entangle him in his words. And they sent their disciples to him, along with the Herodians, saying, "Teacher, we know that you are true and teach the way of God truthfully, and you do not care about anyone's opinion, for you are not swayed by appearances. Tell us, then, what you think. Is it lawful to pay taxes to Caesar, or not?" But Jesus, aware of their malice, said, "Why put me to the test, you hypocrites? Show me the coin for the tax." And they brought him a denarius. And Jesus said to them, "Whose likeness and inscription is this?" They said, "Caesar's." Then he said to them, "Therefore render to Caesar the things that are Caesar's, and to God the things that are God's." When they heard it, they marveled... (Matthew 22:15-22, ESV)

One of the most memorable scenes in the entire *Star Wars* canon is when Darth Vader becomes Anakin Skywalker again in *Return of the Jedi* as he exposes his true identity under that ominous mask. "Luke, help me take this mask off," he says to his son. A concerned Luke responds, "But you'll die." Darth Vader then says, "Nothing can stop that now. Just for once, let me look on you with my own eyes." For most of his life Anakin has been viewing the world and presenting himself to the world through a pretense. His dark, cold mask makes him look stronger than he really is since underneath is a fragile and sad old man in desperate need of unabashed love.

Something similar happens in Matthew's passage about paying taxes to Caesar. The connection is not obvious at first, but an important thing to recognize in this story—and in life in general—is that what one sees in a situation is never all that is really happening. There is always very much more going on below the surface, just as there was with Darth Vader. Through their cunning deceit and indirect communication, the Pharisees and the Herodians inadvertently make some accurate statements about God. Namely, that God is truthful, does not care about anyone's opinion, and is not swayed by appearances. As a matter of fact, Jesus (that is, God) is so perceptive that he sees right through their lying façade, cutting to the heart of the matter beyond the proverbial tip o' the iceberg, leaving his surprised audience dumbfounded.

We are so often like the Pharisees—and Darth Vader—when we approach God in prayer and meditation. We can easily put Him to the test with our metal-black masks on, so long as we need not present our true selves and concerns. The irony is that God, in His infinite awareness, knows the whole truth about us—even better than we do. Strange as it is, such news is of great comfort. We can be utterly vulnerable with God in a way that we can with no one else. There is no need to sew fig leaves together, making flimsy coverings to hide ourselves from his presence. He is not swayed by our false appearance. Perhaps it is to die a death like Anakin when we reluctantly remove our masks, but we gain new life by finally being truly known.

Therefore, let us render our Vader masks to Caesar, and give to God what is God's—that is, nothing short of our entire, true, and unmasked selves.

—Matthew C. Schneider

July 6

...You shall love your neighbor as yourself... (Matthew 22:37-39, ESV)

Over 450 years ago, in the first Anglican Book of Common Prayer, Thomas Cranmer included a collection of Bible verses that would become known as the "comforting words." These passages were read to assure the people before communion that the message of the Gospel was one of forgiveness—forgiveness for the fact that we do not love God with everything, which is manifest in our failure to love our neighbors as ourselves.

Forgiveness—this is the comforting word of the Gospel. This is the unique form of love that comes from God through Christ and flows out to the world through forgiven sinners. This type of love—love which is grounded in the forgiveness of God—is the type that brings us back cyclically to this same Gospel message. It is this self-perpetuating forgiveness that mends fractured relationships, inspires heroic acts of selfless enterprise, and ignites the freedom of the imagination.

So as we hear the injunction to "love God and love your neighbor," know that our love for God flows from a response to the love that God has freely given and the reconciliation that we have with Him through Christ. It is for those of us who have wronged others and who have suffered wrong, because, as we are reminded by the comforting words, "If anyone sins, he has an advocate with the father, Jesus Christ the righteous."

—*Jady Koch*

July 7

> *...He who had received the one talent came forward, saying, "Master, I knew you to be a hard man, reaping where you did not sow, and gathering where you scattered no seed, so I was afraid, and I went and hid your talent in the ground. Here you have what is yours." But his master answered him, "You wicked and slothful servant! You knew that I reap where I have not sown and gather where I scattered no seed?..." (Matthew 25:14-30, ESV)*

A common reading of this parable is that God, like the Elf on the Shelf, is keeping track of your good works and will settle scores with you one day. This reading may be gussied up a bit, and might say that God gives *different* gifts in His grace, and so not everyone is working under the same set of expectations, but the expectations are there anyway, so really the message is the same: "God has invested in you, so do the best with what you've got."

I don't think this is what the Parable of the Talents is after. First of all, God the Landowner gives different amounts of money to each servant—five talents, two talents, and one talent—and this is not to favor one servant over another, but to demonstrate that he isn't interested in the numbers game. Like the Parable of the Sower (Matt 13), God demonstrates His kingdom by sowing seed everywhere, wildly, without concern to production. When God the Landowner returns, those who have traded and added to their talents receive precisely the same welcome: "Well done, good and faithful servant..." Even though one servant brings back a much heavier dividend, he gets no better acceptance than the one who brought back less than half of his. There is no staggered rewards system here—it seems more important to the Landowner that the servants play the game than bring back a surplus.

If this is the case, then what about Mr. One Talent? Why was he punished? The Landowner is not so much angry that he hasn't come back with "growth," but much more upset that Mr. One Talent is all wrong about who the Landowner actually is, namely, a risk-taker and a free-bird. Had Mr. One Talent believed this—and not that the Landowner was a conniving scrooge—he would have felt free to play with his Boss' money and take some risks, too. This belief in God the Landowner as a penny-pinching bookkeeper makes more penny-pinching bookkeepers, who wrap up their gifts in little decorative napkins and bury them below the ground. Maybe you know some of them.

It's interesting that, in this story, those who believe God is gracious and risky take the risks themselves—and both servants come back with double. Maybe that means that, of its own, the Gospel message is self-rejuvenating. So long as it isn't hidden, it does all the work on its own.

Also, could this be what Martin Luther means by "Sin boldly," that the freedom of God's Gospel makes us wild, or turns us into hip-shooting gamblers, rather than prudent lawyers? Could it be that God here is reminding us, in faith, to dirty up the pant legs and take some risks?

—Ethan Richardson

July 8

Peter answered him, "Though they all fall away because of you, I will never fall away." Jesus said to him, 'Truly, I tell you, this very night, before the rooster crows, you will deny me three times." Peter said to him, "Even if I must die with you, I will not deny you!" And all the disciples said the same. (Matthew 26:33-35, ESV)

"Leave it all out the field!" "Give 110%!" "We just wanted it more!" "We control our own destiny!" "It's gut-check time!" Any of these well-trodden sports clichés ring a bell? I love sports. I love watching them. I love watching people celebrate a championship win...the last out, a last-second shot, a touchdown catch as time expires. Love it.

My athletic career can be summed up in one unfortunately true personal anecdote: I played youth league football—special teams, of course. So it's the end of the game, and I'd just gone to the concession stand to get a hotdog and a Coke when the coach comes up and says, "Michaux, you want in the game?" Never mind the fact I'd gone for a snack before the game was even over, but I looked at the coach, then looked at my quickly cooling hotdog, and politely declined. Pretty sure he muttered some words he shouldn't have said in front of kids as he walked away in disgust. Great hotdog, though. Can't remember if we won or lost.

I take a light-hearted detour only to remind myself that no matter what, even if I had been a star athlete or a legendary musician, at the end of the day, I'm still like Peter. On the outside, I'm trying to be the Peter who says, "Even if I must die with you, I will not deny you!" On the inside, in any given circumstance, I'm just like the Peter we find a few verses later. When push comes to shove, my default mode is to save my own skin. I care a great deal about my own comfort. I wish it weren't true, but it is.

That's why I'm not convinced that I just need a cosmic helper— that doesn't do me any good. I need a savior, every day.

—Nate Michaux

July 9

About the ninth hour Jesus cried out in a loud voice, "Eloi, Eloi, lama sabachthani?'—which means, "My God, my God, why have you forsaken me?" (Matthew 27:46, NIV)

When these sorts of questions are asked, the asker is calling out from a deep place of hurt in the heart, not the head. Unfortunately, those of us who try to help answer such questions often make the mistake of trying to answer questions of suffering from the head rather than the heart.

My grandfather dying was my first experience with these sorts of questions. I was 22 at the time and was working a college job in a steel fabrication shop. On this particular morning at work, the secretary called me to the office because my mother was on the phone. She told me that my grandfather had died instantly of a heart attack that morning. He was alone on his daily walk when he died.

I felt now unexpectedly cut off. It wasn't just being left without the chance to say good-bye. In an instant, the world of my youth had been erased and replaced by a new and unfamiliar landscape, in which my loved ones were not permanent, in which death would now make a home in my reality.

I remember openly weeping as I walked back on to the shop floor. Any other time it would have been extremely uncomfortable for me to cry in front of these burly welders and machinists, but I couldn't stop.

While I had been on the phone with my mother, the secretary had let the shop foreman know what had happened, and he had told the rest of the shop. So when they saw me crying, they actually began to cry with me.

And it was in that moment, without a single word spoken, that I knew and realized that each of these men had also known suffering in their lives, that they knew it was beyond words, and so I knew suddenly I was not all alone in this unfamiliar landscape.

This answered my grief in a way that was unexpected and deeply comforting, and in a way that a logical answer could never have done. This was God's answer from the heart, taking in the collective agony of the human experience.

—Jeff Hual

July 10

> ..."My God, my God, why have you forsaken me?" (Matthew 27:46, ESV)

In this cry of Jesus from the cross, it seems paradoxical that these despairing words have given people such comfort. In *Cross-Shattered Christ*, theologian Stanley Hauerwas explains that those who have suffered, who live in the aftermath of Auschwitz or 9/11, are those who seem to quickly identify with this verse: "We do so because we think we have some idea about what it means to be forsaken..." But he continues:

> That we can even begin to entertain such thoughts is but an indication of our refusal, indeed our inability, to believe that this One who hangs on this obscure and humiliating cross is God... This is not a cry of general dereliction; it is the cry of the long-expected Messiah, sacrificed in our stead and thus becoming the end of sacrifice (60-61).

It is the profundity of these words—of God hanging humiliated—that force us to the most abstract flights of speculation, because there really is no appropriate way to "read, mark and inwardly digest" what is being related here. The intricacies and complexities of any theological tradition save people from needing to think about Jesus abandoned on the cross by God. Theological concepts like the *deus absconditus* (the hidden God), or God working *sub contrario* (under the guise of His opposite), or literary

240

allusions (Psalm 22), may be helpful to read about, but ultimately they all stop short of articulating this—the *death* of God's son for the redemption of His people.

In light of this, we do what the church has been doing for 2000 years: "we proclaim the Lord's death until he comes again." We talk about the Man "delivered up for our transgressions and raised for our justification" (Rom 4:25). In these last words of Jesus, we *do* find some comfort, but not in analogies or paradigms or paradoxes, but in our own sufferings and deaths. When we fear or question or cry out, we know that we are not the first, and we are not alone. In fact, as Hauerwas says it, these times are reminders that "the Son of God has taken our place, become for us the abandonment our sin produces, so that we may live confident that the world has been redeemed by this cross."

—*Jady Koch*

July 11

And behold, the curtain of the temple was torn in two, from top to bottom. And the earth shook, and the rocks were split. (Matthew 27:51, ESV)

My family spends a lot of time in Sedona, Arizona. Sedona is the center of the earth for everyone "seeking God." If you want to satisfy the New-Agey "search for the divine," you can gather crystals, crosses, stars, and vortexes, all in one gift shop.

Many of us seek God—maybe that's why you are reading this book. In this verse, we see the veil in the temple, which was a giant, thick curtain that separated the holiness of God from the people, torn in two, from top to bottom. Often this verse is interpreted to mean that now, post-Jesus, we can go *find* God.

However, the truth is, as Paul articulates in Romans 3, no one really goes out looking for God. In our search for the divine, as Sedona attests, we always just turn God into what we think God should be. The importance of the veil being torn in two from top to bottom is not that we can now go to God; instead, it is that God's Spirit is not confined to a tent or temple, and that our search for God is over, because He is now with us everywhere. He is with us now because of the perfect work of God the Son, Jesus Christ. Our search is over, and let's face it, we were never really searching for Him in the first place—by God's grace and mercy, tearing the veil in the temple in two, from top to bottom, God has found us and revealed himself to us in His son Jesus Christ.

—Jacob Smith

July 12

"...Do not be afraid, for I know that you seek Jesus who was crucified. He is not here, for he has risen, as he said..." (Matthew 28:1-10, ESV)

This is the account of the first Easter morning. However, on this Easter morning there is no linen, and there are no brass instruments, no baked hams or Easter eggs, and no large lilac hats. Instead, the initial tone of the first Easter morning is one of hopelessness and great loss. Surely we can call upon moments defined by those two themes: maybe it was a job loss, the death of a loved one, a romantic split; it may be a season of depression or plans gone sour. Maybe you're in one of these seasons now. Here we find a tremendous amount of hope in the midst of bleak situations.

Jesus and the angel appear to these two women, and what they say is important. They do not say, "Hey! Buck up! We're winners!" They do not rebuke their despair, but reassure them, "Do not be afraid." This is profound—often we believe that our despair is faithlessness, and that faithlessness means God must be angry with us. While we may feel faithless, Jesus tells us not to fear—he has triumphed over the faithless despair that defines our world.

I have wondered what I would have done had I been Jesus coming out of the tomb. I probably would have come back for vengeance: "Ladies, tell those disciples, my so-called friends, I am bringing the heat; after I deal with Rome, and those penny-pinching Pharisees, I am coming to put the hammer down." Praise God, I am not Jesus, and there is no hammer. Jesus still calls them brothers, and he tells them to meet him at Galilee, where it all started. What a relief that, sometimes, in the midst of sadness and great loss, as opposed to just moving on, it is best to go back to the beginning, whether it be in relationships, careers, or faith. Christianity is a religion of going back to the Galilee of our lives, where we can be continually refreshed by the grace of God, and we can be reminded again and again that we need not be afraid.

—Jacob Smith

July 13

Now after John was arrested, Jesus came into Galilee, proclaiming the gospel of God, and saying, "The time is fulfilled, and the kingdom of God is at hand; repent and believe in the gospel." (Mark 1:14-15, ESV)

We all have rhythms to our lives—those familiar routines we do over and over again, week after week, that become a part of who we are. For my work life right now, it involves dropping my son off at school, spending the good part of the morning working from a local coffee shop, pastoral appointments for lunch and early afternoon, then a few hours in my study.

We desire this sort of rhythm in our spiritual lives as well. Unfortunately, this has had consequences, and Christianity for many of us has come down to: "Just tell *me* what I have to *do*... Tell me the habits I must form in order to maintain my relationship with God." We can run on spiritual disciplines for a while, but there's eventually a breakdown between what it was meant for and what it has become.

That's why Jesus' words are so comforting.

The rhythm of the Christian life really has nothing to do with behavioral management or "Christian disciplines" or "spiritual formation." Jesus simply tells us this: *repent and believe the gospel.* This *is* the work and the rhythm of the Christian life.

Repentance really just means being honest about who you are. It means admitting there is a giant bedrock of self-centeredness that you can do nothing about. It means being aware of the fact that you're really pretty into yourself, and you need help if anything's going to change.

To believe the Gospel means to believe that help has arrived, that Jesus really is who he says he is and really did what he said he did. This is all we must believe: that, because of Jesus, you are loved and accepted by God, right now, as you are, and not as you should be. Rather than a repeated work through your week, we instead repeatedly return to a work that's already been done on our behalf. Now there's a Christian routine we can stick with!

—*Curt Benham*

July 14

*And a leper came to Jesus, imploring him, and kneeling
said to him, "If you will, you can make me clean"...
(Mark 1:40-42, ESV)*

The Franciscan priest Richard Rohr once said, "Reality is an ally of
God." When we are brought to an honest confrontation with what's
really going on in our lives—usually by way of collision course—the
circumstances have the potential to send us in a beeline to God.

In most of the healings in Mark's Gospel, the character behaves in
the same pattern: he or she approaches Jesus, kneels before him, and begs
to be healed. The sick and the lame are already at the end of reality's
rope, already painfully aware of their disease and their need for help.
They all seem to run without a doubt to Jesus' feet. Where does this
faith come from?

This faith is not gathered with courage or zeal, but desperation; the
sick have the unfiltered advantage of having reality faced for them, and
so reality itself propels them toward saving help.

On the other hand, throughout the Gospels, the "teachers of the
Law" do not cry to Jesus for healing because they believe the Law has
made them good. But Jesus reminds them—and us—that this kind of
self-satisfaction and religious posturing shrouds the reality of our lives
(Matt 23:27). The Law of God has not made us better, but has instead
shown us how sick we really are. When life makes this clear—that we,
too, are sick men and women—reality propels us to the faith of the sick
and the lame.

What about you? Where does reality seem to be evading you?
Where does it feel hardest to be honest in life? Though it may sound
dreadful now, in time, reality will go there, too, and God will come with
it.

—Alex Large

July 15

*A great windstorm arose, and the waves were breaking into
the boat, so that the boat was already filling. But he was in
the stern, asleep on the cushion. And they woke him and
said to him, "Teacher, do you not care that we are*

perishing?" And he awoke and rebuked the wind and said to the sea, "Peace! Be still!" And the wind ceased, and there was a great calm. He said to them, "Why are you so afraid? Have you still no faith?" And they were filled with great fear and said to one another, "Who then is this, that even the wind and the sea obey him?" (Mark 4:37-41, ESV)

"Who then is this?" Many of us know people who are able to refer to God when speaking about spiritual matters, but become uncomfortable when it comes to using "Jesus." Perhaps you struggle with it.

Hollywood certainly has a time with Jesus-talk: there's Ricky Bobby Jesus, Buddy Jesus, Jesus Christ Superstar, *The Passion* Jesus, *The Life of Brian* Jesus, *Jesus of Montreal.* My all-time favorite Jesus, though, is from *The Big Lebowski*, whose purple, rhinestone-studded bowling suit and no-mess attitude make a convincing case for divinity.

It makes sense that we can often stomach humorous (even profane) images of Jesus, while being uncomfortable speaking about the real one. It might be that the real one is seen as outdated or irrelevant, or it might be the opposite—that the true Jesus means confronting a very real and very relevant someone whom we cannot contain or control.

In the calming of the sea, Mark seems to be talking about the human need for control and Christ's trustworthy power in its absence. Both the Jewish and Greco-Roman traditions connect the sea with danger and chaos, making this miracle quite a statement: Jesus is the God of Genesis, who speaks light into darkness and brings order to the deep waters. And this is the foundation upon which the disciples can trust that Jesus—in being *God*—is ultimately in control.

Of course, we tend to be like the disciples in the boat, accusing Jesus of being careless or impotent or aloof. We're as likely to make these accusations when reading the front page of the paper as we are when being cut off on the freeway. We glad-hand God when we're trying to cover our bases and shake our fists at him when we feel that He isn't noticing us.

Jesus, in control, wakes and calms the storm. He knows how fickle our faith is and acts even when we refuse to believe he can. He says: "Why are you so afraid? Have you still no faith? I am here in the middle of all this chaos, doing my work, even if you think I am not."

—*K. Marc Choi*

July 16

Again Jesus called the crowd to him and said, "Listen to me, everyone, and understand this. Nothing outside a person can defile them by going into them. Rather, it is what comes out of a person that defiles them... For it is from within, out of a person's heart, that evil thoughts come—sexual immorality, theft, murder, adultery, greed, malice, deceit, lewdness, envy, slander, arrogance and folly. All these evils come from inside and defile a person."
(Mark 7:14-15, 21-23, NIV)

Jesus is talking about the origin of the great problems of life and how, in response to them, we try to externalize our problems and project them onto other people or circumstances. We naturally dissociate the troubles in our lives by drawing them off to external causes. This is what people mean when they talk about something being a 'bad influence.' We often say that movies or music or the 'wrong crowd' is the problem, but Jesus says that these things don't make someone "unclean."

This presents more problems down the road. Because we think the problem is external, we tend to think that the solution is external as well. This explains the popularity of diets, the new motorcycles of middle-aged men, the search for the most fulfilling job. In light of the problems of our lives, we try to change the externals of our life in hopes that the deeper things might change.

But Jesus says that the problems of our life come from the corruption of our hearts. Out of the heart come the hurtful comments that destroy relationships with children. Out of the heart comes the insensitivity to the obvious needs of others. Out of the heart comes the reluctance to answer an email from an estranged friend.

If the problem lies internally within our hearts, the question is: what can change the heart? The heart is changed through being loved. Or as that great John Newton hymn puts it, "Weak is the effort of my heart, and cold my warmest thought; But when I see Thee as Thou art, I'll praise Thee as I ought."

—*Todd Brewer*

July 17

Then he began to teach them that the Son of Man must undergo great suffering, and be rejected by the elders, the chief priests, and the scribes, and be killed, and after three days rise again. He said all this quite openly. And Peter took him aside and began to rebuke him. But turning and looking at his disciples, he rebuked Peter and said, "Get behind me, Satan! For you are setting your mind not on divine things but on human things." (Mark 8:31-9:1, NRSV)

I was in the store the other day and the 1966 Beach Boys hit "God Only Knows" came blaring through the speakers. This song has made its way onto countless retail playlists and has long been accepted into the canon of mediocre shopping music. Nowadays it more represents consumer fatigue than it does "the most beautiful piece of music ever recorded," as critics have said. I really wish I could hear it for the first time again.

I feel the same way about the "Jesus dying" thing. Having grown up in a Christian environment, at times it seems impossible to hear the Gospel with fresh ears. It doesn't sound so absurd that "the Son of Man must suffer many things and be rejected... that he must be killed and after three days rise again." The story of Jesus' death and resurrection is all too familiar for me, but it's safe to say that back then, no one saw it coming.

Jesus talks very plainly about his death, yet Peter won't have any of it. The idea of God's Son being scorned, rejected and crucified is too outlandish to accept. And who can blame Peter? At this time Jesus has healed the sick, performed miracles, and given groundbreaking sermons, and so is earning a great deal of celebrity. In this position, influential figures *rise* to power—no one, especially at the pinnacle of a career, gives it up.

With 2000 years to theologize and theorize about Jesus, one might assume that the more familiar we become with the story, the more we develop as Christians. And yet nothing about the world has changed. Although the Gospel does manage to powerfully enter our lives, we are still unable to fully grasp its message. A friend of mine describes the state of the Western church as such: "It's as if we have been vaccinated with a mild case of Christianity, which has protected us from catching the real disease." We can't help but delegate the Gospel to grocery store "muzak."

Thank God the Gospel does not require our belief or conviction in order for it to *be true*. Unbelievable as it may be, Christ's death and resurrection happened, and God's abounding grace and forgiveness are real.

—Sam Bush

July 18

And a cloud overshadowed them, and a voice came out of the cloud, "This is my beloved Son; listen to him." (Mark 9:7, ESV)

What kindly pastoral interpreters of the Transfiguration of Christ usually want to say is that it's God's Word from the cloud, His extraordinary word of attestation directed to Jesus should be heard as the divine reassurance that we today, like Christ on the Mount, are beloved children, accent on the "beloved."

Let's start with the plain meaning and see where we go from there. God says that this man is His beloved Son. He also says that people should listen to this man on account of that fact.

I think it is a miracle that God calls *anyone* "beloved." Given the labyrinth of human nature's mixed motivations and unconscious self-deceptions, it's a miracle that anyone partaking of our condition could qualify for this, well, compliment. So we can start there: We all "need a miracle everyday" (Grateful Dead), and here we've got one!

It's like that wondrous "*but*" in the Anglican "Prayer of Humble Access": "We are not worthy so much as to gather up the crumbs under thy Table. *But* thou art the same Lord, whose property is always to have mercy..." Without the "*but*," without the operational existence of a God of mercy, our unworthiness would prove completely fatal, both now and at whatever awaits us at the point of death.

All one's unworthiness gets interrupted at the Transfiguration of Christ, as it did also at his Baptism (Mark 1:11). We only need to add that the sheer existence of such a person, Christ, certified in his compliment from the cloud, makes the same compliment—"This is my beloved son"—a possibility for a person in conscious, humbled flight from the system of this world. The philosopher and mystic Gerald Heard wrote that "escapism" is not a bad thing, because "the verb *to escape* is clear enough—it means to leave a position which has become impossible."

I think we almost all know instinctively, and certainly on the basis of our suffering, that "we gotta get out of this place" (The Animals). God's Word to His Son, on the Mount of Transfiguration, makes that a possibility. Just for it to be a *possibility* is a miracle of miracles.

—Paul Zahl

July 19

"...All things can be done for the one who believes." Immediately the father of the child cried out, "I believe; help my unbelief!" (Mark 9:23-24, NRSV)

For Jesus to heal his son, a father must simply believe, but he cannot. And because the father has too little faith, it would at first seem his son *cannot* be healed. We are often told the same in church: if you just have faith, if you just call upon the Lord, then salvation is yours; sanctification is yours. And yet, what do you make of the stories of countless people who can't kick their addictions, who can't seem to love their spouses or children, who can't even get out of bed in the morning? It seems they are suffering from a lack of belief in the loving God, the redeeming God—if they believed, things would be different, right?

This passage contains both good news and bad, and its downside is that no one, no one, is ever fully faithful or fully believing. We cannot summon this, no matter how much we intellectually defend Christ or how much we talk about him. When brought, like the man in this story, to the place of our own impossibility in even *believing*—let alone *doing*—we're forced to cry out, along with the best of Biblical wisdom, "what is crooked cannot be made straight, and what is lacking cannot be counted" (Eccl 1:15). The life or death of his son depends on his belief, and still the father is forced to admit inadequacy: "I believe, help my unbelief!"

The place of impossibility, however, is the place of grace. God is always our rescuer, and crying out in a state of helplessness is—paradoxically—the most authentic act of faith that's possible in the here and now. The man's belief doesn't come from strength, but weakness, and faith in God amidst weakness ("Help!") is really the only Christian act of faith. The challenge isn't to develop perfect faith; our only task is to recognize how far from belief we really are, and even this vision of desperation is a gift from God.

And so the father in this story has *true* faith, which lives only in the depths of his realization that he is faithless and utterly dependent upon God. It is true for us, too, that in the place of weakness and desperation, we're given the kind of faith that can exist alongside our continuing frustration with our faithlessness.

—*Will McDavid*

July 20

> ...*The disciples said to him, "Then who can be saved?" Jesus looked at them and said, "With man it is impossible, but not with God. For all things are possible with God'...* (Mark 10:17-31, ESV)

Jesus shows an eccentric knack for knowing what's behind the words. All of us strive for that kind of clairvoyance, but often come embarrassingly short. I get myself into "foot in mouth" situations all the time, completely misreading what I thought was so obvious. This doesn't seem to happen to Jesus.

Here he encounters a rich young man who makes the wrong assumption that Jesus thinks he ought to *do* something to inherit eternal life. He admits to keeping most of the commandments, at which point Jesus stops him, looks at him, loves him, and tells him to sell all of his possessions, give the money to the poor, and then to follow him. The young man goes away "sorrowful." Why?

The very thing he thinks he can offer Jesus, Jesus tells him to give away. Jesus finds the bruise—and also, ironically, the accomplishment—in this man's life, and he pushes on it. He does it because the man is not in a place where he can receive the Good News. He has it all—he is wealthy, upstanding, dignified—and these vast resources he feels he can use to benefit the cause, to benefit Jesus. But Jesus doesn't want these.

If you were Jesus, and you were calling for a team of followers, it would be hard to imagine this rich young man *wouldn't* be a frontrunner, right? Jesus does not pick those, though—he has no interest in who the world believes has wisdom, wealth, or wit. He instead chooses those God likes to use: "the foolish things of the world," which bring shame to the wise.

What about you today? What offerings do you hold onto tightly? Or what offerings are being taken from you?

To Jesus you bring nothing to the table. You cannot serve Jesus on your own terms, deciding which gifts will prove most effective. Those who have died—who have left their paltry self-descriptions and silly résumés behind—those are the ones who find themselves being used in ways they never thought imaginable. They find that "all things are possible with God."

—Andrew Pearson

July 21

> *...And they said to him, "Grant us to sit, one at your right hand and one at your left, in your glory." But Jesus said to them, "You do not know what you are asking. Are you able to drink the cup that I drink, or be baptized with the baptism that I am baptized with?" They replied, "We are able'... (Mark 10:35-45, ESV)*

A couple of years ago I read a book by John Maxwell called *Failing Forward*, which is about moving forward when things in our lives do not go as we planned, which eventually happens to all of us. My favorite chapter in this book is called "Get Over Yourself—Everyone Else Has," which describes the dangers of being self-absorbed and self-centered—the dangers of what we call narcissism.

Extreme narcissism is known as "Narcissistic Personality Disorder." Listen to how the Mayo Clinic describes this and see if it rings any bells:

> Narcissistic Personality Disorder is a mental disorder in which people have an inflated sense of their own importance and a deep need for admiration. They believe that they're superior to others and have little regard for other people's feelings. But behind this mask of ultra-confidence lies a fragile self-esteem, vulnerable to the slightest criticism... Narcissistic personality disorder crosses the border of healthy confidence and self-esteem into thinking so highly of yourself that you put yourself on a pedestal.

Narcissism does a lot of damage. It shatters personal lives, torpedoes relationships and marriages, estranges parents and children, and wreaks havoc in church. Narcissism can take down companies, split great rock 'n' roll bands, and keep talented sports teams from winning. The narcissism of others has caused damage in my life, and my own narcissism has caused damage in others' lives. I suspect it's the same with you.

James and John, after hearing again that Jesus will die, say, "Grant us to sit, one at your right hand and one at your left, in your glory." Their response to Jesus' prediction of his impending death and resurrection is a request for power, dripping with narcissism. Jesus responds by letting James and John know that they are clueless: "You do not know what you are asking." Then he asks them a question: "Are you able to drink the cup that I drink, or be baptized with the baptism that I am baptized with?" In their hubris James and John reply, "We are able."

Jesus then calls all the disciples together and cuts to the chase when it comes to narcissism: "Whoever wishes to become great among you must be a servant, and whoever wishes to be first among you must be slave of all." In other words, the antidote to narcissism is death.

Dr. Karl Menninger, a famous psychiatrist, was once asked, "What would you advise a person to do if he felt a nervous breakdown coming on?" Menninger replied, "Find someone in need, and do something to help that person... generous people are rarely mentally ill people" (*Failing Forward* 102-103). The antidote to narcissism is death to self, yet can't we even become prideful about how much we help others? While helping others and being generous can take the edge off, it does not address the root of our narcissism, original sin.

Thankfully, Jesus doesn't stop there. After telling his disciples, "whoever wishes to be first among you must be slave of all," Jesus points to the cross: "For the Son of Man came not to be served but to serve, and to give his life a ransom for many."

—*Dave Johnson*

July 22

"Many will come in my name and say, 'I am he!' and they will lead many astray." (Mark 13:6, NRSV)

People seem to get deceived in one of two ways. Either the deceiver has done a very good job imitating the real thing; or the deceived forgets the real thing, or had never really known the real thing at all, and so he can't tell the difference when the trick comes on. A great example of the first is conniving Jacob, wrapped in wool like his hairy brother Esau, to steal Esau's blessing from Isaac (Gen 27). He must have been convincing, but then again, that story has a little bit of the second way, too: after all, Jacob's ruse never would've panned out had Isaac been able to tell the two apart. Isaac's blindness was key in his own subversion.

More people than can be counted have and will continue to take on "messianic" deceptions of the most epic proportions. It's a safe bet: political heads and activists, mystics and celebrities and popular designers have always created a miraculous and watchful stir. Today, with online communities like Pinterest and Twitter, casual messiahs gain "followers" in minutes with opportune tweets or tags. It cannot be denied that we have more (and, frankly, more *boring*) shepherds today than we have flocks, and the flocks are as fleeting as they've ever been.

If we are deceived for the first reason—that our deceivers play a really convincing messiah—then we've got the wrong Jesus Christ. Jesus, the real one, never seemed to like the limelight much. It seems instead that we fall more into the second category: either we've never *heard* of the real Jesus, or we're incorrigibly bent on forgetting him. Who wants a hero that contradicts our inclinations, who wins by losing, who gains strength by forfeit? Not me, not you, and no one else for that matter. He is our people's messianic antitype—and you know what? This is good news. It means that there will be deceivers, but their ruse will always reach its end at the impossible litmus of death and resurrection. Only one has done this—and he is the real McCoy.

—*Ethan Richardson*

July 23

> *"...Do not be alarmed. You seek Jesus of Nazareth, who was crucified. He has risen; he is not here. See the place where they laid him. But go, tell his disciples and Peter that he is going before you to Galilee. There you will see him, just as he told you." (Mark 16:1-7, ESV)*

An odd fellow in a white robe greets the women who first witness the empty tomb of Jesus. After telling the women about the Resurrection, the angelic figure also tells them a seemingly minor detail about Jesus' next stop—he will apparently rendezvous with the disciples in Galilee. It may seem trivial, but this detail carries everything.

Just before Jesus' arrest, while he had been praying in the Garden of Gethsemane, Peter and the rest of the disciples fell asleep when he needed them most. Later, during his trial and torture, they all fled in outright fear. If this is not enough mettle-proving, Peter, while fleeing, also denied even *knowing* Jesus—*three times!* Peter defined a disciple *fail*. He knew his Lord's expectations—he even really, truly loved his Lord—but he just couldn't help himself.

But after the Resurrection, the women hear that not only will Jesus meet the disciples, as he said, in Galilee, but also he specifically names Peter. Jesus later forgives Peter and commissions the disciples.

In reading this, doesn't it seem adolescent to hear Christians say that we need to be like Jesus? If Peter failed miserably, what chance do we have?

Being like Jesus is a fool's errand. Jesus is the only Jesus, which is why we have this good news. The only "chance" we have is not in trying to emulate the God-man, but in weeping at what we've done and calling upon him for help (Mark 14:72). All Christians are failed Christians. Thankfully Jesus does not punish us accordingly, but he meets us back in Galilee, at the very beginning.

—Alex Large

July 24

> *Afterward he appeared to the eleven themselves as they were reclining at table, and he rebuked them for their unbelief and hardness of heart, because they had not believed those who saw him after he had risen. And he said to them, 'Go into all the world and proclaim the gospel to the whole creation.' (Mark 16:14-15, ESV)*

In this passage, Jesus entitles his eleven ne'er-do-wells Ambassadors to the Whole Creation, just days after they have not only abandoned him in his trial, but also questioned the Resurrection, a magnum opus of the faith. Jesus deliberately comes to eleven ridiculous, hard-of-heart adults and commissions them to be his crew once again—*what?*

I grew up with a lot of guilt about "The Great Commission." Usually, preachers use it to point out how we, the congregation, are not living up to it, and then they exhort us to get on it, quickly. This assumes continuity between the commission and the heart: Jesus tells us to do it, so we do it. What's more, we *want* to. However, in this passage the disciples are *dis*continuous. Here are Jesus' closest companions, he's about to give them his final speech, according to Mark, and he scolds them like teenagers!

They are discontinuous, and so am I. Mark shows how discontinuity equips the disciples to share the Gospel with all of creation: because they know they cannot do what's expected of them, they know they *need* the Gospel—as does everyone else who consistently fails expectations. Of all the louses and losers, these men know they don't deserve Jesus' title. And still Jesus calls them his own. Sinners like them, like me, know that there is nothing to give to anyone except Jesus' message of grace for us all. Needing forgiveness is what equips us to share it with others.

There is comfort in knowing that Jesus knows what we are. The Gospel that he commissions us to share is none other than the forgiveness I am given because he loved me and died for me. This distinction might seem simple, but it changes everything. God chooses to work through stubborn, unbelieving people, starting with me.

—*Kate Norris*

July 25

"...A sword shall pierce through your own soul also, that thoughts out of many hearts may be revealed." (Luke 2:29-35, RSV)

As a baby, Jesus is brought into the Temple by his mother and father—"as was the custom"—and there the relatively insignificant family is spotted by the aged and holy Simeon. Somewhat surprisingly, I imagine, the old man takes the baby into his arms and prophesies. Perhaps it was originally as we find it, in the form of poetry, or song. Or perhaps the message was later worked into a song as early Christians found that what Simeon had said echoed some of their own deepest thoughts about Jesus. Either way, Luke gives us one of the most touching "canticles' in the Bible, and three tensions in the story that are worth pondering.

The first is the tension between holding on and letting go. As Simeon draws the baby close to him he, at the same time, releases himself to God. He senses that once he has seen the "hope of Israel," that is the Messiah, he can let go of life and "depart" this world peacefully (2:29). Simeon might have laid his hands on the child, or simply spoken a blessing. But he takes him up in his arms, signifying a heart that grasps hold of Jesus. At this very moment, he is able to surrender control of his own destiny. We naturally do the opposite: grasp hold of our destinies and, in so doing, let go of Jesus.

The second tension is that between a merely parochial faith and a truly universal one. Simeon's deepest desire is for "the consolation of Israel" (2:25). Correspondingly, we are told in this postmodern age that we can have a personal faith, or be part of our own "faith community," but we are not to foist our religion on others. However, Simeon's gaze extends far beyond his own people. This salvation is "in the presence of all peoples," and is for both Gentile and Jew (2:31-32). I wonder if those who first heard this knew the ramifications of this global vision. They, like we, must have been locked in their own little world.

Thirdly, there is a tension between the glory that Jesus will bring to his people (2:32), and the pain he will bring at the same time (2:35), and no one will experience this inner tug-of-war as deeply as Mary herself. I can imagine Simeon giving her a knowing glance as he speaks this prophetic word: "a sword will pierce through your own soul also." But the simple fact is that Jesus was, and will always be, controversial. Having him in our life will always bring both "agony" and "ecstasy."

—*Peter Moore*

July 26

> *He said to Simon, "Put out into deep water, and let down the nets for a catch." Simon answered, "Master, we've worked hard all night and haven't caught anything. But because you say so, I will let down the nets." When they had done so, they caught such a large number of fish that their nets began to break. (Luke 5:4-6, NIV)*

God's work in the lives of people specially comes in the form of unexpected events. Would Simon really have answered with his been-there-done-that tone if he had known what was about to happen? The work of God is always an intervention; it intervenes upon the tendencies of the fallen world, and against the grain of our own selfish wiring.

Sometimes you will hear a person say, "I don't like surprises." This is the opposite of a faithful posture. It seeks to hold onto control, and to possess that which belongs only to our heavenly Father. Fortunately, He'll fill your nets anyway! Thank God He is not waiting for us to get it together before He will bless us and use us.

Was the Resurrection a surprise to those who knew Jesus? Of course it was! God's grace comes to us always as a surprise. You do not know much of what today will hold.

—*John Zahl*

July 27

Jesus knew what they were thinking and asked, "Why are you thinking these things in your hearts? Which is easier: to say, 'Your sins are forgiven,' or to say, 'Get up and walk'? But that you may know that the Son of Man has authority on earth to forgive sins..." He said to the paralyzed man, "I tell you, get up, take your mat and go home." Immediately he stood up in front of them, took what he had been lying on and went home praising God. Everyone was amazed and gave praise to God. They were filled with awe and said, "We have seen remarkable things today." (Luke 5:22-26, NIV)

Jesus' rhetorical question before the healing seems to be an announcement that we need forgiveness more than we're willing to admit. And Jesus proves he can do the mysterious miracle of forgiving sins by doing the visible miracle of physically healing the paralytic—the man gets up, picks up his pallet, and goes home. And because Jesus *can* do this miracle of healing—something we tend to believe is more miraculous—we're meant to understand from the account that the man's sins have, in fact, also been forgiven.

On May 28, 2009, I was diagnosed with a pituitary adenoma, a non-cancerous brain tumor that had destroyed my pituitary and ruined my health. It was hard going at first, coming to grips with the fact that my life would never again be normal. But in my suffering I was reminded of this story of Jesus and the paralytic, and as I wrestled with my situation I began to see the story in a fresh new way.

The normal way to read the story, that we can believe that Jesus can forgive sins because he proves he can heal, was turned on its head for me, because I already believed that in Jesus I was given forgiveness. And so the story spoke to me in a new, inverted way, meaning that *because* he has forgiven my sins—and I knew that to be very real—I could rest assured that, if he so willed, he could heal my body.

And so I have held on to this in faith for two years now, and it has brought me great comfort in both hope and despair. If he can forgive a sinner like me, then I know that all things are possible, even healing.

—Jeff Hual

July 28

> *"Do you see this woman? I entered your house; you gave me no water for my feet, but she has wet my feet with her tears and wiped them with her hair. You gave me no kiss, but from the time I came in she has not ceased to kiss my feet. You did not anoint my head with oil, but she has anointed my feet with ointment. Therefore I tell you, her sins, which are many, are forgiven—for she loved much. But he who is forgiven little, loves little." And he said to her, "Your sins are forgiven." (Luke 7:36-48, ESV)*

Whole books have been written about this wonderful passage, but I would like to say just three things. First of all, it's clear who she is— she's a prostitute. She has costly perfume because she's a working girl, and she's slept with a lot of men. Everybody knows who she is, and so she's got no hope of ever being any different in anyone's eyes; her history precludes that. Luke only states what is true: she's a prostitute, and it doesn't look like she'll be changing careers any time soon.

I'd also suggest that this is a story focused on upending what we think repentance looks like. We like the moralistic repentance, the brand *we* initiate, first by working up a very sincere heart and then by developing a new game plan for how things will change, and *then*—we think, we hope—God's love and forgiveness is renewed. Instead, Luke illustrates here a woman bound in an inescapable identity. She cannot change, but then she hears a word from outside. She hears about a man who will love her absolutely and unconditionally—even her. She is overwhelmed. Her heart is broken open. It is then that she can repent, because she has been forgiven first.

But what does this repentance *mean*? Well of course, it must mean that she is no longer plying the trade, right? She's joined the Young Ladies Christian League, or gotten out of town and started over, right? Well, if that happens, there's nothing of it in Luke 7. No, Luke shows what real repentance is: contrition and a broken heart. To repent is to simply despair of your self and fall at the feet of Jesus. To repent is to be sorrowful for what you are, not to have a game plan for improving what you do. To repent is to lay everything at his feet and kiss them.

And the last thing I want to say is that this passage is written for me and you. It was written for me because I am both Simon and the woman. It was written for me, the respectable, church-going sneerer. It is also written for me because there is something about me, inside me, just like the woman, something that I can't change and know everyone would hate me for. I won't tell you what it is, but it's real.

May this true story break open our stony hearts today.

—John Stamper

July 29

> ...*"A man was going down from Jerusalem to Jericho, and he fell among robbers, who stripped him and beat him and departed, leaving him half dead. Now by chance a priest was going down that road, and when he saw him he passed by on the other side. So likewise a Levite, when he came to the place and saw him, passed by on the other side. But a Samaritan, as he journeyed, came to where he was, and when he saw him he had compassion. He went to him and bound up his wounds, pouring on oil and wine. Then he set him on his own animal and brought him to an inn and took care of him...Which of these three, do you think proved to be a neighbor to the man who fell among the robbers?" He said, "The one who showed him mercy." And Jesus said to him, "You go, and do likewise." (Luke 10:25-37, ESV)*

"The Good Samaritan"—who hasn't heard some reference to this story? In church, preachers will profile each of the characters in the parable: The Priest, The Levite, The Samaritan. *"Which one are you?"* Of course, the right answer is the Samaritan. And maybe that's true sometimes—maybe we have, at some time or another, found ourselves walking in the sandals in each of the three. However, upon closer inspection, what seems more fundamentally accurate is that we are none of them, but the man in the ditch.

We are the dying man in the ditch who waits for rescue. The Priest passes us by. The religious man, the one who preaches to sinners, walks on by. The Levite, the lawman, the do-gooder, walks on by. But it is the Samaritan, who stands as the opposite, an outcast and a nobody, who shows compassion and mercy to a Jew who ought to have nothing to do with him.

The first two may have had good excuses as to why they didn't stop. The Priest, if he touched us, might be made unclean and then couldn't do his priestly duties. The Levite may have been too busy, may have been worried it was a trap. But the scoundrel stopped and helped.

This is the story of the Christian. We find ourselves in the ditch in need of rescue, but the world and its moral fixtures will not save us. Only the unmerited compassion of one "scorned and rejected" will accomplish that. Jesus condescends and we receive his rescue.

—Andrew Pearson

July 30

But he, desiring to justify himself, said to Jesus, "And who is my neighbor?" Jesus replied, "A man was going down from Jerusalem to Jericho, and he fell among robbers... Which of these three, do you think, proved to be a neighbor to the man who fell among the robbers?" He said, "The one who showed him mercy." And Jesus said to him, "You go, and do likewise." (Luke 10:29-37, ESV)

As a kid, when I was caught doing something I shouldn't, my parents could count on hearing one phrase that, without fail, would involuntarily burst out of my mouth: "It's not my fault!" No matter if I was actually innocent or caught red-handed, I always tried to play the victim-of-certain-circumstances card, full of reasons that I was actually innocent.

Like the man talking to Jesus in this passage, we all scramble to justify ourselves. Nothing displays this more than how readily we justify our withheld love. When confronted with co-workers, friends, siblings, "neighbors" in all senses of the word, we tell ourselves that we've done the best we can. There's the litany of qualifiers: *She's just impossible to deal with. He's had his chance. Honestly, who could deal with the most annoying habit imaginable?* At all dead ends, we find ourselves insisting, "It's not my fault."

Isn't it true that we want to absolve ourselves from the responsibility to love beyond convenience? By saying, "Not my fault," we escape the guilt that accompanies our most self-absorbed conveniences.

Jesus' response to this attitude is a parable about mercy. The unequivocal command, "go and do likewise," insists that loving our neighbors is more mercy than we can handle. Jesus knows full well how miserably we fail to love as we ought, describing the human heart as "a source of evil thoughts, sexual immorality, theft, murder, adultery, coveting, wickedness, deceit, sensuality, envy, slander, pride, foolishness," just to name a few (Mark 7:21). His demand reveals the chasm: that we—in our failure to love and our desperate defensiveness of that failure—are the ones in need of mercy, in need of forgiveness.

The good news is that there's no more justifying ourselves before God. No more lists of reasons or acrobatic excuses. We can just be who we are, as it is said in Titus: "But when the goodness and loving kindness of God our Savior appeared, He saved us, not because of works done by us in righteousness, but according to His own mercy... so that being justified by His grace we might become heirs according to the hope of eternal life" (3:4-7).

—*Liza Koch*

July 31

> *...But Martha was distracted with much serving. And she went up to him and said, "Lord, do you not care that my sister has left me to serve alone? Tell her then to help me." But the Lord answered her, 'Martha, Martha, you are anxious and troubled about many things, but one thing is necessary. Mary has chosen the good portion, which will not be taken away from her." (Luke 10:38-42, ESV)*

I love Martha, specifically here in this moment—it is such a human moment. This isn't to say that Mary—in her stillness before Jesus—isn't human; she just represents a human with the "the good portion," loving

God with all her mind, heart, and soul. But what I love about Martha is that she needs to be brought out of herself, out of all her delusions of control. She is so anxious about everything that she must call out, and I can relate: it seems to me that without first going through what Martha is experiencing, we do not get to the position Mary is in. We cannot recognize the good unless we are called out and brought to it, and there is no better starting place than the place we're in now, which for Martha is issuing her complaint of resentment. She trusts Jesus will do something with it.

And Jesus does do something, but not in the way Martha expects. Rather than command Mary to help her sister, Jesus calls Martha over. He lovingly addresses Martha—overextended, frustrated Martha—and her preoccupation with many things. He tells her he knows she's overwhelmed, "...but one thing is necessary" (10:42a). Oddly, Jesus is preaching himself; he is the good portion, and he's right there with her. He illuminates her anxiety (even heightens her awareness of it), but notice he does not chastise her for it, and he gives her what she needs—himself. There's no chiding, no "Chill out! Stop being so anxious, Martha, it's not attractive!"

This is one of the fundamental differences between the Law and the Gospel: the Law is static, the Gospel is dynamic. The Law can point out your anxiety, but it cannot get you to calm down. It just stands there, it cannot beckon nor plea nor cause you to hear; it can only leave you in static judgment. The Gospel moves, taking the hearer and moving her, walking her to itself. The Gospel seizes the anxious one from her tangled priorities and brings her the good portion, the only necessary thing. This is the same thing as being brought to the Gospel of Jesus, to the foot of the cross.

You and I have more of the story than Martha does. Though this is a foretaste of redemption, we know it points ahead to Jesus' death and resurrection, which happened for the justification of all the anxious ones (Rom 4:25). We are justified by faith apart from our busyness and our work—this is Christ's good news. The gospel message tells us that we are neither defined by our failures nor successes. This is why we need to continually hear this message, continually be reminded of it. In hearing, we are given freedom from our anxiety. We are not told "don't be anxious"—it's not up to us to quell our anxieties—but the justification of the anxious, under God's control, does it for us. We are called like Martha and hear, in the midst of our anxiety, to then respond like Mary.

—Lauren R.E. Larkin

August 1

I tell you, though he will not get up and give him anything because he is his friend, but because of his impudence he will rise and give him whatever he needs. (Luke 11:5-8, ESV)

I feel like it's important to focus on this word "impudence" in this passage, because this passage can be read in a wholly different, even opposing way if that word is misinterpreted. Other translations have "persistence" which is equally tricky. Either way, this is undoubtedly a parable about prayer. It seems plausible to me, and I've actually believed this before, that the passage *could* be saying we can ask enough times or sound desperate enough when we pray, or gesture or genuflect in a way so as to convince the Lord to get out of bed to come to our aid—I don't think it's saying this, though.

The passage instead seems to be offering an answer to a different question; it's not so much "How do I pray?" or "What happens when I pray?," but instead, "Why *does* our Good Friend come to the door to help us?" This seems to be the pertinent question. Not *if* but *why* does he? Why does he get up with his children slumbering beside him—he'll surely wake them up!—to help the one at the door? Why does he get up for the one at the door, who should have called beforehand? The audacity of this visitor! Why, when the world says, "Why didn't you get the job done?" When the world says, "Shop Closed"? When the world says, "Okay, I'll help you out this time," sighs and, in the heavy strain of piety, remarks how he just got these loaves today. *Why* does the friend get up?

It's the *impudence.* The self-evident *need* of the figure at the doorway. The problem is so big that the improper indecencies of "asking for something" or "calling after suppertime" or "waking up the neighbors" or "waking up the children" or "making a scene" are thrown out the window. This is desperation. There's nowhere else to go—this is all there is—the only hope. This is audacity! The friend in bed knows this is a big deal, there's no other reason to be coming by this late, and so he arises.

A friend of mine recently had one of these experiences. His father was about to have his third heart operation in two weeks, and his family—a plane flight away—was understandably at wit's end. Knowing that his family needed him there, he phoned work to let them know he needed to go. He found himself guilt-tripped, his coworkers passively remarking, "Go, but your performance reviews will suffer due to your absence." Arriving at the doorstep in impudence, he found himself at the cold, dark portico of the Law, hearing a numb nothing behind closed doorblinds.

Now a heavier feeling of guilt overshadows his family's need as he boards the plane—what an impossible weight! But this seems to be the way of the world, a reprimand for need, a pre-ordered form for who's getting what.

What does this parable then say in response? The parable, instead, gives us assurance that God is a light sleeper. Like Motel 6—"We'll leave a light on for you"—the door is always open. Our arrival at the door in the deepest reaches of our night is evidence enough, explanation enough that we need something, and our Friend meets us there, our needs in his hands, reminding us that these weights are taken care of. With this, we can rest easy.

—*Ethan Richardson*

August 2

> *He said therefore, 'What is the kingdom of God like? And to what shall I compare it? It is like a grain of mustard seed that a man took and sowed in his garden, and it grew and became a tree, and the birds of the air made nests in its branches.' And again he said, 'To what shall I compare the kingdom of God? It is like leaven that a woman took and hid in three measures of flour, until it was all leavened."*
> *(Luke 13:18-21, ESV)*

When asked what God's kingdom is like, Jesus says it is like a seed that grows into a tree, and that it is also like leaven, or yeast, that gets hidden in some flour.

Two properties come to mind. First, God is interested, and has been for some time now, in trees. Adam and Eve ate from the tree at the very beginning—the tree of knowledge. Jesus "hung upon a tree" to bear the sins of the world (Acts 5:30). And, when it is all said and done, God's people will live under the shade of the "tree of life" (Rev 22:2). Now there are plenty of good theological things to say about trees: trees give protection, they bear fruit on their own, they are powered by the sun. But instead of these great qualities about trees, Jesus is more concerned with the fact that trees are *planted* seeds. The kingdom of God—God's operative structure—is like a very small seed that is buried under ground, that in some way dies, and then brings forth an entirely unforeseen (and very large) purpose.

When Jesus talks about yeast, something he quite likes to do, and its connection with God's kingdom, he focuses on the detail of its *hiddenness* and its *pervasiveness*. Everyone knows you don't need a whole lot of yeast to make a loaf of bread rise, but Jesus is also saying that the yeast is invisible—it is literally "hidden in" the flour. That is to say, there's no telling where God's handiwork is or isn't, until it's already risen to the fullness of its purpose. Only then do you see that it was everywhere all along. Maybe this has something to say about only seeing things clearly in retrospect...

So have you wondered where God's been lately? Has it felt like a dry spell? Do you feel lost? Here, in the mysteries of things buried and hidden, Jesus says this is probably evidence of God's pervasive handiwork.

—Ethan Richardson

August 3

> *"...Then the father said to him, 'Son, you are always with me and all that is mine is yours. But we had to celebrate and rejoice, because this brother of yours was dead and has come to life; he was lost and has been found.'"*
> *(Luke 15:11-32, NRSV)*

Really, there are two lost sons, equally distanced from the heart of their Father. The one son is the easy target—he's finagled the family money out of his Father and blown it in Acapulco on cocaine and whores. For a while, as long as he is buying, he has plenty of company.

And at first, sleeping it off until 3pm in his villa on the beach, stumbling into beach water to come to life, pouring the first Bloody Mary at 4pm for his eye opener in preparation for another long night of living the dream had been what he always dreamed it would be, back when he was working on his Father's farm, always under the stern and supervising eye of his older brother.

But now, he finds that his mental health is running as thin as his wallet. He is a desultory combination of gaunt and bloated. *Um... he thinks, maybe life on Father's farm wasn't so bad after all.* In the words of the King James Bible, "he came to himself" and decides to return to his Father, to "say unto him, Father, I have sinned against heaven, and before thee, And am no more worthy to be called thy son: make me as one of thy hired servants."

The boy's older brother, the one who does what he says and says what he does, the one who lines up the ledger each night right down to the jot and tittle, is just as lost as his younger brother. His sins are interior—cold, calculating, closed up. His wrath erupts as hot as a Caribbean Sun when his lecherous, parasitic, weak-willed brother shows back up and gets received like the King of Spain. *How dare his Father!* How dare his Father show mercy on someone like him! Doesn't he know that this recalcitrant will eat his veal and drink his liquor and rob his silverware and be back on the road in days?

The two sons start out equally distanced from their Father. Only one ends up encircled in his Father's arms. The other remains frozen in time, out in the cold and dark of the courtyard, the party in full tilt inside, His Father pleading with him to come in and get warm. As it is said in the Book of Common Prayer:

> "O God, whose glory it is always to have mercy: Be gracious to all who have gone astray from your ways, and bring them again with penitent hearts and steadfast faith to embrace and hold fast the unchangeable truth of your Word, Jesus Christ your Son; who with you and the Holy Spirit lives and reigns, one God, for ever and ever. Amen."

—Paul Walker

August 4

> *"The younger one said to his father, 'Father, give me my share of the estate.' So he divided his property between them. Not long after that, the younger son got together all he had, set off for a distant country and there squandered his wealth in wild living." (Luke 15:12-13, NIV)*

You remember how the story goes: "Not long after that, the younger son got together all he had, set off for a distant country..." and there he began an internship with a prestigious brokerage house, working in the mail room and finishing his degree at night. With great persistence, he was able to slowly work his way up through the ranks of the company, becoming the youngest VP in their history, and a partner by the age of 34. On top of these amazing accomplishments, our protagonist, the younger brother, also managed to meet a lovely girl, his one true love, whom he married. Their two young children (a boy and a girl) are blonde and precocious.

This, the world's story, is not the one Jesus tells famously in Luke 15. In the world's story, willpower and success are key components. It is fair to say that the world offers basically the opposite of Jesus' story. *His* narrative is much more common. The story is one of self-destruction. The people sound like actual people. You see, God's story is inextricably enmeshed with the facts of life in a fallen world, where people are weak and prideful. God has placed his bets on the wrong horses. And, furthermore, the top-seeded older brother is mad about it!

But the father's angle is full of surprise. It is comforting and encouraging, even in the lowest of low moments. It dresses failures in fine garments and puts rings on their fingers. And the prodigal is in no position to entertain misconceptions about the origin of such worthiness. Actual good status comes from God. Opportunity comes from God, too. The same is true of help and hope. Do you need any of these things? Or have you already gotten everything under control like an older brother? Christianity is probably not the religion for him.

The classic children's hymn "*Jesus loves me, this I know*" is a wonderful song. While its first verse is emblazoned in the minds and hearts of many, the last two verses are rarely heard. They remind us of the unceasing trajectory of the spiritual life. There is the initial encounter with a gracious Father, and then, too, there is the way it plays out for us today, perhaps some time after the fact of that initial home-coming:

> Jesus loves me, loves me still,
> though I'm very weak and ill.
> From his shining throne on high,
> Comes to watch me where I lie.
> Jesus loves me! He will stay,
> Close beside me all the way;
> Thou hast bled and died for me,
> I will henceforth live for Thee.

—*John Zahl*

August 5

> *"But when he came to himself, he said, 'How many of my father's hired servants have more than enough bread, but I perish here with hunger! I will arise and go to my father, and I will say to him, "Father, I have sinned against heaven and before you. I am no longer worthy to be called your son. Treat me as one of your hired servants.' And he arose and came to his father. But while he was still a long way off, his father saw him and felt compassion, and ran and embraced him and kissed him. And the son said to him, 'Father, I have sinned against heaven and before you. I am no longer worthy to be called your son.' But the father said to his servants, 'Bring quickly the best robe, and put it on him, and put a ring on his hand, and shoes on his feet. And bring the fattened calf and kill it, and let us eat and celebrate. For this my son was dead, and is alive again; he was lost, and is found.' And they began to celebrate." (Luke 15:17-24, ESV)*

The other day I was reading the story of the prodigal son with a fresh eye and expectant ear, when out of the blue a new question struck me.

The question arose in my heart, "Was the younger brother repentant or starving?" The statement found here in verse 17 sounds more *pragmatic* than repentant. Could it be that even at the end of our rope, no sorrow lies beneath the boulder of our sin? Could it be that the boulder is too big for us to budge, much less pull out? Could it be that our pragmatic hearts know no better than to come to the father as needy beggars looking for a better job? That's the idea I get from the younger son.

"But when he came to himself, he said, 'How many of my father's hired servants have more than enough bread, but I perish here with hunger!'" In other words, the younger brother's decision is practical: "This sucks! I'm going home where the food is better and the work is easier." This is at least how it appears in this story and in my own story—the heart of returning does not always feel broken. As the hymn says, "All the fitness He requires, is to feel your need of Him."

In verse 20 we see the father meeting the son. "And he arose and came to his father. But while he was still a long way off, his father saw him and felt compassion, and ran and embraced him and kissed him."

The final blow here is not the crushing weight of the Law but the embrace of Christ's love, lavished on the sinner. The prodigal's instinct to find a better job, made out of necessity and not a deeper understanding of his mistakes, shows us the heart does not know what it needs. But our Father does. Our Father doesn't just sit on the bench while we are crushed by the Law—no, the Gospel is the final blow. The Father rises up when we are a long way off and runs to us and falls on our neck with a hug and a kiss. "Come home sinner, come home," He has been beckoning to us. This, the Gospel, is the final blow to the boulder that crushes the life out of us.

—*Jonathan Adams*

August 6

> *He also told this parable to some who trusted in themselves that they were righteous and regarded others with contempt: "Two men went up to the temple to pray, one a Pharisee and the other a tax collector. The Pharisee, standing by himself, was praying thus, 'God, I thank you that I am not like other people: thieves, rogues, adulterers, or even like this tax collector. I fast twice a week; I give a tenth of all my income.' But the tax collector, standing far off, would not even look up to heaven, but was beating his breast and saying, 'God, be merciful to me, a sinner!' I tell you, this man went down to his home justified rather than the other; for all who exalt themselves will be humbled, but all who humble themselves will be exalted." (Luke 18:9-14, NRSV)*

Maybe you've been a Christian for a while now, and maybe you are feeling good about "your righteousness," like the people Jesus is talking about in this parable. Maybe there are moments in your day, or specific situations, when you catch yourself silently judging someone else. More often than not it has nothing to do with them; it's really just that it makes us feel more righteous.

If you had met me in college, I would have told you that I had been a Christian for a while. After a significant experience when I was around 15, I began a sort of quest to *really* know God. My conversion was quite sudden, and I began to read whatever Christian books I could get my hands on; I was reading the Bible regularly; I was praying for long periods of time; I was generally staying on top of things. In modern Christian parlance, I was a "good Christian." Things calmed down in high school, but I still wasn't compromising anything—no swearing, hooking up, getting drunk, or the like. For this reason I tended to look down at those around me that did these things and reveled in the praise it got me in its absence. It's safe to say I felt that my sin was significantly less than everyone else's—I was somehow better, and I felt God knew it. Maybe that's why he saved me, I thought.

But as many of our stories go, I met a girl in college and completely fell head over heels for her. I loved her intensely, even though she wasn't a Christian and did many of the things I felt were *not* Christian. Many of my friends warned me of the perils of dating this girl, especially for my faith. They told me my faith would die, that I would have to choose between her and God. And so, of course, I felt torn in two, my whole life in the balance. All the pressure plunged me into a spiral, and I found myself doing things that, in truth, I never thought myself capable.

By God's grace, I had a friend throughout the whole experience who just listened to me and supported me; when all the pious left, he told me he trusted God was able to support me without berating me. Through this, I was able to see two things: first, that the relationship had to end—something I didn't want to see but already knew was true. He didn't force this on me, but let it come to me in its own time. Second, and more importantly, that I was sinful, and that Christ had died for my sins. This made me like the tax collector, beating my breast and crying out to heaven for mercy. I began to look at others and feel a new measure of compassion.

When we read this parable in Luke, let us remember that Jesus, who saw right through the heart, told it with tenderness to those who were feeling good about their "righteousness." This is good news for the Pharisee in us all, that when we approach him in faith, he will humble us by opening our eyes—first to our sinfulness, and then to his indelible mercy.

—Javier Garcia

August 7

*And being in an agony he prayed more earnestly; and his
sweat became like great drops of blood falling down upon
the ground. (Luke 22:44, ESV)*

Jesus' agony in the Garden of Gethsemane is the conflict in him between
what he wants in his flesh to be (i.e., a surviving human person, skipping
a dreaded painful death) and what he believes he is being called by God
to be (i.e., a person of completely sacrificed ego for the sake of others
whom he loved). This awesome conflict, because it places his core
natural human desire to stay alive in direct opposition to his dedication
to the call of God, causes the sweat of his body "to become like great
drops of blood."

In Renaissance and Baroque paintings, Christ's agony in the
Garden is sometimes depicted with angels holding golden cups to catch
the drops of his sweated blood. In a beautiful song entitled "In the
Garden," Bob Dylan captures this same treasuring of what was
happening there:

> When they came for him in the garden, did they know?...
> Did they know right then and there what that power was
> worth?

I think the conscious decision to lay down your life for another person—
to extinguish your ego with its completely alive and kicking demand to
stay upright "or I'll blow your house down!"—is inconceivable to our
human nature. We may feel it in relation to a child of ours, or to someone
else we love, but that is usually a form of *need*-love. We'd do anything
for *them* because they do so much for *us*.

But to actually vote to cancel your own ego? That, as Bela Lugosi once
said in the character of an old nobleman who wished he were dead, "would
be glow-rious". Who can do this? Who among us is actually able to step
away from human nature's cry, "I want to live." The doing of this, entirely
not in character for human nature, would be, well, worth something.

Christ sweats blood because the powerful action he was
contemplating was "worth," in Dylan's words, far more than anybody
knew. One of the reasons I'm a Christian is because what Christ did is so
beautifully beyond "me and my house" that I desire to worship Him.

—Paul Zahl

August 8

And when those who were about him saw what would follow, they said, "Lord, shall we strike with the sword?" And one of them struck the slave of the high priest and cut off his right ear. But Jesus said, "No more of this!" And he touched his ear and healed him. (Luke 22:49-51, RSV)

This exchange between Jesus and his disciples at an urgent and dangerous moment says more than just a "No" to taking matters into your own hands. It says a great "Yes" to healing, and loving, your enemy. (I resent this, by the way, about Jesus, as he always goes that extra step toward the crumb who hurt you.)

The disciples carry two swords among them, and like Ben-Hur, they are ready to give their lives in service of their teacher and friend. Peter is the one who by tradition takes instant aim at the high priest's slave, and slices off the man's ear. Jesus cries, *Stop!* Then he heals the stricken man. It's in Mel Gibson's *The Passion*, and you can still visit the actual scene, at the foot of the Mount of Olives.

Jesus forbids violence in his defense, and then takes that extra step. This is the rocky part. For myself, I am right with him on the passivity. We have seen and see every day what happens when you try to take matters into your own hands. The better way is to concede things, right down the line—"It's out of my hands!" When you take things into your own hands, it always seems to backfire. Let things come to you. Let the result come to you. And if you're in the wrong, let the result go the other way. I think all of us who embrace the *iustitia passiva* are with Christ here in this lightning encounter. Our theological and personal instincts run in that direction.

But there are limits, right? Do we really have to go the extra mile, and stitch up the minion who "vuz just folloving orrderz?"

The way to look at this is not to ask whether you or I can do it, whether you or I can take that extra magnanimous step. The way to look at it is rather to remember when you or I were in the body of that temple servant, that little man in service of the wrong who was nevertheless helped along to a better path. This is that one extra step— Neil Armstrong's one small but giant step—in service of our fellow earthlings. We are not so much "Peter," who needs to be instructed to put away his sword. We are "Malchas," which is the traditional name given to the temple slave. "I've fallen and I can't get up!" Come, Lord

Christ, and help me get up. I am Malchas and my right ear is lying in a puddle of blood on the ground.

The other day I was with a depressed young man, age 29. His face was completely blank and he could barely get out a word. Turns out he is well educated, graduated from an excellent college, and has a skilled job. But he is depressed and needs help. How could I help him, as he was pretty alienating—no smile, no laugh, dead eyes, no affect of any perceptible kind? The key, for me, was relating to my own depression, my own personal history of depression. The man in my study didn't have to know that, but my love for him was going to have to be tied to one thing: whatever identification I could effect with his disease. Thank God I could. The link was not whether I could reach out in my own strength to this affect-less person, but whether I could reach out to my own personal affect-less self. And that self exists. All I need to do is recollect one long night in Manhattan years and years ago when my wife went into a movie theater to see a movie with Dustin Hoffman and Meryl Streep and I couldn't even go in, but pleaded depression and just walked around the block, at least 25 times, until the movie was over, and we could go back home. Stranger to depression? No. Possibility of connection? Yes.

This is how I can make Christ's magnanimous gesture somehow my own.

—Paul Zahl

August 9

The Lord turned and looked at Peter. Then Peter remembered the word of the Lord, how he had said to him, "Before the cock crows today, you will deny me three times." And he went out and wept bitterly. (Luke 22:61-62, NRSV)

David O. Russell's film *Silver Linings Playbook* (2012) is about Pat (Bradley Cooper), a husband on a restraining order, recently released from a mental institution for his (previously undetected) bipolar disorder. Pat's story soon becomes entwined with Tiffany's (Jennifer Lawrence), a girl with an equally checkered past, who agrees to help Pat cope with his new illness. Eager to get on the healing train so he can get his old life back, Pat at first seems incapable of doing so, mostly because he's unwilling to face the issue himself.

And then there's a kind of breakthrough scene in a diner—it's Halloween and everyone's got costumes on around them—where Tiffany listens to him and discovers, "You think that I'm crazier than you." Pat can't deny it, but later relays the conversation in his therapist's office, that Tiffany said she "likes [the checkered] part of herself along with all the other parts of herself, and can I say the same?" The therapist asks what his answer is, to which Pat responds, "Is that...? You're asking me, you're really asking me that question? With all my crazy, sad—? Are you nuts?"

It is not nuts, and it is not until Pat can see that he is, in fact, *worse off* than Tiffany that he can begin to work on things. And this isn't just true of bipolar disorders. Anyone's desire—and ability—to disassociate themselves from the *truth* about themselves is a scary power. It can kill intimacy in relationships and it can prevent healing help.

This is the same dramatic conclusion made after Peter's third denial. Peter, having rebuked Jesus for his prediction, now sees in Jesus' knowing look what he never would have admitted, even to himself. He goes out and weeps bitterly, not just out of remorse, but probably also out of some kind of release: no longer is he constrained by the poison lie he held to so tightly. The truth is out, and it has exorcised his false pretense.

I have often wondered what that look from Jesus was like. Surely Peter sees in Christ's turning to him—at the moment of his betrayal—a terrible understanding. Surely Peter sees that, if Christ saw this coming, he must have seen everything else coming, too. And still he has not turned his face away.

—Ethan Richardson

August 10

And Jesus said, "Father, forgive them, for they know not what they do." And they cast lots to divide his garments. (Luke 23:24, ESV)

On November 14, 1940, the Nazi German air force blitzed the industrial city of Coventry in England, leaving its surviving citizens in a state of collective nervous breakdown during the days that followed. In the midst of this destruction were the roofless ruins of the city's medieval cathedral. Shortly after the cathedral's devastation, someone used charred timber roof beams to construct a cross to place at an altar made from the rubble. The cathedral's Provost, Richard Howard, then had the words "Father Forgive" engraved in the sanctuary wall behind the altar.

Not only did Howard make it a point to forgive the Germans, but he intentionally wrote only "Father Forgive," leaving out the word "them," since he recognized the need for the people of England to be forgiven as well. Indeed, the Royal Air Force would later carpet bomb the German city of Dresden in similar fashion with an even higher death toll. Nevertheless, you can imagine the audacity at the time of implying that the English were complicit too!

I like to tell this story of Coventry because when I talk about everyday forgiveness with respect to Christianity, people often move to the abstract with me. They might say, that's well and good, but try forgiving a Hitler or an Osama bin Laden. C.S. Lewis, an Englishman who lived through the Second World War, wrote something very similar about forgiveness, calling it the most unpopular Christian virtue:

> Every one says forgiveness is a lovely idea, until they have something to forgive, as we had during the war. And then, to mention the subject at all is to be greeted with howls of anger. It is not that people think this too high and difficult a virtue: it is that they think it hateful and contemptible. 'That sort of talk makes them sick,' they say. And half of you already want to ask me, 'I wonder how you'd feel about forgiving the Gestapo if you were a Pole or a Jew?'

Lewis goes on to say that such questions about forgiveness are typically premature:

> When you start mathematics you do not begin with the calculus; you begin with simple addition. In the same way, if we really want... to learn how to forgive, perhaps we had better start with something easier than the Gestapo. One might start with forgiving one's husband or wife, or parents or children... for something they have done or said in the last week. That will probably keep us busy for the moment.[*]

If we're realistic, much forgiveness is too lofty for us. It's akin to calculus or quantum mechanics. Let's start with some very basic arithmetic instead. Can you forgive your husband or your wife or your parents or

---

[*] Lewis, C.S. *Mere Christianity*. New York: Harper Collins, 2001, pp 115-116.

your children for something they have done or said in very recent memory? Better yet, can you forgive yourself for the things you have done? Stop and meditate on this.

Are you guilty of an infraction that haunts you? Maybe you have never been able to forgive yourself for this thing you did or said. Perhaps you find yourself to be unforgiveable.

"Father, forgive them for they know not what they do." Jesus Christ—our only Mediator and Advocate—is talking about us. He is talking about the Nazis, the citizens of Coventry, our spouse, our children, our parents. He is talking about you and me. We are all there casting lots for his garments. Yet he nails it all to the charred timber beams of the cross. When we can't even find it to forgive *ourselves* for these trespasses, God in Christ forgives it all at once—once for all, the righteous for the unrighteous.

—*Matthew C. Schneider*

August 11

And he said to him, "Truly, I say to you, today you will be with me in Paradise." (Luke 23:43, ESV)

These simple words of Jesus to the "good thief," are a perfect example of how the relative silence of the Gospels forces people to "fill in the blanks." In this instance, we have Jesus, evidently, pronouncing salvation to this man who we know nothing about, save that he is being crucified. People have tried to blunt this picture of pure, unadulterated grace by speculating that this man, were he to have lived, may have warranted eternal life, or perhaps he was being crucified as a good political objector. The tradition has attempted to answer this question in a variety of ways, but they all end up as mere speculation, at best, because his request is all we have.

A lot's been said about this interaction, but I want to highlight the request of the thief, "remember me," in light of the seeming absence of God. While we can confess by faith that we trust Jesus has, in fact, remembered us, in the "presence of God's absence"—the experience of the Hidden God—we are often driven by fear to try and secure our own legacy, validate our own existence.

Were we to have faith that Jesus will, in fact, remember us, then the fears of inconsequence, of not leaving a legacy or making a difference, would fade away. Instead, too often we baptize our careers, families, ministries or anything we can think of to hold up as something by which to be remembered. For our purposes, this is the allure of the Law, which promises that we can establish ourselves and create our own remembrance, that our lives will be monuments to who we were and what we did. As we grow in our appreciation of how unlikely it is that our monuments will be very big (or ever big enough), we're getting close to an understanding of what Paul means by "the curse of the Law."

This is why we need to hear the Gospel every day, because like the "good thief," we can know that our request is simultaneously a confession and a prayer—remember me!—and Jesus' answer was, and is, and is to come: "Truly, I say to you, today you will be with me in Paradise." Thanks be to God.

—*Jady Koch*

August 12

Then Jesus, calling out with a loud voice, said, "Father, into your hands I commit my spirit!" And having said this he breathed his last. (Luke 23:46, ESV)

These words have provided Christians comfort throughout the ages. And they should, writes theologian Stanley Hauerwas:

> ...but that the words comfort us should not hide from us that these last words of Jesus before his death name his willingness to embrace the ice-cold silence of hell...He is no Christ figure' if by Christ-figure we mean the exemplification of a universal pattern of sacrifice for the good of others. Jesus is no 'Christ-figure' if we mean that his death is an exemplification of how we should all die; that is, we should die with the confidence that we have nothing to earn from death. No, this is the real and specific death of Jesus, the Savior of all that has been, is and is to come, who submits to death by our hands. (96-97)

I find this to be a profoundly unsettling point. I would much rather theorize and systematize and turn the event of the cross into a way of explaining my life and the world around me. It's easier to talk about, for example, "the presence of God's absence"—the *Deus absconditus*, not the cross. But I've realized instead that part of the attraction to the concept of the *Deus absconditus*, or any other theological phrase for that matter, even to the distinction between the Law and Gospel, is alluring because it sees through the cross.

Talking about the Crucifix—the reality of God incarnate killed for sinners—is the same as talking about his absence, because in the everyday experience of our crucified lives we wait for and live in hope of the God who saves.

As Hauerwas points out, it is not that we suffer in solidarity with Jesus, but that our sufferings are penultimate to his, because he holds out the promise that "this too shall pass." Because of his sufferings, we have hope. We can hedge, ask questions, and speculate, but at the end of the day, what we have is faith in a completed work, a work of forgiveness, mercy and promised redemption.

This last word of Jesus is his acceptance, his final acquiescence and surrender to the will of his Father, into whose hands he commits his spirit. This is what we hold onto; it is what we profess. When we are crushed under the weight of our own lives, burdened by "what we have done and what we have left undone," we are driven to our knees and point to our only source of hope: "the wood of the cross, on which hung the Savior of the world." We stand with Luther, who wrote in the Heidelberg Disputation, *crux sola nostra theologia*—the cross alone is our theology, and with the Apostle Paul, who endeavored to only "preach Christ and him crucified," and we hold onto those words with passion and tenacity, 365 days a year. Thanks be to God.

—*Jady Koch*

August 13

> *In the beginning was the Word, and the Word was with God, and the Word was God. He was in the beginning with God. All things came into being through him, and without him not one thing came into being. What has come into being in him was life, and the life was the light of all people... The light shines in the darkness, and the darkness did not overcome it. (John 1:1-5, NRSV)*

Emily Dickinson said it well:

A WORD is dead
    When it is said,
    Some say.
I say it just
    Begins to live
    That day.

Rather than words, we prefer images: lots of them, and in rapid succession. We tend to devalue words. Image is everything. But this is where we can get into trouble. Words not only describe; they can also do. When the priest says "I now pronounce you man and wife," you are married. When the judge says "not guilty," you are set free. Words can do things.

One of the most powerful things a word can do is *promise*. An image can't quite do that. When someone promises, "I'll be there for you," they are committing themselves to that person.

God has done this in his creative word. Through his word, he creates the world. Through this word he promises to be there for the world, to watch over it and take care of it. Through his Word, he himself enters our world, ultimately to take on all its pain and violence, for the very purpose of taking it away. And creation is itself a promise. It is God's guarantee that he will take care of you, along with all other creatures. God's creative word always delivers a gift. Your life is a gift of God, as the lives of all others. In this gift, community is established; we are joined in fellowship with fellow believers—and indeed with all creatures. Even our disagreements can't destroy this bond.

God's word is a word that does what it says and says what it does. In the word that gives the risen Jesus Christ to us, God finds an ear to receive this good news. With God speaking, no other sounds can distract. And through our ears, we learn that God is true to his word. He forgives us our sins and opens us to new horizons for growth and service.

Also, God's word is alive and efficacious. Having created the world and all that is, God wants also to recreate us to be people of faith, people who will both fear and love God. Sin is not the last word about us sinners. No. God has the last say, and His promise to us is so very clear: you are mine; you belong to me.

With such good news in the ear, what else can we do but thank God and want to share this word to others where and when it is appropriate? We also want to keep hearing this word because we know that our very lives depend on it.

Gracious, merciful God, you share yourself with us. We thank you for your word and we ask that we would be true to your word, even as you are true to us, all of our days.

—*Mark Mattes*

August 14

Yet to all who received him, to those who believed in his name, he gave the right to become children of God. (John 1:12, ESV)

Receiving, believing and becoming. This verse encapsulates Christianity. While many have turned the first two stages into the science of how to get saved, I am not convinced we know what it means to *become* God's child. Jesus came into the world not to run us through the how-to-get-to-heaven crucible, but instead to gather creation under two bloody wings. Another devotional writer Oswald Chambers wrote, "In the history of the Christian church, the tendency has been to avoid being identified with the sufferings of Jesus Christ. People have sought to carry out God's orders through a shortcut of their own. God's way is always the way of suffering—the way of the *long road home.*"

This world has and always will clamor about new rights issues, and these issues may have merit, but a friend of mine likes to say, "Christians have no rights in this world," and I think he is correct. At least in the sequence of receiving, believing and becoming, there is no entitlement. *Becoming* is not code for a life of ease. It's also not code for a re-evaluation of motives or ethics or preaching. Becoming a child of God involves much more than theological catchphrases.

Jesus assures us we may very well be despised by people we try to assist. With family, friends, and neighbors, there's no reason to expect that the "children of God," whatever their theologies, will be welcomed any more than the Son of God was. Receiving Christ is an inheritance serving a life-and-death sentence: you are loved more than you could imagine, and you don a crown of thorns. To put it in a creedal sense, this is the essential "descent into hell" that always precedes rising from the dead. Looking at it this way, the appeal of the evangelist becomes a call to one's own funeral as much as it is a call to believe, and this cannot be avoided.

Nevertheless, this is not hopeless or bleak: it is this identification with the Man of Sorrows that makes sense out of families and jobs and getting older. Though it is difficult to walk into the fringe with our "new birth" certificates in hand, and walk away from the Dylan Thomas adage to "Rage, rage against the dying of the light," we enter into the honest, but unpleasant, heritage of souls whose names pepper the pages of our Bible. Like Jesus himself, who became the outcast of Eden, who knew the rough kiss of betrayal, we are the sons and daughters of a terrible affliction and a deep resurrection. This is something of what it means to *become* a child of God.

—*Dylan Potter*

August 15

> *When the steward of the feast tasted the water now become wine, and did not know where it came from (though the servants who had drawn the water knew), the steward of the feast called the bridegroom and said to him, "Every man serves the good wine first; and when men have drunk freely, then the poor wine; but you have kept the good wine until now." (John 2:9-10, RSV)*

The "moral" of Christ's miracle at the wedding at Cana seems to be that he not only turned water into wine, but he turned it into *good* wine. The steward, an independent witness who did not know the "back story" of its existence, attested the quality of the wine.

John emphasizes this almost quaint story, quaint because we know how unintendingly meaningful were the steward's words. Because always-otherwise-profound John emphasizes this "first of his signs," I think we need to ask why.

The meaning is simple. God's activity, seen in Christ's miracle, is "top drawer." He doesn't cut corners or decide to become "penny wise, pound foolish." *Only the best!* Or rather, only the right and proper.

Often my wife and I have stayed in Christian hostels or conference centers. They could be part of the "liberal" church or part of the "conservative" church. Almost invariably, the soap was bad. Tiny little ancient cubes of a hardened gray or beige substance, to which the wrapping paper invariably stuck when you tried to open it—which could take a half hour. This told us that the soap packets used in the hostel or center were about ten years old, not to mention the size of postage stamps.

There were exceptions to this apparent tightwad culture about spending money, but not many. A few times in Germany you could stay in a clean and well-equipped Protestant Church hotel—with better soap. But in general, nobody was "keeping the good wine until now."

I like the generosity and high standards observed by Jesus at the wedding at Cana. I think John liked them, too. Let's hear it for some signature soap!

—*Paul Zahl*

August 16

Now there was a man of the Pharisees named Nicodemus, a member of the Jewish ruling council. He came to Jesus at night and said, "Rabbi, we know you are a teacher who has come from God. For no one could perform the miraculous signs you are doing if God were not with him." In reply Jesus declared, "I tell you the truth, no one can see the kingdom of God unless he is born again. "How can a man be born when he is old?" Nicodemus asked. "Surely he cannot enter a second time into his mother's womb to be born!" (John 3:1-4, NIV)

Naïve—and also a bit slippery—Nicodemus has the credentials, the studies and the status that a professor today might have, but John sheds light on some of his less attractive qualities. First, he comes to Jesus by night, perhaps a bit embarrassed by his fascination with the Son of God, or embarrassed by its association with the losers of the world.

More than that, though, Nicodemus doesn't seem to understand a word Jesus is saying! Much more interested in theological questions than the heart of the matter, Nicodemus is stuck on the mechanics of "new birth" ("How can these things be?"). It is in the context of this discussion that we hear the famous words "For God so loved the world," but we never get Nicodemus' response. After Jesus delivers these concise words of comfort, Nicodemus fades into the background, leaving only the impression of his frustrated and floundering speculation.

Perhaps this first glance at Nicodemus gives us a warning about theologies in general. It's no wonder people tend to cringe and wince when people start talking theology; it is so often disconnected from what's really going on, and it's often an opportunity for navel-gazing more than it is for any kind of good news. Speculative study—while having merit of its own—can be like a nighttime visit, providing more opportunities for evasion than for honesty, and this is totally Nicodemus' state of affairs. It is sad, because what use is it knowing any of it if it doesn't bring us to reality? What good are the questions if we never reach the love of God in Christ?

The good news is that God knows we sidestep and is infinitely patient with us in our sidestepping. What's more, He draws us back to Him. Jesus responds to Nicodemus' shortsighted questions with the truth. As we see Nicodemus in our thinking, how great it is that God redirects us to the heart of all theology: Jesus Christ and him crucified.

—*Javier Garcia*

August 17

He must increase, but I must decrease. (John 3:30, ESV)

I grew up thinking that "sanctification" was all about me. I thought that I was saved by Jesus, but then it was up to me—in my *cooperation* with the Holy Spirit—to become a holy person, a good person. In my mind, my obedience and disciplines were what sanctified me, what helped me climb the ladder to glory. Sanctification is the word used to describe the life between "being saved" and going on up into God's glory. "Sanctification is a process," I had been told.

Now I have a new vision of sanctification—and it really is a *vision*. It's not based on merit, but on reality. It kind of looks like this:

I am standing in front of a gravestone. It is grey and wet, predawn, and the breeze is brisk at first. I have a shovel in my hand and I am digging. The digging is easy for a while, but then, about a foot down, I hit clay and the digging becomes harder. After a while I'm completely covered in red mire, this refuse of years of decay. Then dawn breaks. The sun rises over the cruciform headstone, and its shadow passes over me. Not long after, I am completely under its shadow. I cannot escape the depths of digging, but I cannot escape the morning shadow of the cross, either. The sunlight seems to filter around the cold stone, heaven a cross-shaped keyhole through the pit that I have dug for myself.

To me, this is a more insightful vision of sanctification. The deeper we dig, the more we realize Christ's boundless depth of love.

—*Keith Pozzuto*

August 18

"...Everyone who drinks of this water will be thirsty again, but whoever drinks of the water that I will give him will never be thirsty forever. The water that I will give him will become in him a spring of water welling up to eternal life..." (John 4:13-26, ESV)

Jesus is saying here that he doesn't buy into all the things we pretend to be. These are all portions of the same shallow water—the human propensity to "be okay." We all posture in this way—sometimes we forget we're even doing it because it has become such a part of us.

At work, in front of my boss, "I'm okay" is to look motivated, maybe periodically make note of my "job effectiveness" in the past months. At night, "I'm okay" is getting exercise, dressing meticulously without looking meticulous, knowing when stop talking about myself for so long, after a couple—but not too many—bourbon-gingers. Amongst the religious-folks, "I'm okay" is theologizing *everything*, using Latin terms, saying things like "the human condition." I have many faces. Whitman said it: "Do I contradict myself? Very well then...I am a multitude of multitudes."

Have you ever felt a friend of yours watching *you* talking to another friend from another circle? Did your multiplicities become embarrassingly transparent? It is confusing, and sometimes a little scary, that our saccharine satisfaction with our relationships is often a satisfaction with how well we played the face, how well we "pulled off" the roles of Hard-Working Employee, Witty Suitor, Self-Understanding Christian. In other words, how we say "I'm okay" is, in a lot of cases, a testimony to what's *not* okay. Where we pose most in our lives is likely where we suspect we would be rejected if we were honest.

The good news is that Jesus cuts to the chase. We may hedge and say, "Let's keep this ambiguous—theoretical—noncommittal." This woman at the well is obviously someone who needs some company, being the socially ostracized woman in marital strife she is, and yet she is *still* playing the game. Jesus doesn't cut to the chase to condemn, but to illuminate that he *knows* and still *loves*. He needs her to know that he sees the face behind the faces and still comes to her. Jesus, in love, renders to a pulp her fragments of pretense. And as much as we are this woman, the same is true: we are offered this grace, that behind our many faces we are cut to the heart—and fully loved there.

—*Ethan Richardson*

August 19

He told me all that I ever did. (John 4:39, ESV)

What do I really want? What would make me feel better? How would I even know when I had it? In the midst of an aching feeling that there's something missing, that I want something and don't know what it is, I ask myself these kinds of questions.

Sometimes I think it's an Audi R8. I know it wouldn't solve my problems, but it might help. Other times I know it's something more profound like *freedom*. While it is definitely true that freedom is something I crave, *freedom* just sounds abstract. The answer that seems to connect most, that I'll find myself saying out loud, is "I just want to go home."

The funny thing is that I have muttered this to myself when I *am* home, just sitting on the couch. I know it's not a physical location, but rather a belonging, a kind of acceptance. I want to be in a place of rest, where I am fully known and fully accepted. Being with my family in my house is certainly the context in which I feel this more often than not, but there are plenty of times when I do not feel at home in my own home, in my own skin even. When I feel like this, there is nowhere on earth I could go that would make me feel like I belong.

This is where Jesus surprises us, just as he did the woman at the well. He surprises us because he knows who we are and what we've done, and he stays with us.

—*Sean Norris*

August 20

...When Jesus saw him lying there and knew that he had been there a long time, he said to him, "Do you want to be

made well?" The sick man answered him, "Sir, I have no one to put me into the pool when the water is stirred up; and while I am making my way, someone else steps down ahead of me." (John 5:2-8, NRSV)

Saint Augustine says that the sick man, at the edge of this pool with its "five porches," is symbolically sitting upon the five books of the Torah, the Jewish Law. "These five porches signify the law which bears the sick but does not heal them, discovers them but does not cure them." The sick man can sit there as long as he wants, but he will always be a sick man, sitting upon a standard that will always "step down ahead of him."

In light of this, an emphasis is put on the question that Jesus asks the sick man and the response he gives. "Do you actually *want* to be made well?" Besides being an insulting thing to ask a cripple, the question itself says Jesus might not be so sure he actually *does* want to be made well. The sick man's response seems to support this: he offers Jesus a non-response by laying down the victim card. Rather than say whether or not he'd like things to change, he can't help but tell Jesus what circumstances have kept him from changing. In his very public sickness, he has developed a defensive self-pity that's quarantined him from help.

Public or not, we tend to sidestep inquiry in the same way. When questioned, sometimes we might play the martyr, and drone on about circumstances that *just made it impossible*; other times we play the hero and get irritable defending the unblemished decisions we've made. Self-pity and vainglory are really two sides of the same coin of self-defense. They are two ways we choose to refuse the help we need.

What's wonderful here is that Jesus doesn't need the right response to get on with the work of healing. He understands that sick people balk at help, and he helps anyway.

So, what questions have you been sidestepping (or completely avoiding) lately? Who or what has prompted them? Where have you felt the need to explain away an inquiry? It could be that there you sit, as the sick man, upon a hopeless or unattainable standard. But God isn't waiting for you to figure out the right response. His work of healing is prerequisite to your shaky desire for it.

—Ethan Richardson

August 21

The Father judges no one but has given all judgment to the Son, so that all may honor the Son just as they honor the Father. Anyone who does not honor the Son does not honor the Father who sent him. Very truly, I tell you, anyone who hears my word and believes him who sent me has eternal life, and does not come under judgment, but has passed from death to life. "Very truly, I tell you, the hour is coming, and is now here, when the dead will hear the voice of the Son of God, and those who hear will live. For just as the Father has life in himself, so he has granted the Son also to have life in himself; and he has given him authority to execute judgment, because he is the Son of Man."
(John 5:22-27, NRSV)

Listen again to these words from our Gospel lesson: "The Father judges no one but has given all judgment to the Son... He has given him authority to execute judgment."

The unavoidable word in these passages is *judgment*. It is a word that causes people to bristle, the kind of word that, when we encounter it, feels a bit like a speed bump, even a roadblock. It brings to mind a wagging finger, "*tsk tsk*" sentiments, *shame-shame-shame* fingers. Judgment stops us in our tracks, seemingly holding us down under the giant Platonic form of a heavenly thumb.

So we need to think about what it means for Jesus to be our judge. Let me offer two thoughts.

First, if Jesus is the one who has been given by God the authority (as God) to judge the world, then it is also means that you and I have been relieved of any similar obligations. In life, it is not our job to judge. When we find our selves doing it, when we find ourselves looking down our noses at the people we come in contact with, we have stepped out of proper alignment with God. We have, in some sense, simultaneously tried to usurp His role, and have ceased to trust Him.

Second, if Jesus is judge, this is good news. You *want* his judgment! His justice is full of mercy. As a theologian has said, it is fair to say that, in Christ, "*the judgment of God is forgiveness.*" I don't know about you, but that's the last judgment I ever expect reckoned to me. It's the one verdict that I rarely offer myself. It's incredibly good news that, once and for all, our final judgment has come down from cosmic officials, as a deep, all-encompassing, counterintuitive, refreshing acceptance. He has pled our case with three short words: "Father, forgive them."

—John Zahl

August 22

How can you believe, when you receive glory from one another and do not seek the glory that comes from the only God? Do not think that I will accuse you to the Father. There is one who accuses you: Moses on whom you have set your hope. If you believed Moses, you would believe me; for he wrote of me. But if you do not believe his writings, how will you believe my words? (John 5:44-46, ESV)

There is a very strong courtroom motif throughout the Gospel of John. At the end, John actually frames his account of Jesus' life like a courtroom eyewitness testimony (21:24). Here it is certainly true: Jesus is dealing with the legal accusations of a group of Pharisees who have objected to his healing miracles. Earlier in this chapter Jesus very boldly claims, "the Father judges no one, but has entrusted all judgment to the Son" (5:22). In God's courtroom, Jesus is not the defense attorney; he is the Judge. Jesus goes on to state here that Moses (the Law) will serve as the prosecution.

It must be understood that while God's Law shows us the divine moral ordering of the universe, it also *always* accuses sinners of their sinfulness. The Law shows no one is right with God—and that was the Pharisees' problem. And ours too. The fact that they—and we—overlook the truth about our legal standing means that we end up missing our need for a savior.

When we hear talk about God's holiness or glory, very often the response is pie-eyed delight, not run-and-hide Edenic fear. Many contemporary worship songs go on and on about God's holiness and grandeur, but they also fail to recognize the fact that God's holiness shames us. Next to the perfect, the imperfect is obliterated. It's true.

But the Gospel of John tells us something else entirely. Way back in the introduction to the Gospel, John writes that "The law came through Moses, but grace and truth came through Jesus Christ" (1:17). The Gospel tells us that Judge Jesus is also Jesus the Condemned. The reason Jesus can make a non-condemning ruling and declare sinners righteous is that the price for not keeping the Law has been paid in his own blood—the judge takes all the blame himself, freeing us from the defendant's chair.

—*Ben Phillips*

August 23

> *...When they were satisfied, he told his disciples, "Gather up the fragments left over, so that nothing may be lost." So they gathered them up, and from the fragments of the five barley loaves, left by those who had eaten, they filled twelve baskets. When the people saw the sign that he had done, they began to say, "This is indeed the prophet who is to come into the world." When Jesus realized that they were about to come and take him by force to make him king, he withdrew again to the mountain by himself. (John 6:5-15, NRSV)*

When you hear about God's deliverance, what image springs to mind? For the Jews of Jesus' day, it was a combination of a new Moses—someone who would give them the Law—and a new David, a political leader who could fulfill the nation's "manifest destiny" of political hegemony.

Jesus reproduces Moses' greatest feat of provision, which is free bread all around. People love this and are deeply impressed. Indeed, the whole miraculous-power ministry is so effective that Dostoevsky, in *The Brothers Karamazov*, asks why Jesus doesn't just stick to it. It certainly works for making people believe.

But unfortunately, it's the wrong kind of belief they're buying into. They want a strong, powerful Messiah who makes sense to them. Later, Jesus tries to correct their view, using his newfound publicity to make a point about eating and drinking his body. The crowds leave in droves.

Sometimes when we think we're following Jesus the most, we're actually attaching our own hopes of political power, self-improvement, or any other sense of "being in the right." Encountering the Gospel always turns this upside-down. Karl Barth said that the Bible, honestly read, "makes straight for the one point where we must decide to accept or reject the sovereignty of God." Unfortunately, we all avoid this point by projecting our own hopes onto Christ—whose ministry was actually meant to free us from petty, navel-gazing self-improvement and our perpetual need to be in the right.

So what does true faith look like? Admitting our weakness and lack of faith, first off. But that's not the takeaway here. Moses had demanded faith from the Israelites in the wilderness, strictly forbidding them to gather leftovers, so they were forced to "let go and let God." But in Jesus' *lived* retelling, there are twelve baskets of leftovers. Instead of "let go and let God," God just *provides*, to point of excess, despite knowing we'll somehow fashion his provision with our own ideas for God (we don't "let" Him do a thing). But still He provides, regardless of how weak our faith is or how we feel at any given moment.

Again, what springs to mind when you think of God's deliverance? If you and I are honest, it's probably not exactly what Jesus had in mind—maybe it's deliverance from singleness, the resuscitation of a loveless marriage, a way out of what seems to be a dead-end job. But the good news is that regardless of how well we think we understand or how much we fail to "get it," God still, always, provides fully.

—Will McDavid

August 24

All that the Father gives me will come to me, and whoever comes to me I will never cast out. For I have come down from heaven, not to do my own will but the will of him who sent me. And this is the will of him who sent me, that I shall lose nothing of all that he has given me, but raise it up on the last day. For this is the will of my Father, that everyone who looks on the Son and believes in him should have eternal life, and I will raise him up at the last day. (John 6:37-39, ESV)

Through Jesus, God actively reaches into our chaos, pain, and confusion to grasp us. He initiates the relationship with us: "I have come down from heaven to do God's will." This relationship is secure; it cannot be driven away, forgotten, or lost.

Jesus here is assured that many will come to him in faith. God doesn't turn any away who come to Him, nor will He ever disown them. In a world of overwhelming complexities and insecurities, God has fixed an eternal gaze on us and will not let anything get in the way. Our future is not pending; our future is resurrection.

This fixedness doesn't mean we aren't still bent toward independence and infidelity. If the security of our salvation depended on *our* ability to keep our gaze on Christ, then not only would salvation slip from us, but we would all the more jog the treadmill of self-centered schemes of righteousness. Thankfully, it all depends on God to keep up. He is the one "not willing that any of these little ones should be lost" (Matt 18). He assures us, his little ones, that "No one can snatch them out of my Father's hand" (John 10).

—*Justin Holcomb*

August 25

Jesus stood up and said to her, "Woman, where are they? Has no one condemned you?" She said, "No one, Lord." And Jesus said, "Neither do I condemn you; go, and from now on sin no more." (John 8:10-11, ESV)

Levels of anxiety have skyrocketed in the last twenty or so years. In 2011, Slate.com reported that "The average [American] high school kid today has the same level of anxiety as the average psychiatric patient in the early 1950s."[*] Everyone accounts for the rise slightly differently—technology, workaholism, narcissism, religious decline, etc—but no one denies the problem. The comforts of modern life have not come without a mental and emotional cost.

Perhaps more worrying are the ways we've chosen to deal with our collective anxiety. We self-medicate with substances and entertainment. We spend more than we make. We put on a happy face, both in person and online. We do whatever we can to avoid feeling bad.

Some would say that we've embraced a general "feel-goodism" that does us more harm than good. Pain is fought and denied rather than tolerated or confessed. Sadly, the same is true in the church. Instead of defeat and failure, we talk about struggle. We hedge our prayer requests in phrases meant to exonerate God from culpability. We condemn

---

[*] http://www.slate.com/articles/arts/culturebox/2011/01/its_not_the_job_market .h tml

ourselves (and are condemned by others) for our less-than-savory feelings. "I shouldn't feel this way." "A Christian doesn't feel such things." It may be endemic, but that doesn't prevent it from being emotional quicksand. Our intolerance toward pain makes the pain worse.

Jesus understands this. When confronted with a woman caught in adultery, he does not heap condemnation upon condemnation. He doesn't affirm her wrongdoing—of course not. But neither does he condemn her. Walker Percy once wrote that "We love those who know the worst of us and don't turn their faces away." Christ sees the worst in her and doesn't turn his face away.* And that's enough. The simple absence of judgment when it is most expected (and maybe even deserved) is a saving act for this woman.

If you've ever experienced this sort of non-judgment in the face of real wrongdoing, you know that when it happens, *it's a miracle.* Fortunately, God sending His son into the world is a miracle. But perhaps the greater miracle is that God "sent his son into to the world not to condemn the world but to save it" (John 3:17). Jesus does not condemn you for your anxieties and fears, however founded or unfounded they may be. He does not hedge or deny or put a band-aid on your pain, and He is not asking you to, either. Instead, like the woman caught in adultery, the place of rawness and weakness and guilt and vulnerability is the place where His love for us becomes real, where we encounter the Friend of Sinners in all His counter-intuitive glory.

So how are you refusing to "go there" today? Where are you telling Christ that he is wrong not to condemn you? That you know his business better than he does? Well, he doesn't condemn you for your inability to give up on your self-destructive compulsions. He didn't turn his face away then, and he does not turn his face away today either. Amen.

—*David Zahl*

August 26

Again Jesus spoke to them, saying, 'I am the light of the world. Whoever follows me will not walk in darkness, but will have the light of life." (John 8:12, ESV)

---

* Percy, Walker. *Love in The Ruins.* Picador, 1971, p 106.

Robert Louis Stevenson, author of *Treasure Island*, who lived in Scotland in the 19th century, was intrigued as a boy by the work of the old lamplighters who went about with a ladder and a torch, setting the street lights ablaze for the night. One evening, as young Robert stood watching with fascination, his parents asked him, "Robert, what in the world are you looking at out there?" With great excitement he exclaimed, "Look at that man! He's punching holes in the darkness!"

This is what Jesus means in John 8, that he punches holes in the darkness. It means that while we are powerless to push against the gloom that closes in, this gloom is Jesus' place of operation. Our hope is not that we can be strong enough to "bring light into dark places," but that Jesus is powerful enough and willing to do something about it.

Perhaps the darkness within is something you live with, something you keep doing. Maybe you have this horrible sense that since that you made your mess, you have to deal with it or clean it up. Perhaps it is something that has been done *to* you. Maybe you are the victim, and somebody trampled your trust or abused you in some way. Maybe your experience of darkness is not a matter of guilt or victimization, perhaps it is a situation. Maybe it is the hovering weight of your depression or anxiety. Maybe the broken relationships in your life. Maybe you feel trapped. Or maybe your future looks dark and confusing.

These darknesses are not the final word, but we cannot "tough love" ourselves out of the situation—God doesn't work that way. We need the one who *is* the light to *see* the light. It may dominate how you feel right now or maybe it will show up later, but either way it is not your final condition, because Jesus is the savior who takes on the darkness so that we can have the light. Instead of death, decay, and darkness, Jesus gives us the light of life.

—*Justin Holcomb*

August 27

When [Jesus] had said this, he spat on the ground and made mud with the saliva and spread the mud on the man's eyes, saying to him, "Go, wash in the pool of Siloam" (which means Sent). Then he went and washed and came back able to see. (John 9:6-7, NRSV)

Here we read about a man born blind, whom Jesus enabled to see. You can imagine the huge reorientation this must have brought to the life of its recipient. Indeed, he couldn't keep from telling the whole town about it, for his entire experience of life had been (suddenly) altered for the better. What joy, what grace!

Similarly, the Christian faith completely changes one's perspective. It causes us to see new things. We see the ways that we can help others. We discover the value of putting their needs ahead of our own. We discover the value of humility, and that regret can lead us to more deeply appreciate God's forgiveness, which ultimately leads to peace (2 Cor 7:10). We see that people, when they act terribly, are no different from us, the victims of the warring emotions that arise from within them. They, like us, are sick and in need of mercy. And with faith, too, comes hope. It looks into the unknowns of life, into the dark, and anticipates an end that cannot be expected, but which is surely trustworthy...and ultimately good.

Jesus changes the way we see. What is he showing you?

—*John Zahl*

August 28

Jesus wept. (John 11:35, ESV)

Jesus has been called because his friend Lazarus is sick; he intentionally delays coming, knowing that Lazarus will die and that he can bring him back to life—and then he weeps, though we're surprised because it would seem like he "knows better" than to cry. We too often want to distance ourselves from our suffering—from the loss of our job, the death of friends or family, the tragic divorce—and we do so by analyzing it, somehow thinking that the right perspective, or the right amount of faith, or the right theology, will cushion or annul the blow. We shouldn't weep, people think, because our friend is in a better place, because God is working through it—and we wouldn't be sobbing or screaming or paralyzed if we "just had faith" or "had our heads on right."

Christ proves all of these attempts to minimize or avoid suffering to be utterly wrongheaded. Not only does Jesus know that Lazarus is headed to a better place, but he also knows that his friend will be brought back to life almost immediately. And yet that knowledge doesn't make the anguish go away. He sobs for his friend's death even though he knows it's only temporary; he sobs for Mary and Martha's grief even though he knows that it, too, will soon turn to joy. It's not just that he gives us permission to grieve, but he grieves himself, even though his "faith" and "perspective" and all those other traits—inevitably hapless clichés to actual sufferers—are really there; they're real. He cannot outthink his grief, and there's no possible way that we can.

Jesus grieves for the sickness, the death, and all the other physical and emotional ailments that plague the world. He knows, better than anyone, that all will be redeemed, but this gives him as little real comfort in the moment of suffering as it gives us. Christ's ability to grieve isn't an act, and he perhaps grieves not less than us for being the Son of God, but more. It is his compassion, his divine sadness, and his unique share in the collective distress of humanity that allow him to save the world. Human sin and suffering affect him on such a deep level that he wants to take the entire weight of guilt, pain, and death upon himself as his body becomes the eternal, crucified lament of an abject humanity. And it's ultimately Christ's ability to weep that saves us. Jesus is certainly most human during his weeping and loss and anxiety and guilt, but it's also perhaps here that he is most divine.

—Will McDavid

August 29

Now is the judgment of this world; now will the ruler of this world be cast out. (John 12:31, ESV)

Jesus is referring to his imminent death by crucifixion. He has entered Jerusalem and the Jewish leaders are plotting his death, and the Romans are willing to go along with it. Surrounded by critics and corruption, his world is as ours is today, so it makes sense that the Messiah proclaims judgment. But when Jesus refers to the "judgment of this world," he means that God will bring judgment upon him. Now is the time: Christ, the Judge, will fulfill justice upon the "rulers," but he'll do so by being himself "cast out."

The ruler of this world stirs it all, cultivates the fearful thoughts that drive our anxiety—how the bills are going to get paid, when the promotion will come, where our daughter will go to college, what happiness has been lost or sorrow gained, and the fear hinging all fears, death. Whether you call it the devil, the pressures of life, or the inner-ego, Jesus says now is the time this ruler is cast out. He does so by casting himself out with it, through his own death.

So when we're sure we feel God's displeasure, that He is angry we've messed it all up, remember that God's judgment *has* passed. In judging his Son instead, the rulers of this world have no sway. Sin has lost its sway—as well as all the reverberating shadows it casts upon our daily lives. This means no corrupt government has the last say; neither does social acceptance, career failure, or your own interior, condemning voice. Jesus casts out the power of the ruling critics on the cross.

—Kate Norris

August 30

> *Jesus, knowing that the Father had given all things into his hands, and that he had come from God and was going back to God, rose from supper. He laid aside his outer garments, and taking a towel, tied it around his waist. Then he poured water into a basin and began to wash his disciples' feet and to wipe them with the towel that was wrapped around him. (John 13:3-5, ESV)*

Jesus washing the disciples' feet deconstructs our "normal" conception of what gods do. Creating, judging, and rewarding—yes—these are appropriate divine activities, but not washing feet. Jesus' lowly service is a practical inversion of our normal view of authority and power. His un-self-conscious act of service is a picture of God's upside-down approach to our world and to us.

Dostoevsky gives us a picture of this upside-down approach in his book *The Idiot*, which is about the gentle and unlikely Prince Myshkin, who throughout the novel interacts with rage-filled, backbiting, power-hungry, and envious antagonists. They struggle for accolades and live like beasts. Yet Dostoevsky does something dramatic with his Prince Myshkin; he is dropped in the middle of this depravity and then forced to struggle with it. Frail and simple, his way is astounding! He speaks clearly and without lies. He loves everyone he comes into contact with, especially the peasants and the servants. He is not self-aggrandizing. And for all of his love and kindness, his meekness and his tenderness, the world around him dismisses him as an idiot.

Jesus Christ is like this. Our world, in all its wisdom, finds him and the meekness of his cross foolish. He is the penniless and powerless prince, who came to serve: "I have come to serve, not to be served, and to give my life as a ransom for many" (Matt 20:28 and Mark 10:45).

—*Justin Holcomb*

August 31

> *I am the true vine, and my Father is the vinedresser. Every branch in me that does not bear fruit he takes away, and every branch that does bear fruit he prunes, that it may bear more fruit. Already you are clean because of the word that I have spoken to you. Abide in me, and I in you. As the branch cannot bear fruit by itself, unless it abides in the vine, neither can you, unless you abide in me...* (John 15:1-5, ESV)

When we think of being "pruned" by God, it's easy to think of minor cuttings, small challenges that do us good, but perhaps harder to think of the severe changes that might drastically affect our lives in too painful a way.

To the gardener, however, pruning a plant looks like cutting off living branches—taking significant lengths off of a perfectly healthy branch to encourage new growth. This is true of what Jesus is saying, too: being pruned oftentimes feels very painful, as if some large part of you that was once deeply connected to life has been severed. It can feel as though one's wounds have been left raw to face the elements. It can feel like God has deliberately disconnected Himself, and one's protests are met only with silence.

We can take heart from Christ's words: God prunes every branch that doesn't bear fruit, so that it will be even more fruitful. Every saint who has been "fruitful" has dealt with the emotional loss of having been pruned. The Gardener is lovingly ruthless. He severs parts of our connection to the vine—even connections that do not appear in need of pruning—so that we can bear more. Because He abides in us and we in Him, we can be certain that even the most painful pruning experiences are for the sake of His great love.

—*Bonnie Poon Zahl*

September 1

As the Father has loved me, so have I loved you. Abide in my love. If you keep my commandments, you will abide in my love, just as I have kept my Father's commandments and abide in his love. These things I have spoken to you, that my joy may be in you, and that your joy may be full. "This is my commandment, that you love one another as I have loved you. (John 15:9-12, ESV)

Where are you having a hard time loving the people around you?

Maybe someone got in the way of something you want and you've lashed out. Maybe your kids aren't making decisions the way you think they should and you're growing resentful. Maybe your spouse isn't giving you what you think you deserve and you've become cold.

Run a book search on Amazon for "loving others" and you'll get over 41,000 results, almost all of them self-help books offering techniques on loving people better. This certainly tells us we have a problem on our hands, but it also tells us the answer isn't a simple one. This becomes especially problematic in light of this passage: Jesus is commanding us to love others *as he has loved us.* Right. Let's get on that one.

We can try to "get better" at loving people. We place an emphasis on ourselves, on tips and techniques to help us work at it. This inevitably leads to frustration, because not one in 41,000 ever fully works. And honestly, this is the death we must die. Rather than empower us, Jesus' command kills—who can love this way?

Thanks be to God, that's not the end of the story. When our loveless propensities have done their number on us, God is faithful to raise us to new life through His own, one-way love in Jesus: "As the Father has loved me, so have I loved you." Jesus loves us the way the Father loves him! The same love that raises Jesus from the dead is what raises us from our dead lovelessness, day after day.

This love is the only thing that can generate this crazy, outlandish one-way love in us. Hearing this good news takes our eyes off our successes and failures in the love department, and places them on the One who loves us perfectly. Only when we rest in God's perfect love for us will we begin to know what loving others even means.

—Curt Benham

September 2

> *"Nevertheless I tell you the truth: it is to your advantage*
> *that I go away, for if I do not go away, the Advocate will*
> *not come to you; but if I go, I will send him to you. And*
> *when he comes, he will convict the world of sin and*
> *righteousness and judgment..." (John 16:7-15, NRSV)*

In this chapter of John's Gospel, Jesus is explaining to the disciples why it is better for him to go away than to stay. We can all relate to the disciples' question. Wouldn't life be easier if Jesus were still here, in flesh and blood, to talk to, to learn from, to minister to us, to answer our questions? Instead we are left with an invisible God, and it is not always easy to believe in something invisible. How could this be better than having Jesus with us?

Jesus' answer is that he has gone away for our own good, so that he could send to us an Advocate, the Spirit, whose involvement in our lives and in the world will be even more wonderful than Jesus' own.

This Spirit is an Advocate, a Paraclete. He is *our* advocate, in the world and before God. The Spirit is always on our side, and the Spirit is always with us. You cannot escape God's advocacy. "Whither shall I go from thy Spirit? Or whither shall I flee from thy presence? ... Even the darkness is not dark to thee." (Psalm 139:7, 12). There is nowhere you can go to get away from being known and loved and defended and sought by the Spirit of God.

And this is true whether we like it or not. In verse 8 we are told that this Advocate is also the one who convicts us of sin. The Spirit is the one who reveals the truths we want to keep hidden and who looks at what we think is the best of ourselves and sees it for what it is.

Sometimes I wish I could stay in the darkness rather than face such light. "Even the darkness is not dark to thee." Sometimes I am afraid of this Advocate, this fire from heaven that burns in order to heal, this Spirit of truth who sees through my lies. At the end of the chapter, Jesus says it straight: "you will have pain, but your pain will turn into joy" (John 16:20). May it be so.

—*Simeon Zahl*

September 3

> *Jesus answered, "My kingdom is not of this world. If my kingdom were of this world, my servants would have been fighting, that I might not be delivered over to the Jews. But my kingdom is not from the world." Then Pilate said to him, "So you are a king?" Jesus answered, "You say that I am a king. For this purpose I was born and for this purpose I have come into the world— to bear witness to the truth. Everyone who is of the truth listens to my voice." Pilate said to him, "What is truth?" After he had said this, he went back outside to the Jews and told them, "I find no guilt in him." (John 18:36-38, ESV)*

How would other "gods" have responded to Pilate? Zeus would have his thunderclap. The Messiah everyone wanted would have called an army down to conquer the Romans. The possibilities for divine extrication are endless, but none would have selected crucifixion. Voluntary, ultimate worldly defeat is not "godly" in the traditional sense. Our concept of higher powers—God or Rome or money—determines our understanding of truth.

Nietzsche calls Pilate's Socratic response to these words, "What is truth?" "the only saying that has any value" in the New Testament. Undoubtedly, Pilate is puzzled by Jesus' enigmatic "defense." Betrayed and denied by his followers, Jesus does not even offer any argument for acquittal.

Pilate does not wait for, or expect, a response to his question. As a Roman prefect, he has been criticized for his treatment of Jews and Jewish customs. Despite his misgivings regarding Christ's guilt, to avoid further Jewish unrest and accusations about him to Rome, he seeks the "truth" by turning to the congregated masses. Truth was not objective but only what would serve Roman order and his personal interests.

Nineteenth Century Russian painter Nikolai Ge's painting *Quod Est Veritas (What is Truth?)*, contrasts Jesus, a ragged vagabond, before stately Pilate, well polished in his finely-folded toga. Pilate poses the question Socratically, while already turning from Jesus to the waiting crowd. The light of Rome shines from behind Pilate but does not grasp Jesus, almost void of form, and unreachable to those who are not yet "of the truth," who cannot listen to his voice.

Jesus does not become man to conquer this world. If, in response to Pilate, Jesus and his "servants" vanquished his Jewish and Roman oppressors before ascending to heaven, we would be left with the Law of God, "Be ye therefore perfect, even as your father which is in heaven is perfect." And, though many religions or theories, including versions of Christianity, do see religion as continuous striving to emulate moral perfection, perfection is not attainable. We require atonement for our sins, so that we may be freed from the condemnation of the Law.

The truth is that Christianity is necessarily linked with death. Christ bears witness to this truth, not through his achievements in this world, but through his death on the cross, so that by him and through him, we may be given life by the Spirit that raised him from the dead.

—Ron Flowers

September 4

…"I thirst." (John 19:28, ESV)

If there is a particularly enigmatic word among Jesus' last from the cross, this is it. "How can the Second Person of the Trinity thirst?" wonders theologian Stanley Hauerwas, answering that "surely this must be meant metaphorically. But if this is only a metaphor—something said for our benefit to insure that in spite of being the second person of the Trinity Jesus tries to identify with our lot—the cross is just a cruel joke" (71).

Going back to the first century, there has remained within Christianity a docetic tendency to turn the cross into an object lesson, a huge graphic parable that God uses to show us how bad we are, how much we're loved, how bad the Romans are, etc. But none of these attempts (which are alive and well up to this present day) have been able to do justice to what we see happening here.

This cry of Jesus helps emphasize an aspect of the cross that we wrestle with. That the cross is a punishment is clear, but that it is also the substitutionary death of the One who thirsts on our behalf, so we will have to thirst no more, is something we've often missed.

This is where a proper distinction between Law and Gospel becomes crucial, because even though we all thirst, the Law exposes the deadly, destructive futility of our wells. As Jesus told the Samaritan woman, "Everyone who drinks of this water will be thirsty again, but whoever drinks of the water that I will give him will never be thirsty again" (John 4). The Law exposes, convicts, and leads to the Gospel, the fount of living water.

In light of this universal thirst, we have simply this proclamation of the Gospel to offer, a sip of wine and a bit of bread to slake people's thirst and ward off hunger. This seems unfortunate because, certainly, we would love to offer more. Promises of health, wealth, and security are nicer to make, but "those and 13 dollars will get you a cup of coffee at Starbucks," as they say.

Like nomads in the desert, we have found an oasis of living water in the message of "God's one-way love to sinners," and trust that we will be among those referenced in the book of Revelation, of whom it is said:

> They shall hunger no more, neither thirst anymore; the sun shall not strike them, nor any scorching heat. For the Lamb in the midst of the throne will be their shepherd, and he will guide them to springs of living water, and God will wipe away every tear from their eyes (Rev 7:16-17).

—Jady Koch

September 5

"It is finished." (John 19:30, ESV)

In my church stand two crosses. One, the crucifix, shows Jesus in all of his tortured agony. The other stands gleaming white and empty, a potent symbol of the promise that in Jesus "death has lost its sting." And as much as we profess faith in the victory, it is telling that the crucifix stands over the pulpit and the empty cross over the Lord's Table; one signifies where we are, and the other signifies where we will be "when he comes again in glory." Until then, these words from the cross remain our hope.

Living in the "sufferings of the present age" means living with the lot of wanting more. In this agony where Christ hung, he calls out, "Father, forgive them, for they know not what they do." John's Gospel puts it only slightly differently: "It is finished." This is what we have, the basis of our faith, that holds on, as David Ford says, during our *overwhelming*. "This overwhelming," writes Stanley Hauerwas, "[allows] us to live not because we have answers to all the world's troubles, but because God has given us a way to live without answers" (88).

But before we grow our beards out, throw up our hands and retreat into the mystery of 24/7 Eucharistic adoration, let us be clear about what we *can* say, because too often the "sufferings of this present age" force pastors and theologians—and I am as culpable as anyone—to unanswered, unfinished speculation about the cross that subverts Jesus' very cry.

What's worse, today's moral teachers, across the political and theological spectrum, have turned this end into a beginning. "See," it is argued, "Jesus did it all, now get going and do (or stop) x-y-z, because that can't really be all there is to it." This is a tragic irony: the very words signifying an actual *end* to something are parlayed into motivational grist for the mill of the suffering soul.

In direct and steadfast opposition to this, we never tire of insisting that "it is finished" means just that. Everything that ever needed to be done or ever *will* need to be done by us to be reconciled to God has been done. God is in control. He is redeeming the world. We cannot mess up His plan because, well, "it is finished." We are free to live as people in the "sufferings of this present age," living squarely in the shadow of the crucifix, "always being prepared to make a defense to anyone who asks a reason for the hope" (1 Peter 3:15). In this hope we wait, because although our end has not yet come, the only "it" that matters is already finished.

—*Jady Koch*

September 6

> *Now Thomas, one of the Twelve, called the Twin, was not with them when Jesus came. So the other disciples told him, "We have seen the Lord." But he said to them, "Unless I see in his hands the mark of the nails, and place my finger into the mark of the nails, and place my hand into his side, I will never believe." Eight days later, his disciples were inside again, and Thomas was with them. Although the doors were locked, Jesus came and stood among them and said, "Peace be with you." he said to Thomas, "Put your finger here, and see my hands; and put out your hand, and place it in my side. Do not disbelieve, but believe." Thomas answered him, "My Lord and my God!" (John 20:24-28, ESV)*

"Doubting Thomas" is an inaccurate title. Let's simply call a thing what a thing is. Disbelieving, distrusting, betraying Thomas. Thomas witnesses the amazing miracles Christ performed, including the raising of Lazarus from the dead; he has been journeying with him for years now. It is astonishing that, in spite of all the glorious acts and miracles, Thomas does not altogether apprehend Christ as his Savior (John 14:1-14). Thomas has no excuse. He is damnable—a skeptic who has spent all this time with the Son of God, witnessing everything, and still does not believe. If anyone is worthy of the lake of fire, Thomas is.

What if *you* do not believe? Thomas does not believe, and he receives no short shrift for it. But of course, the scary—and true—thing is that we can all relate to this kind of skepticism. Maybe he's upset. I know that I would be depressed and bitter just like Thomas. I would make outlandish if-then ultimatums, too, "If..., then...I will never believe."

Being God as he is, Jesus has a word for Thomas, and his verdict runs contrary to Thomas' disbelief. Instead of Thomas getting a scolding, Jesus carries the wounds in his hands. And not only does Jesus invite Thomas to see his wounds, the wounds that are holding all of Thomas' sin, but also he allows Thomas to place his fingers in them, to feel the wounds which bear his sin. In short, Christ shows Thomas what's been taken from him.

Christ wishes to be known to you as the forgiver of your sins, and even if you deny it, he's coming to you. He died for your sins and was raised for your justification (Rom 4:25). The one who reveals to you the holes in his hands has atoned for all your flaws, all your betrayals, all your mistakes. Though you may want to take responsibility and have ownership over your own sins, the truth is your "sin" no longer belongs to you (Gal 3:13).

—*Matthew McCormick*

September 7

> *[Christ] said to him the third time, "Simon, son of John, do you love me?" Peter was grieved because he said to him the third time, "Do you love me?" and he said to him, "Lord, you know everything; you know that I love you." Jesus said to him, "Feed my sheep." (John 21:17, ESV)*

A quick recap of Peter's "greatest hits" in the New Testament:

a) When Jesus tells him to walk on water, Peter is afraid and sinks.

b) Peter tries to persuade Jesus that he will not have to die, to which Jesus responds: "Get behind me, Satan! You are a stumbling block to me; you do not have in mind the things of God but the things of men."

c) He falls asleep in Gethsemane, three times, after being asked three times not to do so.

d) He denies Jesus three times, despite his protestations after being told in no uncertain terms that he was going to do so.

e) He draws his sword in Gethsemane and is rebuked for it.

f) He gets rebuked asking about John, the beloved disciple ("what is it to you?").

g) We are even told that, after the disciples first hear reports of the Resurrection, Peter loses the race to the empty tomb.

It would seem that nearly everything Peter does in the Gospels ends in a correction, a rebuke, or a red-cheeked failure. With one notable exception, of course: when asked by Jesus, "Who do you say that I am?", Peter acknowledges that Jesus is the Christ, the Son of God, and he is the first of the disciples to do so. Otherwise, though, one almost wonders whether Jesus' name for him, which means "rock," was an ironic gesture. Far from acting as a stable leader of the faith, when it was time for action, he could be relied upon to *fail*. Indeed, short of him rejecting the faith entirely, it is hard to imagine a *worse* Christian than Peter. And yet in this passage, the resurrected Christ gives Peter even more authority than he had before. Why?

In his early novel *The Cabala,* the great American writer Thornton Wilder gives us a clue: "All gods and heroes are by nature the enemies of Christianity... Only a broken will can enter the Kingdom of Heaven. Finally tired out with the cult of themselves they give in. They go over. They renounce themselves."

It is no coincidence that Peter is both the weakest and the one who recognizes who Jesus is. He can recognize the savior because he knows how much needs one. The archetypal Christian is not a person who looks like Jesus, but a person who looks like she needs Jesus. Many of us are full of shame deep down because of our private failures and our private fears. Like Peter, we question whether God would love us and care for us if He really knew what went on—and how we really feel—

and if He really knew how little we think about Him some days, and how often we choose our own desires over His commands.

The comfort that Peter finds on the beach is our comfort, too, that the only thing God requires of you and me is our deep-seeded and ongoing need. Like Peter, we are met in our shame and embarrassment and to our great surprise, given the opposite of what we deserve.

—*David Zahl*

September 8

"It is not for you to know the times or dates the Father has set by his own authority." (Acts 1:7, NIV)

The last words of any great person demand attention. Sometimes they are curious, as when U.S. president John Adams died saying, "Thomas Jefferson survives." Other times they are profound, as when Martin Luther took his last breath clutching a piece of paper that read, "We are beggars."

What message did Jesus feel deserved his final moments? Basically, that in the film of our lives, we are actors, not directors. But there is a director, who is God. This sentiment may sound self-evident, but it is not. In fact, it remains as controversial as it is comforting.

Woody Allen once observed, "Luck guides our lives much more than we care to admit. Coming out of an age of psychoanalysis, people tend not to feel that way. They tend to feel, 'I'm in control.' ...My observations in life have *not* been that. Luck plays a much greater role— a frightening role in our lives." Replace the word "luck" with "God," and you have something pretty similar to what Jesus is trying to communicate here.

We are not in control of our world—hurricanes and recessions and accidents tell us that much. But a far less popular conviction is that we are not in control of our own lives, that we do not have authority. I was speaking to a woman recently who had just fallen in love. She told me that at first she had strongly resisted the relationship, saying, "It just wasn't part of my plan. I figured I would be much more established in my career before something like this happened." She had come face to face with the futility of her plans. In her case, they almost derailed the happiness they were designed to achieve. Sound familiar?

We have been relieved of an authority we never had in the first place. The authority belongs to God, and He is not like the policemen and politicians and parents that we normally associate with the word. He has exercised His authority by laying it down, and He did so for you and me, that we might be relieved of our endless, vain attempts to seize it back. In this way, the last words of Jesus transform fear into freedom and give rest to those who are exhausted. Father actually does know best, and that bears repeating.

—*David Zahl*

September 9

> *When the day of Pentecost arrived, they were all together in one place. And suddenly there came from heaven a sound like a mighty rushing wind, and it filled the entire house where they were sitting. And divided tongues as of fire appeared to them and rested on each one of them. And they were all filled with the Holy Spirit and began to speak in other tongues as the Spirit gave them utterance...* (Acts 2:1-11, ESV)

The Day of Pentecost: the birthday of the Church. It's a dangerous day. It's dangerous because the central figure of Pentecost—the Holy Spirit—is not someone you can control. The author Annie Dillard is talking about the Holy Spirit when she says, "It is madness to wear velvet hats to church; we should all be wearing crash helmets. Ushers should issue life preservers and signal flares; they should lash us to our pews."

Pentecost is all about power, and the proof is in the pudding: Peter the Sandpile becomes Peter the Rock. The disciples heal people who are sick. Their lifestyles change—they start living in community, they share their possessions in common, they give to the poor with extravagance. Some of them are killed for their faith. Finally, they convert the Roman Empire.

What's the vital factor that took these weak, divided individuals and molded them into one strong body? The key to Pentecost power is, well, weakness. As St. Paul puts it, "I will all the more gladly boast of my weakness, in order that the power of Christ may rest upon me" (2 Cor 12:9).

An example of Pentecost power in weakness happened in Northern Ireland some years ago. You may remember it, because a photograph of the incident became quite famous. Two British undercover agents were driving a car near a funeral of the Irish Republican Army. They turned down a wrong street and drove too close to the funeral procession, and a gang of IRA men stopped them, dragged them from the car, stripped them, beat them, shot them, and left them to die.

Out of the door of the local church and into the street came a Roman Catholic priest. Here was a moment of utter weakness and failure on all sides. But this priest was a person who had faced and acknowledged his own weakness, and had heard the risen Jesus say to him, "Peace be with you." So out of the door and into the street he went. He walked up to one of those fallen undercover agents. He knelt beside him, crouched over him, pressed his lips to the lips of his political enemy, and tried to breathe life back into his body,

And in that moment on that little side street, one priest did what all those bombs and bullets could not do. He broke down the dividing wall of hostility—and Love had the last word.

Whenever the disciples are weak, Jesus says to them, "Peace be with you." So remember a weak moment in your life, either this past week or a long time ago. Picture Jesus standing right in front of you at that exact moment, looking you in the eye, and saying to you, "Peace be with you." This is the key to Pentecost power.

—Jim Munroe

September 10

When they heard this, they raised their voices together in prayer to God. "Sovereign Lord," they said, "you made the heaven and the earth and the sea, and everything in them. You spoke by the Holy Spirit through the mouth of your servant, our father David: "Why do the nations rage and the peoples plot in vain? The kings of the earth take their stand and the rulers gather together against the Lord and against his Anointed One.' Indeed Herod and Pontius Pilate met together with the Gentiles and the people of Israel in this city to conspire against your holy servant Jesus, whom you anointed. They did what your power and will had decided beforehand should happen. Now, Lord, consider their threats and enable your servants to speak your word with great boldness. Stretch out your hand to heal and perform miraculous signs and wonders through the name of your holy servant Jesus." (Acts 4:24-30, NIV)

I am not an optimistic person. Even under the best conditions, I am the one who fears the worst, who is always thinking: *This is just too good to last*, or, *what's the rest of the story?* If I won the lottery, I would be worried about the tax consequences. If the doctor told me that I was in fairly good shape for a man of my age, weight and personal habits, my "takeaway" would be "What did he miss?" or "That's what they all say before the big one hits."

The response I usually get for my admittedly sour outlook is that I need to "have more faith" and "trust God with the future," or worst of all, that passive-aggressive advice-in-the-interrogative, "Have you prayed about it?" Well, no, of course I haven't, and if I did it would just be a prayer of pure anxiety with a "Dear God" prefix and an "In Christ's name" conclusion!

So what can be made of this passage from Acts, this shockingly optimistic, confident prayer, in which God is seen as in control, even of those who had crucified Jesus, to do His loving and perfect will? Is this prayer an early version of "Let go and let God?" It just doesn't strike me that way. Because it seems like a genuinely happy prayer, not a prayer that is trying to be theologically correct, not a contrived, ginned up, "have faith" kind of show-prayer. I think we all want this prayer, this optimism and even joy, but where does this come from?

Not from me, that's certain. And not from God—that is, not from God in the abstract, not "God is in heaven so all is right with the world." God as a conceptual part of "the life equation" may have produced some successful dissertations, but not much palpable joy. And God as a coping mechanism has always been prone to mechanical failure when a cancer diagnosis surfaces.

What I love about this prayer is that it is prayed by people who are as afraid of life and the future as I am. So how can Peter and the puny church pray this way? It is, it seems to me, not the prayer of the faithful, but of the forgiven. The joy and confidence that spills from this prayer seems to come solely from the free gift of God's love and forgiveness in the crucified and risen Jesus. Peter has denied the Lord three times at the crucial test of his faithfulness. In return, he has been loved, forgiven, and given a promotion! Many of the others praying this prayer had surely cried "crucify him" not long before. Yet they, too, "cut to the heart" by the knowledge of who they really are and what God has done, receive not only forgiveness from God, but also the gift of His Holy Spirit. They have experienced a God who comforts his assassins.

That alone, I believe, can calm the anxious heart. It can give those—like me, who regret the past, fear the present and dread the future—a ground for hope, and even for some real, come-what-may joy. That, anyway, is my little prayer for you and me today.

—*Michael Cooper*

September 11

> *...But Peter said, "Ananias, why has Satan filled your heart to lie to the Holy Spirit and to keep back for yourself part of the proceeds of the land? While it remained unsold, did it not remain your own? And after it was sold, was it not at your disposal? Why is it that you have contrived this deed in your heart? You have not lied to men but to God..."* (Acts 5:1-11, ESV)

It's easy to think that the deaths of Ananias and Sapphira are brought on more by their selfishness than their dishonesty. The distinction may seem negligible, but it's important. Without it, it's easy to come away from this passage thinking that they are expected to give away everything, when instead they are punished for *claiming* to have given everything when they really haven't. But it still sounds very crude: why would such an action provoke so unmerciful a response? Is lying really their death sentence, or is there a deeper issue present in their situation?

I believe the root of Ananias and Sapphira's deception stems from not wanting to give anything at all. Deep down, they want to keep all the money from the property to themselves, but aware that others in the church have donated all their money to the church, the two want to save face. They are more concerned about the outward appearances of Christian love than being honest about where they stand.

Rather than being a fable about lying, though, this passage conveys that Ananias and Sapphira should not have felt obligated to give anything at all. "Sincerity" in this context would have meant being open with the church about their desire *not* to give. I think their lives would never have been in jeopardy had they kept every cent of the money for themselves instead of pretending to be generous.

So honesty, and the freedom which stems from it, seem to be the key issues here. Peter questions Ananias, "Didn't [the land] belong to you before it was sold? And after it was sold, wasn't the money at your disposal?" Peter makes it clear to Ananias that he had been under no obligation whatsoever to give all, part, or any of his money to anyone. Because Christ has come, because he has taken our debt and paid in full, our God-appeasing tithe is covered. Through Christ, all God's requirements for us have been met.

What's terrifying, then, is that Ananias and Sapphira don't drop dead for deceiving or withholding truth from God, but for believing what is untrue of God. They believe they must *give* something; that in order to be acceptable before God and church, something is required. Ananias and Sapphira hold as truth their requirements and pretenses, and reject the truth of Christ's freedom. Because they believe their lives are being tallied, God takes their lives, leaving them in the only thing Jesus needs for their resurrection: their death.

—*Jeremy Coleman*

September 12

> *"Repent, therefore, of this wickedness of yours, and pray to the Lord that, if possible, the intent of your heart may be forgiven you. For I see that you are in the gall of bitterness and in the bond of iniquity." And Simon answered, "Pray for me to the Lord, that nothing of what you have said may come upon me." (Acts 8:22-24, RSV)*

In this passage, Simon the magician has seen the power the apostles have been given and has come to belief. At the same time, he wants their power for himself. When Peter calls him out on this, he attributes Simon's desire to one cause in particular: his bitterness. Despite Simon's conversion, and the sincerity of his belief, he is still bitter at some level towards the apostles, perhaps for stealing his thunder. Coming to faith has not solved all of his problems. You could say that he is conflicted: both grateful and bitter at the same time.

What burdens, what "bonds," have you brought with you into the life of faith? Perhaps you still have a violent temper that sneaks out when you least expect it. Or you are a hopeless snob, just like before. Or are you still in the "gall of bitterness" toward someone—a parent, an ex-boyfriend, a sibling, an old friend who ditched you, a minister who let you down?

Even as Peter has pretty harsh words for Simon here, he also views the ex-magician with mercy: he calls Simon's iniquity a "bond" or (in other translations) a "chain." In other words, Peter sees that Simon is bitter, but also that he cannot help feeling this way. Acknowledging this, about ourselves and about others, is the beginning of mercy and a firm foundation for prayer.

—Simeon Zahl

September 13

> *Now there was in Joppa a disciple named Tabitha, which, translated, means Dorcas. She was full of good works and acts of charity. In those days she became ill and died, and when they had washed her, they laid her in an upper room. Since Lydda was near Joppa, the disciples, hearing that Peter was there, sent two men to him, urging him, "Please come to us without delay." So Peter rose and went with them. And when he arrived, they took him to the upper room. All the widows stood beside him weeping and showing tunics and other garments that Dorcas made while she was with them. But Peter put them all outside, and knelt down and prayed; and turning to the body he said, "Tabitha, arise." And she opened her eyes, and when she saw Peter she sat up. (Acts 9:36-43, ESV)*

Luke tells us that Tabitha, or Dorcas, is "full of good works and acts of charity," yet she falls ill and dies. A disciple, filled with the beneficence of God, gets sick and dies—how is that fair? Doesn't she deserve to be healed? Often this cry is thought in our hearts, but the truth is that we don't know what fair means. A small child can make this observation; having never known "fair," they have an innate sense that the bad and the painful, the consequences of this life, are often "undeserved" or "unfair." Tabitha does not deserve to die, we say—her hard work has earned life, hasn't it? Why, if God is good, would God let the good die?

Our side of the story is *quid-pro-quo*. According to our ethic, you get what you work for, what you put in is what you get out, and good people get good stuff. This may be our side of the story, but it's not the full story.

The Old Testament certainly doesn't paint this picture—humanity seems completely deserving of the death of entire peoples, destruction of temples, God forsakenness. Here humanity is, in fact, incapable of anything that warrants a "Well done!" from the Almighty.

Yet in spite of the incredible failures that we are, the New Testament tells of the light of redemption. Humankind doesn't deserve these things: we, prior to Christ, lie dead in all our good works and noble efforts, waiting for a miracle of salvation from death, just like Tabitha. Just like Tabitha, our good works can't and don't resurrect us—we need the mercy of saving grace.

In Christ, our works are not weighed, good or bad. In Christ, we are given life, for Christ's saving breath enters our souls and we rise out of death, completely upending our impressions of fairness (Eph 2:5).

—Lauren R.E. Larkin

September 14

> *"When we had all fallen to the ground, I heard a voice saying to me in the Hebrew language, 'Saul, Saul, why are you persecuting me? It hurts you to kick against the goads.'"*
> (Acts 26:14, NRSV)

In his song "Riding for the Feeling," Bill Callahan (of the band Smog) describes a character in front of a room of questioners. This character—perhaps Callahan himself—wonders if he's "said enough," but everyone else, despite having no more questions, asks him to stay, because they've got nowhere else to go. The speaker doesn't seem to want to go either:

> I kept hoping for one more question
> Or for someone to say,
> "Who do you think you are?"
> So I could tell them
> With intensity, the drop evaporates by law
> In conclusion, leaving is easy
> When you've got some place you need to be
> I'm giving up this gig for another season

Sometimes when we must go—whether it's skipping town or breaking up or quitting work—the "letting go" is the hardest thing to do. Knowing we must do so, we still tend to wait around for one more question or acknowledgment or paycheck before we ride off, and we find ourselves in the territory of "kicking against the goads."

This seems to be the way Paul explains his conversion on the road to Damascus. Usually we just read that Paul was riding, gets blinded out of nowhere, and his commanding influence as persecutor is retrofitted for the stadium preaching circuit. Here, as he explains it to Agrippa, it seems more like Jesus comes to him to compassionately point out, "Paul, you've been feeling this way a while now. This is stupid. It's hurting you not to yield!" Jesus says what Paul has not been willing to see or admit to himself, namely, that he *wants* to "give up this gig for another season."

Can we surrender like this, though? Could the *Apostle Paul* do this? Does *Jesus* think we can do this? Just "die?" Just "let go?" It's like trying to grace oneself into a cold swimming pool; there's no real way to do it.

I keep having this dream where Jesus is asking me to jump out of an airplane in faith. (I'm terrified of heights.) I'm holding this steel bar with my jumpsuit on, plane hatch now spilling wild space air into the cabin, and all I have to do, at 24,000 feet or whatever, is *let go*. Just *let go*. I will fly and fall into the wild air of God's mercy and therein find new, free, strangely secure life.

It doesn't matter that Jesus is my parachuting captain—the thought is crazy. I will not let go. The only way I'm coming off that plane, in the air, is if my sweaty palms lose their hold—or if Jesus "kills" me, actually jerks me from my death grip, to fall into the unknown. This is no low estimation—this is what must happen.

Thankfully, this is what *does* happen. Though we are not able to "give up the gig," to say goodbye to old selves, to let go of old habits, God's gracious light violently dismounts us. As Paul is thrown from his horse, so, too, does God kill us, to resurrect a "new season" in dead bones.

What about you? Where are these "dead bones" in your life? Where in life are you "kicking against the goads," and how are you kicking them? Where do you find yourself incapable of saying goodbye, incapable of yielding? Our only hope for these places is demonstrated in Paul's testimony, where the Lord meets us on the road to glory and graciously throws us to the ground.

—*Ethan Richardson*

September 15

When neither sun nor stars appeared for many days, and no small tempest lay on us, all hope of our being saved was at last abandoned... The bow stuck and remained immovable, and the stern was being broken up by the surf. The soldiers' plan was to kill the prisoners, lest any should swim away and escape. The centurion... ordered those who could swim to throw themselves overboard first and make for the land, and the rest on planks or on pieces of the ship. (Acts 27:20, 40-44, ESV)

This passage from Acts finds the apostles Paul and Luke (the author of the passage) on a boat in the middle of a terrifying storm. The wind is relentless. They are at the mercy of the elements. Verse 15 graphically describes their predicament: "when the ship was caught and could not face the wind, we gave way to it and were driven." They recognize their impotence and yield.

Trying to save themselves, they start taking well-intentioned steps to control the situation. This is a normal human response. First, the crew girds the ship by tying ropes around the hull. This doesn't work. So the next day, they throw cargo overboard. This also fails, so they throw the tackle overboard. Rational steps, right? But in the end, they have made no progress.

Will God now step in and rescue them? No: verse 20 reads, "And when neither sun nor stars appeared for many a day, and no small tempest lay on us, all hope of our being saved was at last abandoned." These are shocking words, especially coming from Saint Luke, the writer of two books of the Bible, in the company of Saint Paul, the greatest missionary of all time. And yet he says it: they abandoned all hope of being saved.

When we face storms in our life—internal and external—we usually try to control them, like Luke and his shipmates. But our attempts usually fail. We try to make the right person love us; we try to beat an addiction through willpower; we try to change a spouse's behavior; we try to perfectly develop a career; we try to attract a wayward child home through cajoling, pleading, or yelling. But our efforts fail. Despite all Luke and Paul's efforts, they are shipwrecked. In fact, the surf totally destroys the boat. Paul and his companions are washed on shore, clinging to broken pieces of the ship.

This kind of shipwreck story is a paradigm for the Christian life. For all of us, storms will come and all hope will be lost. Of all people, Christians should remember that death must come before resurrection. The problem is that many of us are working really, really hard to keep the ship together. We've strapped ropes around the ships of our lives in a desperate attempt to keep them afloat. We tell ourselves that things are not that bad, our spouse will change, our job will change, *we* will change.

Such self-deception is exhausting. This passage tells us that sometimes the ship must break apart. There must be a moment when we realize our marriage has failed, our child has cut herself off from the family, our career is at a dead-end. This admission is honesty with ourselves and with God. In other words, repentance—because when we realize how bad it is, we call out for help. And in doing so, we trust God. This is the place where, in religious terms, we are saved.

God, in His mercy, may let the whole ship, everything around you, break apart. And you may be washed on shore with only the clothes on your back, metaphorically speaking. But God is at work, and you may be surprised where you wash ashore. As Jesus said, "Truly, truly, I say to you, unless a grain of wheat falls into the earth and dies, it remains alone; but if it dies, it bears much fruit." (John 12:24)

—Aaron Zimmerman

September 16

> *...From morning till evening he expounded to them, testifying to the kingdom of God... He lived there two whole years... proclaiming the kingdom of God and teaching about the Lord Jesus Christ with all boldness and without hindrance. (Acts 28:23-31, ESV)*

This passage finds the Apostle Paul at the end of his life, under house arrest in Rome. In verse 28, Luke tells us that Paul was "testifying to the kingdom of God." In verse 31, we read that Paul was "preaching the kingdom of God." So: testifying to and preaching the kingdom. This is how Paul ended his life. So we would do well to make sure we understand what this kingdom is.

Google-searching "kingdom of God" yields over ten million hits. It's also one of those Christian buzzwords you hear if you move in evangelical circles. There's talk of "kingdom professionals," "kingdom builders," and living by "kingdom principles." Christian organizations have mission statements that speak of "establishing God's kingdom." New churches talk about the *way* of the kingdom, with a heavy emphasis on actions and habits. Common to all this talk of the kingdom of God is the idea that the kingdom is primarily about what Christians do. We make the kingdom happen.

If you look at how Luke describes Paul's actions vis-à-vis "the kingdom," Paul simply testified and preached. That is, he was a witness to the kingdom as something already here—that's what a testimony is. And second, the kingdom was a message to proclaim. Paul announced the kingdom. Not much building or establishing here. Just talking about something that God has already done.

This flows directly from Jesus' talk about the kingdom of God. Take a look at Mark 4:26-27: "The kingdom of God is as if a man should scatter seed upon the ground, and should sleep and rise night and day, and the seed should sprout and grow, he knows not how." God is the actor behind the kingdom. He establishes it; He makes it grow. The farmer—that is, us—doesn't even know how it happens. Also note Jesus' words in Luke 10:9: "The kingdom of God has come near to you." It comes near to us. The movement is from God to us. We don't bring it down.

Finally, two other statements from Jesus about the kingdom are worth a look. In Mark 10:14-15, Jesus famously says, "Let the children come to me, do not hinder them; for to such belongs the kingdom of God. Truly, I say to you, whoever does not receive the kingdom of God like a child shall not enter it." And in Matthew 21:31 we hear Jesus say, "Truly, I say to you, the tax collectors and the harlots go into the kingdom of God before you." What both these passages convey is that the kingdom of God is something powerless, sinful people enter; it is not some kind of world system that triumphant Christians build.

The bottom line is that the kingdom is something *God does*, and brings about apart from human effort. Secondly, it is for the powerless, the sinners. Thus Paul rightfully understood that the kingdom is something you announce, you testify to, you preach, because it is something God has established. It is a place where sins are forgiven and the weak and sinful can come in. And once you're in, God continues to be the one to do the work in you. As Jesus says, the kingdom grows, but we don't even know how. It grows in you, but not because of your effort. It just happens.

—Aaron Zimmerman

September 17

(Indeed, when Gentiles, who do not have the law, do by nature things required by the law, they are a law for themselves, even though they do not have the law, since they show that the requirements of the law are written on their hearts, their consciences also bearing witness, and their thoughts now accusing, now even defending them.) (Romans 2:14-15, NIV)

I grew up watching Saturday morning cartoons, and one of my favorites was G.I. Joe. After a 30-minute adventure of search and rescue, the end would inevitably bring a new moral to learn. The show always ended by saying, "Now you know, and *knowing* is half the battle." The first chapter of Romans quite differently defines immorality as un-dependent on knowledge. Merely *knowing* right and wrong does not work to persuade or dissuade.

Oftentimes I think back on past mistakes and think of how foolish I was. In retrospect I realize how myopic my decision-making was, or how blinded I was by ambition or selfishness. I often think, "If only I had *known* then what I know now," then things would be different. If I'm truly honest, I know that knowing more doesn't guarantee that I would act differently. In fact, most times I know the possible consequences of my actions, and still I make the same mistakes.

For instance, I know that eating large amounts of ice cream with brownies is going to make me fat. I know that the food pyramid recommends that I eat some 6-8 fruits and vegetables each day. Yet on days when I am particularly stressed, just try to stop me from heading to the freezer and the microwave. I don't think I'm alone here; it is not that the troubled teenager, the deceitful banker, the alcoholic, the rude neighbors do not *know* the right thing to do; the right thing to do is beyond their reach. Or as a friend of mine put it, "It's not that I don't know what to do, it's that I can't do it."

In the same way, St. Paul understands that sins do not occur from a lack of knowledge, but because of a sinful heart. I sin because I am a sinner and can't help myself. I am powerless, against both my rational and subconscious impulses, to look out for myself.

More knowledge, understanding, or wisdom will not be our knight in shining armor. It is not enough to know the difference between right and wrong. What we need is for the Savior to rescue us from ourselves.

—Todd Brewer

September 18

Do we then overthrow the law by this faith? By no means!
On the contrary, we uphold the law. (Romans 3:31, ESV)

Time and time again, Christian people stumble on this question of the Law.

The question I get, time and time (and time) again, is this one: How will I know to do right when grace and forgiveness are everything? Don't we need a few tips, or pointers, say, from the Bible? Won't people take advantage of grace?

That is the question you always get when you present the Gospel. You don't get it from "non-believers," who respond to the Gospel with incredible relief and assurance.

You get the question from "Christians," believers for some time, who seem fearful of it, or maybe even jealous, I don't know. "Christians" just can't seem to understand that grace always ends up "upholding the Law" in practice. You don't have to worry. The Holy Spirit automatically creates works of loving from prior love.

Even so, I don't think the ministers of grace are ever going to "persuade" the Christian community that grace applies to Christians. I have failed utterly at this for well over 30 years. Outsiders love the message; insiders resist it, even hate it. Probably we just have to "let them go"—the "Christians" I mean. Something about the way the religious (sub-)culture works just makes it impossible to hear the grace word there. I'll try to keep on going, and "I won't... back... down" (Tom Petty and the Heartbreakers). But have no illusions: You'll never persuade the "religious."

Better maybe just open up a hospital for these people when they crash (they always crash). Take 'em in then, offer the Old, Old Story, and maybe then, after crashing and burning, they'll hear it with new ears.

—Paul Zahl

September 19

And to the one who does not work but believes in him who justifies the ungodly, his faith is counted as righteousness. (Romans 4:4-5, ESV)

I once had a kind friend in college who, like most us, was profoundly confused and deeply conflicted due to some difficulties in his past. The outward bearing of this resulted in, shall we say, an achievement gap of sorts—so much so, in fact, that his grades in school were consistently catastrophic, which really only exacerbated his issues.

On one particular occasion, after a spring semester, he and his father were together when the mailman came by and happened to deliver my friend's grades. As expected, my friend's father opened the envelope, scanned the grades, looked at my friend, said, "Well, that's pitiful," and walked off in disgust. As he told me, I was reminded of Hank Williams' famous "Men with Broken Hearts," which goes, "Have you ever watched with helpless hands while the heart inside you dies?" My friend could help what was happening inside no more than he could help his father's reaction.

Did he *deserve* the rebuke? I suppose his father's reaction was just. He hadn't done enough work, he hadn't gotten the grades, therefore he hadn't gotten the praise that comes from *achieving* the grades. And his father's expectations for achievement were not unfair or cruel in itself. I happen to know his father loved him, and for the most part, parents generally want their children to succeed and be happy.

And yet his father failed to see what was *really* going on. That's nothing new—any parent or boss or civic entity denies the deeper realities of bondage and deep hurt. Albeit unwittingly, this denial can sound an awful lot like cruelty to the "Men with Broken Hearts." The higher-up's rebuke may be intended in loving interest; it still sounds like cruelty.

The message of Christianity is Romans 4:5, the good news of "justification by grace alone, through faith alone." It is exactly the inverse to the cruel, manipulative language of achievement. When my friend's paralysis took him to a dark cave, he helplessly watched his own heart inside him die. Feeling alone and doomed, he found company in Jesus Christ and his cross, who made his home in that self-same cave, with the dysfunctional, paralyzed, and hurt. When the world walks out on us, muttering "Pitiful," our Lord turns to us and says, "Surely I am with you, even to the end of days."

—David Browder

September 20

...delivered up for our trespasses and raised for our justification. (Romans 4:25, ESV)

In 1763, a man named William Cowper was invited to assume "Clerkship of Journals" in the English House of Lords. Consumed by anxiety and agony over the impending examination of his credentials, he had a complete breakdown that led to three suicide attempts. Shortly after his third attempted suicide, Cowper, an accomplished writer, wrote a hymn entitled "Praise for the Fountain Opened." The words are a vivid, graphic and bold expression of what is known theologically as the atonement:

> There is a fountain filled with blood drawn from
> Emmanuel's veins;
> And sinners plunged beneath that flood lose all their guilty
> stains.
> Lose all their guilty stains, lose all their guilty stains;
> And sinners plunged beneath that flood lose all their guilty
> stains.

His continuing recovery led him to Olney, the parish of noted former slave trader and author of "Amazing Grace," John Newton. There, in 1779, Newton asked Cowper to contribute to a hymnal called the Olney Hymns.

The power of Cowper's hymnody lies in its vivid, sharp, and often brutally human imagery. Without such concrete language, when we are led to abstract ruminations on the concept of God, we are in danger of further detaching our faith from everyday life. God floats back up to heaven and inhabits the sometimes intangible realms of peace and tranquility. In Cowper's hymns, however, the reality of the cross—in the wood and the blood—destroys abstract pretension and proclaims the message of God to the world: Jesus was "delivered up for our trespasses and raised for our justification."

Only from the cross can the everyday ramifications of the Gospel—the daily cycle of forgiving, receiving forgiveness, and reconciliation—be understood. This is what Cowper knew, and it is why the beauty of his hymns continue to haunt, convict and encourage:

The dying thief rejoiced to see that fountain in his day;
And there have I, though vile as he, washed all my sins
away.
Washed all my sins away, washed all my sins away;
And there have I, though vile as he, washed all my sins
away

—Jady Koch

September 21

*...More than that, we rejoice in our sufferings, knowing
that suffering produces hope, and hope does not disappoint
us, because God's love has been poured into our hearts
through the Holy Spirit which has been given to us.
(Romans 5:1-5, ESV)*

In his autobiography, *Days of Grace*, tennis champion Arthur Ashe
wrote: "I have always been a firm believer in the therapeutic value of
adversity. Of all people, athletes must reach an accommodation with
losing, and learn to make the best of it." Ashe died of AIDS received
through an injection given by a tainted needle. He wrote his story
knowing that he was leaving behind fame, fortune, and a lovely family.

For every Olympic athlete we watch as they receive their gold
medal, there are thousands of others who almost made it, but didn't. I
was present when a friend lost his chance of going to the 1964 Tokyo
Olympics by a hair. His non-Christian father was mortified at his failure,
but my friend grew through it into a strong servant of Christ.

Compare that with the sign on the walls of the Princeton
University boathouse: "Show me a good loser, and I'll show you a loser."
The secular mind dismisses the "therapeutic value of adversity" as
weakness.

But Paul invites us in Romans 5:1-5 to "stand" in a different place,
the place of "grace." In this place, we discover a past in which we are at
peace with God, a present in which we have full access to His mercy, and
a future hope in sharing in His glory. But these gifts were won at the
cost of suffering, namely Christ's, and remain ours as we rethink the role
of suffering in God's world.

Looking at verses three and four, suffering has such a therapeutic
role in our lives that, rightly received, it enables us to endure the present

while looking in hope to the future. This, says Paul, is the root of *character*—something that is always hammered out on the anvil of pain.

Fortunately, we do not have to gut this out as if it were up to us to manufacture character with steely determination. There is a waterfall of love cascading down on our heads, which turns character-building into spontaneous excitement, and suffering into joy.

—Peter Moore

September 22

> *What shall we say, then? Shall we go on sinning so that grace may increase? By no means! We died in sin; how can we live in it any longer? Or don't you know that all of us who were baptized into Christ Jesus were baptized into his death? We were therefore buried with him through baptism into death in order that, just as Christ was raised from the dead through the glory of the Father, we too may live a new life. (Romans 6:1-4, NIV)*

If you've felt stuck lately, if you've exhausted all attempts to prove yourself, or fallen short of some prescribed expectation, these words in St. Paul's epistle are truly hopeful ones. He is saying here that we are not justified by our works or abilities to follow the expectations, but instead true freedom comes by our faith in the redeeming blood of Christ.

In response to this pardon, many pose the question to themselves, "Now that I have been forgiven in full, will I keep on sinning? Will I be forgiven again?" The answer, of course, is yes, we are *still* unable to keep ourselves from sinning, but Paul isn't really asking this question—he is asking, "*shall* we go on sinning?" to which his answer is, "By no means!" The distinction is that while God's Law still remains and the sins go along with it, we are no longer *beholden* to it because we have been set free by the love of God. He has taken our sins and given us salvation.

Now then, are we like the young undergraduate, freshly separated from the control of nagging parents, thus confusing the absence of authority with "freedom" to partake in sin and promiscuity? "By no means!" While the Gospel does free us from the reign of sin and the anxiety brought by the Law, it does so with love and atonement rather than simply removing itself from the picture entirely. After all, the college freshman inside us all, released from the bondage of our parent's dos and don'ts, isn't really acting out of freedom, but instead out of rebellion against a power that still plagues us. We can still hear their voice from miles away.

It is only once we return home to find a father and a mother who look at us as we are and say, "Son, I am pleased with you" that we experience the Gospel. It is only in this place that we may bury the guns and stop rebelling. No longer are we haunted by the voice of displeasure, but rather we are carried by the tune of great pleasure and acceptance.

What is so freeing and rejuvenating about the Gospel and the grace of God is not the absence of God's authority, but the presence of God's love. Now that we are in Christ, we are free from the reign of sin and now bound under the love and grace of God. The Gospel shows us that love is the only thing truly capable of generating love.

—Josh Bascom

September 23

If we have been united with him like this in his death, we will certainly also be united with him in his resurrection. (Romans 6:5, NIV)

I try to imagine how to approach a verse like this, one that stands with such vast profundity in such simple brevity. What words could be placed beneath these, which seem to carry such a weight as to move whole epochs? And yet it is wonderfully and maddeningly simple: the verse very simply dispels the ultimate fear that binds our timid hearts, that keeps someone from believing and trusting that for him or for her—for you and for me—there is the possibility of forgiveness.

This is a word for those for whom hell on earth is not hard to imagine, where it seems all too close to reality. It is a word for those who are so gripped with remorse from something in the past that living in its wake is like death to them. It is a word for one whose "gig is up," who has received a quick and public exposure. It is a word for the one suffering a silent, slow death—a twisting and lonely life. It is a word for anyone who can resonate with the image that we each are the "walking dead."

The wounds we carry (given or self-inflicted) are never to be minimized; it is no accident that our risen Lord carried with him the scars of his crucifixion. But as Tim Keller once observed, deeply wounded people are often deeply selfish people: they cannot *not* think of themselves and their wounds.

Where are these wounds for you? What afflictions do you find yourself brooding on or pushing into conversations with others? With these words from Paul, we are given hope that someone lifts us from the self-absorption our wounds crave. This is the collision of God's grace into our wounds. Something besides me resurrects me.

Paul has no naïve understanding of people. He squares up to our bounden relationship to death, and still he asks, "Don't you know that you have died to sin; how can you live in it any longer? As you have died to it, are you going to assume the position of giving it power, vivifying it for your own pain and pleasure? No, you cannot—you have died to sin! As we have died to sin, we have shared with Christ in his baptism into death; if we have been united with him into his death, we will certainly also be united with him in his resurrection." United in *his* resurrection—this is something besides us restoring life to our wounded souls.

—Gil Kracke

September 24

> *So, my brothers, you also died to the law through the body of Christ, that you might belong to another, to him who was raised from the dead, in order that we might bear fruit to God. For when we were controlled by the sinful nature, the sinful passions aroused by the law were at work in our bodies, so that we bore fruit for death. But now, by dying to what once bound us, we have been released from the law so that we serve in the new way of the Spirit, and not in the old way of the written code. (Romans 7:4-6, NIV)*

In this passage, Paul is talking about what he's always talking about: God's Law, human sin, and human freedom from the penalty of the Law in Christ. He's explaining that through baptism we die to the contract that we were under with the Law, and we enter a new union of freedom with Christ.

But this freedom sometimes feels abstract in a church environment. Years ago in a Sunday school class, a woman said, "I have never felt free as a Christian." I believe she's not alone. This is where mainstream Christianity fails many of us: all too often the message being preached from pulpits is that trying to be good is good enough for God. This kind of sermon leaves us indebted to the Law, so that the only room left for grace is gap-filler theology: the idea that when we do occasionally stumble, God says, "that's O.K."

This is so completely contrary to what Paul is saying in Romans 7, but it doesn't change the fact that many people approach "God" and "religion" this way. This belief does fail eventually, though it doesn't tend to happen in church pews on Sundays—it's in the hospital lobby, or late on a sleepless night, or with that impending decision your boss has yet to make.

At these points, when the chips are down—when we really need someone, when we see we can't change things, when we feel guilty— then we find it hard to justify why we've gotten there. At that place and at that moment, our need overshadows however well-behaved we believe we've been in the eyes of God.

But this is also when freedom becomes real, when we see what grace truly means, because we realize that everything we could have tried to do would have come up short at this moment. At this point, when our preoccupation with our own earning and obedience is suppressed, suddenly nothing stands between us and God, and we finally have the freedom to simply say, "Lord, help me, a sinner!" Here the relationship is clear: He comes to us in our hour of need, and sits by our side, to let us know we belong to His love.

—Jeff Hual

September 25

I do not do what I want, but I do the very thing I hate.
(Romans 7:15, ESV)

You might know how it typically happens: someone becomes a Christian after hearing the Gospel. It's good news on a personal level, and they think about the changes they could make in their life, and suddenly they've never felt so gung-ho about anything, ever.

And then it wears off, usually after exactly three months. They find themselves slipping back into all the old ways of thinking and being. It's a letdown because they feel as though their change of heart had been genuine, but it's also a letdown because they feel that if it *had* been a genuine saving experience, it should have lasted.

By this time, they've begun to feel guilty, they've begun to wonder if the God that sent His Son down is pretty upset with His down-payment, because they're certainly not holding up their end of the arrangement. They might worry if they ever genuinely felt anything at all. Surely this feeling is only exacerbated on Sundays, where they come face-to-face with a room full of veteran churchgoers who are, from the looks of it, *definitely* better people.

Maybe this was you, maybe it still is. But take heart—it wasn't you who got it wrong.

Moralism—all the stressful talk to "Be like Moses" or "Be like David" or "Be like Jesus"—it isn't what Jesus died for, though it has sadly become the face of Christendom. There are far too many Christians offering the love of the Gospel as a conditional bait-and-switch, but there is nothing conditional about what Christ did for you on the cross.

We will always share Paul's experience in Romans 7 where our thoughts and behaviors do not match up with our new heart, but we will also share in the comfort that he finds in the unconditional love and mercy of God.

—Mike Burton

September 26

Wretched man that I am! Who will deliver me...? (Romans 7:24, ESV)

I've always been interested in the different ways people arrive at their interpretations of this passage, because I've discovered that I've been left with little choice in the matter when it came to my own.

Admittedly, there were times in my life when I read it with contempt, as if this were the description of the "non-committed" Christian. Surely, I thought, Christianity has to offer more hope for victory than this tormented soul is experiencing. Then, with greater frequency, I found myself crying out in desperation *with* the speaker, and as I began to see myself more and more aptly described by the anguish of the speaker in this passage, I began to question my initial commitment to Jesus or the reliability of the entire Christian message. I came to the point where this passage either described *the* Christian life, or I was not a Christian—there was no other option. Fortunately, I was not alone.

In the year 427, St. Augustine, referencing his earlier written book entitled *An Explanation of Certain Passages from the Epistle of the Apostle to the Romans*, completely changed his previous interpretation, he writes:

> In [that] book I said: "However, when he says, 'We know that the Law is spiritual; but I am carnal' adequately shows that the law can be fulfilled only by spiritual men, the kind that the grace of God transforms," I certainly did not want this applied personally to the one who was already spiritual, but to the man living "under the "Law" but not yet "under grace.""...I reflected upon this more deeply and I saw that his own words can also be understood about the Apostle himself...

Like Augustine—and many other Christians throughout history—the experience of my life as the same one described by this passage exposed the depth of my own need for the Gospel and forced me to re-evaluate all of my prior assumptions.

I could no longer view sin as a choice or action but rather as a more fundamental problem lying at the root of my life—even all the good things! I was forced to see the Law as that just and righteous standard of God that was attainable only through faith, and that by which I was still being judged to the extent that I lived "in the flesh." Finally, I saw that I had been living in a super-spiritualized reality where I believed that my "flesh" was that which was evil and I was, deep down, a purely good and well-intended person crying out for holiness. What I came to realize is that my "flesh" is the totality of who I am and what I do, and that totality did not need to be healed, but needed to be saved.

I used to view life as manageable with a little help from Jesus. I was not aware of the depth of God's love for sinners in view of what was accomplished on the cross. Now, the amazing depths of my enduring and constant need are proportionate to the heights of Gods never-ending mercy, and this is why, as counterintuitive as it may be, Romans 7 remains a bedrock source of comfort, security and joy.

—Jady Koch

September 27

For God has done what the law, weakened by the flesh, could not do. By sending his own Son in the likeness of sinful flesh and for sin, he condemned sin in the flesh...
(Romans 8:3, ESV)

It was early in the morning, and I was in my car. I came to a stop at a corner, and I wanted to turn right. A sign read, "No Right Turn on Red." I looked to the left, the right, forward and back—not a car in sight. I checked the sidewalks—not a person in sight.

I took my foot off the brake, shifted into first and started to ease up on the clutch when suddenly, out of the corner of my eye, I saw in the rear view mirror a car pull up behind me—with a big bubble light on the roof and a man in uniform behind the wheel. I put my foot back on the brake, waved, and waited for the light to turn green.

At that point, two things did *not* occur. First, I didn't tell myself, "Oh good! I was about to break the law, but now someone's keeping an eye on me, and I can't wait to obey all traffic signs from now on."

The other thing that did not happen was that the police officer did not get out of his car, come over to my car, get in on the passenger side, smile warmly and say, "Jim, my dear brother in Christ, I know you're frustrated, because of wanting to turn right on red. I want to be here for you. What don't we pray together?"

Which is to say, the law was able to keep my actions momentarily in check. But my heart and will remained untouched. I still wanted to turn right on red. The vision of obedience was in front of me—I could see the promised land of obeying traffic signs clearly. But the power to obey eluded me. I was stuck on the far side of that chasm between vision and reality.

There's an AA button that reads, "I didn't quit. I surrendered." That's the invitation—to give up trying to conform to a set of rules I can't keep, and instead just collapsing, surrendering, and yelling for help.

So where is the power to obey eluding you? Where do you find a chasm between where you'd like to be and where you are? More importantly, where are you being stirred to surrender? Grace says that there is always an answer.

—*Jim Munroe*

September 28

For all who are led by the Spirit of God are sons of God. For you did not receive the spirit of slavery to fall back into fear, but you have received the Spirit of adoption as sons, by whom we cry, "Abba! Father!" The Spirit himself bears witness with our spirit that we are children of God, and if children, then heirs—heirs of God and fellow heirs with Christ, provided we suffer with him in order that we may also be glorified with him. (Romans 8:14-17, ESV)

Think for a moment about the most famous orphan of all time. No, not Little Orphan Annie. I'm talking about a certain privileged young boy who lost his parents in a robbery gone wrong. A boy for whom orphanhood would come to define the rest of his life and inspire many great deeds (and films). I'm talking, of course, about Bruce Wayne. And while Batman may not be the most serious example, he certainly embodies the "slavery to fear" to which the Apostle Paul is referring in a startling way. Bereft of parents to protect and provide for him, the weight of the world falls on young Bruce's shoulders. There is no one to look out for him, and no justice other than that which he can make for himself; the only solution to his problems is himself. That he might respond to such a lonely, godless universe by turning himself into an all-powerful "übermensch" makes perfect sense. And in our own little ways, we all seek to control our environment and ourselves in Bat-like ways. In other words, we are all functioning orphans.

I once had the opportunity to watch a friend and his wife go through the process of adopting a child in the state of New York. When I asked him what the most profound thing about the experience was, he responded in the following way: "We got vetted and they put us on a list of couples waiting for a child. They made it very clear that there was no guarantee that anything was going to happen, no timeline to go by. Then, one day we woke up and got the call. We went to the hospital and signed some papers, and our lives were forever changed. In a single moment, we went from being husband and wife to being mother and father. But more importantly, for us, this baby became our son. All this happened before we had even met the baby! And it's irrevocable. There's no divorcing a child. Come what may, that boy was our son, with the privileges that entails."

One of the many beautiful things about adoption is that it is initiated by the parent(s). The child is a passive recipient and beneficiary. His security is assured by the efforts of a benevolent third party, independent of anything he might bring to the table, good or bad. And this is precisely what happened when Jesus Christ came into the world. He died so that we might become children of God—and he signed the papers in blood. He did not do so in order to be arbitrarily gruesome, but to underline the permanence of our adoption. Nothing you or I do or say can erase that signature. Like a little baby, our relationship to our heavenly Father is defined by our need and helplessness, and His love for us.

You are not the only possible solution to your problems. There is nothing to fear. Not even bats.

—David Zahl

September 29

For there is no difference between Jew and Gentile... the same Lord is Lord of all... (Romans 10:12, NIV)

In this passage, the Apostle Paul denies the legitimacy of a particular strain of categorization. He suggests that "there is no difference between Jew and Gentile." He wants to get rid of something that runs rampant in each and every society, and in so doing, achieves something incredibly rare. What does he want to get rid of, and what does he hope to accomplish?

"Jew and Gentile" are racial and religious distinctions. Paul assumes that his audience is used to being grouped into one of these two categories. Either they are born Jewish, or they are not, making them "Gentile." Today, the majority of the world's Christians are "Gentile," so it may not seem like a radical suggestion. But it was, and it still is. Paul is completely unconvinced by racial distinctions. They are, to him, unpersuasive and tertiary. They deal with things that are only skin deep. To his way of thinking, outside differences hold no merit. The human nature beneath the surface of every racial category is the same. All people, no matter where they are from, need God's love.

He elaborates upon this same idea in Galatians: "There is neither Jew nor Gentile, neither slave nor free, nor is there male and female, for you are all one in Christ Jesus." Paul is not content only to dismiss racial distinctions. He is also unconvinced about distinctions that have to do with prestige and occupation: "There is neither...slave nor free." Are you an investment banker? Are you unemployed? In God's eyes they are the same; both need God's love.

There is a saying on the East Coast of the United States: "The difference between the North and the South is that in the North, the first question a person asks you is, 'What do you do for a living?,'" while in the South, the first question asked is, 'Where are you from?'" You see, even after 2000 years, people are still very much hung up on this type of differentiation. What do you do? Where are you from? Who do you know? What do you have? How do you look? What is your gender?

In God's eyes, these characteristics do not hold merit. They do not interest God. This comes as good news to those who feel, in some sense, that they do not "make the grade." But this also comes as bad news to those of us who relish certain achievements and qualifications about ourselves. In each instance, and no matter where we fall on the spectrum of pedigree and accomplishment, we separate ourselves from our fellows. People are either "in" or they are "out." It is so unhelpful.

And so, in getting rid of these concerns, we begin to see a picture of life that unifies. There are no distinctions. But there is equality. We all stand before God in weakness and need. And if you don't mind the stigma that comes with being adopted, you will see that His love for you has given you foolproof standing, total justification, and an end to the games and putting stock in them. Thank God for this alternative, unifying perspective.

—*John Zahl*

September 30

...for the gifts and the calling of God are irrevocable.
(Romans 11:29, ESV)

As a kid, one of the rules of life was always *no take-backs*. This meant that once you gave something away, you could not ask for it back. "No take-backs" applied to every case when a classmate gave away a valuable commodity to another classmate, like a pencil or magic marker, a baseball card, a finely crafted paper football, or the rarely-gifted Snack Pack or Hostess Cupcake. If you gave one of these valuable commodities away, there was to be no asking for it back. If someone asked for it back the offended party would simply say, "No take-backs," and that was the end of it. If that wasn't the end of it, doom awaited you on the playground.

In this verse, Paul says that "the gifts and the calling of God are irrevocable." The gifts and the calling of God are not to be changed or recalled or undone. Basically, with God there are *no take-backs…* in the best kind of way.

Throughout the Old Testament we see again and again that God gives these gifts to Israel and does not take them back. We see again and again that God calls Israel His chosen people and never takes that back. Many of the prominent leaders of the Old Testament are sinners, like Jacob who deceives his own brother and father, Moses who has a short temper, Samson who chases prostitutes, David who commits murder and adultery, Hezekiah who caters to the heathen—it goes on and on. And yet, in spite of their disobedience, God does not disown them. In spite of their unfaithfulness, God remains faithful.

This, of course, is not just the case with Israel, but with you and me, too. This is good news, because our life experiences are replete with take-backs. When it comes to the gifts people give one another, there are often strings attached. And these take-backs can involve things much more important than baseball cards and cupcakes.

Sometimes a company will take back an offer made to an excited new employee and offer the job to someone else. Sometimes the gifts people give one another are yoked to unspoken expectations and run the risk of being taken back. Take-backs often occur in relationships. In his song *Lonesome Day*, Bruce Springsteen articulates the heartbreak this creates:

> Once I thought I knew
> Everything I needed to know about you
> Your sweet whisper, your tender touch
> But I didn't really know that much
> Joke's on me
> It's gonna be okay
> If I can just get through this lonesome day

On top of the take-backs the world dishes out, our own lives are also filled with "acts of foolishness" that cannot be taken back. These permanent experiences of bad news, though, are overshadowed by the permanently *good* news of the Gospel: that out of love for all of us Jesus Christ gave his life for us on the cross, an act the Greeks of his day considered utter foolishness. But as Paul wrote to the Corinthians:

"God's foolishness is wiser than human wisdom" (1 Cor 1:22-25). This wisdom, the stubborn forgiveness of God in a world of take-backs, will never be shaken. No strings attached.

—Dave Johnson

October 1

For God has consigned all to disobedience, that he may have mercy on all. (Romans 11:32, ESV)

A plausible first reaction to this verse is certainly "Not fair!" It always has been and always will be offensive to say that we are innately wired in opposition to self-control. It also seems a part of our wiring to shake fists at God, feeling entitled to a free will we just know we've always had.

In saying this, St. Paul isn't changing the rules of the game in some way, but describing life as it already is. We might feel duped or lied to, but the truth is that we never have the autonomy we think we have.

If you think about it, our lives seem inherently characterized by the rub between what we know we should do and what we actually do. Knowing I shouldn't play with my dad's lighter under his bed, and then doing it anyway, and watching the bed go up in flames. Knowing I shouldn't let my sisters take the fall for said fire, and then doing it anyway. Knowing I shouldn't lie to the police officer in front of my parents about the broken window at the school, and then doing it anyway. The examples go on and on.

If life is about bringing together the "is" with the "ought," we need some serious help. It only gets heavier if you consider the Sermon on the Mount (Matt 5). What about the thoughts you've thought, even about the people you love? What about the things you've said you would do that you didn't do? What does your search history say about you? What about all of the people you haven't really liked throughout the years?

St. Paul exposes our desperate need once again, and thankfully provides the answer. God's plan all along has been to take from us this faith in ourselves, so that, in our daily disobedience, we find His mercy anew.

—Sean Norris

October 2

Rejoice with those who rejoice, mourn with those who mourn. (Romans 12:15, NIV)

It's almost everything you need to know about effective ministry, and, more importantly, about the way that faith typically informs the bulk of human relationships, all in a single verse. *"Rejoice with those who rejoice; mourn with those who mourn."* Sounds easy enough.

The only problem is that we almost always get it wrong. We (1) mourn with those who are wanting to rejoice, and (2) rejoice with those who are in the midst of mourning. For example: "That's great that you got a new job that you're excited about... *But does it have benefits?*" Or: "Don't feel bad about the break-up; there are plenty of other fish in the sea." The world abounds with such instances. It's the difference between "helping" and just listening.

The 1956 film *Friendly Persuasion* illustrates this point brilliantly. As the teenage son of a Quaker family decides to take up arms for the Union during the Civil War, his mother is eager to dissuade him, citing the pacifism that is a defining characteristic of their denomination. But the boy will not listen. So mother turns to father and says: "You have to stop him from going!" Father replies: "I'm just his father; I'm not his conscience." The movie goes on to affirm both the father's decision with regard to their son, and also the mother's personal adherence to a nonviolent expression of faith.

But usually, like the mom in *Friendly Persuasion*, we don't really think that God can work without our getting involved (as a third party) in a conversation meant for two. After all, who likes to be interrupted? The same thing applies to the dialectic that exists between God and the people that concern us, but with one noteworthy difference: God actually won't let you interrupt the thing He's doing in the life of your friend. Try as you might. Go ahead, just try to change someone's mind by taking issue with their train of thought. Surely we've all experienced the exasperating futility of trying to change people.

And yet God can and does exactly that with great regularity.

—*John Zahl*

October 3

Owe no one anything, except to love each other, for the one who loves another has fulfilled the law. For the commandments, "You shall not commit adultery, You shall not murder, You shall not steal, You shall not covet," and any other commandment, are summed up in this word: "You shall love your neighbor as yourself." Love does no wrong to a neighbor; therefore love is the fulfilling of the law. (Romans 13:8-10, ESV)

My wife and I just had a little boy, and it has been quite a joy to ponder all the mud puddles, puppy dogs, ball games, and baited fish hooks. It has also been an opportunity to re-acquaint myself with the documentary and book *Raising Cain: Protecting the Emotional Life of Boys*. It is plain to see, in the book's diagnosis of children, the bondage to self-assertion rather than a will that acts freely through objective choice:

> When school is not a good fit for a boy, when his normal expressions of energy and action routinely meet with negative responses from teachers and classmates, he stews in feelings of failure—feelings of sadness, shame, and anger, which can be very hard to detect beneath that brash exterior. Unable to "talk out" the emotional pressure, boys typically act out through verbal or physical aggression that walls them off emotionally from others, straining or severing emotional connections to the people and circumstances they find painful.

I usually describe it to my class as the difference between a brain hemorrhage and a nosebleed. If there is a brain hemorrhage (internal) and its symptom is a nosebleed (plainly visible), it is always our first instinct to treat the symptom without regard to that which we cannot see. So we stuff Q-Tips up our noses and call it a day. But it is a symptom! Its status as outward manifestation is totally irrelevant compared to the brain hemorrhage that exists away from plain view!

It is the same way with the Law. Christianity has engaged itself (to its detriment) primarily in the realm of ethics. Good deeds. Like the frustrated boy mentioned above, behavior is emphasized and regulated with almost total ignorance of what is actually driving it.

The Law is love, and love is a disposition through which its manifestations arise. This is the kind of love that empties itself in love for God and neighbor. It is not a kind of love that we can generate; it is the sort of love with which He loves us. The interesting thing is that the love with which we are loved by God—one-way love—is what begins to heal the internal condition. Being loved, we actually begin to love through a touched disposition. In this love, the internal and the external are fully addressed in powerful ways.

—*David Browder*

October 4

Accept one another, then, just as Christ accepted you, in order to bring praise to God. (Romans 15:7, NIV)

If we are to "accept one another" in the way that "Christ accepted" us, we should consider how it is exactly, that God loves us.

Christianity brings with it the great insight that real love is always built upon a foundation of forgiveness and not merit. This is why, in the Episcopal liturgy, we affirm that God accepts us, "not weighing our merits, but pardoning our offenses." God's love is forgiving love, not a reward for good performance; it's truly unconditional.

In 1979 Jimmy Senyah released a little known disco song in France called "Weakness for Your Sweetness." He sings to a girl he is smitten with that he's "got a weakness for your sweetness" repeatedly. She flutters her eyelashes, and his heart melts. It is because she is so lovely, that he loves her. I wish I could ask Jimmy, "But what about when she's not being sweet?"

Having a weakness for sweetness is not the kind of love the Gospel teaches, because it conditional. It's there for you—as long as you stay sweet.

Instead, in Christ, we learn of the compassion God has for us when we are feeling low, and stuck, and not very pretty. In effect, God has a "*sweetness for your weakness*," the kind of comfort you can only hope for in a world obsessed with keeping things even-steven. Sweetness-for-weakness reflects the dynamic that Paul wants us to have for each other, because it's the kind of love God has for us. It's the kind of love that comes as a surprise (Luther called it "alien love"), and when we connect with it, the darndest thing happens: we actually become a little sweeter.

—*John Zahl*

October 5

Accept one another, then, just as Christ accepted you, in order to bring praise to God. (Romans 15:7, NIV)

The topic of Romans 14:1-15:13 is love and Christian liberty. Those who are "strong," Paul says, tend to look down upon the "weak," and their attitude is counterproductive to genuine Christian community. It's certainly no less tempting now to gauge others: in the work place or in church Bible studies, the everyday appraisals are everywhere. In the previous chapter, Paul reminds the church in Rome not to allow their familiarity with grace to become a "stumbling block" to other believers— I shudder to think that he is writing about me.

Acceptance is a word we value in principle, but we'd rather not act on it. Acceptance simply goes too far for our tastes: we talk about "tolerance" or "hospitality," but to think of acceptance in terms of Christ's self-emptying kind of acceptance is veritably repulsive. At every corner we are inclined to say we have earned our stripes, that we have merited the privileges we so quickly withhold from those around us. A pastor once told me we only invite presumption and promote despair when we impose metrics upon others. He is correct because the word "accept" in 15:7 seems as if God is asking me to accept others as I've been accepted, and that acceptance isn't one of my character traits.

The New Testament records numerous accounts when the early believers stumbled over this very same stone: Jew and Greek, male and female, slave and free. In fact this section is essentially Paul's call for the Jewish believers in Rome to accept their Gentile counterparts, not as interlopers, but as brothers and sisters. The curious thing is that there is something about accepting the other that brings praise to God, perhaps because it best summarizes the condescension of Christ—to accept the other in Christ is to tell another person that we are just as shocked that God would welcome us. To view ourselves as Gentiles—this is still our stumbling stone! But most importantly, who knew that his resurrection was itself the confirmation that we are accepted by the Father every bit as much as he is accepted?

—*Dylan Potter*

October 6

To the church of God in Corinth... together with all those everywhere who call on the name of our Lord Jesus Christ—their Lord and ours. (1 Corinthians 1:2, NIV)

When I lived in New York City, my roommate and I often found ourselves walking from one place to another at night. Coincidently, it seemed like every time we did this, a random streetlight would suddenly burn out. This happened so many times to my friend that we both began to think he possessed some special power over the street lamps of New York City.

Obviously this was a delusion, but it is not unlike the way many of us try to live our lives, as though we are in control of the events that happen to us, reading our agency and influence into situations when they aren't necessarily there. We live as though we are our own saviors, as though the only way that we can find help in the midst of difficulties is to try harder, dig deeper, and rely more upon our own efforts. It is a terrible, and exhausting way to move through the world, and rather than solving problems, the self-as-savior approach to life actually creates problems, encourages self-centeredness, and thereby brings about friction between us and our fellows.

Alternatively, Christians "call on the name of our Lord Jesus Christ"—we ask God to be our Savior, and we turn our lives and difficulties over to Him, that we might experience the relief that comes when we no longer have to be our own savior. The Christian faith is generated largely by the failed project that the world calls self-reliance. How nice it is that we can be honest about our own limitations, wherein we find the One who has none!

—John Zahl

October 7

[God] will sustain you to the end, guiltless in the day of our Lord Jesus Christ. God is faithful, by whom you were called into the fellowship of his Son, Jesus Christ our Lord. (1 Corinthians 1:8-9, ESV)

The opening to Paul's first letter to the Corinthians shows both Paul's deep personal involvement with the church in Corinth and his abiding concern for theological precision. In the first paragraph alone, Paul covers all the "-ologies:" ecclesiology, Christology, soteriology, eschatology.

What this means is that right off the bat, Paul is especially concerned with the Corinthians getting their theology right. This is interesting because, to an outside observer, the Corinthians' main problem is their behavior. The Corinthians, by all accounts, have gone off the rails. Later sections of the letter reveal that the church is riven by "pastor wars," sexual immorality (a man has shacked up with his stepmom), and spiritual arrogance. But Paul does not begin with their behavior. He begins with their theology.

In these first sentences, Paul reminds the Corinthians of foundational Christian truths. I'd like to point out two. The first centers around the word "guiltless" in verse 8, which means Christians are, by virtue of Christ's merits and death, guiltless before God. This is good news in a world where everyone is constantly keeping score. Have you seen Wes Anderson's *The Darjeeling Limited*? In the movie, three brothers are unable to reconcile their own bitterness toward each other, the root cause being a total lack of grace and forgiveness. Instead, there is control, manipulation, and deceit. Their operating principle is "an eye for an eye." You hurt me, I hurt you.

The vast majority of human relationships are like this. In Christianity, however, God declares us guiltless. That doesn't mean we stop being sinners. Rather, it means God chooses to see us through the lens of love. He regards us as guiltless. He removes the stain. And the grammar is important here: God is the subject, the one who acts. "You" (and that includes you!) is the object; God acts, we receive the action. God will "sustain you to the end" in this guiltless-ness. God is the one who makes you guiltless in His sight, sustains you in guiltlessness, and will eventually judge you guiltless at "the day of our Lord Jesus Christ," i.e., the end of the world. In short, God does the work.

The second thing to note in this passage is in verse 9 and centers on the word "fellowship." Paul sums up here the whole point of Christianity: God has called you into fellowship with Jesus. This, again, is another rebuke to those Christians who would say our religion is mostly about what we do. This is a big idea these days: orthopraxis (right doing), not orthodoxy (right believing). This is implied when Christians ask other Christians, "How's your walk with the Lord?" The focus is on what you are doing. But Paul here says that God has called us into fellowship. That is, a relationship with Jesus. A relationship is something based on love, not doing. Rules don't operate here.

—Aaron Zimmerman

October 8

For the word of the cross is folly to those who are perishing, but to us who are being saved it is the power of God. (1 Corinthians 1:18, ESV)

You've heard the spiel. It's practically a Christian summer camp mantra: you have a God-shaped hole in your life, but you've been trying to fill it with non-God-shaped stuff. And that's why you suffer or feel empty. So if you'll just fill the void with God-shaped stuff, you'll feel a whole lot better.

I've worried if anyone would stick around if they had an inkling of what new life looks like "after God takes over." Contrary to what the majority of the Bible says about human experience, the collective consciousness is somehow haunted with the idea that new living destines us for financial stability, deep relationships, or glowing health. But this picture is unreal; it does not account for certain future pain and difficulty, nor does it prepare us to see that God's chosen way is often through these roads of suffering.

The Corinthian people, much like us, are enamored of the mountaintop perception of theology and life—of moral superiority and health-wealth gospels. Paul, instead, fixes his attention to the crucifix, something he permits is foolishness to the world, but is also the wisdom of God.

It is true that in light of Christ's sacrifice, we are guaranteed his resurrection, but this does not mean we have inoculated ourselves to the cross. A clearer picture of the reality of Christian life lights upon the counterintuitive-ness of the power of death; God disarms us by operating through death and resurrection, not through our multistep successful living schemes. While we're busy twittering ourselves into a tizzy, God covertly communicates his power in the "weakness" of the cross.

—Matt Johnson

October 9

And I, when I came to you, brothers, did not come proclaiming to you the testimony of God with lofty speech or wisdom. For I decided to know nothing among you except Jesus Christ and him crucified. And I was with you in weakness and in fear and much trembling, and my speech and my message were not in plausible words of wisdom, but in demonstration of the Spirit and of power, that your faith might not rest in the wisdom of men but in the power of God. (1 Corinthians 2:1-5, ESV)

Paul does not preach a message of Jesus-Plus. Many in the church think that the message of the Gospel is simply not enough, or that the Gospel message is more than the forgiveness of sins. There is an attempt to add something to it to make is more appealing and plausible—advocacy groups, intentional living dinners, accountability partners. Paul is careful to make sure this simplicity is not compromised. It's not that Paul thinks these things aren't good; it's more that his prayer is that their "faith might not rest in the wisdom of men but in the power of God."

When I became a Christian in high school, I was excited about my newfound faith and looked for any and every opportunity to grow deeper. My question was always, "Now what?" I dove into every devotional—my favorite was this one with a bodybuilder benchpressing a cross, called *Cross Training Manual*. I signed up for mission trips. I participated in this Christian outdoorsman camp, culminating in a 13-mile run with a 40-pound pack. Though I may have learned some Bible, in the end I felt just like everyone else—restless, insecure about my relationship with God. I never felt that I was doing enough.

Over time I started skipping morning "quiet times," but when friends in my Bible study asked me how they were going, I would tell them they were going great. I had done all the scaling I could do, but found myself feeling Jesus less and less with every climb. "What was I doing wrong?" I asked myself.

I think I had begun to believe in this idea of Jesus-Plus, the lie that I was supposed to try as hard as I could, and *then* Jesus would pick up where I left off. I believed that if I did my part then he would do his. Basically I began to think the message of the Gospel was true only insofar as I helped bring it to bear.

The Gospel is sufficient of its own, and its work is never finished. Destroying the old self that seeks to supplant the Gospel with our own efforts is the work of the cross, not ours. Our only confidence is in this life-saving message, and nothing else. This is what Paul means to "know nothing... except Christ and him crucified."

—Andrew Pearson

October 10

I planted, Apollos watered, but God gave the growth. So neither he who plants nor he who waters is anything, but only God who gives the growth. (1 Corinthians 3:6-7, ESV)

Here again we see Paul addressing the bickering problems among the Corinthians. But rather than addressing the external behavior, Paul realizes the real problem is internal and theological.

Paul knows that there are two approaches to life for all human beings. The first approach is human-centered. Men and women in this camp see themselves as in control of their lives. This is like *The Office's* Dwight Schrute quoting Billy Zane's character in *Titanic*: "A man makes his own luck." In other words, human beings have the ability to judge people and events, map out their lives, and control their destiny. Students at elite colleges positively ooze with this kind of thinking. This is the human-centered view of life. In the spiritual realm, this view is called justification by works: making oneself acceptable to God through good behavior.

The second approach to life is God-centered. In this view, people are seen as they are, flawed and broken, prone to compulsive acting-out. Like the Harvard student who plays a video game for 10 hours straight, despite the fact that he has a paper due and is already on academic probation. Or like the suburban mother who regularly spends thousands of dollars on clothes she doesn't need. Or the executive who is a furtive alcoholic. Or the high-achieving honor-roll student who is anorexic and cuts herself. Or the Bible study leader who obsesses over pornography. Thus, unlike in the human-centered view, the clear thinking God-centered man or woman no longer places the burden of "getting better" on the ones who are ill. The God-centered view knows that people need a divine rescuer—like sick people need a doctor—and that this never stops being true, even for "serious" Christians.

The Corinthians are decidedly human-centered. As a result, as we see in this passage, they quarrel about their spiritual leaders. Since they believe their personal growth is their responsibility, they know they better pick the right guru! Paul attacks this view. He steers them back to reality: God is the one who calls, redeems, saves, and continues to heal. Paul says that he and his co-pastor Apollos are nothing. An amazing thing to say! Can you imagine TV preachers saying that? But Paul says conclusively: only God gives the growth.

Do you feel like you control your closeness to God? Is your "walk with Christ," your "spiritual journey," all up to you? Paul says only God gives the growth. See the illustration Paul uses to close the argument: God is the gardener, and you are simply a plant in the field. So don't do something, just sit there!

—*Aaron Zimmerman*

October 11

> *Let no one deceive himself. If anyone among you thinks that he is wise in this age, let him become a fool that he may become wise. For the wisdom of this world is folly with God. For it is written, 'He catches the wise in their craftiness," and again, "The Lord knows the thoughts of the wise, that they are futile." So let no one boast in men. For all things are yours, whether Paul or Apollos or Cephas or the world or life or death or the present or the future—all are yours, and you are Christ's, and Christ is God's. (1 Corinthians 3:18-23, ESV)*

The "wisdom of this world" tends to sound something like these maxims: "If you're not going forward, you're going backward." "You need to climb the ladder to get to the top." Staircase terminology is certainly overused in Christian lingo, and it's almost always tied up in sanctification. Believers climb toward Jesus, who sits at the top, and we'd better not disappoint. Striving upward, onward, ever higher to maturity and glorification.

Paul is saying this talk is futile. From God's perspective it's a waste of time, and as many of us know from experience, it is destructive. There are countless crashers and burners lining the bottom of staircase-climbing anthropology.

So when the "wisdom of this world" has destroyed us, what's a boy or girl to do?

Paul says you become a fool. The "foolishness of this world," applied to Christianity, means there is no forward or backward. You are just fine, standing right where you are—Jesus has made it so. The ladders and staircases have fallen because there's nowhere to climb to—Jesus came to you and died right where you stand, rather than forcing you to climb all the way to heaven.

So rest. He has given everything to you. He is yours and you are his. You can forget about yourself now because he did it all. It really is finished. What's "best" for you has already been given—there's simply nothing left to do now, except maybe think about what you *want* to do with all that free time...

—Curt Benham

October 12

And such were some of you. But you were washed, you were sanctified, you were justified in the name of the Lord Jesus Christ and by the Spirit of our God. (1 Corinthians 6:11, ESV)

Someone I respect very much once told me that he has been a Christian all his life, which means he has done all his sinning as a Christian. I had never thought of it that way, but I guess I am in the same category.

The Apostle Paul, who calls himself the "chief of sinners," is speaking to the members of this community who have been defrauding and suing each other and then going to TV court to sort it out. He reminds them that they used to be wild and wicked but then were forgiven; he exhorts them to live out that forgiveness in like-minded love for others, but things don't seem to turn out that way.

Surely it doesn't for most of us—within or without the church. Consider families: the bitterness harbored against an absent father, the coy manipulation of a six-year old to take what isn't hers, the sibling rivalries that turn every exchange into a reflection of favoritism. Call it harsh, but it seems in line with how Jesus elevates the Commandments to their highest pitch: "But I say to you...whoever says, 'You fool!' will be liable to the hell of fire" (Matt 5:22b). We exhibit in the most casual encounters our inability to forgive.

"To have lawsuits at all with one another is already a defeat for you. Why not rather suffer wrong? Why not rather be defrauded?" (6:7). We are a people shown mercy who cannot show mercy ourselves.

And yet Paul writes, "But you were washed, you were sanctified, you were justified in the name of the Lord Jesus Christ and by the Spirit of God." God sent Jesus to forgive the unforgiving, to cover in love a people who cannot help themselves. He sent Jesus not to condemn them but to wash them, to make them clean.

This is the message of the cross: that when the weight of our mistakes comes crashing upon us, as it has for the Corinthians, God's word to us is that He loves us still. Because of Christ, we are clean, even though, if we're honest, it certainly doesn't look it. That's God's "crazy love" (Van Morrison), that He covers you in guiltlessness to walk you through this time.

—Kate Norris

October 13

Now concerning food offered to idols: we know that "all of us possess knowledge." This "knowledge" puffs up, but love builds up. If anyone imagines that he knows something, he does not yet know as he ought to know. But if anyone loves God, he is known by God. (1 Corinthians 8:1-3, ESV)

In his 2011 book *Thinking Fast and Slow*, the Nobel Prize-winning social psychologist Daniel Kahneman wrote something very interesting: "There's a notion out there that self-awareness is a form of salvation, that if we know about our mental mistakes, we can avoid them...But it turns out self-knowledge is surprisingly useless; even when we know why we stumble, we still find a way to fall." Kahneman is even brave enough to admit that his decades of groundbreaking research haven't significantly improved his own mental performance. "My intuitive thinking is just as prone to overconfidence, extreme predictions, and poor planning as it was before I made a study of these issues," he writes. Wow. If an expert like Dr. Kahneman hasn't been able to effect change in himself through self-knowledge, what hope is there for laymen like you and me?

Perhaps it should come as no surprise that the Apostle Paul juxtaposes knowledge with love in this passage, subordinating the latter to the former. Knowledge, after all, is partial. There are so many things we can't know, and that we don't know, both when it comes to ourselves and to the world around us. And even those things which we think we know for certain can change. I was taught growing up that Pluto was a planet. But astronomers have since declared it to be nothing more than a large hunk of rock!

Nowhere is the "uselessness" of knowledge more apparent than in personal relationships. We convince ourselves that if (enter name here) just knew how alienating some of their habits are, they would change. It's our job to inform them when they're chewing with their mouth open, laughing too loudly, blindly defending the hurtful behavior of their family members, etc. Such nit-picking and nagging may never work—it may even have a destructive effect on the relationship—but that rarely stops us from trying.

The Gospel frees us from the illusion that if we only knew more, things would be better. This is because the Gospel is not about knowing; it's about *being known*. It is not about loving so much as being loved. The two are related, and in precisely the way Paul suggests. You can know someone and not love them, but you can't truly love someone without knowing them.

Imagine if I locked my dog and my wife in the trunk of my car. After an hour, only one of them is going to be glad to see me. The dog's love is unconditional, but it is ignorant. He doesn't know what I've done. My wife's love, on the other hand, is slightly more tenuous. She knows what I've done, and it can't help but affect her feelings for me, at least for the moment. Perhaps we think God is like our dog, that He loves us as long as He doesn't know what we've done. Or perhaps we think he is like our wife/husband, where He knows too much to feel good about us. The miracle of God's love is that it is both. He knows us *and* He loves us.

So where are you putting faith in knowledge today, rather than the One who knows? Rest assured, it has not caught Him off guard. He loves you still. And there is nothing partial about it.

—*David Zahl*

October 14

> *...The eye cannot say to the hand, "I have no need of you,"*
> *nor again the head to the feet, "I have no need of you." On*
> *the contrary, the parts of the body that seem to be weaker*
> *are indispensable, and on those parts of the body we think*
> *less honorable we bestow the greater honor, and our*
> *unpresentable parts are treated with greater modesty, which*
> *our more presentable parts do not require... (1 Corinthians*
> *12:12-31, ESV)*

I have spoken a number of times with exasperated people in the church who are confounded at how few others are doing the things that they value. "I volunteer down at the soup kitchen and no one else wants to come down with me from the church," or "I was the only person who noticed so-and-so, a newcomer this Sunday, and welcomed them." These are common statements, and I completely understand the sentiment. How many times I've started a sentence with "Why don't they..."

What we really want, though, is for our own values and actions to be validated by others. The problem with this thinking is obvious, but we often disguise it by couching our motivations in righteous terms. "I just think we should be intentional about..." or "We ought to be reaching out to..." They certainly seem like fair statements. Jesus commanded that we serve the poor, the orphans and widows—and so we *should* do things like serving in soup kitchens and loving our neighbors.

What we often fail to realize is that sometimes, the soup kitchen is located in a church and already staffed by Christians. While wagging fingers, it is easy for our view of "the church universal" to get very myopic. We forget that the church is much bigger than we can often see, and that it has many parts. If we are the left pinky, it is easy to forget that the eye does not help anyone by trying to be another left pinky like us.

Jesus has freed us from needing to decide what's indispensable. Instead, in freedom we serve as the Spirit moves us to serve; that is always going to be different than how another is moved, and that is okay.

Jesus says a lot of things about how we ought to live, but with his commands we must remember his description of the Kingdom: "So the last shall be first and the first last." (Matt 20:16). The things of God are confusing, and most often they oppose the way we think they "ought" to be, but rest assured, God is in control. May this be a source of peace and not consternation.

—*Kris McInnes*

October 15

Now we see but a poor reflection as in a mirror; then we shall see face to face. Now I know in part; then I shall know fully, even as I am fully known. (1 Corinthians 13:12, NIV)

One weekend, my wife and I went antiquing in rural South Carolina. We were looking for a new coffee table. Soon after entering a small shop in Walterboro, my wife discovered a beautiful, old, wrought-iron flower box, which, she quickly became convinced, would make a perfect coffee table if we just turned it on its side and got a piece of glass cut for the top. The owner, a very nice lady, asked us where we were from and we told her: Charleston. She mentioned that she had grown up in Charleston, on Sullivan's Island. My wife commented that I, her husband, currently worked on Sullivan's Island. The lady mentioned briefly that her father had served as an Episcopal priest at the little church there, a place called Church of the Holy Cross. Flabbergasted, my wife responded: "My husband is one of the ministers at that church!" Everyone got the chills.

Clearly God wanted us to have this coffee table, and through a seemingly random, far-fetched series of events, had made it obvious that our entire day had been part of a much bigger plan. We returned home, with our new coffee table component in tow, excited to finally get it into the home where it had been destined to serve.

An hour later, we were home, carrying the flower box through the front door and into the living room. We sat it down in the middle of the room, up-ended so that we could see what it would look like. It was not right at all. It looked terrible.

God is certainly in our midst, but what exactly He is doing in a life at a particular moment is rarely a thing that can be easily perceived.

—*John Zahl*

October 16

If for this life only we have hoped in Christ, we are of all people most to be pitied. (1 Corinthians 15:19, NRSV)

People like to say, "Don't worry." But have you ever been told that when you've actually been in a really serious spot, one that you can't see your way through? It's generally meant well, but it almost always comes off as unhelpful. It makes me think of *Men in Black*, when the alien cockroach breaks into the morgue and holds Laurel hostage. Will Smith and Tommy Lee Jones enter to prevent the alien from escaping and save the girl (and the world). Will Smith says, "It's okay, Laurel," as she is being held around the neck by the alien in a decaying fleshy Edgar suit, and Laurel responds, "How is this okay?!" Will Smith responds, "I'm saying it's *gonna* be okay!" I jokingly use this phrase with my wife when we get overwhelmed about something. She's always skeptical of this pacifier in the face of real problems because, she rightly objects, "How do you know it's going to be okay?"

And how do we? The trouble with faith is that it is uncertain. We do not know instinctively that things are going to be okay. It is this uncertainty that stirs the pot of doubt for some of the Corinthians, who have begun refuting the existence of the resurrection. Paul's answer here is that "If for this life only we have hoped in Christ, we are of all people most to be pitied." If there is no resurrection, we do not have hope, and our belief is ridiculous.

Ridiculous or not, worried or not, the assuring thing is that it isn't up to us. What we don't always believe is still objectively true; it doesn't become less true because we haven't conjured up enough belief in it. Besides, our faith is not something that we maintain or conjure up, but something *given* to us. Like everything else with God, we are the passive recipients of faith—God is the author and sustainer of our faith, and He will attest to Himself. This is what the Holy Spirit does in those moments when we ask, "How is this okay?" The Holy Spirit reminds us of what has been done, that no matter what, God is faithful, and from that knowledge faith begins to spring. This is where we hear those words of comfort: "It's gonna be okay."

—Sean Norris

October 17

> "Death is swallowed up in victory. O death, where is your
> victory? O death, where is your sting?" The sting of death is
> sin, and the power of sin is the law. But thanks be to God,
> who gives us the victory through our Lord Jesus Christ. (1
> Corinthians 15:54-57, ESV)

Because the "wages of sin is death," redemption from death is the whole story of the Bible from beginning to end, and Jesus' resurrection is the core of the redemptive theme. Death is swallowed up in Christ's victory, giving us the freedom of life everlasting.

And yet we die. Everything dies—humans and animals suffer and die, whether by natural causes or natural disasters or cancers or famines or wars or murders. In wake of these deaths we feel worry, condemnation, shame, and despair. Though we strive against it, death always has the last word.

It is for this reason that, if we don't pin our hopes for redemption on the cross of Christ, we are left to feeble strategies to fight the perpetual tides of death. One particularly odd strategy for dealing with death is seen in a piece of art by British artist Damien Hirst. In 2007, he unveiled his masterpiece: a diamond-encrusted platinum cast of a human skull priced at $98 million. The skull, cast from a 35-year-old 18th-century European male, is coated with 8,601 diamonds, including a large pink diamond worth more than $8 million in the center of its forehead. His explanation of the work is fascinating: "I hope this work gives people hope—uplifting, take your breath away....It shows we are not going to live forever. But it also has a feeling of victory over death."

We don't need diamond encrusted skulls that give the feeling of overcoming of death. We need sin and death to *actually* be overcome. Paul says in Romans that "Jesus Christ died for our sins and was raised for our justification" (4:25). This overcoming of death reaches all the way to you here, to the memories of smaller deaths in your life; to your depression now, your fears and insecurities, your shame for what's been done to you or the impulses you cannot control.

In the cross and in the resurrection, God has taken sin and death. Though it may not be visible, Christ has overthrown them, taking sorrow captive and ruling over death for all eternity. Love has replaced darkness, joy has replaced despair, and peace has replaced fear.

—*Justin Holcomb*

October 18

Blessed be the God and Father of our Lord Jesus Christ, the Father of mercies and God of all comfort, who comforts us in all our affliction, so that we may be able to comfort those who are in any affliction, with the comfort with which we ourselves are comforted by God. For as we share abundantly in Christ's sufferings, so through Christ we share abundantly in comfort too. (2 Corinthians 1:3-5, ESV)

This passage is all about the comfort-giving nature of our Father in heaven, that He actually delights in generously giving out mercy and comfort to His frightened flock. Though his flock may fear or feel unworthy of the gift, He does not tire of doling out comfort for the afflicted.

It is easy, then, to believe that there are variations of affliction—but with God there is no pecking order. He doesn't discriminate; God, by nature, presents Himself in "any affliction." This is something the Church experiences together—as we share in Christ's suffering, we too share in the comfort of God's love. This does not mean that affliction must be sought after—it comes as surely as we live, and Paul calls us to see that somehow these afflictions have been made Christ's own. It is mysterious, as Luther puts it, that "Christ our Head, makes our afflictions His own, so that when we, who are His body, suffer, He is affected as though the evils were his own."

Paul then describes how we are to use this experience of comfort to comfort those around us. This is something we've largely forgotten how to do. Though we're needy of comfort, we often end up pushing ourselves and others to lead, as Thoreau said, "lives of quiet desperation," instead of seeing the freedom Christ has won for us. We feign the "all is well" persona, perhaps because we want to draw from the well no more than anybody else. We naturally fear our own weakness, but Paul here is saying this weakness is all we need for the fount of comfort.

Though it is true that this is an audacious claim, let us be audacious enough to seek this comfort amidst the afflictions of our lives. God understands where we are. His Spirit shares in our afflictions.

—*Javier Garcia*

October 19

For all the promises of God find their Yes in Him.
(2 Corinthians 1:19-20, ESV)

"Yes" is a gracious word. Yes, please come in. Yes, please stay for dinner. Yes, I would love to go with you. Yes, of course, take all the time you need.

"No" is a forbidding word. No, you may not come. No, there isn't room for you. No, I'm too busy. No, it was due yesterday.

Human beings are both Yes and No. Most children learn to nod "yes" and shake their heads "no" before their first birthdays. The Beatles sang, "You say yes, I say no, you say stop, and I say go, go, go, oh no!" We are a thousand different people every day.

And in our world of subterfuge, denial, mixed messages and motivations, we often say "yes" while shaking our head "no." Have you ever considered responding to an invitation you dread by saying, "I'd love to... but I really don't want to?" I'm hoping one day to have the courage to say that instead of saying, "That would be great. I'll just check my calendar at home." Of course, I'm always a no-show.

I am like the first son in Jesus' parable about the father who sends his boys to work in the vineyard. The first says, "Yes" and then doesn't go, and the second says, "no" and then goes to work. With human beings, it is always "yes" and "no," often at the same time.

But in Jesus it is always Yes, as the Apostle Paul tells us. Jesus is God's Yes to a world that has for once spoken a resounding and univocal "NO!" to Him. No, God, we don't want you. No, God, we'd rather run our own show. No, God, go away. Our "no," of course, found its final expression in the nails and spear and thorns of the cross. Our "no" killed God.

But God says "Yes" anyway. All the promises of God find their Yes in Jesus. To us, the naysayers, God says, "Yes, please come in. Yes, please stay for the banquet. Yes, I know all about who you are and what you've done and what you've been trying to hide. And Yes, I love you now and always."

—Paul Walker

October 20

Now if anyone has caused pain, he has caused it not to me,
but in some measure—not to put it too severely—to all of
you. For such a one, this punishment by the majority is
enough, so you should rather forgive and comfort him, or he
may be overwhelmed by excessive sorrow. So I beg you to
reaffirm your love for him. (2 Corinthians 2:5-8, ESV)

We tend to be more troubled than encouraged by Paul's call to forgiveness in this passage. This is mostly because Christians have a hard time absorbing the deep sinfulness of the Church. As Luther describes it, "There is no greater sinner than the Christian Church." This seems a hard pill to swallow today: while the Church ought to be The House of Forgiveness for the Repeat Offender, it more often feels like a community of believers inoculated to shortcomings and crises. We may like to talk about the "new creation," about "bringing on the Kingdom of God," but we don't want to talk about the "flesh" that remains in our experience as it did before—and it's no surprise this has had an impact on church attendance. Dark barrooms and social media networks have taken its place as the appropriate place to cry for help.

In this passage, Paul describes a very common scene in churches: a member's slipup caught wind and made a mess of things. Surely we know how this goes down, in or out of church: some details are uncovered, and a dramatic electricity spreads amongst the group. Feelings get hurt, trust is betrayed, and impressions are shattered. Suddenly things can never be the same again.

It's no different for the Corinthian church, but Paul makes it clear here that the natural consequences wrought by the wrongdoer are punishment enough, and the buck should stop there. He anticipates the human impulse to lord the past over a wrongdoer—an impulse we all have—and disassociates it from the message of the Jesus. As withholders of forgiveness, Paul calls the Corinthians to reaffirm their love for those who have fallen. That is to say, in the name of Christ, the rebuke requires a complete reversal: a kiss on the face, an embrace, a patient empathy in the process of recovery.

So where is forgiveness withheld in your life? When have you been the withholder; when were you the withheld-from? Perhaps it's been uncovered, or perhaps you see no way it could be covered enough, but the wrong is there and you both know it. Perhaps the silent tension is punishment enough.

The house of God is a house full of those in need of forgiveness. Let us ask God to bring Paul's words of instruction to us and to our churches. This will happen when people—starting with you and me—can be honest about our sufferings. This honesty comes from the knowledge that in Christ, forgiveness shall not be withheld.

—Javier Garcia

October 21

Now if the ministry of death, carved in letters on stone, came with such glory that the Israelites could not gaze at Moses' face because of its glory, which was being brought to an end, will not the ministry of the Spirit have even more glory? For if there was glory in the ministry of condemnation, the ministry of righteousness must far exceed it in glory. Indeed, in this case, what once had glory has come to have no glory at all, because of the glory that surpasses it. For if what was being brought to an end came with glory, much more will what is permanent have glory. (2 Corinthians 3:7-11, ESV)

Paul has come to the conclusion here that the Law has done its job. How? Put simply, though the Law cannot cure the chronically self-inclined human nature, it exhibits human nature with crystal clarity. In laying our natures bare, our profound need for a Savior is laid bare with it. The Law is useful in setting us up beautifully for our own demise—and for the resurrecting work of an atoning God. Now the Law, according to Paul, having performed its "ministry of death," is set aside for the "ministry of righteousness." The Gospel, the eminently permanent presence of God's love for humankind, is now here to stay!

But this is where the questions come in. Isn't my *faith* a contribution to salvation? I am called to *believe*, aren't I? What about my actions of obedience? Don't I need to show God that my faith is real by how I live my life? If I love the Lord, I should love His Law too, right?

We have a propensity for these kinds of protests of the Gospel message, dimming down the bright end of our death in Christ. We prefer the control Pelagianism offers, the hope we might be able to contribute to the divine contract.

It is not abnormal to find circles in which "salvation" means the admission ticket to God, but "Christian Living" is thereafter the maintenance fee. In these circles Christianity—a faith based upon God *taking* control of your life for you—looks more and more like any other moralistic balance beam. Returning to the Law as one's mettle testing—more than being a dishonest portrayal of Christ's ministry—is fraught with needless hazards, leading believers back into the "ministry of death." In modern parlance, the return to the Law creates psychological burnout. It kills, and it cannot make alive.

The Christian is not under this penalizing and paralyzing power of the Law. The Christian walks under the umbrella of grace, covered by grace, and moved to life and faith and holiness by grace. This is the Christian message, the "ministry of righteousness" that gives us hope.

—*Ethan Magness*

October 22

> *But their minds were made dull, for to this day the same veil remains when the old covenant is read. It has not been removed, because only in Christ is it taken away. Even to this day when Moses is read, a veil covers their hearts. But whenever anyone turns to the Lord, the veil is taken away.* (2 Corinthians 3:14-16, NIV)

Do you know anyone who takes everything personally? Somebody who seems like they're actively looking to take offense? Maybe a person around whom everyone walks on eggshells? Someone who, in other words, sees the world through a veil of judgment?

A veil of judgment is much like any veil: it separates us from other people. It blocks out the light and obscures our vision so that all we can see are potential judgments. Some of us wear that veil like a pair of glasses. Paul claims here that such a veil exists whenever the old covenant—the Law—is read. We don't hear something beautiful and holy being described. All we hear is accusation.

Veils of judgment exist most plainly in relationships. Maybe we've wronged someone or they've wronged us. Maybe they said something hurtful, and it got back to us. The next time we see them, a veil of judgment will have fallen between us, a coldness that prevents us from experiencing them in any way that isn't laced with condemnation. We hear criticism where it's not intended. Instead of "blah blah blah," it's "law law law."

I remember getting some uncommonly wise advice from a friend about a problem that had been bothering me. When I got home that evening and told my wife, she just stared at me. "I told you the exact same thing three months ago!" The veils of judgment that exist between spouses (or between siblings, or between parents and children) are often the most intricately woven.

Gary Ridgeway, the "Green River Killer," was one of America's most notorious serial killers, responsible for the deaths of nearly 100 women in the 1980s and 90s. Finally captured in 2001, when he was put on trial, the victims' relatives were given the chance to express the pain and grief that his crimes had caused. He sat there stone-faced as family member after family member berated him. They called him an animal. They told him he would burn in hell. They wished him an agonizing death. And then the father of one of his victims, a large man with a white beard, approached the podium. In a measured yet warm voice, he said, "Mr Ridgeway, there are people here that hate you. I'm not one of them. You've made it difficult to live up to what I believe: what God says to do, to forgive. You. Are. Forgiven, sir." Ridgeway immediately started crying, and later that day gave his first statement that showed any remorse. The veil of judgment dropped, and for the first time he could see what he had done. Forgiveness accomplished what judgment—even the most just kind—could not.

Can you relate? Where in your life, and with whom, have veils been lifted—and where have they fallen? When Christ was crucified, the veil that hung in the temple, the one that separated human beings from God—the underlying and ultimate veil—was torn in two. Try as we might to sow it back together, it has been permanently set aside. We may see the world through a veil of judgment, we may see others and ourselves through one, but God, when He sees us, does not. You. Are. Forgiven.

—David Zahl

October 23

Now the Lord is the Spirit, and where the Spirit of the Lord is, there is freedom. (2 Corinthians 3:17, ESV)

Does your faith feel like freedom? Does it energize you to face the world? Is religion a source of creativity and joy and insight for you? Does it give you encouragement and help? Does it provide a place to bring your sorrows and your joys? Is it a refreshing blast of honesty and humor in a dull, serious, trivial, narrow, uninspired world?

Or is it a muffle, a dampener, a nagging voice of guilt—a stream of half-joking "sin" caveats (e.g. "I know I have all sorts of selfish reasons for wanting to do this, but...")? A duty, a chore, a social obligation? A "sincere" judge, faking nice, who will turn on you should you misbehave? Does your religion constrict and tighten your path in life instead of opening strange new possibilities?

The Spirit brings freedom, not a muffle. Muffle religion, reprimand religion, constriction religion, has nothing to do with God's Spirit. For the Spirit is the Spirit of Jesus Christ, who "came that they may have life, and have it to the full" (John 10:10).

—Simeon Zahl

October 24

For it is God who said, "Let light shine out of darkness," who has shone in our hearts to give the light of knowledge of the glory of God in the face of Christ. (2 Corinthians 4:6, NRSV)

Our brains are instinctively programmed to recognize faces; it's that psych-101 gestalt thing. It's why the fronts of cars seem to have personalities or why we can see "the man in the moon," or like Cliff Clavin on *Cheers*, can imagine that a potato is the spitting image of Richard Milhous Nixon. It's in us to humanize things. The verse above talks about what it would mean for God to humanize Himself, to give Himself a face. I mean, how *really* does that face appear to us?

People I now consider very dear friends cautioned their friend, now my wife, to rethink dating me, because at the time I was not a Christian. Their concerns were genuine and motivated by care. I knew about these concerns (she had told me about them and how she took them seriously), and I remember the feeling of judgment hurt deeply. In the end, however, her love for me—which, like all true love, was unmerited and undeserved—won out. I will be eternally grateful for that, because all conversations and books aside, it was her love for me, regardless of my not being a Christian, which brought me to Christ. Her acceptance of me as I was was life-changing, and in it I was touched by "the light of the knowledge of the glory of God in the face of Christ" as I had never seen it before.

Theologian Jürgen Moltmann described love as "an event in a loveless, legalistic world: the event of unconditioned and boundless love which comes to meet man... unloved and forsaken... and gives them a new identity..."

As we recognize one another through faces, God comes to us in the same way, in the face of Christ that comes to us as love "in a loveless, legalistic world." It is a real human face, one that does not assess, judge, or condemn. It is the disfigured face that could have called down legions of angels in his defense, but chose humiliation and death on the Cross at the hands of those he loves. And it is this face, one of love without conditions, that takes our voids, the absolute nothings we have to offer, and creates out of them new lives free from judgment, through which the light of Christ's freedom and peace can shine out of the darkness. And that face changes everything.

—Leonard Finn

October 25

"...and he died for all, that those who live might no longer live for themselves but for him who for their sake died and was raised." (2 Corinthians 5:14-15, ESV)

If good stories told in novels and movies are any indication, most of us want to be caught up in something bigger than ourselves. It is odd, because the truth is that we spend most of our time thinking about ourselves, serving ourselves, and helping ourselves to the exclusion of almost everyone and everything else. And yet, ironically, this kind of self-orientation is entirely uninspiring, if not embarrassing to us, when brought to light. No one wants their narcissism unveiled.

But enjoying a story often means imagining yourself within it. Like the characters in the really memorable stories, we want to be caught up in something great, something outside ourselves—to be in love, for example. No one wants to see the story end with, "And she left love for the big opportunity at Bank of America." Even though we spend most of our time going after things for ourselves, the things that truly inspire us always seem to draw us out of ourselves.

I work with teenagers in a church, and it doesn't take much to see the nature of their internal struggle with religion. For a lot of them, at least, it looks like this: "What I want to do" vs. "What God wants me to do." Freedom is defined as being your own person and getting to do what you want. So naturally, slavery is being God's and doing what He wants. I remember having a similar outlook. And if I'm honest, I still do, even now. Self equals freedom. God equals slavery. This is our mantra, covertly or overtly.

Against this mantra, St. Paul comes out swinging, telling us what all the best stories have been telling us—that the exact opposite is in fact the truth. God (and Love) is freedom from the slavery of self. Christ's death, Paul says, has not only saved us *from* something but *for* something. The cross has delivered us out of death and sin and into a world of meaning and love, where we finally have something to live for that is bigger than ourselves. No longer slaves, we have been set free to live as we were meant to live, for him and for others. Through his death, we become characters in the story we always longed to be in. It is His love that draws us out.

—*Ross Byrd*

October 26

Therefore, if anyone is in Christ, he is a new creation; the old has passed away; the new has come. All this is from God, who through Christ reconciled us to himself and gave us the ministry of reconciliation; that is, in Christ God was reconciling the world to himself, not counting their trespasses against them, and entrusting to us the message of reconciliation. Therefore, we are ambassadors for Christ, God making his appeal through us. We implore you on behalf of Christ, be reconciled to God. For our sake he made him to be sin who knew no sin, so that in him we might become the righteousness of God. (2 Corinthians 5:17-21, ESV)

Paul here talks about the reconciled becoming reconcilers. God reconciles Paul to Himself through Christ and, second, He gives Paul the ministry of reconciliation. Paul is the only New Testament writer to use the noun "reconciliation" and verb "to reconcile." Reconcile means "to bring back to friendship after estrangement, to harmonize." The picture is to re-establish an original peace that once existed. In Paul's writings, God is always the reconciler. The initiative is God's, who changes a relationship of enmity to one of friendship, and this is accomplished through Christ, through his death on the cross.

The recipient, he then says, is the world. This means that reconciliation is comprehensive and all-encompassing. God's reconciliation is done in forgiveness—by not "counting against us" the amount of a debt we owe. Like late charges on a credit card for which we are legally responsible, God doesn't post the debts to our account that should rightfully be ours. This is because Christ so closely identified with the plight of humanity that their sin became his.

This is our great hope—that Christ's death took the consequences of our sins, that his perfect life is attributed to our account, that where sin abounds, grace abounds even more, that where we are weak, God is strong. This is what it means to be an ambassador of Christ, simply and honestly communicating our weakness, helping others with the pressure they feel to display to the world their infinite and paltry successes. If it's already covered, and the account is settled, why are we wasting so much time and energy displaying our self-righteousness? Why not boast in weakness?

—Justin Holcomb

October 27

> *But he said to me, "My grace is sufficient for you, for my power is made perfect in weakness." Therefore I will boast all the more gladly about my weaknesses, so that Christ's power may rest upon me. (2 Corinthians 12:9, NIV)*

You want to be in control, but you are not. Because of this, the heart-felt experience of faith will always entail a kind of personal deconstruction, rather than some kind of building up. The more you get to know the God who loves sinners, the more you will see your own need for Him.

Sometimes people ask God to build in them all the things that they think they need in order to face life successfully. He will do no such thing! Why would He turn you into a vessel that has no need for Him? Faith means trusting Him to be all the things you need Him to be, despite your own inadequacies, and, for that matter, in light of the fact that you don't actually know what you need or what success actually looks like. He won't give you strength; He will be your strength. God deconstructs. God intervenes. God prevents.

—*John Zahl*

October 28

> *For through the law I died to the law, so that I might live to God. I have been crucified with Christ. It is no longer I who live, but Christ who lives in me. And the life I now live in the flesh I live by faith in the Son of God, who loved me and gave himself for me. (Galatians 2:19-20, ESV)*

Crucified with Christ? Paul certainly knew something of crucifixion: five times whipped with the thirty-nine lashes, three times beaten with rods, stoned once, thrice shipwrecked, a day and night adrift at sea, constantly dealing with enemies and false brethren (2 Cor 11).

Jesus' crucifixion saves us by absorbing all our sins—and even God's accusation against sin—by nailing them to a cross and burying them, never to rise again. While Christ's is the only crucifying work that's ever going to save the world, Paul's circumstantial crucifixions bear fruit insomuch as they make him more and more like Jesus. Paul, in his sufferings, discovers that the attempt to control life makes things no more or less manageable. All he has left for himself is sheer dependence in God.

Would you say your relationship with Jesus is *working* for you? If you find yourself in a cruciform season of life, it's probably not working in any way that keeps you in charge. But your hope is that what looks like death—all those things over which you have no control—actually makes up the fertile ground for God's resurrecting life. In your deaths and desolations, you may discover God's beautiful power and rich love to walk you through all things.

Christ hasn't just died for us—Christ lives in us. Indeed, we die by letting go not only of all those things over which we have no control, but even our very selves are taken. Through these things, our crucifying experiences, God puts us to death. We were goners anyway, but Christ hastens the end by uniting us with his own death. This is the end that is a new beginning. A resurrection. Christ—our strength in "every riven thing" (C. Wiman) in our lives—guarantees that it's not us but Christ who walks our walk and lives our life. With it all under control, we don't have to understand it all or wait to feel it hit—God allows good fruit to come from good seed. Though we may be oblivious to Christ in us, unaware of his work, we bear the Christ who lives in us to others in their needs and concerns.

—*Mark Mattes*

October 29

> *Is the law then contrary to the promises of God? Certainly not! For if a law had been given that could give life, then righteousness would indeed be by the law. (Galatians 3:21, ESV)*

"Eat your vegetables!" We are advised by parents, school administrators, and the US Government to eat our vegetables. But does this constructive advice work? A *New York Times* article by Kim Severson examines the efficacy of decades of public guidance regarding vegetable consumption:

> Despite two decades of public health initiatives, stricter government dietary guidelines, record growth of farmers' markets and the ease of products like salad in a bag, Americans still aren't eating enough vegetables...
>
> The results fell far short of health objectives set by the federal government a decade ago. The amount of vegetables Americans eat is less than half of what public health officials had hoped. Worse, it has barely budged since 2000... [A doctor involved in the study], like other public health officials dedicated to improving the American diet, concedes that perhaps simply telling people to eat more vegetables isn't working. "There is nothing you can say that will get people to eat more veggies..."

The study does not mean that no one *eats* vegetables. Many enjoy vegetables, others willingly eat them as part of their desire to fulfill a healthy or organic lifestyle. Over time, though, we do not continue eating or start to eat vegetables because of parental guidance or government campaigns.

If eating vegetables is good—which is undoubtedly true—and their consumption may even be helpful to the environment—which is also true—why don't people abide by the campaigns?

The Apostle Paul's insight in this verse is vital but almost always ignored: "If a law had been given that could impart life, then righteousness would indeed be by the law." Like "eat your vegetables," the Law is good, and the Law is not "contrary to the promises of God," but advising someone to follow the Law does not better the chances for its fulfillment. When given advice, even recognizably good advice, our selfish wills naturally rebel.

Paul's insight is clarified through parenting toddlers. Instantaneous negative reactions to directions, frequent emotional and physical outbursts to directives—if they don't want to do something, they won't do it. Aside from some acculturated disguises, adults are no different.

Thankfully, we are not loved by our vegetable intake, or by following any commands from the Law. Christ gave it all so that through him our sinful nature is revealed, and by his grace our hearts may begin to actually *desire* what the Law commands. May Christ through grace fix our hearts to desire those good things—even salad in a bag.

—*Ron Flowers*

October 30

> *But the Scripture imprisoned everything under sin, so that the promise by faith in Jesus Christ might be given to those who believe. Now before faith came, we were held captive under the law, imprisoned until the coming faith would be revealed. So then, the law was our guardian until Christ came, in order that we might be justified by faith. But now that faith has come, we are no longer under a guardian...* (Galatians 3:22-25, ESV)

Several years ago, *The Onion* news magazine ran a commentary attributed to the CEO of Gillette, outlining the company's competitive strategy. For years, men's razors contained two blades. Two blades were sufficient for shaving, and no one complained about needing more blades. Then, Gillette introduced the Mach-3 razor, with *three* blades! The Mach-3, a hit, stirred the pot amongst its competitors. As a result, Gillette enhanced its 3-blade razor by adding an aloe strip for moisture, placing the company at the pinnacle of innovation in the razor industry.

But to the CEO's surprise, as he explains, "the bastards went to four blades... Moisture or no, suddenly we're the chumps." What follows is his competitive reply and angry reaction to this setback:

"Sure, we could go to four blades next, like the competition. That seems like the logical thing to do. After all, three worked out pretty well, and four is the next number after three. So let's play it safe... Why innovate when we can follow? Oh, I know why: Because we're a *business*, that's why!"

Faced with the law of competition, the CEO changes course: "We're going to five blades... You think it's crazy? It *is* crazy... We didn't claw our way to the top of the razor game by clinging to the two-blade industry standard. We got here by taking chances. Well, five blades is the biggest chance of all."

While fictional, *The Onion*'s story demonstrates a common captivity. I often feel that a particular accomplishment or experience will bring me the success or peace I need. I strive to achieve, expecting peace to follow, and often don't succeed. When I do, however temporarily, like with the three-blade razor and aloe strip, success is fleeting and another obstacle arises, often immediately. The Law increases its demands through four blades, and its infinitely demanding character imprisons us. We cannot satisfy the craving of fulfillment. There is always one more blade to add. Like the faux-Gillette president, resentment grows with the burden.

Whether we seek to fulfill God's Law or the laws of Achievement, Society, or Power, the Law destroys us. Yet it also shows our need and leads us to Christ. Faith is revealed to us, and we are freed from our shackles. Our justification comes not from the next rung of the ladder but through the priceless gift of grace.

—*Ron Flowers*

October 31

God has sent the Spirit of His Son into our hearts, crying "Abba! Father!" (Galatians 4:6, ESV)

Faith in Christ means that the Holy Spirit has been sent to our hearts. Christianity has often made a mess of this gift of the Holy Spirit, turning it into a possession manipulated for purposes of worldly power. Once the Holy Spirit was given quite visibly, as when Christ was baptized in the Jordan by John or when tongues of fire were placed on the heads of Christ's new preachers at Pentecost. This was needed because of hard disbelief among the righteous and unrighteous alike according to the Law. Presently the Holy Spirit comes hiding in the Word of preachers or, as we sometimes say, "through the bare word alone." This gives us what we call an "internal" testimony, or voice that we hear assuring us, that God is pleased with us because He is so pleased with his only begotten Son, Jesus Christ, who went all the way to the cross. That is, instead of hearing the voice of the Law saying, "What have you done?", we hear Christ alone, who stands victorious over all other powers and voices that want to claim us.

This is enough to know that we have the Spirit, but there is also what we might call an "external testament" to the Spirit's presence in our hearts. We actually find that our feelings and thoughts are changed, since we now enjoy hearing Christ all the time. We stop taking our internal religious temperature and start clinging to an external word. Peace and certainty arrive to us as wonderful gifts that are unknown but for the Gospel. Certainty is impossible to come by in this old world. It must be given as the gift of the Holy Spirit, the Spirit of the Father's Son.

But faith is attacked as long as we remain in this old world, attacked by all our old enemies, including Satan, the Law, and my own sinful self. The moment I hear Christ, Satan prowls about holding a mirror up to me, saying: "Look for yourself, I see only a sinner, don't you?" In fact we soon feel the opposite of certainty and peace, and the moment we remove our ear from Christ's words, the old black magic of doubt enters more strongly than ever before. But here we have a great promise given in Paul's letter to the Galatians. The Spirit is given to go to work for us in precisely these situations of doubt. He exercises faith in us, which means to apply faith when it is really needed in times of trial when we do not see or feel Christ's presence. This can be the terror of the Law coming back and telling us what we have not done. It can be the tremor of death, which seems greater than even Christ can handle, and it can be the roaring of the Devil who tells us to stop listening to Christ and look only at ourselves.

In these times we have the promise of the Holy Spirit, given to us for the purpose of becoming our own intervening voice, taking our complaint to God in the form of a child's plea: "Abba! Father!" The Holy Spirit does not whisper; He yells, and yells louder than any law or sinner or devil, so that none can snatch us away from Christ. So what if we do not feel strong—Christ's strength is made perfect in our weakness (2 Cor 12:9), and this means the Holy Spirit takes over for us. Our faith is not in our power to persevere, but in the Holy Spirit's power to claim the Father's ear and our own all in one terrific shout. The Gospel, remember, is a short word, and so the Holy Spirit never has to pray long, just loud. With Him on our side we can be certain of our salvation since it is Christ who accomplishes these things, not us.

—*Steven Paulson*

November 1

For freedom Christ has set us free; stand firm therefore, and do not submit again to a yoke of slavery. (Galatians 5:1, ESV)

So often the language around the cross of Christ insinuates a means to an end. Through Jesus' great sacrifice we *can* have "our best life now," or we *can* have that patience we've not had with our spouse and children, or we *can* achieve the things we couldn't before. All of these things, while desirable, are not the impetus behind the cross. St. Paul says it plainly here in this verse: "For freedom Christ has set us free." Freedom for freedom's sake is God's underlying motivation in the cross, and true freedom is found nowhere else.

The obvious question arises, "Free from what?" The modern vernacular doesn't leave much room for talk of bondage or slavery, even on the interior, but it is undeniable that we are consumed by everyday concerns. The new baby, the dwindling 401-K, the knocking noise coming from under the hood of the car, the impossible boss, the impossible parent. Surely, it must mean freedom from these things.

But it is not freedom from difficulty, but freedom from our own sinful inclinations to carry on a charade. Just like the Galatians, we often think that the moment of freedom comes at conversion; after that, we just get serious about living it out. Ironically, then, our expressed need for Jesus has gone because "we're changed." As Paul says in verse 4, "You are severed from Christ, you who would be justified by the Law; you have fallen away from grace."

This seriousness about our role in living it out only lasts as long as we can keep up the charade of "the new man" or "the good wife" or "the patient employee." Something will crush us, every time, that will be too big for us, and we will die again at the cross—where He has set us free.

—Sean Norris

November 2

For in Christ Jesus neither circumcision nor uncircumcision counts for anything, but only faith working through love. (Galatians 5:6, ESV)

Much of the problem that Paul deals with in the letter to the Galatian church has to do with a combination of snobbery and fear. There is no place in the Christian Gospel where these motivations can find a defense. Much like the Galatian church, Christians often find that no matter how long they have been believers, snobbery and fear of what other people think of them constantly reemerge.

Is there something about you that you think gives you an advantage over your fellow human beings? It might be your background, your schooling, your job, your looks, etc. In human terms, these things can inflate our self-understanding, but they are, in fact, poison to the spiritual life. They divide us from our fellows, and they can only serve as liabilities where our attempts to love are concerned.

God's blessings are born of His mercy to us; they are not indicators of our own righteousness. They may enable you to serve others in a unique way, but your advantages do not belong to you, so don't take them personally. Remember, all of God's children are adopted!

—John Zahl

November 3

For the whole law is fulfilled in one word, "You shall love your neighbor as yourself." (Galatians 5:14, RSV)

"Brad and Lucy, Lucy and Brad!" (*The Searchers*, 1956)

Love and judgment, judgment and love! They are mutually exclusive. And they really are! You can't love somebody if you are judging them, I don't care who you are. And you don't judge somebody if you are really loving them. Judgment and love are un-mixables.

Yet here we read that judgment is fulfilled in love.

This does not mean that we are wrong when we observe that judgment and love are un-mixables. It means that our picture of judgment is wrong, and our understanding of how love works is wrong.

When we love somebody, we give them the matchless and unique space to, well, judge themselves. This is what the world seldom understands. When you are loved, especially when you are forgiven, your blood curdles, your hair stands on end, you become ill, and thus you find yourself. Kerouac wrote that the "book of pure truth is a bunch of mirrors bound together." Love equals the "space" for another person to see himself, or herself. It is a bracing look! Yet it has huge effect. You cannot stay the same when you really see yourself. And when you do see yourself, you actually start to become the person the Law stated you should become.

It's like that moment in the Gospel of John when Peter, having denied Christ, is in the courtyard and Jesus walks by, bound, and he simply looks at Peter. Nothing more—no expostulating words, no accusation, no "hard feelings"—just a look. We know it was the "Look of Love" and that Peter crumbled and melted. Christ combined truth with love in his unique way. It is the unique way of the universe. Love without judgment, which is the only real love at all, creates self-knowledge, and actually self-loathing, which leads to self-forgetfulness. And self-forgetfulness instantly transforms itself into loving your neighbor as yourself. You merge, as it were, with your neighbor. He or she is no longer a stranger, no longer an "other." The stranger is you.

It is amazing how many of us still believe, inveterately and impenetrably, that judgment can create a change, that "telling someone what to do" (euphemistically, "speaking the truth in love") will result in their doing it. It is an almost universal fallacy, and it exists just as much among Christians as among everybody else in the world. *Tell "em to love and they'll love.* It never works. It always fails. What works is love, without judgment, which creates, *eo ipso*, the very thing that judgment tried and failed to create.

The world almost never seems to grasp this. After all, the world does everything wrong on purpose. But the New Testament says it. Love creates the thing that judgment could not, cannot, and never will do. Love issues in love.

—Paul Zahl

November 4

> *Praise be to the God and Father of our Lord Jesus Christ, who has blessed us in the heavenly realms with every spiritual blessing in Christ. For he chose us in him before the creation of the world to be holy and blameless in his sight. In love he predestined us to be adopted as his sons through Jesus Christ, in accordance with his pleasure and will—to the praise of his glorious grace, which he has freely given us in the One he loves. In him we have redemption through his blood, the forgiveness of sins, in accordance with the riches of God's grace that he lavished on us with all wisdom and understanding. (Ephesians 1:3-8, NIV)*

The other day, while watching TV, a commercial's motto was: "Actualize Your Best You." Commercials have been saying this for years; it's nothing new: *doing* leads to *being*. Cause-effect. Want six pack abs? Just buy the Muscle Milk, or the Bowflex, and give the core-regimen 110% for some weeks, and you'll see results. *Doing* helps us make sense of our achievements and results.

As delightful as it may be, "Just Do It" mistakes how knowledge connects with willpower. We may want to do it; we may even need to do it, but often we can't just do it—or at least we can't do it for very long.

In a world that divides losers and achievers by the "Just Do It" principle, the Bible says we're really just the same. Abs-of-Steel and Sadsack-3am-TV-Watcher are really two sides of the same person, though they don't seem to have anything in common. The same diagnosis rests upon the narcissist and the depressed: the Reformers called it *homo incurvatus in se*—humankind's state of being curved in on itself, inclined toward bellybutton gazing. We are naturally self-obsessed, with our abilities or our problems. In all cases, our common denominator is *self* and the self's acceptance.

The remedy, then, is to have our spines straightened out, in order to see that hope comes from with*out*, not within. This passage is an elated riff on that hope, that "in Christ, you are blessed with every spiritual blessing." The answer is in Jesus, not you, who takes the pressure off. Jesus inverts the logic of *Do* vs. *Can't Do.* In Christ you just *are*—without ever needing to have *done* anything. It's already been done. So now, *doing* can just be a response to already *being.*

What in your life challenges you to "Just Do It?" We all have a longing to belong—both overachievers and self-loathers carry this anxious pride, and it doesn't make either more or less acceptable to God. This is good news, that "He chose us in him before the creation of the world." His choosing happened *before* the willpower dilemmas confronting you today. You were lovingly adopted before you ever did a single thing.

—Matt Johnson

November 5

> *For by grace you have been saved through faith. And this is not your own doing; it is the gift of God, not a result of works, so that no one may boast. For we are his workmanship, created in Christ Jesus for good works, which God prepared beforehand, that we should walk in them. (Ephesians 2:8-10, ESV)*

Have you ever wondered why Paul begins with grace rather than faith? Paul opens up chapter two by describing our state before Christ, and it's not good—he does not describe us as sick or weak, but dead. He makes perfectly clear, using the word "dead," that there is absolutely no help or life within us. Therefore Paul must begin with grace, the free gift of God, because dead people can't have faith. It is purely by grace that we have any faith and can experience God's rich mercy.

This is a powerful passage because it articulates to us that Jesus Christ is not only our justification, but our sanctification as well. I was once in a Bible study where everyone was emphasizing verse 10, the good works that He has prepared for us to walk in. The question in Bible study went something like this: "Okay, now that we have been saved, what good works do we need to walk in?" What we see in this passage is that God is the author and finisher of our salvation and the good works He has prepared for us to walk in. Therefore, since He has brought you to life, He will lead you to the works you can do. The question to ponder today is not, "What works should I be doing?", but rather "What works do I want to do?" Those are the works that are led by the Holy Spirit, and the works that He has prepared for you to walk in.

—*Jacob Smith*

November 6

For you were once darkness, but now you are light in the Lord. (Ephesians 5:8, NIV)

Of all the emotions associated with darkness, none is more powerful than depression. Those of us who have experienced it know that, like darkness, depression is frightening. The great American writer David Foster Wallace was not exaggerating when he described depression as a "large dark billowing shape," "the billowing black sail of hell."

Sigmund Freud theorized that depression is anger turned inward. Child psychologist Dorothy Martyn defines it as "a loss of stature in your own eyes." As we all know, anger at oneself and loss of stature can be justified. In my own life, depression has always had a trigger, usually a perceived failure of some kind—something as significant as the break-up of a relationship or as trivial as the purchase of the wrong kind of air-conditioner.

Still, anyone who has been depressed, or dealt with a depressed person, knows that it is a sickness that cannot be cured by the sufferer. No amount of telling a depressed person not to be depressed—or explaining to them why they shouldn't be—has any effect, other than often making the situation worse. In fact, the condition feeds on itself to the point where the depression can become indistinguishable from the person. To a depressed person, the Apostle Paul's assertion that apart from the Lord we are not only in darkness, but that we are the darkness, does not sound so far-fetched.

So what is the answer? Can a depressed person be helped? How does the light get through? Sometimes nothing works, not even medication. But other times, the "black sail" is pierced by compassion.

Someone, maybe a good therapist or pastor, tries to understand and empathize with the pain rather than oppose it, and as a result, the depression begins to lift. Light shines into the darkness from outside, in the form of a loving and patient advocate.

It is not surprising, then, that Jesus is called the Light of the World (John 8:12). He was and is the very embodiment of Compassion, the one who died for people who have every reason to be depressed. But through his death and resurrection, we are made light. Our feelings, as dark as they may be, no longer have the final word. We can boldly join The Smiths in singing, "There is a light that never goes out."

—David Zahl

November 7

And I am sure of this, that he who began a good work in you will bring it to completion at the day of Jesus Christ. (Philippians 1:6, ESV)

There's a lot of talk in church and culture about "growing" and "maturing" and "next steps." Maybe you get anxious when people ask you, "What are you doing these days?" or "What are the next steps?" Maybe you worry about your relationship with God feeling stagnant or stale.

For our relationships with God, we generally seek to remedy the anxiety with wishful thinking about being more "fruitful." We worry that maybe we should spend more time in prayer, read the Bible, spend more time or money or resources on others. We obsess over our desires. We tell ourselves we ought to be more thankful. The list goes on.

It is possible from this verse to look at the situation from a wholly different angle: you *have been* called by God and according to His purpose. He's not waiting for you to make right decisions before He moves you forward. He doesn't *need* you to make the right decisions—with all of our anxieties and hopes, His dexterous work will be used on you. He has promised to bring to completion what He's started.

As Ryan Adams observes, "I was trying to find me something, but I wasn't sure just what. Funny how they say that some things never change." While much of the time it seems to us like some things never change, we can rest assured that things have changed, are changing, and will change, albeit mysteriously and invisibly. He who calls you is faithful.

—*Mike Burton*

November 8

For to me, to live is Christ and to die is gain. (Philippians 1:21, NIV)

When I first read this passage, I was struck by St. Paul's joy in the face of imminent death. How can he say, "to die is gain?" During a chaplaincy internship I had at a hospital, I had the awful privilege of attending an autopsy of a young man in his mid-twenties. His death was sudden and completely unexpected. As I watched the gruesome autopsy, I was overwhelmed by the reality of my own death. I recognized that one day I, too, will donate my organs to science. Or as Victor Hugo says, "Men are all condemned to die, though the stay of execution varies."

What is it about death that can make people so uncomfortable? For many, death signifies their unfulfilled hopes and dreams. It means the end to what they hope would be a promising career. Death means tragically leaving loved ones behind. Death entails many unresolved regrets. In light of death, we regret all the strained relationships that are left unreconciled, whether it's the distant friend or the estranged family member. We worry about remembrance, or even whether some people will be glad we're gone.

But St. Paul says that to die is gain! Why? What can possibly be gained in death? For Paul, the answer is twofold. He says this because in many ways he has already lost everything. He has lost his career, his family, his reputation and all his financial assets (Phil 3:8). He has already lost almost everything there is to lose in this life.

St. Paul also says that to die is gain because he knows that death is not the end. But in some senses for me this sounds like a consolation prize. The idea of an afterlife seems abstract and removed from our daily toils. But as I think about it more, it is not that the afterlife is a disembodied existence with wings and harps. Paul knows that in death he gains Christ (Phil 1:23). He knows he will spend eternity with the One who loves him unconditionally. Paul's death is not marked by the loss of his career or family, nor is it marked by regret over those things he did not accomplish. But Paul's death means gaining the One who loves and forgives him. In light of God's surpassingly great love for us, may we too say boldly that to die is gain!

—*Todd Brewer*

November 9

> *But what things were gain to me, those I counted loss for Christ. Yea doubtless, and I count all things but loss for the excellency of the knowledge of Christ Jesus my Lord: for whom I have suffered the loss of all things, and do count them but dung, that I may win Christ, and be found in him, not having mine own righteousness, which is of the law, but that which is through the faith of Christ, the righteousness which is of God by faith: that I may know him, and the power of his resurrection, and the fellowship of his sufferings, being made conformable unto his death; if by any means I might attain unto the resurrection of the dead. (Philippians 3:7-11, KJV)*

There is an inverse correlation, it seems, between "life" as we see it and Christianity. Paul here is rejoicing in the fact that he's lost everything he had been working for in his life—the grooming, the scholarships, the social standing, the moral rectitude. He really rejoices he's lost it. He says that losing all these things has actually brought him closer to the Lord. Everything he had been working for, he now sees, is rubbish, "dung." It's not that he hasn't "suffered" the loss of these things, but the loss of them he counts in the win column, now that he knows a new life and new power.

What if this is not meant to be abstract in any way whatsoever? What if "losing" things—your edge, your cool, your sleep, your touch, your marbles, your car keys—really, in the most straightforward sense, brings one closer to the heart of God? What if death and suffering are, quite literally, the places of "the fellowship" and the groundwork for "the power of his resurrection?" What would that say about today, your dreams deferred and your plans ahead? What would that say for the things you're currently trying to "keep alive?" What would that say for the things you've lost and continue trying to recover? It would suggest, as Robert Farrar Capon writes:

We never recover. We die. And if we live again, it is not because the old parts of our life are jiggled back into line, but because, without waiting for realignment, some wholly other life takes up residence in our death. Grace does not do things tit-for-tat; it acts finally and fully from the start.[*]

If this is true—that loss and death are companionable partners with "Christian" life and power—then the good news is twofold. First, the Gospel of Jesus Christ exposes all the chasings of "livelihood"—the momentary successes, the daily primping and planning—for the hogwash it is. We are freed from its hold on our standing (and our sanity).

Second, and perhaps more beautifully, our losses and deaths are not absent of God, but instead access points *to* God, doorways to God. This is not a platitude, but a transfiguration: the "loss of all things"—call it your "low point" or "breakdown" or "rock bottom"—actually *becomes* for you that hardy shelter Jesus talks about, where "the rain descended, and the floods came, and the winds blew, and beat upon that house; and it fell not: for it was founded upon a rock" (Matt 7:25).

The wild contradiction of "Christian Living" is this unsightly comfort, that our firm ground stands in "being conformable unto his death," and thus falling into the "power of his resurrection."

—Ethan Richardson

November 10

But our citizenship is in heaven, and from it we await a Savior, the Lord Jesus Christ, who will transform our lowly body to be like his glorious body, by the power that enables him even to subject all things to himself. (Philippians 3:20, ESV)

When I was an infant, my mother tells me, I suffered regularly from ear infections. A particularly painful infection reduced me to a fit, and my mother, who tells me she was completely undone by my screams, took me to the doctor in panic. New decibel levels ricocheted against the linoleum floor and the high gloss wall-paint in the examination room. Frazzled, she couldn't help the doctor; I obviously couldn't either. The doctor took me

---

[*] Capon, Robert Farrar. *Between Noon and Three*. Grand Rapids: Eerdmans Publishing, 1997, p 77.

in his arms and laid me down on the table. Gently he held me securely down and stilled my head with one large hand, and with the other he examined my ear.

We enter the world like this, as babies raging against the world, and we live our lives in much the same way onward—though perhaps sometimes a bit more socialized. And yet sometimes, the more we rage against our various illnesses, the worse things seem to get.

As Delirious sings, "Love will find a way to break through." This is the hope of the Christian faith. God broke through as this Love in the person and work of Jesus Christ. Jesus forgave all those who raged against God; he made the sick well. His promise is that we will realize the full scope of what he did for us when he comes again; he will transform our lowly body to be like his glorious body. He has the power to overcome our worst tantrums and even our death. Perhaps today something is hanging over us: a fear, a regret, a loss, an addiction. He knows our problem more than we do, and he will subject that thing— even the big thing in our lives—to himself for healing.

—Kate Norris

November 11

> *Once you were alienated from God and were enemies in your minds because of your evil behavior. But now he has reconciled you by Christ's physical body through death to present you holy in his sight, without blemish and free from accusation. (Colossians 1:21-22, NIV)*

Everyone, at some point, has been dumped. The subsequent feelings are some of the worst you can have. Sadness, hopelessness, and shame gnaw at you until what you never thought would happen happens, and you "get over" the person that dumped you. At its core, being dumped is accusation. You wonder what you did or said or *were* to drive away another person.

Such self-doubt isn't irrational: the adage "It's not you, it's me," is false ninety percent of the time. One person often breaks up with another because of some perception of the other's awkwardness or inadequate level of cool. This is a running motif in *Seinfeld*. For each of the countless girlfriends Jerry dates, he always finds some flaw upon which he fixates, and he breaks up the relationship because of it.

And it's true for relationships in general. One person wrongs the other in some way, and injury and guilt breaks the friendship. I know someone who, because of one critical word said at a Thanksgiving dinner, hasn't spoken to the offending parent for years. It takes one mistake to ruin a friendship. Think of wedding invitations: no matter how small the wedding, if a close friend feels slighted, it is likely that they will not talk to the couple again. Relationships always break because of some form of guilt and accusation.

St. Paul says that we were alienated from God and were His enemies. Because we rejected His love, our relationship with God was broken—we had turned away, and there was no going back. But thankfully, God chose not to leave the relationship broken. Because of Christ, we are free from the breakup we asked for. In a world of relationships broken by guilt and accusation, God does not accuse us, but pardons us in a continual pursuit. Though people constantly judge us by some measure of performance, God does not. In God's eyes, we can do no wrong. We are without blemish, free from quick accusations or painful breakups.

—*Todd Brewer*

November 12

And you, who were dead in your trespasses and the uncircumcision of your flesh, God made alive together with him, having forgiven us all our trespasses, by canceling the record of debt that stood against us with its legal demands. This he set aside, nailing it to the cross. He disarmed the rulers and authorities and put them to open shame, by triumphing over them in him. (Colossians 2:13-15, ESV)

Think about all the demands that press on you on a daily basis. There are demands on balancing your time: meetings, schedules, picking up the kids. There are demands on your energy. Your boss probably demands a certain level of performance at work, your children or spouse make demands to be present, to be loving. You are demanded legally, too: you must pay taxes, fulfill jury duty. It is hard not to view the world as one long list of ceaseless demands.

But there is another dimension to this bleak vista. Everything mentioned above only addresses the demands on us at a horizontal level, but there are the vertical demands from On High, too, aren't there? It's ironic that we will go to great lengths to talk about and work away at the horizontal variety, but the idea of a command from the Big Guy is just not cricket. Aren't we the ones who get to make demands of God?

Scripture tells us differently; we are, as Paul writes in this passage, dead in our trespasses. In short, we aren't really in any position to make demands. God demands instead, and God demands perfection. Jesus said, "Be perfect, therefore, as your Heavenly Father is perfect" (Matt 5:48). This is the summation of the Law of God.

However, God does not only reveal himself to us through His demands, but also through love, and He "has made [us] alive together with him, having forgiven us all our trespasses." Paul tells us that the vertical demand upon us, particularly what Paul calls a "record of debt," has been canceled, nailed to the cross of Christ.

The debt owed to God is not money or time or energy, but your very life. You cannot give it, but the Gospel—God's good news—is that we are no longer crushed by its consequences. In view of this polar shift, the Gospel tells that all horizontal demands get put in their place. We are freed from them. They don't go away, to be sure, but by God's grace our ways of approaching them are newly liberated.

—*Ben Phillips*

November 13

If with Christ you died to the elemental spirits of the world, why, as if you were still alive in the world, do you submit to regulations—"Do not handle, Do not taste, Do not touch" (referring to things that all perish as they are used)— according to human precepts and teachings? These have indeed an appearance of wisdom in promoting self-made religion and asceticism and severity to the body, but they are of no value in stopping the indulgence of the flesh. (Colossians 2:20-23, ESV)

When Martin Luther was a young Augustinian monk—prior to becoming the great reformer—he was plagued with an incessant need to make sacramental confession. According to medieval tradition, grace was only available through the sacraments on the precondition of confessing one's sins. Luther, unlike any of his monastic brethren, obsessed over whether he had actually confessed every single sin he committed, no matter how trivial. This greatly annoyed his fellow monks who were called to be his confessors at all hours.

Of course, along with confession, and monastic life more generally, came many forms of making penance, and other daily requirements for performing rituals in order to stand in right relationship with God. Try as hard as he might, Luther found these ascetic disciplines never fully worked for him. In fact, they often made matters worse despite the outward appearance of his piety, which burdened him greatly:

> I was a good monk and kept my rule so strictly that I could say that if ever a monk could get into heaven through monastic discipline, I was that monk... And yet my conscience would not give me any certainty, but I always doubted and said, "You didn't do that right. You weren't contrite enough. You left that out of your confession."... Although I lived a blameless life as a monk, I felt that I was a sinner with an uneasy conscience before God. I also could not believe that I have pleased him with my works. Far from loving that righteous God who punished sinners, I actually hated him... I was in desperation... I kept my three vows devotedly day and night and yet I felt no repose in maintaining my duty so purely.[*]

What Luther recognized was that all this activity of austere self-denial had, as Paul says to the Colossians, an *appearance* of wisdom, in promoting "self-made religion and asceticism and severity to the body," but it was of no value in stopping the indulgence of the flesh. In other words, neither the problem nor the solution are in our outward activities—in what one does or does not do. Rather, as Jesus Christ says, "It is not what goes into the mouth that defiles a person, but what comes out of the mouth; this defiles a person" (Matt 15:11). The problem thus lies deep within us—original sin is inherent to our very nature, written on our DNA. Try as much as we like, there is no gene therapy for purging our nature.

Understanding this is helpful, not just theologically but also psychologically. There is no spiritual apparatus we can or must use to earn God's favor. Believing otherwise will lead us, like Luther, to desperation. Please don't let me be misunderstood: Yes, disciplines like fasting, or Bible reading, or yoga, or the newest trends of veganism, all

---

[*] Mullett, Michael A. *Martin Luther.* New York: Routledge, 2004, p 42.

have value. Too often, though, we pervert these "disciplines" into misguided technologies for preventing sin and earning God's grace.

Thankfully God does not operate by "helping those who help themselves"—a popular aphorism not from Scripture but from Ben Franklin. Rather, God helps wretches, like Luther, and me, and you, who cannot help themselves. I repeat: God helps those who *cannot* help themselves. He did so, is doing so, and will do so through Jesus Christ, the Righteous. Thanks be to God!

—*Matthew C. Schneider*

November 14

For you died, and your life is now hidden with Christ in God. (Colossians 3:3, NIV)

Imagine that you suddenly find yourself, without any preparation, standing on a stage and being watched by an enormous audience. How would wearing a mask over your face affect your level of comfort? If you're like me, the answer is: immensely. It's like being able to tell someone something that you've always wished someone would say to them, but without them knowing that it was you who said it. Wearing a mask enables you to feel either detached from or, at least, less associated with anything of yourself that you might regret exposing.

When we are given security that is not contingent upon our own intrinsic abilities, fruit is born, as if by reflex. It is life lived in the absence of condemnation.

As far as today is concerned, there is no rehearsal, but the performance must go on. In a very real sense, God has already covered your life with His Holy Spirit. "Your life is now hidden with Christ in God."

—*John Zahl*

November 15

We give thanks to God always for all of you, constantly mentioning you in our prayers, remembering before our God and Father your work of faith and labor of love and steadfastness of hope in our Lord Jesus Christ... you turned to God from idols to serve the living and true God, and to wait for his Son from heaven, whom he raised from the dead, Jesus who delivers us from the wrath to come. (1 Thessalonians 1:2-10, ESV)

Hope is what fuels many of our actions and motivations. We routinely need something to look forward to on the calendar, or something to keep us from facing our pain and difficulty today. Much of the time our hope is false. Either it is based on our own abilities to make things better—the upward slope, as it were—or it is placed in ephemeral conditions (e.g. "Things will get better when we're married," or "I'll feel right once I'm in a routine"). But what if things are not getting better? What if you look at your life today and see the same struggles you had yesterday? Or if you're faced with things that you have no control over, like losing your job, having a rebellious child or unrelenting parents, or an illness you can't kick?

When we talk about hope, we need more than just the same old clichés about the little engines that can, and lemons turning into lemonade, because our problems are usually much bigger than us. We need more than a short-lived fix: we need a resurrection. Paul says here, "[God] raised from the dead Jesus, who delivers us from the wrath to come." Christ has given us permanent hope. This good news relates all the way down to today's malaise, to the memories of old wounds and current addictions, and to the fears and anxieties about what's to come.

This is why we rejoice—because faith, love, and *hope* are possible for you in Jesus. They are, indeed, the works of God in us.

—*Justin Holcomb*

November 16

Now may the God of peace himself sanctify you completely, and may your whole spirit and soul and body be kept blameless at the coming of our Lord Jesus Christ. He who calls you is faithful; he will surely do it. (1 Thessalonians 5:23-24, ESV)

Christians, like everyone else, are prone to worry about their standing in the face of judgment. We believe that the work of Christ is the one thing that's made it possible for us to stand before God at all, but on a practical level we rarely believe it to be enough. We fret about whether we've said or done the right things, whether we're "seeking God's will" in all we do, whether we're "discerning God's call." We rarely trust that sanctification is something that God imparts.

Paul's prayer is that we would realize it is *God* who sanctifies us: "may the God of peace *himself* sanctify you completely." To be made holy and blameless is the work of God in Jesus, not the work of man. To be kept blameless is also the work of God, not the work of man. We will stand in Christ's likeness because, mysteriously and often unnoticeably, the God of peace sanctifies and will continue to sanctify the sinner. Paul's prayer closes with a firm reminder and assertion that it is God, not us, who makes and keeps us blameless: "He who calls you is faithful; he will surely do it."

—*Bonnie Poon Zahl*

November 17

The one who calls you is faithful, and he will do it. (1 Thessalonians 5:24, NIV)

It is no secret that we live in a world completely saturated with do-it-yourself solutions. From building an economy to removing signs of aging to a backyard birdhouse, we seldom flinch when given new imperatives. The church is no exception to the rule. In fact, it does not matter whether we receive instructions from the pulpit or the talk show; we tend to welcome new tips and strategies for self-improvement as much as the rest. At first the health-and-wealth message sounds attractive, like a late-night infomercial on financial freedom, or the Ab Roller Plus 15-Minute Power Program. But unsurprisingly, all of the tapes and foam and aluminum eventually end up gathering dust in a corner of the buyer's garage.

How different is this can-do attitude from the Apostle Paul's tone in this letter to the church in Thessalonica? Though we're buried under tons of hopeless solutions from the self-help sector, Paul outlines God's model of the universe: we Christians do not do for ourselves, but *God does for us.*

One of my friends, who went to a well-known fundamentalist college in the South, recounted (bitterly) the way he was appealed to "recommit" at almost every chapel service. It got to the point where students did not even know why they walked down to the altar, time after time. I wonder how many of the students still worship on a regular basis after four years of high-intensity pleading from the school figurehead and numerous guest speakers during those chapel services.

Such *counter*examples of Christ's uninhibited acceptance help me consider the radical nature of the Gospel all over again. Paul begins this benediction in verse 23: "May God himself, the God of peace, sanctify you through and through. May your whole spirit, soul, and body be kept blameless at the coming of our Lord Jesus Christ." What is so striking here is that Paul bypasses the can-do in you and me. This is a word of assurance that people like us need to hear over and over again—God Himself will sanctify you, every part of you; He will keep you together.

—*Dylan Potter*

November 18

> ...*God chose you as first fruits to be saved through sanctification by the Spirit and belief in the truth...* (2 Thessalonians 2:13-17, ESV)

The best definition of sanctification is "the art of getting used to justification," as Gerhard Forde says. It is the art of understanding that I no longer rely on myself or my performance in order to be loved and accepted. It is the art of leaving behind the old regime of "If... then" and getting used to the new world of "Because... therefore."

Sanctification is saying good-bye to the thought that "If I keep engaging in this or that sin, then I'm a bad Christian," and hello to "God has forgiven all my sin and taken away all condemnation; therefore there is nothing I can do to make Him love me more or less, and there is nothing that I can do to get in His way of transforming me into the image of his Son."

And the best news is that sanctification is by the Spirit; it is not by you or your discipline or your effort. As Paul says, sanctification is by the Spirit and is triggered by belief in the truth. Every day, the Spirit sanctifies us by the renewing truth of the Gospel. And what is this truth that sanctifies?

Will Campbell, a desegregationist who lived in the South during the sixties, understood the truth that sanctifies. An agnostic once asked Campbell the following question: "In ten words or less, what's the

Christian message?" His quick answer was, "We're all bastards, but God loves us anyway."

The more Campbell reflected on his knee-jerk answer, the more he liked it. We are not born children of God; because of sin we are born enemies of God. Yet God wasn't content to leave us bastardized—He sent his own Son to take on bastard status so that you and I could be adopted as sons and daughters of God.

All this Gospel saving was thought up by God, executed by God, signed, sealed and delivered by God—100 percent of it, leaving 0 percent for the bastards, if you do your math. This is justification and sanctification by the Spirit. Since our will is bound and, as the 1928 Book of Common Prayer says, "we have no health in us," then we must look completely outside ourselves for help. And God is the helper of the helpless. He does not help those who help themselves, but those who cannot help themselves.

This is the Gospel of the God "who loved us and gave us eternal comfort and good hope through grace." It is the only message worth getting used to.

—*Paul Walker*

November 19

May the Lord direct your hearts to the love of God and to the steadfastness of Christ. (2 Thessalonians 3:5, ESV)

More often than not, when confronted with a hard time or a friend's hard time, I am not comfortable not fixing the problem. Suffering gives a knee-jerk propensity to fixes—I want it to stop, and I want it to stop now. With another's suffering, I want to be sensitive to their needs and I want to "allow room," but I don't want it to take long.

Do you find this to be true? In the presence of a breakdown, what do you do? Of course we do not want our loved ones to suffer, but more often than not we are less concerned with their comfort level and more focused on our own. It's like the classic scenario played out in the amazing 1980 movie *Airplane!*, during which a woman begins to become hysterical, and the passengers line up, one by one, to literally smack some sense into her. Some just use their hands, but others brandish bats, crowbars, boxing gloves, etc. While dark, this is a true illustration of how people suffering around us make us feel. In *Airplane!*, they just want her to shut up; otherwise, they all might begin to consider the danger they are all faced with.

We want to quiet down the outward sign of pain and suffering because it is an all-too-painful reminder of where we, too, live, at least at some point or other. It is too great a thing for us to face. But this is where the rubber meets the road with Christianity—it is what makes it matter in everyday life. In the midst of suffering and pain, when we want to simply stamp down whatever is boiling over, we can know that God Himself will direct our hearts to His love and faithfulness. He will be the one to give an answer to our problem.

—Sean Norris

November 20

Now may the Lord of peace himself give you peace at all times in every way. The Lord be with you all. (*2 Thessalonians 3:16, ESV*)

There are a couple things I keep coming back to in this well-loved benediction: first, there is a Lord of peace and the presupposition that we are peace-less. Peace does not exist inside of us, nor can we fabricate it. Second, this implies that we need to be *given* peace.

We would all like to think of ourselves as peaceful people, but on most mornings, our minds are a clutter of things to do and fears to keep at bay. Here believers in Christ are reassured that they can have peace in every situation, but do we really feel that way in light of an economic recession? In light of continued global strife? In light of our child's weekend drinking? In light of our deadlines? In light of our most criminal thoughts and actions? Or even in light of this passage, which tells us we *should* feel peace?

We don't have peace because we worry; we worry because we are afraid. We are afraid that we will be condemned. Whether it be the standards at work, a father's expectations, the ideal weight, or the Ten Commandments, we are terrified of falling short. In his book *Who Will Deliver Us?*, Paul Zahl writes that "It is possible to deduce that the long chronicle of 'man's inhumanity to man' has roots in an aggregate of personal imprisonments from fear that bind everyone who has ever been born" (15). Fear drives us to fight both against each other and against ourselves.

On the night of his betrayal, Jesus says to his disciples, "Peace I leave with you; my peace I give to you. Not as the world gives do I give to you. Let not your hearts be troubled, neither let them be afraid" (John 14:27). Jesus speaks this to people who have good reason to fear. But Jesus has not come to condemn them or us, but to save us, to give us the very peace he has with God. Jesus comes and extinguishes our fear with God's love for us. There is no sin he hasn't forgiven. There is no fight he hasn't overcome.

—*Kate Norris*

November 21

> *...though formerly I was a blasphemer, persecutor, and insolent opponent. But I received mercy because I had acted ignorantly in unbelief, and the grace of our Lord overflowed for me with the faith and love that are in Christ Jesus. The saying is trustworthy and deserving of full acceptance, that Christ Jesus came into the world to save sinners, of whom I am foremost. (1 Timothy 1:12-15, ESV)*

Beginnings are both important and telling for most relationships. If you are married, the way you began to fall in love says a lot about both you and your relationship with your spouse. The way he loved you even when you finally became vulnerable and told him all about your past. The way she supported you when your career had fallen apart.

While others judge and criticize your failures and imperfections, a loving relationship reminds us that we need grace and not law. We do not need to be told by others that we have messed up, lost favor or fallen short. Instead we need to be loved and supported there, in the midst of the failures. The birth of a loving relationship is so amazing because it is not tethered to achievement. When you are loved as you are—scars and demotions and all—you find that there is nothing more freeing.

The Apostle Paul reminds his young apprentice Timothy of the beginning of his own relationship with Jesus. It had nothing to do with performance, prayer, or perseverance—or any of the other descriptions fitting a "healthy relationship" with God, for that matter. Paul didn't love Jesus or pray to Jesus; instead, he was persecuting Jesus. In the light of God's eyes, Paul deserved judgment. Instead, Jesus met Paul on the road, and Paul received the overflow of mercy.

Being a Christian is not based on performance standards, which is why Paul can tell Timothy that the Gospel is the most important thing to remember. We do not become Christians, nor do we remain Christians, based upon what we do. Instead, we are told, "Christ Jesus came into the world to save sinners, of whom I am the foremost." Amen.

—Alex Large

November 22

...For there is one God; there is also one mediator between God and humankind, Christ Jesus, himself human, who gave himself a ransom for all. This was attested at the right time. For this I was appointed a herald and an apostle (I am telling the truth, I am not lying), a teacher of the Gentiles in faith and truth. I desire, then, that in every place the men should pray, lifting up holy hands without anger or argument. (1 Timothy 2:1-8, ESV)

Alcoholics Anonymous has a popular saying: "Expectation is a planned resentment." We expect to get the promotion at work, and when we don't, we are resentful. We expect our fellow motorists to follow traffic laws (and common sense), and when they cut us off, we are resentful. We expect our spouse to meet all our needs, and when they don't, we are resentful. We expect the church to be a functional, loving institution, and when it isn't, we are resentful. Yet resentment is useless, like a weapon aimed at a target that always, somehow, boomerangs back at the shooter. And over time, resentment can turn into bitterness, or worse, hate.

When we resent other people, we stop communicating with them. We hold back. We avoid them. When we resent institutions, we rebel against them. Resentment is relationship poison. Yet we don't just resent other people or institutions. We resent ourselves when we fail to meet our own expectations or standards. One shorthand for depression, after all, is "anger turned inward." So what's the answer? Reason certainly doesn't seem to make much of a difference. That is, people are seldom argued out of their anger. Anger is fundamentally irrational. Just think about fighting in sports. No, for resentment to dissipate, something has to happen.

When Paul talks about Christ as a ransom for all, as our mediator, he is pointing to Christ as the end of expectation. God's expectation has been met in Christ. In other words, judgment has been removed as a factor in the way we relate to God. This is what it means to be reconciled, that the Father now resents none of us, ever.

So where is resentment holding you hostage? Where is it blocking your communication with other people? With God? Our resentments are not binding. Our anger has been nailed to a cross. The channel is open, and we can lift up "holy hands without anger" or resentment.

—David Zahl

November 23

For there is one God, and there is one mediator between God and men, the man Christ Jesus, who gave himself as the ransom for all, which is the testimony given at the proper time. (1 Timothy 2:5-6, ESV)

In 1492, there were two prominent families in Ireland, the Butlers and the Fitzgeralds. They were in the midst of a bitter feud.

Sir James Butler and his followers took refuge in the chapter house of St. Patrick's Cathedral in Dublin. They bolted themselves in, seeking protection from Gerald Fitzgerald and his men.

As the siege wore on, Fitzgerald had a change of heart. Here were two families, living in the same country, worshipping the same God, in the same church, trying to kill each other. So Fitzgerald called to Butler, inviting him to unbolt the door and come out. Butler, understandably wary of treachery, refused.

So Fitzgerald seized his spear, cut away a hole in the door large enough for his hand, and then thrust his entire arm through the hole. Fitzgerald's arm, extending into the chapter house, was completely vulnerable, totally undefended, and utterly available for being chopped off.

James Butler grasped Gerald Fitzgerald's hand with his own and then opened the door. The two men embraced, and the feud was ended. Thus was born the expression, "Chancing the arm."

That door and that hole still exist today. You can go to St. Patrick's Cathedral and see that evidence of chancing the arm.

But you don't have to go to St. Patrick's Cathedral to be encountered by the one who chanced his arm for you. For you, and whatever feuds you face with whatever enemies stand behind your door, that arm through the door is the arm of Jesus Christ. Chanced for you, his arm through the door bears on its hand the scar of a nail hole. It is offered to you, barricaded inside all of your own inner-chapter houses.

—*Jim Munroe*

November 24

> *Command and teach these things. Let no one despise you for your youth, but set the believers an example in speech, in conduct, in love, in faith, in purity. Until I come, devote yourself to the public reading of Scripture, to exhortation, to teaching. Do not neglect the gift [charisma] you have, which was given you by prophecy when the council of elders laid their hands on you. Practice these things, immerse yourself in them, so that all may see your progress. Keep a close watch on yourself and on the teaching. Persist in this, for by so doing you will save both yourself and your hearers. (1 Timothy 4:11-16, ESV)*

Poor Timothy—what a load! Paul, his "father in the faith," has left town, sticking him with quite the laundry list. And yet that sounds an awful lot like typical Christianity, doesn't it? Taking the burden from your shoulders and laying a dozen in its place. Hit atonement like a drive-thru, and with that bag in hand, speed off to the highway of "the Christian life" of moral responsibility, Scripture reading, character-building. Christianity somehow became a life of holy burdens.

There in the middle of all that is given him to do, though, is that which is given to him wholly and fully. The *sine qua non*—neglect it and it will all fall apart—is the *charisma* (gift) in him.

The certainty with which Paul approaches the ministry is the same certainty under which Timothy gets to operate: if the Lord has put him to it, the Lord himself will do it, and the Lord has certainly put him to it. Is Timothy the one saving or preserving himself and his hearers, or is God Himself the Savior of all, including Timothy and his hearers? Paul says it is not an either/or: God saves, and Timothy is responsible for the saving where he has been placed. It is not God *without* Timothy, nor is it God x% and Timothy x%, but God fully and Timothy fully. Whatever saving Timothy is set to be doing, it will be the Lord doing it, and that goes for the ordering, reading, preaching, teaching and the rest of this grand, long list of things given to do along with the gift given.

Where do you feel you and God are working 50-50? Where does God feel absent or dormant? Where does his presence feel all too present?

What is to be done in the Church is what God himself *gives to be done.* Toward that doing He gives gifts. Tasks given, gift given, to Paul and Timothy and others who are surely put in place; it is the Lord, the Savior, seeing to the whole show.

—Jonathan Mumme

November 25

So do not be ashamed to testify about our Lord, or ashamed of me his prisoner. But join with me in suffering for the gospel, by the power of God. He has saved us and called us to a holy life—not because of anything we have done but because of his own purpose and grace. This grace was given us in Christ Jesus before the beginning of time, but it has now been revealed through the appearing of our Savior, Christ Jesus, who has destroyed death and has brought life and immortality to light through the gospel. (2 Timothy 1:8-10, NIV)

U2 enigmatically dubbed their 2004 album *How to Dismantle an Atomic Bomb.* There isn't much in the track listing that gives an indication about munitions, though, or becoming a member of your local bomb squad; but if you were sucker enough to buy the, ahem, "Deluxe" Edition disc, you'll find an actual epigraph. "I am death, the mighty destroyer of the world"—a phrase taken and paraphrased by Oppenheimer on the first test of the atomic bomb in 1945. The album, written largely on the heels of the death of Bono's father, is about dismantling death.

Which brings us, not surprisingly, squarely to Paul's opening words to Timothy: "This grace was given us in Christ Jesus before the beginning of time, but it has now been revealed through the appearing of our Savior, Christ Jesus, who has destroyed death..." I am struck by how bald that phrase stands—Christ Jesus, the Lamb of God, the One Who Was Slain, The Destroyer of the Destroyer of the World.

For Paul, this changes everything, as the letter starts here and works backward. Fear not, do not be ashamed, join with me in suffering. Just as we didn't do anything to destroy death, nothing shall happen to us in life or death now; the power of God shall prevail. We know the end of the story, even as we are in its midst—this is the basis of our hope.

How is death, the atomic bomb, dismantled? By the appearing of the Power of God in the Flesh, known to us as love. Love came down at Christmas, love came back to life again at Easter, and love (as Bono would write) is the end of history. Death has been destroyed, and it is not our end; immortality has been given in its stead. Love will be the last word of our history, written in arrears. As Paul wrote another time, "For now we see only a reflection as in a mirror; then we shall see face to face." This present darkness shall not last, for a light shines in the darkness, and Christ Jesus, the Destroyer of Death, himself the answer to the question posed by the album's title, has brought life and immortality to light.

—Gil Kracke

November 26

Remind them to be submissive to rulers and authorities, to be obedient, to be ready for every good work, to speak evil of no one, to avoid quarreling, to be gentle, and to show perfect courtesy toward all people. For we ourselves were once foolish, disobedient, led astray, slaves to various passions and pleasures, passing our days in malice and envy, hated by others and hating one another. But when the goodness and loving kindness of God our Savior appeared, he saved us, not because of works done by us in righteousness, but according to his own mercy, by the washing of regeneration and renewal of the Holy Spirit, whom he poured out on us richly through Jesus Christ our Savior, so that being justified by his grace we might become heirs according to the hope of eternal life. (Titus 3:1-7, ESV)

After reading the first couple verses of this passage, we might expect Paul to make some exhortation to go out and live differently. Paul, instead, spins it on its head. We think that life after the cross is somehow different than it was before we first heard the message of grace. We think that now we will be able to do what we could not before. "Hey, thanks for the help. I've got it from here." But we are prone to the same wickedness as those who are not in Christ. Believers and non-believers alike are in the same bag. For Paul there are no such categories as "good people" and "bad people;" there are just people, all capable and guilty of the same faults.

Think of what Paul says in Romans 3, "No one seeks after God. There is none righteous. No, not one." All of us are bad. If our works made us good or worthy in some way, then we would not need salvation anyhow. We would not need mercy. But Paul clearly shows that we did and still do. The point here is that Paul is turning our attention away from ourselves and onto God.

Do you ever have this problem, the so-self-focused-I-lost-all-perspective problem? It seems first-nature to think everything is up to us, even if the problems we face are too big. Every day presents tons of things that warrant worry or concern, from catching the subway to getting dinner ready, and we get in over our heads. But innately we believe we must break through it—heads down, push forward.

Paul points elsewhere. Taking our eyes off of ourselves—all the ill motives and vain attempts—he reminds us of God's mercy. He takes our everyday despair and focuses the everyday upon God's merciful action toward us.

This pointing away from ourselves to the mercy of God is our hope. We stand on the receiving end of God's undeserved grace. Looking inward, who we were before conversion and who we are now is just the same. And yet we are still saved because it never depended on us anyway: everything that matters most is solely dependent on the perfect sacrifice, and this has given us hope.

—Lauren R.E. Larkin

November 27

I thank my God always when I remember you in my prayers, because I hear of your love and of your faith that you have towards the Lord Jesus and for all the saints, and I pray that the sharing of your faith may become effective for the full knowledge of every good thing that is in us for the sake of Christ. For I have derived much joy and comfort from your love, my brother, because the hearts of the saints have been refreshed through you. (Philemon 1:4-7, ESV)

One of the ways God bestows grace is by refreshing us continually through other saints, or fellow believers, in Christ Jesus. We should venture an understanding of how this is even possible, given that so much of the time "being refreshed" —that is, "fellowship" —seems so stultified by bitter clashes, rampant judgmentalism and political nonsense.

Paul begins these verses by stressing his thankfulness toward Philemon, specifically because of his love and faith in Jesus. The second part of this sentence has been translated various ways but, it seems to me Paul is indicating that a certain amount of faith is required when dealing with the saints. That is, we have to believe that beyond what we may see in a passing conversation or e-mail, God is working through us and in us. Despite how impossible it may seem, we have to dare to believe and to act in the belief that God is active in all of His broken vessels.

This is important to keep in mind, because who doesn't cringe over certain aspects of church life, if not every aspect of it? Remember Anne Rice? How she renounced the Church and Christianity altogether while still claiming to be "committed to Christ," and how millions of people on the internet championed her cause? Whether it's the quibbles over music, the opinionated who won't stop politicizing the weekly Bible study, or those people who just don't "get it," Paul urges us to hope against hope. This regard for the church—seeing the Church as one sees oneself—is a disposition of the heart that only God can create and foster.

Though it is a dysfunctional family—a family that wishes it were not a family sometimes—I, for one, would not be a Christian if it were not for certain refreshing brothers and sisters. When I had just about had it with everything, and nearly "pulled an Anne Rice," God provided people who loved me rightly, as if God knew the exact right people, at the right time, when I most needed it. The funny thing is, once this happened, and when it happens in general, I began to believe again that God works in His Church, and I was drawn to love it despite its frequent ugliness. By no means does this mean that I don't struggle with the Church or its members. *Au contraire!* But God refreshes me in opportune times through special people, to show how the wholeness of the Gospel includes a love and faith for the saints. Though perhaps you can't say the same, I hope you've known what this experience is like.

Lord, give us comfort and gratitude for the saints you have provided in this complex and clumsy family.

—*Javier Garcia*

November 28

So if you consider me your partner, welcome him as you would welcome me. If he has wronged you in any way, or owes you anything, charge that to my account. (Philemon 1:17-18, NRSV)

I grew up in Northern Virginia, and there was an elderly man in our church we called "Maj." None of us knew his real name, but we knew he had been a major in the U.S. Army and was a veteran of World War II. Everyone looked up to him. A widower of average height, thin and wiry, he always wore the same tweed jacket and fedora every single Sunday. During the school year on Sundays after church, Maj would treat any middle and high school students to the all-you-could-eat buffet at Shakey's Pizza Parlor in Annandale (I don't think it's there anymore). Parents would drop us off at Shakey's after church and pick us up an hour or two later. As a middle school student with a metabolism through the roof, I was in heaven. While we were eating, Maj would smile and walk around the tables, talking to each of us, cutting up with us. He paid for all of us—the buffet, the drinks, all of it his treat. I thought there had to be a catch, but there was no catch. Maj welcomed us and paid for everything.

Philemon had a slave named Onesimus, who had stolen from him and run away to visit Paul in prison. Apparently Paul led Onesimus to become a Christian, because he refers to him as "my child, Onesimus, whose father I have become during my imprisonment." Paul wrote his letter to Philemon to encourage him to welcome Onesimus back. It is a personal recommendation letter similar to the recommendation letters that I find myself writing each year for students applying for college or seminary, a personal letter on someone else's behalf. In fact, Paul encourages Philemon to welcome back Onesimus not as a slave, but rather as "a beloved brother."

This kind of prodigal welcome is a defining characteristic of Jesus' ministry. Throughout Scripture, Jesus warmly welcomes sinners before they even *think* about getting their act together, because he knows they can *never* get their act together. Jesus welcomes sinners with open arms, open arms that are later stretched and affixed to a cross. Paul is encouraging Philemon to welcome Onesimus back, though he has run away and stolen, and to welcome him back as a brother.

Jesus' welcoming sinners is a major part of the Gospel, but it is not the *entire* Gospel, and in his letter to Philemon Paul not only urges him to welcome Onesimus back as a brother, but he also continues: "If he has wronged you in any way, or owes you anything, charge that to my account. I, Paul, am writing this with my own hand: I will repay it."

Paul knows that the issues of running away and theft cannot be overlooked or brushed aside, but must be dealt with head on. Paul does not ask Philemon to overlook the ways Onesimus has wronged him. Paul does not ask him to let bygones be bygones or to "just let it go." Instead, Paul takes Onesimus' burden upon himself: "If he has wronged you in any way," he tells Philemon, "or owes you anything, charge that to *my* account." Like Maj, Paul does not expect Onesimus to pay the price himself (or to want to), but takes care of all of it. The message of the cross is no different—not only does Jesus welcome sinners, but also he takes the burden of all the ways we have wronged God upon himself, and he pays everything owed. And he did this for sinners—"while we were still sinners," God proves his love for us once and for all in Jesus' death on the cross (Rom 5:8).

—Dave Johnson

November 29

If he has done you any wrong or owes you anything, charge it to me. I, Paul, am writing this with my own hand...
(Philemon 1:18-19, NIV)

Put it on my account. Charge it to me. Let me get the check. We speak these words casually when out to lunch with friends or colleagues. But what about when the ante is upped, and one offers to place something more substantial on their account?

There's a short story by Walter Wangerin called "Ragman." The Ragman goes around exclaiming, "Rags! Rags! New rags for old!," strangely absorbing the addiction of the alcoholic when he exchanges blankets with him, and putting on the lame arm of the disabled man as his own when they exchange jackets. It was as if "the hopes and fears of all the years" rested on this sin-eater, this John Coffey.

In a display of understatement and courage in two parts, Paul befriends the runaway slave of Philemon, whose name is Onesimus: to run away from one's service as a slave was an offense punishable by death. Remarkably, Paul—in full knowledge of this offense—asks that the punishment be placed on *his* account. Just as remarkable, Onesimus, having a courage that comes only by faith, is now the courier of a letter addressed to the one who rightfully has a claim on his life and his death. And still he goes.

What comes off the page and shows itself, these thousands of years later? There really is no *if* to it; it is more certainly an *as*: "as another does you any wrong or owes you anything, charge it to me." Paul assumes that we will both wrong others and be wronged by others. How can Paul—or any of us, for that matter—place yet more debt on the account? By virtue of our common nature, he has no credit-worthiness; his ledger is no cleaner or less overdrawn than others. Paul, like us, is so indebted that he could be said to have *no account*!

Paul is expressing, in a real situation, what Luther expressed so many centuries later: "A Christian is a perfectly free lord of all, subject to none. A Christian is a perfectly dutiful servant of all, subject to all." Paul knew with a deep, soul-changing knowledge that his national-debt sized bill had been utterly forgiven by Christ, absorbed as Christ exchanged his news clothes for Paul's old rags: Paul was made perfectly free, subject to none. No strings attached. Zero balance. That alone allows him to speak with such command and confidence as to send a runaway slave back to his owner with the word, "put it on my account—I am perfectly and completely and wholly bound to this man." Likewise, that alone allows Onesimus—a runaway slave—to walk freely back into the lion's mouth, to what would be a just sentence of death. It is the peculiar and wonderful freedom of a Christian that ties us fully and freely to another; indeed, the only way we can be freely bound to another is if we are free indeed. It is for freedom that Christ has set us free.

—*Gil Kracke*

November 30

> *Therefore, as the Holy Spirit says, "Today, if you hear his voice, do not harden your hearts as in the rebellion, on the day of testing in the wilderness, where you fathers put me to the test and saw my works for forty years. Therefore I was provoked with that generation, and said, 'They always go astray in their heart; they have not known my ways.' As I swore in my wrath, 'They shall not enter my rest.'" Take care, brothers, lest there be in any of you an evil, unbelieving heart, leading you to fall away from the living God. But exhort one another every day, as long as it is called "today," that none of you may be hardened by the deceitfulness of sin. For we share in Christ, if indeed we hold our original confidence firm to the end. (Hebrews 3:7-14, ESV)*

This passage in Hebrews has a strong "today" thread in it. Verse 13 says, "Encourage one another *daily*, as long as it is called *today*, so that none of you will be hardened by sin's deceitfulness." Verses 7-11 are quoting Psalm 95, "*Today*, if you hear his voice, do not harden your hearts." I think Paul is saying there are big consequences if one is *not* living in *today*: the "heart hardens," the believer "falls to the power of sin." But is the writer exalting a "Live in the Moment" philosophy, which happens to be pretty strong these days? No. There is something deeper at stake.

The warning in Psalm 95 is based on a past event where Israel had rebelled against God. Psalm 95 encourages Israel, "Do not harden your heart as you did in the rebellion on the day of testing in the wilderness." In other words, our pasts have an absolute impact on our present. If we fail to address the past now, today will bring natural consequences. This is a descriptive truth for human beings; it is why therapists and doctors and attorneys have jobs. We are shaped by our past, the present is always *becoming* the past (and visa versa), and the future is often envisioned by our quiet projections from these pasts. All this to say, the past is alive and well in us.

How many people do you know, yourself included, who have events and relationships left unresolved or with regrets? If these things aren't reconciled "today"—and in many cases they aren't—they will continue to be a source of deceit and pain. This is why we need the

Gospel today, because only the grace of God can touch those past places we cannot return to or resurrect. Pain often doesn't go, but the peace of Jesus Christ can and will be present in, over, and within that past.

This is also why your need for encouragement, as the passage says, is a *daily* need. This is not "Buck up, little camper" encouragement, which is often vapidly disconnected and utterly useless in giving solace to your past. But it's the encouragement of grace; the assurance that, while you remain tied to the past's shipwreck, Christ died for you and, in so doing, has killed your past and resurrected it to new life. These are the words of life today, and tomorrow, and tomorrow after that, words that balm the wounds of yesterday.

—Ben Phillips

December 1

Since then we have a great high priest who has passed through the heavens, Jesus, the Son of God, let us hold fast our confession. For we have not a high priest who is unable to sympathize with our weaknesses, but one who in every respect has been tempted as we are, yet without sinning. Let us then with confidence draw near to the throne of grace, that we may receive mercy and find grace to help in time of need. (Hebrews 4:14-16, RSV)

He's not *The Mikado*'s "Lord High Executioner!" Though "Great High Priest" sounds pretty impressive. The point of this passage is that the Perfect Man "who has passed through the heavens" is *sympathetic* and came in peace.

In 1959, a pretty ragged little movie appeared in drive-ins that was called *The Cosmic Man*. It portrayed a supremely powerful alien from space that came down in what looked a giant spherical egg. The alien wore a dark raincoat, very large sunglasses, and talked like John Carradine. The movie's key scene, however, revealed that he was really *good*. Even as the military tried to blow him to kingdom come, the alien cured a little boy of polio. If you're a Christian, you probably can't help liking this well-intentioned movie, low-budget as it is.

One of the supreme powers of Christian faith lies within the interplay of vast might and tender human sympathy. This interplay is heightened here in chapter four, because the "Alien" has "in every respect... been tempted as we are." The qualifying phrase "yet without sinning" was added to preserve the vast might of the Alien—He has to exist somehow apart from human nature—but the emphasis is on the sympathy. It is more important, for us, at least, that God be sympathetic than that He be perfect. The sympathy—for us!—trumps the majesty.

The application of the passage is simply that we can come to God "in time of need," and without hesitation. This is because God knows, from inside out, what need feels like. Can anyone really explain this? Phrases and figures of speech are sometimes used in theology to "protect" one idea against the impact of another idea. They're just phrases and figures of speech, though; intellectually defensive qualifiers, we might say.

Here, the "golden apples of the sun" (Ray Bradbury) are these: we can come to God "with confidence," "we may receive mercy" from God, and we will find in God "grace to help in time of need."

All this is another way of saying, rent *The Cosmic Man.*

—*Paul Zahl*

December 2

Indeed, under the law almost everything is purified with blood, and without the shedding of blood there is no forgiveness of sins. (Hebrews 9:22, ESV)

"I am not bound to please thee with my answers," says Shakespeare's Shylock in scene 18 of *The Merchant of Venice*, as he sues for justice before the Venetian court. He has a pound of flesh coming his way, and he is bound to have it. There is to be no mitigation, no tempering down of justice by some degree of mercy, no matter how eloquently Portia will plead. What is written is written; the law is the law. And that is exactly his assertion: "I stand here for law."

God, so long as He is God, is not bound to please us with His answers, either. The early church rejected the Marcionite heresy—the one which sought to prune the canon of Scripture back to a corpus that modern, civilized Romans could handle; gone the bodily and the Hebrew, remaining the spiritual and the Greek. So, too, have the moderns sought to redact God's blood-wrath. The problem of all the blood in Hebrews 9:22 is not that God is unjust or even incomprehensible, but rather that the knife's blade points here, at our own breast. *Shylock*: the name has since become a byword for severity, callousness and a grim insistence on the rigid letter of the law. God, according to the letter to the Hebrews, is a Shylock of the first order. To blood He is entitled, and blood He will have.

As with many references in literature, in media or the silver screen, we may see theological lines running through *The Merchant of Venice*, and they work, as they often do, in the language of the Law. When it comes to the Law, God is Shylock. Where God distinguishes himself from Shylock is not in the percentaged tempering of His wrath, or in making more palatable demands. Rather God, in the person of Jesus Christ, places *Himself* at the pointed end of the knife, as the object of His own blood-thirst. Jesus Christ's *new* covenant (Heb 7:22, 12:24) is not *new* by way of founding some no-blood, sophisticated, spiritualized religion. It is new because Christ enters God's full demand with *his own* blood. What the blood of creatures could never fulfill, the blood of God Himself does. Full demand, without mitigation; full justice, without temperance; full mercy through the blood of Christ—our sins not just rationalized, or understood, or accepted with the caveat of our improving, but covered over in blood, atoned for, and remembered no more (Heb 8:8). This is our new covenant, still signed in blood.

—*Jonathan Mumme*

December 3

> *He has appeared once for all at the end of the age to remove sin by the sacrifice of himself. And just as it is appointed for mortals to die once, and after that the judgment, so Christ, having been offered once to bear the sins of many, will appear a second time, not to deal with sin, but to save those who are eagerly waiting for him. (Hebrews 9:26-28, NRSV)*

It was not just shame and guilt that grew out of the disobedience of Adam and Eve, but death as well. God's intent was that life might reign, but with sin, death came into the picture, along with decay and rust. And as much as we wince at the thought, we, each of us, have been grafted into the family that must face a last day.

My wife and I are Texans now. Any good Texan soon learns he or she has to make a kind of Lone Star pilgrimage to The Alamo, which we did within weeks of our move across the state's border. The trip to this place, that "nexus" point of history and tragedy was humbling—and disquieting—reminding me of my first trip to the USS Arizona's "remains" in Pearl Harbor nearly four decades earlier in my life.

Most know the battle cry, "Remember the Alamo," and the very dark events that surrounded those hallowed grounds were, in a very real way, a kind of tangible fertilizer that empowered the people of the future Texas to eventually defeat Santa Anna at the Battle of San Jacinto on 21 April, 1836. Strange how something dark, even perhaps ominous, can in some way be redeemed.

In the capture of the Texans, Santa Anna decided, as punishment for the attempted escape, that one man for every ten would be executed. Blindfolded, each man was required to draw a bean. If a white bean was drawn, the prisoner lived in jail; however, if a black bean was drawn, the prisoner was shot by a firing squad on March 25, 1843.

There is a "black bean" at the Alamo with the appropriate "write up," and a letter that one young man wrote to his mother after he had drawn one of Santa Anna's "black beans." It was daunting indeed to read the young fellow's words of dread, of knowing his death was only moments away. But then he did hope—in a sense, pray—that his death would bring meaning to his life.

On Good Friday, we contemplate when the Lord draws the black bean. It is a vivid reminder that someday, each one of us will draw ours as well. There is a connection we need to make here. The passage from Hebrews begins to lay that out that connection for us.

I would have hated to be one of those prisoners who reached in Santa Anna's "bean" bag, but I know that in a sense I already have. We have all drawn the "black bean," and there is no getting around that. May this be our prayer for reflection:

> God is eternal light.
> May I die at peace with my God.
> Lord, stay by our door.

—Russ Levenson

December 4

Let us draw near to God with a sincere heart in full assurance of faith, having our hearts sprinkled to cleanse us from a guilty conscience and having our bodies washed with pure water. (Hebrews 10:22, NIV)

Whether we see it or not, we come to God as baptized individuals. This is something that, if forgotten, leaves us spending a lifetime needlessly currying the Lord's favor. We see that Jesus even submitted himself to baptism, to the shock and protest of John the Baptizer. The fact that our Savior plunged his head beneath the waters is one thing, but what makes it all the more profound is that he intended for people like you and me to have "our bodies washed with pure water."

In the movie *O Brother, Where Art Thou?*, two of the folk fugitive crew participate in a riverside baptismal service, and the minister tells one of the men, named Delmar O'Donnell, that all his sins have been washed away as he emerges from the water. As ne'er-do-well Delmar remarks, he's even forgiven for when he stole that pig and was convicted. His friend protests, "But you said you were innocent of that!" To which Delmar responds gleefully, "I lied... and that's been washed away too!" Like Delmar, this verse from Hebrews reminds us that our relationship to God is not based upon an ability to produce a "sincere heart" or "full assurance." It is, instead, a cleansing—a burial and resurrection. God, not the minister, not the baptized, is the promise-maker during baptism; He promises to seal the weak and helpless child with His approval all the way until the child is a weak and helpless old-timer.

No matter what we might say about the sacraments, at the very least they remind us that our life is inextricably linked to the cleansing work of Christ. Our baptism is not a rite of passage; it is a drowning and rebirth. It is an execution witnessed by God and the Church. It is a testimony to our inclusion into Jesus' death and resurrection. In Luther's commentary on Romans, he wrote, "When we are baptized into everlasting life and the kingdom of heaven... it is necessary that we should be baptized into Jesus Christ and his death." In short, we relive the event in the Jordan where God pronounces His eternal benediction: "You are my beloved child, with whom I am well pleased." This is why we cling to our baptism, because it is a new and living demonstration of God's pleasure with us before we could even respond.

—Dylan Potter

December 5

But recall the former days when, after you were enlightened, you endured a hard struggle with sufferings, sometimes being publicly exposed to abuse and affliction, and sometimes being partners with those so treated. For you had compassion on the prisoners, and you joyfully accepted the plundering of your property, since you knew that you yourselves had a better possession and an abiding one. (Hebrews 10:32-34, RSV)

There is this ever-recurring conception—it is a conception, nothing more—that having become a Christian, or given over your life to Christ, the problems of life will fade and the sufferings of life abate. Every "theology of glory" wants to believe this. Every personal "glory story" wishes intensely to claim this.

And who doesn't wish for and want a life without suffering? We reify the hope of a life that is purely positive and, more importantly, purely under the control of our desire for absolute avoidance of the negative. I understand this. You understand it. Everybody concedes the power of such a hope.

Yet this little text from Hebrews demolishes it. "After you were enlightened," says the text, "you endured a hard struggle with sufferings." The vexing, accurate words are "endured," "struggle," and "sufferings." Did I sign up for this when I "became a Christian?" B. C. (Before Christ) life was hard enough. In my life A.D. (The Year of Our Lord) things are *supposed* to lighten up. The passage says otherwise.

The "otherwise" is true to the experience of Christian sufferers throughout all time and everywhere. The Latin phrase is *semper et ubique*, always and everywhere. Universal suffering, spread evenly. Kerouac put it this way: "We human beings are hopeless lost fools wandering mournfully in a general rain of woe that falls evenly everywhere." Another way of putting it is Luther's expression *simul iustus et peccator*, which is to say that Christians are always and forever "justified and still sinner," which means "beloved yet always still human." Even though you have given yourself over to the Nazarene Other, you are still in your human nature. You will never not be marred with suffering, transiency, and insubstantiality. Life is a dream, even for Christians.

The letter to the Hebrews underscores this. Even after your "enlightenment," sufferings came piling on, with persecutions and unpopularity. And to what hope does the author point? Where is the balm in Gilead, some positive spin on the recurring afflictions that inhere among faithful and convinced Christians?

The hope is of an abiding—lasting—possession that is ours beyond this world and therefore enduring. Nothing here lasts. Nothing here exists without suffering piled on to it. Nothing here has anything but the solidity of a dream. The abiding possession is love, which is our belovedness from God and our consequent "works of love" (Kierkegaard) in relation to our fellow sufferers. The human works of love are the sort of electricity of lasting Being.

Whenever I watch the legions of skateboarders milling around the odd enigmatic statue of Phillips Brooks by Trinity Church, Copley Square in Boston, the statue of Bishop Brooks with the hooded figure of Jesus behind him (I have read it was the last public statue in the USA to depict Christ), I am drawn to the text at its foot. I have read enough about Phillips Brooks to no longer worship him as a hero. He was flawed and mixed like everyone else. But the text in stone is sublime: "He loved his fellow man." This is the electricity that binds everyone together, and it is almost always the fruit of belovedness, the belovedness that comes from God to Kerouac's "hopeless lost fools." Love from outside, conferred on people as they are, creates love from us to the others around us. As it did with Bishop Brooks, the darling of his age who died so young. But he really did love his fellow man. He had a better possession, an abiding one.

If only the skateboarders, who are Boston's "angry young men," could hear and receive the words on the statue by which they literally whizz a hundred times a day.

—Paul Zahl

December 6

Now faith is the assurance of things hoped for, the conviction of things not seen. (Hebrews 11:1, NASB)

When you look at your career, your marriage, your health—do you spend more time thinking about what you don't have than what you do? Even a casual inventory reveals how little we are hardwired for gratitude. Or maybe you tirelessly compare yourself with everyone you come across. Other people become either an affirmation or condemnation of your worth, their very existence a comment on yours. Everyone has some situation where they are plagued by "things unseen," a place where they are in need of assurance.

There are differences among "assurance" and "reassurance" and "self-assurance." Oftentimes, religion boils down to a strategy of reassurance. Reassurance is a pat on the back. A pep talk. A hug even. "Hang in there, it's going to be alright." At best, reassurance is a reality check, a reminder of how things really are. At worst, it is a pie-in-the-sky way of dismissing another's fears or doubts. Either way, reassurance depends on the reassurer. It may feel good to be comforted for a while, but then the difficult questions settle in: How do they know everything will be okay? Can they see into the future? However well-intentioned other people's attempts to reassure us are, the psychologist's truism "reassurance never reassures" has some basis.

Self-assurance, on the other hand, is a way of creating our own hope, reacting to those "things unseen" by attempting to bring them into being ourselves. Self-assurance is tied to our performance and ability; as such, it works well when the stakes are small, or when we're in our comfort zone. Not so much when we've exhausted every avenue. What happens when our best isn't good enough?

The message of Christianity is one of assurance—assurance to people who are losing hope, drowning under the weight of "things unseen." Perhaps it is not surprising that the crucifixion itself looked like the opposite of what it was. It looked like a hopeless situation. When they saw their Lord arrested and executed, the disciples must have been acutely aware of "things unseen." But the resurrection of Christ seems to indicate that God is at work in the place where things seem most hopeless. He's not waiting for us to do something, or to figure out the right tactic.

Thankfully, the assurance of Hebrews goes beyond our circumstances, intentions and abilities. It is based instead on something outside of us, something objective, something *sure*: the unassailable love of God revealed in the risen Christ. Where the unseen became seen, once for all, now and forever.

—*David Zahl*

December 7

By faith we understand that the worlds were prepared by the word of God, so that what is seen was made from things that are not visible. (Hebrews 11:3, NRSV)

"Do you think people ever doubt that God exists?" This was the question one of my pre-adolescent children asked, as we stood in line waiting outside a barbeque joint near the Gulf Coast of Florida. Actually, when the question popped out, I was thinking about something that was kind of weighing me down—and yet, here one of those "little children" that Jesus was so fond of telling others we had to be like. One of those was thinking on even weightier matters than me! It was, however, a good question, an honest one—and one that helped me get out of my mood.

In the course of my service as minister, I've often had that question put to me, more by grown-ups than youngsters. And of course, the answer (if I am honest) is "Yes." I think, during these times, that perhaps the underlying question is often, "Is it okay to doubt the existence of God?" My answer is usually only slightly squishy—"It may not be okay, but it is quite normal!"

Whenever I do get this question, I realize it usually means the one with the query is not running away from God, but toward Him—they are on a search. They have opened their minds and hearts to begin really exploring faith.

It is certain that much of what we know in Christianity seems worthy of thoughtful skepticism. But is that all bad? I remember a line that has been of help to me over the years—from Mary Shelley's *Frankenstein* of all places—"Without doubt there would be no need for faith."

It is *faith* that gets us through the doubts. Doubts are normal. Alongside the apostles, we are in good company. But at some point we might want to remember Jesus' gentle, loving, though clear reprimand to the most famous doubter, Thomas: "Do not doubt but believe" (John 20:27).

The passage from Hebrews is known as the "Great Faith Chapter" of the Bible because it retells the incredible miraculous story of God working with His followers over the centuries—and how faith played a key role in each case. But faith, like all good things from God, is finally a gift. It cannot be bought or earned, but only received. There are many things that may block our faith—our reason, our intellect, our reluctance, our fear, and yes, of course, our doubt.

"Do people ever doubt the existence of God?" Well yes—I have. "Is it *okay*?" Such doubt is normal—it is something with which we all struggle, but ultimately, we are given comfort in the place of faith. How does one have such faith? Know that God wishes to give it. It is a gift. Pray for it.

—*Russ Levenson*

December 8

> *Keep on loving one another as brothers and sisters. Do not forget to show hospitality to strangers, for by so doing some people have shown hospitality to angels without knowing it. Continue to remember those in prison as if you were together with them in prison, and those who are mistreated as if you yourselves were suffering. (Hebrews 13:1-3, NIV)*

As Christians, we are encouraged to disregard the world's standards of merit and favor instead a humble position before God. We understand ourselves to be the recipients of divine mercy, and are grateful for it. We come to digest the idea that our good standing with God has not been earned at all. Quite the contrary, it has been bestowed upon us because God loves us more than we can begin to fathom.

Remembering this good news also enables us to have compassion and collegiality with those who have fallen especially short on "the ladder of success." They are not so different from even the most well-put-together Christians among us. Before God, in fact, we stand on the same footing with them.

This is an idea that needs to be conveyed, especially to those who will appreciate it the more for its surprise factor. Who is it that you should love, but do not? Who is it that you should care for, but instead have neglected? Have you, for example, ever visited a prison before? Perhaps God will present you with a fresh opportunity to do something of this variety, something that will stretch you beyond the confines of your daily comforts and familiar associations.

Not only can God love (with enduring patience and steadfastness) *even* them, but so also do *we* need to stop justifying our lack of love, instead asking God to soften our hearts the way He softened his own heart toward the human race in sending his Son.

A few years ago, in an attempt to engage more effectively with some very involved members of my congregation, I agreed to participate in a ministry-related visit to a maximum-security prison. I'll never forget the experience of visiting a group of men on death row. I walked up to one of the tiny cell windows and looked inside. There, sitting on the end of a cot, I saw man reading his Bible. He got up from his bed, and offered me his hand through the little slot. Then he asked me if he could pray for me, and if there was anything going on in my life that I was seeking prayer for.

He took my hand and we prayed together, brothers in Christ, standing on the same stage before our heavenly Father, with that big metal door between us.

—*John Zahl*

December 9

Do not be deceived, my beloved brothers. Every good gift and every perfect gift is from above, coming down from the Father of lights with whom there is no variation or shadow due to change. (James 1:16-17, ESV)

James here teaches us how to praise and worship God in our everyday lives, while at the same time warning us of a deception that is always lurking at the door. He has rightly separated what we often would confuse. Yes, evil and temptation exist in the world, and while God may work *through* evil and suffering, they are not a part of God's character. Instead, James says, "Every good gift and every perfect gift is from above..." People are often deceived about this, and it seems like the confusion comes in one of two ways: either we think that evil is part of God's character, or that our good things come from below, from here—from ourselves, from nature, from the circumstances we've lined up. We are chronically tempted to believe, he seems to be saying, that what we enjoy on earth is not from God, but from ourselves.

This can open a whole new perspective on the mundane goings-on as well as the more extraordinary matters of everyday life. It is impossible to contemplate the entire scope of God's gifts: the food we enjoy comes from God—Mexican food, Japanese food, French food, German food, Turkish food, Arabic, American. What is delicious and nutritious comes from God. God is the author of good meals, good meals with friends and family. He is the purveyor and financier of dining establishments worldwide!

More than this, the "Father of Lights" puts people in our lives and takes them out; He displays mountain ranges and valleys and glaciers and estuaries and parks. The stars and the moon and the sun—the expanse of the universe comes from God. If you wake up to a spouse and children who are the delight of your heart—not necessarily today, but some days—they have come from God. If you are single and have the time to study and meet with friends, give thanks because such blessings also come from God. If you are more advanced in years and have had a myriad of rich experiences from your past, give thanks, because these years and experiences have been given by God. If you are working, in whatever job you might have—banker, teacher, real estate agent, minister, whatever—there God works through you in the world. If you are out of a job, give thanks that God sustains you. Whatever your situation in life, God is present in the good and perfect gifts He provides.

This is not to blanket the pain and difficulties of these things, or to say that one must always understand the vast glory of one's daily existence, but James describes a Father who has made life from nothing, who will be this generous into eternity. Not only does God provide what we need here on earth, but also what we need when our short time here is up.

This same Father of Lights sends Jesus Christ, in his death and resurrection, to guarantee for us an everlasting hope. Whereas God now bestows universal grace for all people, eternal rest is promised to those who have faith in Christ. So, as we read James, let us look up toward the Father of Lights, and wonder at the vastness of His glory in the things He provides and the works He does, both in what is obvious and what is hidden. Whatever is good on earth and in heaven, in the present order of things and in the way they will be—it all comes from the Fount of Every Blessing.

—*Javier Garcia*

December 10

Know this, my beloved brethren. Let every man be quick to hear, slow to speak, slow to anger, for the anger of man does not work the righteousness of God. (James 1:19-20, RSV)

On the Mount of the Beatitudes on the north shore of the Sea of Galilee, the Catholic Church there, a place of frequent pilgrimage, displays the Beatitudes of Jesus in glass. Dazzling for me, most recently, was the Seventh Beatitude: Blessed are the peacemakers, for they shall be called the children of God.

The association that flipped to mind immediately was to the pathology of anger. Non-peacemakers are angry. They eat the apple of discord, wherever they see it on the tree. And then division and dreadfulness come spitting out.

I realize this sounds pretty psychological, but it's the result of observation. It is as if anger, in angry people, is free-floating. It attracts itself to different objects and different people. It seems almost arbitrary. Angry people bite your head off one day, but someone else's head the next. Maybe you are the angry person.

The Epistle of James, for all its reputation as being in tension with St. Paul, is pretty sound experientially. "The anger of man does not work the righteousness of God." I see this every day. My anger, somebody else's anger, does little to rectify things that are wrong or unjust. It just makes me "seethe" and burn, and build massive bonfires of resentment. Remember *Hangover Square*, the Laird Cregar horror movie in which the murderer disposes of his victim by pretending it's a "Guy," as in Guy Fawkes, and places the body on a November 5th bonfire in plain sight? The limp corpse of the person he has just strangled takes its place, like another cord of wood, on the vast screaming blaze. Hollywood macabre, straight to the bone.

Anger is like this. It's "another brick in the wall." It is consumed, and it consumes us. In short, it murders. It does not work the righteousness of God.

St. James' words are immortal because they are empirically, descriptively true. Listening is ever best ("Let every man be quick to hear"). Wise men say that he who knows the most says the least ("slow to speak"). Anger is human, judgmental, self-righteous, infected, and finally terminal.

I wish "conservatives" would take this aboard. I wish "liberals" would take it to heart. I wish everybody would, well, just "Stop! In the Name of Love."

—*Paul Zahl*

December 11

But be doers of the word, and not hearers only, deceiving yourselves. For if any one is a hearer of the word and not a doer, he is like a man who observes his natural face in a mirror; for he observes himself and goes away and at once forgets what he was like. But he who looks into the perfect law, the law of liberty, and perseveres, being no hearer that forgets but a doer that acts, he shall be blessed in his doing. (James 1:22-25, RSV)

When you drive to and from the airport in Birmingham, Alabama, there is always this brick church you pass with letters on the tower that say, "Doers of the Word Church." Sounds pretty good. But then you look more closely, and you see the church is defunct. It is all closed up, and the church van nearby—"Doers of the Word" painted on it—looks junked and forlorn.

The building is a kind of parable. Telling people to be "doers of the word," as in the passage here, sounds good. Until you try it. Then it runs out of gas. People become exhausted. They start to fight. Pretty soon the tires are flat and the engine is dead.

Years ago, a nice woman in Scarborough, New York told me she had stopped attending a nearby church because the pastor's sermons, coming down on Westchester County wealth for the sake of social justice and the poor, had simply tired her out. No one knew more keenly than she did that conscience pricks the "rich" as well as the "poor." But the pastor was giving her no aid, no comfort, no balm—just guilt and more guilt, and innumerable Sundays of exhortation.

But hey, I don't think James is talking about guilt and more guilt. I think, rather, that James is speaking a descriptive word, and a powerful one, at that. People who do not love as a result of being loved are like the man in the letter who "observes his natural face in a mirror; for he observes himself and goes away and at once forgets what he was like." Actually, when you see yourself as you are, you become almost instantly compassionate. *Presto!* It is really true. Every time a person takes just one look at his or her true condition, it discomfits so inwardly. It lights a revolution. It sparks the breakdown, which the Bible calls repentance. When you see your true self, it creates compassion, and this compassion spreads to others. You don't forget what you are like. You are literally appalled, like Ebenezer Scrooge, into a change of heart.

And one more thing: Anybody see the Hammer horror classic from the '70s entitled *Vampire Circus*? I don't recommend it particularly, but there is one amazing scene in which the citizens of a plague-ridden village pass by a series of mirrors that distort the image. What the people actually see is their pathetic and vulnerable mortality, their thinness, their fatness, their reality, their sin. And the vision is horrible. And that's when the vampire strikes. It is not corny. Yet there is no hope.

For us, the looking into the mirror is filled with hope. God, after all, made us and knows us. Nothing is hidden from Him. Yet He still loves us. That is the Christian confession. No vampire strikes at the moment of truth. Grace comes at the moment of truth. Jesus comes at the moment of truth. The presence of Jesus in the mirror is what St. James means by the phrase, "the law of liberty." The mirror is not judgment, the mirror is love. And you can't walk away from such a mirror and be the same person. You act, as it were, automatically.

One day I hope to go to Birmingham and see the old broken-down church with a new lamp lit, and a new church bus. I also hope they don't change the name.

—*Paul Zahl*

December 12

For whoever keeps the whole law but fails in one point has become guilty of all of it. (James 2:10, RSV)

One of my favorite musicians is Jim James from My Morning Jacket. He has a lyric in one of his songs that says, "Trying gets nothing done." I have several close friends and family members who are in twelve-step recovery programs. Over the years, I've heard many of them "share their stories." One guy is fond of quoting a founder of one of those programs: "...we shall find no enduring strength until we first admit complete defeat."

I'm very interested in this concept of surrender, both as a theological abstraction and as a practical reality. Except for those aforementioned friends and family, I haven't come across many people in life who understand so deeply the value, dare I say necessity, of giving up. But you don't have to be an alcoholic or drug addict to relate.

Ever experienced unrequited love? Didn't get that promotion? Turned down by the co-op board? Just can't seem to appease that in-law? Pick a topic and go with it. I actually like this verse in James because it reminds me how futile my efforts are where it really counts. If I'm honest with myself, then I admit the standard of the Bible isn't to try harder. It's to be perfect. Right now.

Yikes! Where does that leave me? Well, possibly with the best of all scenarios. The law is good and perfect, but there's also zero room for error.

The cross! Thankfully, the cross satisfies that completely onerous demand. I'm going to paraphrase something I've heard many times, but it still means a lot to me: because I don't *have* to do anything, it frees me up to do everything. For me, that's good news!

—*Nate Michaux*

December 13

For judgment will be without mercy to anyone who has shown no mercy; mercy triumphs over judgment. (James 2:13, NRSV)

Back in the mid-90s my family and I lived in Wyoming, where I served in youth ministry. We attended the local high school graduation, joining a family with whom we'd become good friends. The parents were so excited to see their one and only child graduate from high school. They asked me to videotape the graduation for them so they could simply sit back and enjoy the commencement ceremony. I was honored by their request and arrived early and took the time to set up the camera at a great angle, etc. I videotaped the whole ceremony, sure that I had done a great job.

A couple evenings later we all gathered at their house to watch it. There was just one snag: while the audio was great, the screen was black. We could hear everything, but we couldn't see a thing. For all my efforts in trying to capture great camera angles and the like, I had neglected to take the lens cap off.

Today's reading from the letter of James is a well-known passage about faith and works, and there has been much argument and discussion about the idea that faith without works is dead, that if we're saved by faith and not by works, what does it mean that faith without works is dead? But in the midst of these arguments and discussions we forget to take the cap off the lens and are therefore blind to what stands at the root of this passage. The main point of the Gospel is not faith-versus-works, because faith and works have to do with our response to the Gospel, and the heart of the Gospel is not what *we* do for God, but what God *has done* for us in Jesus Christ. The heart of the Gospel is these four words... "*mercy triumphs over judgment*" (2:13).

Of course, our culture is obsessed with judging others. Many of the most popular "reality" television shows are centered on judgment. One show, *Toddlers and Tiaras*, is about beauty pageants for toddlers. Little girls, three-, four-, five-year-olds, primped and postured and pronounced by their appearance. But it's a booming business. (By the way, my guess is that along with the fast-growing industry of beauty pageants for toddlers, there will be an equally fast-growing need for child psychiatrists.)

And then there's *American Idol*, centered on what judges think about a contestant's singing ability. Randy may say something like, "Yo, yo, keeping it real, dog—you did your thing—you got *pipes*!—props to you, *dog*!," while Simon may say something like, "That was absolutely awful—I felt like I was watching a poor attempt at karaoke in a cheap hotel bar," and Paula may say something like, "I... I... I just... I just love you... you are a bright and shining star!" Of course, millions of Americans join in the judging and phone in their verdicts.

But being judged is not just a mainstay on television; it is an integral part of our culture, an integral part of human nature. Judging and being judged is a part of life from cradle to grave. We're judged by our circumstances, by the color of our skin, by our neighborhood, by our school—how we dress, whom we marry, what we drive, where we *belong*, how smart or athletic our kids are, where *they* go to college, where we then retire... cyclical judgment never stops.

The good news is that God gives us mercy in Jesus Christ, because God in Christ took upon Himself our due judgment. The Greek word "mercy" in the New Testament, *eleos*, is proactive and focuses on meeting the needs of the recipient, regardless of whether or not the recipient has a claim on the giver. In other words, when it comes to the mercy of God, God is the one who proactively takes the initiative and gives us mercy in spite of the fact that we have no claim on it whatsoever. God gives us His mercy, and this triumphs over the judgment of our works.

—Dave Johnson

December 14

But no human being can tame the tongue—a restless evil,
full of deadly poison. (James 3:8, RSV)

So I was at a Bible study, and the leader was going on about gossip. It's terrible, she said, this tendency we have to gossip. Watch it! Stop gossiping, for heaven's sake, and we'll all have a much happier office and staff team. We all nodded our heads—I winced inwardly—and went our way.

Not ten seconds had gone by, after the Bible study ended, when one of the participants walked into my office and proceeded to say terrible things about a co-worker who had just been present with us. Horrible things, vicious things she said of her colleague. Not ten seconds! ("Give us Barabbas!")

This little encounter taught me again, for the umpteenth time, that the tongue is a "restless evil," as St. James writes; but also that "no human being can tame the tongue." Gossip cannot be legislated out of existence, slander is always and everywhere around, no "libel" laws can tame internet commenters or restrain heated bloggers. Speech is most easily corruptible.

Incidentally, this is why the Eightfold Path of the Buddhist faith contains the promotion of Right Speech. "Wrong speech" is everywhere. Right Speech is always a sign of goodness and un-self-serving intent.

So what to do with the description in James? If the tongue is untamable, does that place us forever at its mercy?

Yes and No. We will never live in a world where libel and verbal accusation, and the "concealed hatred and conditions" (Jack Kerouac) that lurk behind most versions of human love, are not standing at the door of situations. But No, too, for love has the winsome power to restrain the tongue. I find that people who are (somewhat) secure within love are less likely to criticize, more likely to encourage, less likely to judge, more likely to forgive. When you are satisfied in love, your level of verbal contempt goes down. What we want to be is a realistic forgiver. What we want someone else to be is a realistic forgiver. I know that mean, malicious thoughts are always close at hand. Always. Romans 7 taught me this. Life has taught me this. But when I am treated with a little mercy, I definitely get nicer.

I felt undone when that church worker came in after the exhortation concerning gossip; and gossiped, gossiped bad. But I shouldn't have been surprised. I do know, however, that she was insecure, and surely not feeling loved, and precious. Maybe things at home will lighten up—or maybe heat up, if that is required. But when she "breaks," to quote Dylan, the love of God may do just the thing, and heal the tongue. Not until then, however.

—*Paul Zahl*

December 15

...knowing that you were ransomed from the futile ways inherited from your forefathers, not with perishable things such as silver and gold, but with the precious blood of Christ, like that of a lamb without blemish or spot. (1 Peter 1:18-19, ESV)

Peter's use of "ransom" here would surely have conjured the notion of slavery to his first readers. A slave receives freedom if somebody "ransoms" them, pays the price for their freedom. Using this idea, Peter underlines a helpless human situation. We, apparently, need a ransom— we don't need a "push in right direction," we don't need to "follow our hearts," we need freedom from a captor.

Nobody likes to think of himself or herself as a slave. We instead think of autonomy and strength. But if we're honest, we can see how our lives in sin—our deeply contorted compulsions and propensities—are more like slavery than just a few correctable slipups. This isn't just a theological proposition; it's also experiential: in addictions, dysfunctional relationships, emotional impulses—wherever we feel caught or stuck.

Where are these for you? (It probably doesn't take long to figure out.) By these we are mastered, the cruel taskmasters we both love and hate. They are our inner-progenitors of despair, of death.

God's response to our need is as dire as our captivity. God pays our terrible ransom with the blood of sacrifice. This is why Jesus said, "The Son of Man came... to give his life as a ransom for many" (Matt 20:28). It is why Paul says we "were bought at a price" (1 Cor 7:23).

Peter has the Passover lamb in mind when he refers to Christ being "without blemish or spot" (Ex 12, Lev 22). As in the Passover, it is all about substitution—Jesus is the fundamental lamb of sacrifice, whose blood is the perfect replacement, absorbing the marks we bear from our masters and demons, whether physical, emotional, psychological, or spiritual. In his death and resurrection, God, in loving sacrifice, absorbs our wounds and gives new life.

—Justin Holcomb

December 16

> *But you are a chosen people, a royal priesthood, a holy nation, a people belonging to God, that you may declare the praises of him who called you out of darkness into his wonderful light. Once you were not a people, but now you are the people of God; once you had not received mercy, but now you have received mercy. (1 Peter 2:9-10, ESV)*

Acceptance and belonging are undeniably and fundamentally human. Certainly their power is pronounced in their absence, in rejection: whether it is the person whose attention you need but don't have, or the law firm that hasn't called you, or the date that didn't call back, or the fraternity that didn't give you a bid, or your own voice in your own head. Perhaps for you it was religious judgment, or an angry ex, or recent weight gain but, deep down, don't we have a primary need that seems to get triggered by any sense of rejection?

Sometimes it is deserved, sometimes not—but all rejection in some form or another *feels* deserved. And life in fear of rejection can make paralytics of us all.

On the other hand, acceptance is sometimes deserved, but *undeserved* acceptance is God's operating principle of grace. It somehow changes guilt into assurance and makes beauty out of ugly things. It strikes us when we are weak, not strong. It meets us in pain and restlessness. It meets us when we feel that our exclusion is deeper than usual, when our disgust at our exclusion has made us intolerable company. It meets us when longed-for progress does not appear, when old compulsions re-emerge, when despair destroys joy and courage. Grace has the uncanny ability to accept our most unacceptable moments.

In these darknesses, God says, "Because of Jesus, you are accepted. You *belong*, to Me. You don't need to try to do anything right now. Don't seek after anything; don't perform anything; don't capitalize; don't intend. Just *be*. Simply *accept* the fact that you are accepted."

Of course you are flawed and sinful and, most of the time, not that great of an investment! But you are more accepted and loved than you can know. This is because in Christ, you are chosen: you are part of "a chosen people, a royal priesthood, a holy nation, a people belonging to God."

—*Justin Holcomb*

December 17

Make every effort to supplement your faith with virtue, and virtue with knowledge, and knowledge with self-control, and self-control with steadfastness, and steadfastness with godliness, and godliness with brotherly affection, and brotherly affection with love. For if these things are yours and abound, they keep you from being ineffective or unfruitful in the knowledge of our Lord Jesus Christ. (2 Peter 1:5-8, RSV)

The Second Epistle of Peter contains a lot of Law. Parts of it, including the section at the end where Peter "takes on" the teaching of St. Paul, are hard to read when you are in a Grace state of mind. But what might be there for us?

Let's say this: There is certainly nothing wrong with "virtue," and "knowledge," and "self-control;" with "steadfastness," and "godliness," and "brotherly affection," and surely not with love. There is not one single thing wrong with these high integrities.

We took a trip not long ago to Israel, and also the West Bank, with our whole family. There were several moments of uncertainty—like when a church and site we had so longed to visit was closed. Or when a restaurant we really needed, for we were thirsty and hungry and exhausted, proved not to be in the place we had thought it was. (It materialized a quarter mile away and proved to be a high point, right down to the flakey torch-song by Celine Dion that was on repeat throughout the meal.) These were moments of serious uncertainty within an already uncertain Middle Eastern setting. And in each case of uncertainty, we came to a solution.

This is why virtues like steadfastness, not to mention self-control and knowledge, are devoutly to be praised.

And, as Peter says in the eighth verse, they are expressions of fruitfulness and effectiveness. Faith without such "works" is dead. Such works are the Chef's signature "blue plates!" When Christians are awful, and mean, and gossipy, and dress up self-righteousness as some kind of helpful advice, and compartmentalize their dark side, they show by this that they have missed the boat. The synapses are not connecting.

Thus I read this "Law"-appearing text from St. Peter as simply a description of what happens in life. Faith results in virtue, with knowledge, and so on. These things are fruit, and they are sustaining.

Now back to that Celine Dion hit. Hit? Just picture it: ten nice Americans in a restaurant on the West Bank—we are probably the first guests they have almost ever had—the waiter has to sprint out to the market around the corner to even buy the vegetables—we, the guests, are beyond starvation in July Holy Land heat—and Frau Celine is belting it out, on repeat, maybe 25 times for us (there is no one there to change the setting on the CD player back in the kitchen). This is the Christian life. This is the fruit of Christ's grace, the absurd joined to meaning, and it is sublime.

—Paul Zahl

December 18

But do not ignore this one fact, beloved, that with the Lord one day is as a thousand years, and a thousand years as one day. (2 Peter 3:8, RSV)

Here's a different tack: a "metaphysical" expression from the Bible. It says that to God there is no experience of time such as we have. There is no long and no short, no *Rip Van Winkle* wakeup to the "normal" way that time goes by, no "Long Live Walter Jameson" coming to terms with ultimate mortality. (The reference is to an ancient episode of *The Twilight Zone*, in which a roguish academic lives for 120 years, only to confront in 1961 a wrinkled, worn former lover. Her anger at her ever youthful seducer does him in. He turns to dust on the floor!) God does not age! The Deity is apart from all passage of time.

God is not a part of time as humans measure it. I use the politically correct word "humans" here, because we are now in the realm of sci-fi, where the big distinction is not between races and peoples, or men and women, but rather between earthlings and aliens. God is alien in this sense, for He does not relate in time.

I think of the Time Traveler in H.G. Wells' (and George Pal's) immortal *The Time Machine*, in which the Rod Taylor character travels at least 25,000 years into the future, while his friends back in London wait on the night of December 31st, 1899 over after-dinner drinks for him to "get back." Yet, as you remember from that movie and novel, only love matters. The Time Traveler is finally uninterested in his speculations about time. He becomes un-obsessed by them. Instead, he becomes interested only in his true love, played by Yvette Mimieux in the film, and he gambles 26,000 years on her. All other preoccupations turn literally to dust.

What I would hope to say about the metaphysical passage before us is that it is true. Conceptually, and in any world of reasoned speculation in which we might live, God is out of time. God has to exist out of time. Otherwise, He would not be God. Christians confess that God "entered" time, in the Person of Christ; and that "Incarnation" has made all the difference. But God as God must by definition exist out of time. So what do we know that is eternal that we can also still see in time? What exists among us now that is both in time and out of time?

Love is the sure answer to that one. Love exists in the now, and love is the attainment of forever. It is the only thing that seniors want just as much as adolescents do. Love is what you want on your gravestone, and love is what you want for your infant grandson, and your adult daughter. Love, to quote St. Paul, never ends. It is why the Wells/Pal hero makes a completely satisfying decision, so far as the readers and the audience are concerned, when he chooses love over time, even if she is only to be found in the impossibly distant future. Love trumps time, trumps ontology, trumps physics, trumps metaphysics. Kerouac wrote, "The Buddha—philosophy's dreadful murderer." I say, "Love—time and eternity's scythe."

—*Paul Zahl*

December 19

My dear children, I write this to you so that you will not sin. But if anybody does sin, we have one who speaks to the Father in our defense—Jesus Christ, the Righteous One. He is the atoning sacrifice for our sins, and not only for ours but also for the sins of the whole world. (1 John 2:1-2, NIV)

During my college years I worked in a genuine country "general store." It has long since closed, and even then it was a dying breed—selling everything from horse shoes to human shoes to hoop cheese to nails to fish hooks. But this store somehow held on, not really making any money, but remaining open due to the fact that the family that owned it kept it open in honor of the family patriarch, Mr. P, who had toiled in it for over 60 years. Mr. P's health was failing, and at the time I worked there he was confined to his bed. His son had taken up the torch, but not with the same enthusiasm. Times change, but this little store in its day, I came to learn, had been part of the fabric of community life for four generations, and it was much more than a commercial venture.

In fact, many of the people I met there who came in to shop on the weekends, both black and white, came from Chicago or other big cities. They had moved away many years before, but came back to this store as a kind of pilgrimage because, as I learned in time, they had a lot of affection for Mr. P. They wanted to see if the store was still there and seemed to take great pleasure in just wandering around the place, sitting by the pot bellied stove and talking about how it used to be.

Despite it not being the most efficiently run business, a few of the stories circulating told me why people came back to this little backwater place after 30 years, and it had nothing to do with nostalgia. Instead, every single one remembered some kindness that Mr. P had done for them 30 or 40 years before. In particular, I was told of a family that had fallen on hard times and had over time bought quite a lot of things, food and clothing and animal feed probably, from Mr. P on credit. While their account kept increasing, Mr. P never sent them a bill, but they knew what they owed, and it was a lot—more, in fact, than they could ever dream of paying. They were ashamed of this debt, and because they were ashamed they quit coming in to the store. After a while, Mr. P noticed that he had not seen them in some time, and he asked one of their neighbors if something was wrong. He was told that they felt bad that they owed this huge debt and they didn't have the money to pay it, and that they couldn't stand to come to the store and face Mr. P, and they surely were not going to ask for anything else "on credit." When Mr. P heard this, he promptly wrote them a letter telling them that whatever it was they owed, they didn't owe it anymore, because he wanted to see them back at his store more than he wanted or needed money they didn't have anyway.

I think about that story whenever I read this passage from 1 John. Instead of "consequences," John offers his readers the promise of complete forgiveness, and even more than that, he offers them an Advocate for them as "sinners" before the Father: "But if anyone does sin, we have one who speaks to the Father in our defense—Jesus Christ, the Righteous One." John says that we who are debtors are defended by the One who is righteous, by the one who has already paid every debt. Our defense is based on our debt being paid and cancelled by "Jesus Christ the Righteous," not on our promise and good intentions to pay in the future, or our excuses for not having paid in the past. Mr. P knew that the only way he was going to see the folks he loved again was if he absorbed and cancelled their debt. Thirty years later they were still coming back.

John knew the same: God keeps us close to God, even in the midst of our failure and brokenness. He does this by the power of His unmerited grace in a way that no threat of judgment and no amount of fear-induced spiritual effort on our part could ever achieve. These are "comfortable words" indeed.

—Michael Cooper

December 20

See what love the Father has given us, that we should be called children of God; and that is what we are... (1 John 3:1, NRSV)

Several years ago a crabby older man wanted to take me to lunch. I knew something was up, but I accepted his invitation anyway. (Perhaps you know the joy of being unexpectedly invited to that kind of lunch.) We met at a restaurant, and after the initial small talk, the axe fell and he unloaded on me: "Why do you always preach about God's love? People need to hear about God's judgment and wrath. People need to straighten out their lives. People need more than touchy-feely sermons—they need 'balanced' preaching." Crabbiness in overdrive; he was on a roll. It was a delightful meal. I listened to him, but I disagreed with him. I still do. The heart of the Gospel is God's love, and God's love is anything but "balanced."

"Balanced" preaching has nothing to do with the Gospel. People are unable to "straighten out" their lives, and the Gospel is that God takes our place, atones by *substitution.* The Bible is explicitly clear that love and compassion (Jesus' entire ministry) are one-sided. Those who really think the Gospel is about straightening out their life can become—well, crabby—and it can ruin an otherwise perfect lunch.

The heart of Gospel is the love of God in Jesus Christ—a love that transcends all bounds, a love that is unconditional, a love that cannot be measured or bullet-pointed in a dry theological textbook; a love for sinners whose lives are a complete train wreck—a love with no ulterior motives, no strings attached, no catch; a love that sounds too good to be true and yet is true; a love that gives hope to the hopeless; a love that brings relief and comfort to the beat-up, the bedraggled, and the burned-out; and, finally, a love that makes all things new.

—Dave Johnson

December 21

By this we shall know that we are of the truth and reassure our heart before him; for whenever our heart condemns us, God is greater than our heart, and he knows everything. (1 John 3:19-20, ESV)

Last summer, I had the privilege of being the chaplain at a camp. At one point, I found myself with a group of high school students who were trying out an exercise called "The Leap of Faith."

This exercise involves climbing up to the top of a telephone pole, using big metal staples on the sides of the pole. The challenge is then to very slowly stand up on top of the pole, which at this point is some 30 feet off the ground and swaying back and forth. Then, the object is to shout "three, two, one" and leap off the pole into space—and then, after the belay rope catches your leap, to enjoy the ride back down to earth.

One young woman gave it a try. She got halfway up the pole before coming back down. A bit later, she tried again. This time she got all the way to the top—and then climbed back down. She tried it one last time. She went up, managed to sit on top of the pole, and finally leaned forward and fell off it. Not a graceful leap of faith, exactly, but she did it.

As the belay rope lowered her, the others were cheering and clapping, and she had a big smile on her face. Then, as her feet touched the ground, and as her friends gathered around to hug her, she started to cry—and they were sweet, sweet tears. Her tears had nothing to do with making it up the pole. They had everything to do with trusting the rope and the belayer and all of us enough to give it a try. They had everything to do with the arms that awaited her as she came down. They had everything to do with being adopted, adopted into the strength and freedom and love of the family of Jesus Christ.

They had everything to do with—as the passage above says—God being greater than her heart.

—Jim Munroe

December 22

No one has ever seen God; if we love one another, God abides in us and his love is perfected in us. (1 John 4:12, RSV)

This verse sums up "in quintessence" (Squeeze) the two most important themes of the Bible:

The absolute otherness of God and the total accessibility of God through human love. That's a big claim!

But think about it: St. John is struck by the inability of human beings to have eye contact with God. "No one has ever seen God." He is beyond human perceiving. Yet John insists that God is there, "abiding" in us, when we love. Or rather, if we love. (Most of the time we don't love but are "looking out for number one.")

We might label this verse a "liberal" sentiment. Ernst Käsemann told the story of a pretty tough Dutch layman, who once asked his minister the question, "Is it possible, dominie, that Jesus may have been a liberal?"

Whatever the right answer to that question is, this verse *sounds* "liberal." First, it seems to knock out the anthropomorphic idea—God is not corporeal in any way we could grasp. (John does state in the prologue to his Gospel: "No one has ever seen God; the only Son, who is in the bosom of the Father, he has made him known." This means that the one clear window into God's actuality would be the historical Jesus.)

Second, the verse locates God's love within human love. "If we love *one another*, God abides in us." Love is horizontal. Or better, the only way to confirm the presence of God is to see whether people who talk about loving God are actually loving their neighbor.

Religion is vertical, and probably so vertical that we start swaying when we get more than eight rungs up the ladder, and it just collapses with our trying. On the other hand, God is completely horizontal, in the here and now, when we find ourselves showing a little heart to our fellow sufferers.

1 John 4:12 is a kind of ancient paraphrase of that show-stopping number from *Damn Yankees*, the Broadway musical, when the Washington Senators, down in the dumps but on the eve of their resurrection, sing: "You gotta have heart. All you really need is heart." Then the miracle happens.

—Paul Zahl

December 23

> For everyone who has been born of God overcomes the world. And this is the victory that has overcome the world—our faith. (1 John 5:4, ESV)

How strange, that faith is victory for a Christian. It is so small and entirely passive. It does nothing, but receives all in the form of a gift only by hearing. Faith, after all, is trust, and trust emerges not from within a person, but from outside. Trust depends upon another, not ourselves, and is called out from us by another making a promise. Trust is created in us by Christ making a promise. A promise is not yet seen, but faith is already, presently, actually created. This is why John does not say faith will be our victory one fine day; it is our victory already, right now, even though we have not yet seen what it will give. "Faith is in things not seen," after all, as Hebrews 11 says.

Should we not then say that faith is Christ's victory, not ours? That we perhaps look on and cheer Him to victory, but plainly the day belongs to Him and so the victory too? Christ is the Lord, is He not? Christ is the victor, and to the victor go the spoils. Justice, after all, as Aristotle teaches us, is that each keeps what is one's own, and does not take what belongs to another. How, then, can we claim faith is our victory?

A victory means an enemy is conquered; John says "the world" fights against us. That is a rather formidable enemy indeed: death, the devil, and their one instrument for destruction, which is the Law of God itself. Yes, even though the Law is holy, right, and pure, it was misused specifically by faith. Faith came to trust the Law instead of Christ, and sought its righteousness through works of the Law instead of by faith in

426

Christ alone. This engenders a great struggle for those of us who grow up like little children under the Law, as it always points out what we have not done. Trust in it begins to shout so loudly that we can't hear anything else, and so we come to conclude that God is angry with us, and that somehow we need more time to get things right before our Lord comes for us.

However, at the right time, God's only Son was born to redeem those "who were under the Law" (Gal 4:5). He brought the Law to an end by removing its power to judge us. In other words, "He fought the Law, and the Law won." But, when the Law won against its own Lord on the cross, calling Christ the greatest of sinners, the Law lost its accusatory curse upon sinners. Christ's victory is to lose all, willingly, on the cross, though he is innocent and sinless.

Christ's victory *becomes* mine because, raised from the dead, he is now Lord of a new kingdom where there is no Law. Christ peoples this new kingdom with sinners whom he simply forgives. He chases the Law out of our consciences and replaces it with his own promise: "I am pleased with you." By this promise, Christ gives birth to faith in us who had lost faith, or put it in the wrong things. Faith is our victory because Christ ceases to be a Law-giver and becomes truly a redeemer who speaks the new word of forgiveness while we are yet ungodly.

—Steven Paulson

December 24

> We know that we are from God, and the whole world lies
> in the power of the evil one. And we know that the Son of
> God has come and has given understanding, so that we may
> know him who is true, and we are in him who is true, in
> his Son Jesus Christ. He is the true God and eternal life. (1
> John 5:19-20, ESV)

There are times when our lives seem to fit neatly and comfortably into our world and what it offers and demands. Then there are days when nothing seems to fit at all, when the world rains on in unrelenting blows that leave us black and blue, chewing up and spitting out what little remains of our confidence.

Whichever sort of a day today may be, and whatever the world may bring before us today, we *can* be confident in this: we are from God, even as the whole world seems to be going down in flames. Knowing this, the world becomes less overwhelming, less surprising, and the momentary comforts you experience today can be held just as open-handedly as the discomfort you experience on another day. Our certainty lies not in the provisional promises that the world offers, because the world's promises are not eternal. Instead, we can be certain in the knowledge that the Son of God has come, and it has overcome the unrelenting blows of a frenetic world. Jesus gives us comforts of assurance in a world harried by changing circumstances, by being "true God and eternal life."

—Bonnie Poon Zahl

December 25

Any one who goes ahead and does not abide in the doctrine
of Christ does not have God; he who abides in the doctrine
has both the Father and the Son. (2 John 1:9, RSV)

So often there's a need to do something more with Christianity—to feed the hungry, shelter the homeless, stop war, protect the environment, or even just let your spouse control the remote for the evening. In one sense, that desire to do something is a response to love, to the incredible gift of God's forgiveness in our lives, and in that sense, it's healthy. And it's also extremely helpful to the world around us that suffers.

However, when what we *do* becomes the *test* of what we *believe*, or the litmus of the sincerity of our faith—whether that test is in our own minds or is a judgment by others—we deal with something very, very different. In C.S. Lewis' *The Screwtape Letters*, the diabolical Screwtape bemoans to his apprentice, Wormwood, the threat of Christians being "merely Christian." "What we want," he explains, "if men become Christians at all, is to keep them in the state of mind I call 'Christianity And.'"

The hard pill for our egos to swallow (but the only one that saves us) is that there is no "And." Christianity is not a moral code, a guide for living, or an agenda—it is a doctrine of belief that we need only abide in and take comfort in. It is a doctrine of belief in the work of one man and one man alone, who was God incarnate, Jesus Christ; and no one gets to the Father except through Him (John 14:6). Our good deeds are wonderful in that they help our neighbors, strengthen our relationships with one another, and maybe even stave off global warming (maybe). However, in terms of "being Christian," in terms of salvation, they are all completely after-the-fact, because "It is finished" (John 19:30). All that is left is belief.

—Leonard Finn

December 26

Now to him who is able to keep you from stumbling and to present you blameless before the presence of his glory with great joy... (Jude 1:24-25, ESV)

In the Original Garden, blame is everywhere. After Adam and Eve sin, they try to hide from God. Guilt that rightly deserves blame makes you want to go into hiding. But God finds Adam and asks him if he has eaten the fruit of the forbidden tree. In response, Adam blame-shifts: "The woman whom you gave to be with me, she gave me fruit of the tree, and I ate." He is unable to give God what every parent wants from his or her child: a straight answer. The man from whom we all inherit our immaturity and defensiveness not only blames the woman but also blames God! ("The woman whom *you* gave to be with me!") And if there weren't enough denial and projection, the woman blames the serpent: "The serpent deceived me, and I ate."

The scene from Genesis constitutes the Original Blame Game, a game that has been played out at all times and in all places since. It is played out in marriages that finally break under the weight of blame, in families that fracture amidst cross-generational accusation, in cities whose inhabitants lay blame along racial lines, and among nations who blame a global crisis on a neighboring country's ideology.

Where does blame actually lie? We have a favorite children's book called *David Gets In Trouble*, by David Shannon. It's the story of a boy named David who spends his day drawing on the living room walls, torturing the cat, burping at the table, breaking windows with baseballs and generally living the life of a mischievous boy. When David gets in trouble he always says, "No! It's not my fault!" Or "I didn't mean to!" Or "It was an accident!" or "No! It wasn't me!" Most of us, whether we're old or young, live David's life, Adam's life—getting in trouble, then shifting the blame. When we are honest, however, we know that the blame really lies with us.

How then could Paul say that we will be presented to God as blameless? Because the Bible says that all the blame-shifting in the world shifted finally to one man. Jesus Christ, the only blameless man, accepted the blame on our behalf. For our sake He who was without sin and without fault said on behalf of you and me, "Yes! It is my fault. The blame stops here." Because of Jesus Christ, those who trust in him are blameless forever.

The news of the One who took the blame is the news that will finally penetrate your defenses and end the blame game. At the end of *David Gets In Trouble*, David cries out in the dark of his room before going to bed, "Yes! It was me! I'm sorry." His mom comes in and lays her hand of blessing on his head. Happily, unburdened of his guilt, he says, "I love you, mom." His response of love is the response of all who know that Jesus has taken the blame. Yes, it was me, Lord. Thank you for taking my blame. I love You.

—*Paul Walker*

December 27

Behold, I stand at the door and knock. If anyone hears my voice and opens the door, I will come in to him and eat with him, and he with me. (Revelation 3:20, ESV)

No one likes being sick, especially if it involves nausea. If you've ever had to vomit, you know what I'm talking about. Jesus says of the church in Laodicea in verse 16 that, because they are neither hot nor cold (i.e. useless), he will spit them out. The Greek word translated as "spit" can mean "vomit." Here is a church that has become so repellant as to warrant being vomited out of Christ's mouth. What on earth could they have done to warrant such a grace-less judgment?

The Laodiceans were rich. Very rich. In fact, when an earthquake destroyed most of their city they didn't need Roman federal funding—they repaired the city out of their own pockets. Verses 17-18 indicate that wealth had made them to think they needed nothing else, when, in reality, they were "wretched, pitiful, poor, blind, and naked." This church is thus standing in the ultimate seat of denial. Their perception of reality stands at odds with the foundations upon which their church was founded. But I'll bet they had great self-esteem!

It is this self-centered, "victorious" church that thus rejects its own Lord and consequently becomes useless (neither hot nor cold). This is a passage first and foremost of Law. It is a call to repentance in the face of judgment, not to the individual *per se*, but to the church. Ironically, and inappropriately, Revelation 3:20 is a favorite of evangelists: "Behold, I stand at the door and knock. If anyone hears my voice and opens the door, I will come in and eat with him, and he with me." In context, this is not a picture of Jesus knocking on the door of a bad boy's heart, pleading for an altar run, but a picture of Jesus calling to a church that has kicked him out! But even if this did refer to an individual, could someone so supremely self-indulgent—like you and me—really have it in them to hear Jesus' voice and let him in? The answer, I think, is no. And let's be honest, how many of us know people who are not in church today because of something someone in the church did to them? "I can't go back there, not after what those women said to me when my marriage fell apart."

So where is the Gospel in all this? Jesus says that those whom he loves he rebukes. While that sounds at first like a non sequitur, sometimes the only way the love of Christ steals into our hearts or into the church is by deconstructing the "lies that bind." Only then can the light of his grace and power be any comfort at all. Jesus is very bad-mannered in this door-knocking scene—but then again, wouldn't it be more bad-mannered to leave us dead in our own house? I love this passage because it shatters tame versions of Jesus, and I love this passage because it tells me that Jesus has to shatter me in order for me to live.

—Ben Phillips

December 28

Then I saw a great white throne and him who was seated on it. From his presence earth and sky fled away, and no place was found for them. And I saw the dead, great and small, standing before the throne, and books were opened. Then another book was opened, which is the book of life. And the dead were judged by what was written in the books, according to what they had done. And the sea gave up the dead who were in it, Death and Hades gave up the dead who were in them, and they were judged, each one of them, according to what they had done. Then Death and

Hades were thrown into the lake of fire. This is the second death, the lake of fire. And if anyone's name was not found written in the book of life, he was thrown into the lake of fire. (Revelation 20:11-15, ESV)

At least in the apocalyptic thriller *2012* there were signs, warnings, and scientific data. According to St. Peter, even the scientists will likely be surprised by the final day coming, as Peter says, like a thief in the night (2 Pet 3:7-12). Signs and wonders there will be, but Charlie Frost will not be broadcasting from the top of a mountain when all things flee before the throne of God, as He rolls back the heavens and the earth to make room for His court and the hearing of all the cases that have piled up since Adam and Eve took that which was not given them.

Recently, simply the prospect of a few more degrees centigrade has been sufficient to make all mankind sweat, regardless of their zip code. On February 3, 2007, the headline of the *Bild*, Germany's most widely read newspaper, proclaimed in bold letters over the backdrop of a sickly looking globe, "*Unser Planet stirbt!*" ("Our Planet is Dying!"). What then of the prospect of not dying, but burning in a "lake of fire?" And if that were not enough, then there are these books.

How many are there? St. John, the author of Revelation, does not say. Perhaps one for each of us—"The Book of the Deeds of Jamie?" Would a single massive tome cut it for you? How many printed pages would your internet cache take? How many gigabytes would the video file of your whole life on CCTV be? According to St. John, it is going to get dicey, very dicey, for every one us. At least Dante left some wiggle room in *The Divine Comedy*; the noble pagans are given a castle in limbo, not subjected to the actual fires of the inferno. According to St. John the only place that our deeds are getting any of us is the lake of fire, a second, big death after our first, little death.

Over against the books and the fire stands *the* book, a single one. It is not your book, nor mine, but our names may be written in it. It is the Lamb's *Book of Life*, composed before the foundation of the world, in view of the culmination of the world (Rev 13:8). The book is his, and the names written in it are judged according to his, the Lamb's, credentials, and destined for a long life with him and the Father in a new heaven and new earth, new creatures in a new creation.

Whose names are in the book? More importantly, a pretty decisive question in the face of such hot judgment: "Is *my* name in this *Book of Life?*" This gets answered by the baptismal waters of belief: "I baptize

you in the Name of the Father and of the Son and of the Holy Spirit"—
this is the decision of approval, "signed, sealed, delivered." To be in
Christ is not to be headed for the lake of fire, but washed as a new
creature in the new creation. The waters of the font keep us cool on this
apocalyptic day, and every apocalyptic day, for all the fires between now
and then.

—Jonathan Mumme

December 29

> *Then I saw a new heaven and a new earth, for the first
> heaven and the first earth had passed away, and the sea was
> no more... And I heard a loud voice from the throne saying,
> "Behold, the dwelling place of God is with man. He will
> dwell with them, and they will be his people, and God
> himself will be with them as their God. He will wipe away
> every tear from their eyes, and death shall be no more,
> neither shall there be mourning, nor crying, nor pain
> anymore, for the former things have passed away." And he
> who was seated on the throne said, "Behold, I am making
> all things new." (Revelation 21:1, 3-5, ESV)*

I have a peculiar habit when it comes to reading *The New York Times*: I
always skip sections A and B. I ignore International, National, and
Regional, and head straight for the special-interest sections like Science,
Food, Design, Arts & Leisure. It is only when I have exhausted the non-
news articles that I turn to the "real" news.

Why? Well, while the news may inform me of recent events and
developments, it does not tell me anything *new*, really. It only reinforces
what I already know, that the world I live in is in poor shape. The wars
of this year, the hunger and violence and need—I already know them
quite intimately. I find them in the pain I know and experience in my
own immediate life. I am a world, a country, a region in strife: loss,
conflict, sickness, sadness—these are the constants in this, our human
situation.

This isn't to say there isn't real joy to be found, only that it is often
not nearly as vocal as life's difficulties. As the Jayhawks sing, "Trouble,
that's what we had / And everything that goes around / Comes around

in a bittersweet lament / Well my heart's already broken down / Looking for a sweeter sound / Looking for a brighter day."

Against such a backdrop, this passage is a blast of fresh air. It tells us that this world and its tears will pass, that "a brighter day" *is* coming. In pointing us to a future where there will be no tears, our tears in this broken world are made both legitimate and peaceably illegitimate. We can finally confront our pain, knowing that this world is not our answer, and that no matter how deep, senseless and unbearable the suffering we see and experience is, we are not terminally bound to it.

So, wherever you are, here it comes to you today, the vision of "a new heaven and a new earth." May it allow you to confront today honestly—may it also affirm you and comfort you. May it stir in you a hope and confidence that God is with you here, and that God is indeed trustworthy to make all things new.

—K. Marc Choi

December 30

And he said to me, "It is done! I am the Alpha and the Omega, the beginning and the end [telos]. To the thirsty I will give from the spring of the water of life without payment." (Revelation 21:6, ESV)

On November 22, 2010, hip-hop artist Kanye West released his album *My Beautiful Dark Twisted Fantasy* to universal acclaim. A couple of months later, *The Onion* commented with the headline, "Fully Validated Kanye West Retires To Quiet Farm In Iowa," reporting that "Kanye West announced Wednesday that he had finally received the exact amount of approval he needed to attain and had therefore retired from the entertainment industry to live on a small farm in Iowa."

The picture is absurd. On *this* side of heaven, we're always going to need more money, more approval or prestige—and it all boils down to a need for affirmation, for self-worth, in light of our deep knowledge of our own failures, our limitation and guilt. And we pursue them by effort, earning and sacrifice. "You've got to pay to play," as the old saying goes.

Fortunately, we're on the most solid ground in the world with our need. Early in his ministry, Jesus the physician claimed not to call the healthy, but the sick; not the righteous, but sinners. And even after Jesus' work was "finished"—even after God's work in history is "done"—it's the thirsty who receive. We don't magically become well because of Christ's work on earth, and even after all things are made new, we remain the thirsty.

What do we thirst for? Affirmation, belonging, solidarity, forgiveness—in a word, *grace*—and God himself gives "living water" (Jn 4:10). Though our imperfect remembrances of God's love and forgiveness will never fully set us at rest for "the time being," John's picture of us enjoying His grace is of an infinite river where the thirsty find rest.

The word "end" here means end of time, or climax, but it also means purpose, or goal. All of our strivings and failings and wants and needs are directed to this one—the endless grace of God, for us, without payment.

—Will McDavid

December 31

> *Then he showed me the river of the water of life, bright as crystal, flowing from the throne of God and of the Lamb through the middle of the street of the city; also, on either side of the river, the tree of life with its twelve kinds of fruit, yielding its fruit each month; and the leaves of the tree were for the healing of the nations. (Revelation 22:1-2, RSV)*

The Bible ends on this very high note. Bishop Jakes refers to the author of its last book as "St. John the Revelator." It came alive to my wife and me when we sailed to the island of Patmos a few years ago, and stood in the spot where John received his Revelation. The place is full of atmosphere, and it has a kind of aesthetic simplicity that sets it off from other holy places in that part of the world. Fewer icons and a contagious quiet.

What is most visionary here, at the close of Revelation, is John's extremely hopeful expression that the leaves of the tree of life are "for the healing of the nations." The apocalyptic vision does not concern rivers of blood (Enoch Powell), nor the lake of fire. That dismantling of "what is" has, by this time in the Revelation, taken place. The smoke is now cleared. God's final and enduring purpose, you might say, is for the first time glimpsed, "beyond the horizon" (Bob Dylan). God's purpose is benign. It is unconditionally and perfectly benign. God's tree of life exists for the healing of the nations.

We were in Bethlehem recently, where the healing of the nations is definitely not taking place. The separation-wall constructed to seal the Palestinians "in" and keep them "out" is a sort of visual triumph of non-meekness, a quality that definitely seems to be inheriting the earth. It is "theology of glory" over there, and the mourning, the hungering and thirsting, and the meek of the Beatitudes are getting no slack. "Guns and Moses," as the t-shirt says.

From an "All Things Must Pass" perspective (George Harrison), there is no way ultimately that the injustices inherent in that scene are going to triumph. Nothing in this world lasts, and this includes even the separation-wall. Go to Berlin! Checkpoint Charlie is now a giant souvenir stand. You would never for a minute know—unless you did— that World War III almost began there—literally almost began at that precise point—in 1968. Ultimately, the same thing will happen to the separation-wall, even if it is impossible to imagine it now. Read "Ozymandias!" All things must pass—no exceptions.

But this final chapter says more. It is not just that injustice is transitory. No, injustice will be replaced by healed and healing reunion. Angry scars will be turned to baby skin. Inflammation will be replaced by softness. Division will be reunion. New Jerusalem will not just be absent of strife, but it will contain the beauty of refined feeling, the heart of sacrificing love, the mutual affect of compassion—what "the world needs now" (Jackie DeShannon). "Beyond the horizon" is a utopia of powerfully underwritten peace.

This is how the Bible ends. It ends not with a whimper.

—*Paul Zahl*

436

GLOSSARY

ANTHROPOLOGY

Everyone has something in mind when they use the phrase, "We're only human." This is because everyone has an anthropology, a conception of what human beings are like, their potential and their limitations, about what constitutes humanity. Some hold a more optimistic estimation of the human race, a "high" anthropology if you will, while others are more cynical or pessimistic, maintaining a "lower" view. Jesuit scholar J. Patout Burns, in his book *Theological Anthropology*, explains that *theological* anthropology is simply "[the investigation of] the resources, the limitations, and the destiny of the human person." Such an investigation is not only beneficial; it represents the crucial first step of any philosophical or theological project. We try to learn our anthropology from Jesus, who "knew what was in man" (John 2:25) and prayed for forgiveness for his own executioners because they "know not what they do" (Luke 23:34). We believe that the problem with being "human, all too human," as Friedrich Nietzsche once wrote, is deeper and more fundamental than any philosophy, instruction manual or moral system can address; it might even shed some light on why our Hero was crucified.

ATONEMENT

When contemplating the "work of Christ," one is entering into the realm of Christian theology that is known as the "Atonement," AKA the question of what exactly Jesus accomplished on the Cross. In the *imputation* model of atonement, God is interested in people giving up any idea at all of there being a price that could be paid to earn His love or forgiveness. It does away with all models of merit in our relationship to God. Jesus saved us purely "by giving his life as a ransom for many" (John 3:17). Rather than seeing the human condition as one merely of sick people needing to be cured, this approach views us more along the lines of "the walking dead" who need to be brought to life.

Dead people do not merit anything; they can only be raised with Christ. Until our own deaths, however, this raising with Christ can only be anticipated by faith; it can only be confessed. We confess that by imputation, God has given us the only thing that has *ever been needed:* to be "reckoned Righteous" before God through faith (cf. Gen 15:6).

GOSPEL

We stand in the tradition that sees the Gospel as just what the word means: Good News. Specifically, the Good News that "Jesus Christ came into the world to save sinners." (1 Tim 1:15). "[Christ] was delivered over to death for our sins and was raised to life for our justification" (Rom 4:25). The Gospel is a proclamation, rather than an invitation or command, yet it always addresses sinners and sufferers directly, i.e. you and me. People have gone wrong throughout history when they have reduced this Good News to its effect on those who have heard it, e.g., peace, love and understanding. These are wonderful things, to be sure, but they should not be confused for the Gospel itself, lest it become a means to an end, rather than an End in itself.

GRACE

Broadly speaking, grace can be understood as God's unmerited favor toward human beings, His one-way, sacrificial love for sinful men and women who deserve anything but. It is a gift with no strings attached. Grace is the answer we receive in Christ to the question of God's disposition toward troubled people like you and me. Grace, of course, does have horizontal meaning as well. While humans tend to attach strings to the gifts we give, acts of mercy and charity that occur in spite (or because) of ample reason for them not to could be considered gracious. We often experience grace in such terms, being loved when we feel unlovable, praised when we deserve reproach, rewarded when we should be punished, etc.

IMPUTATION

How does a good and holy God reconcile Himself to hurtful and hurting men and women? One particularly inspiring answer involves the theological concept of imputation, the idea that God reconciles sinners to himself by declaring them to be righteous on account of Christ. In and of themselves, they remain the same sinful person. Conversely, God does not justify believers by infusing them with His own goodness or righteousness; He justifies them by imputing Christ's righteousness to them. We are judged by God on the basis of Christ's action and identity which, through his death and resurrection, have been given or reckoned or imputed to us by faith, rather than on the basis of our own action. As one classic summary puts it, "Christ's merits are given to us so that we might be reckoned righteous by our trust in the merits of Christ when we believe in him, as though we had merits of our own" (*Apology of the Augsburg Confession* XXI).

LAW

Law is a theological term that refers to one of the two ways God speaks to human beings. In his treatise "The Freedom of a Christian," Protestant Reformer Martin Luther hit on an essential element of Christian theology when he wrote, "the entire Scripture of God is divided into two parts: commandments [Law] and promises [Gospel]." The basic distinction is straightforward: the Law tells us what we *ought* to do; the Gospel tells us what God has *done*. The Law, with its 'you must's or 'you must not's, both defines the universal standard of divine goodness and reveals human weakness. It typically does its work of accusation in the form of a *commandment attached to a condition.* "*If* you do/are (blank), *then* you will (blank)."

While the Law, in its biblical expression, is true and good, it is also impotent in inspiring what it calls for. In fact, it tends to create the very thing it seeks to avoid. As a motivating agent, it is not just impotent but actually counterproductive. Which is where the Gospel comes in. As St. Augustine once wrote, "The law... contributes nothing to God's saving act: through it he does but show man his weakness, that by faith he may take refuge in the divine mercy and be healed."

SANCTIFICATION

The concept of "sanctification" is taken from the Latin word *sanctificare,* which is a combination of *sanctus,* "holy," and *facere,* "to make." Sanctification, then, refers to the process of becoming more holy/righteous/good/etc, of growing or maturing in faith. While not unique to Christianity, the topic of sanctification has a long history within our tradition, particularly the question of how it relates to the concept of Justification. In other words, how does "being made right with God" (justification) relate to "being made holy" (sanctification)? Theologian Gerhard Forde saw the two as one and the same, describing sanctification as "coming to grips with your justification." Imagine a person who has been given an absurdly expensive gift by someone who not only refuses to be repaid, but considers any attempt at repayment to tarnish the gift itself. The only course of action is to deal with the free gift, to dwell on its lavishness, to internalize its beauty, to live out of a profound sense of gratitude. This can be an uncomfortable position, much less popular than the "corporate ladder" that has masqueraded as Christian teaching throughout much of its history, mainly because it takes the whole process out of human hands. A plant does not will itself to produce fruit, after all.

THEOLOGY OF THE CROSS

Christianity's defining symbol is the cross where Jesus Christ was crucified at the climax of his ministry. At the center of a religion of hope, joy, and love is an image representing death, failure, and pain, and this paradox is central to the meaning of the Christian religion. Most broadly, a "theology of the cross" is simply a theology that takes the image of the cross, and the event that took place upon it, extremely seriously. It also means viewing Christ's death on behalf of sinners—what in theology is called the atonement—as the and center of his work in the world.

A "theology of the cross" (*theologia crucis*) in this sense contradicts the assumptions we normally have about life. It says that God is most reliably present not in our strengths or our successes or the things we like best about ourselves. Rather, God is present and working in the world exactly in the place where a person is falling apart, where they are discovering the limits of their power instead of its possibilities. It also means that God is always involved with people and situations exactly as they currently are, instead of as they could be or might be or used to be.

THEOLOGY OF GLORY

A helpful way of understanding being a "theologian of the cross" is in contrast to what Luther calls being a "theologian of glory." Theologies of glory are approaches to Christianity and to life that try in various ways to minimize difficult and painful things, or else to defeat and move past them, rather than looking them square in the face and accepting them. In particular, they acknowledge the cross, but view it primarily *as a means to an end*—an unpleasant but necessary step on the way to good things in the future, especially salvation, the transformation of human potential by God, and the triumph of the Kingdom of God in the world.

One window into understanding this is to look at the ways people talk about painful experiences. If someone has just undergone a difficult and unwanted break-up, for example, they often say things like "well, it wasn't a good relationship for me anyway," or "but I've really learned a lot from this whole experience." This kind of thinking is rationalization—it basically tries to make something sound like a good thing that is in fact a bad thing. It is a strategy for avoiding having to look pain and grief directly in the face, and for not having to acknowledge that we wish life were different but are powerless to change it. In the church, one hallmark of theologies of glory is unwillingness to acknowledge honestly the reality of ongoing sin and lack of visible transformation in Christians. A theology of glory is often operative when faith feels like a fight against these realities instead of an open invitation to acknowledge them.

AUTHOR INDEX

BIBLICAL REFERENCES INDEX

DAILY OFFICE LECTIONARY GUIDE

This Daily Office Lectionary guide offers readers a way to read *The Mockingbird Devotional* that takes the church calendar into account. While reading the Bible from start to finish is a wonderful way to engage with God's word, it is worth noting that some denominations and traditions have taken a different approach. *The Book of Common Prayer's* "Daily Office," for example, offers a person a way to read the entire Bible in two years while aligning the readings with the various holy days that punctuate the Christian year. For each day of a particular week, there is a passage and devotion whose corresponding page number is in parentheses. Reading this devotional using the chart below will ensure, for example, that on Easter Day, one can read a devotion that deals explicitly with events related to the empty tomb. This approach to the devotional offers another angle for experiencing the Bible, as well as providing an added layer that can helpful for Christian ministry in liturgical churches. Think of it as two books for the price of one.

Week of 1 Advent:

Sunday	Amos 5:18-24 (185)
Monday	1 Thess 1:2-10 (381)
Tuesday	2 Pet 1:5-8 (419)
Wednesday	2 Thess 2:13-17 (384)
Thursday	2 Pet 3:8 (420)
Friday	Matt 22:1-14 (233)
Saturday	Jude 1:24-25 (429)

Week of 2 Advent:

Sunday	Matt 22:37-39 (236)
Monday	1 Thess 5:23-24 (382)
Tuesday	1 Thess 5:24 (383)
Wednesday	2 Thess 3:5 (385)
Thursday	2 Thess 3:16 (386)
Friday	Haggai 1:6 (195)
Saturday	Haggai 2:3-5 (197)

Week of 3 Advent:

Sunday	John 5:44-46 (288)
Monday	Luke 22:49-51 (272)
Tuesday	Luke 22:61-62 (273)
Wednesday	Rev 3:20 (430)
Thursday	Matt 25:14-30 (237)
Friday	Matt 11:2-6 (222)
Saturday	Isa 10:27 (147)

Week of 4 Advent:

Sunday	Isa 42:2-3 (151)
Monday	Zeph 3:14-17 (194)
Tuesday	Rev 20:11-15 (431)
Wednesday	Titus 3:1-7 (392)
Thursday	Rev 22:1-2 (435)
Friday	Gal 3:21 (363)
Dec. 24	Isa 35:1-4 (149)

Christmas Eve Gal 3:22-25 (364)

Christmas Day and Following:
Christmas	Matt 1:21 (205)
1ˢᵗ Sun. after	Luke 2:29-35 (255)
Christmas	
Dec. 29	2 John 1:9 (428)
Dec. 30	1 Sam 1:15-18 (91)
Dec. 31	John 8:12 (292)
Holy Name	Isa 62:1-4 (159)
2ⁿᵈ Sun after	Isa 65:17 (161)
Christmas	
Jan. 2	Judges 3-5 (84)
Jan. 3	Heb 11:1 (405)
Jan. 4	Heb 11:3 (407)
Jan. 5	1 Cor 1:2 (339)
Eve of	Rom 15:7 (337)
Epiphany	

The Epiphany and Following:
Sunday	Isa 52:7 (153)
Monday	John 9:6-7 (293)
Tuesday	Isa 55:8-9 (156)
Wednesday	John 5:2-8 (285)
Thursday	John 6:5-15 (289)
Friday	Col 3:3 (381)
Saturday	Psalm 118:4 (130)

Week of 1 Epiphany:
Sunday	John 1:1-5 (278)
Monday	Gen 1:1-5 (25)
Tuesday	Gen 1:14-31 (26)
Wednesday	Gen 1:28 (27)
Thursday	Gen 4:7 (38)
Friday	Isa 42:2-3 (151)
Saturday	Eph 2:8-10 (371)

Week of 2 Epiphany:
Sunday	John 4:39 (285)
Monday	Isa 43:25 (152)
Tuesday	Heb 4:14-16 (399)
Wednesday	Eph 5:8 (372)
Thursday	Gen 11:4 (39)
Friday	Mark 4:37-41 (244)
Saturday	Psalm 148 (136)

Week of 3 Epiphany:
Sunday	Heb 10:22 (402)
Monday	John 5:22-27 (287)
Tuesday	Gen 15:1-6 (40)
Wednesday	Gal 2:19-20 (361)
Thursday	Heb 9:22 (400)
Friday	Heb 9:26-28 (401)
Saturday	Heb 10:32-34 (404)

Week of 4 Epiphany:
Sunday	Heb 11:1 (405)
Monday	Heb 11:3 (407)
Tuesday	Gen 21:6-7 (42)
Wednesday	Gen 22:1-18 (43)
Thursday	Mark 8:31-9:1 (247)
Friday	Gen 23:17-20 (44)
Saturday	Mark 9:23-24 (249)

Week of 5 Epiphany:
Sunday	Mark 10:17-31 (250)
Monday	Heb 13:1-3 (408)
Tuesday	2 Tim 1:8-10 (391)
Wednesday	John 8:10-11 (291)
Thursday	Isa 60:1-2 (157)
Friday	Isa 61:1 (158)
Saturday	Psalm 34:6 (119)

Week of 6 Epiphany:
Sunday	Gen 29:31 (45)
Monday	1 Tim 1:12-15 (387)
Tuesday	1 Tim 2:1-8 (388)
Wednesday	1 Tim 2:5-6 (389)
Thursday	1 Tim 4:11-16 (390)
Friday	Isa 64:5-6, 61:10 (160)
Saturday	Gen 32:24-28 (46)

Week of 7 Epiphany:

Sunday	Matt 5:3-10 (208)
Monday	Matt 5:4 (209)
Tuesday	Matt 5:7 (210)
Wednesday	Matt 5:17-20 (211)
Thursday	Matt 5:23-24 (212)
Friday	Matt 5:27-30 (214)
Saturday	Psalm 148 (136)

Week of 8 Epiphany:

Sunday	Mark 10:35-45 (251)
Monday	Prov 16:25 (138)
Tuesday	Matt 6:19-24 (217)
Wednesday	John 13:3-5 (296)
Thursday	2 Cor 12:9 (361)
Friday	Matt 7:16-19 (220)
Saturday	Phil 1:6 (373)

Week of Last Epiphany:

Sunday	John 12:31 (295)
Monday	Prov 27:6 (139)
Tuesday	Prov 31:10-31 (140)
Ash Wed.	Luke 18:9-14 (269)
Thursday	Deut 7:6-8 (69)
Friday	Hab 3:18 (193)
Saturday	Titus 3:1-7 (392)

Week of 1 Lent:

Sunday	Dan 9:1-19 (178)
Monday	1 Cor 1:8-9 (339)
Tuesday	Heb 3:7-14 (398)
Wednesday	1 Cor 2:1-5 (342)
Thursday	1 Cor 3:6-7 (343)
Friday	Heb 4:14-16 (399)
Saturday	Judges 7:2-3 (87)

Week of 2 Lent:

Sunday	1 Cor 3:18-23 (344)
Monday	Jer 1:1-9 (162)
Tuesday	Rom 6:1-4 (323)
Wednesday	Rom 6:5 (324)
Thursday	1 Cor 6:11 (345)
Friday	Rom 2:14-15 (318)
Saturday	Psalm 23 (113)

Week of 3 Lent:

Sunday	Rom 3:31 (319)
Monday	Rom:4:4-5 (319)
Tuesday	Gen 44:34-45:1 (49)
Wednesday	1 Cor 8:1-3 (346)
Thursday	Rom 4:25 (321)
Friday	Rom 5:1-5 (322)
Saturday	Psalm 14:1-3 (112)

Week of 4 Lent:

Sunday	Gal 5:1 (367)
Monday	Rom 7:4-6 (325)
Tuesday	Isa 6:5 (147)
Wednesday	Rom 8:3 (329)
Thursday	Rom 8:14-17 (330)
Friday	1 Cor 12:12-31 (348)
Saturday	1 Cor 13:12 (349)

Week of 5 Lent:

Sunday	Jer 23:29 (166)
Monday	Jer 29:4-7 (167)
Tuesday	Jer 31:31-34 (168)
Wednesday	Rom 10:12 (331)
Thursday	Rom 11:29 (332)
Friday	Rom 11:32 (334)
Saturday	Rom 12:15 (335)

Holy Week:

Palm *Sunday*	Matt 21:4 (232)
Monday	Psalm 51:12 (125)
Tuesday	Isa 53:3-5 (154)
Wednesday	Job 19:25-29 (110)
Maundy Th.	Jer 20:7-9 (165)
Good Friday	Lam 3:14-18, 21-23 (170)
Holy Saturday	Lam 3:55-57 (171)

Easter Week:

Sunday	Matt 28:1-10 (242)
Monday	Mark 16:1-7 (253)
Tuesday	Mark 16:14-15 (254)
Wednesday	Micah 7:1-7 (190)
Thursday	Ezek 37:4-6 (175)
Friday	1 Cor 15:54-57 (351)
Saturday	Psalm 104:30 (129)

Week of 2 Easter:

Sunday	John 20:24-28 (303)
Monday	Exod 14:10-13 (52)
Tuesday	Exod 14:14 (54)
Wednesday	Exod 14:21-22 (54)
Thursday	Exod 16:2-3 (55)
Friday	Dan 3:29 (176)
Saturday	Dan 4:28-37 (177)

Week of 3 Easter:

Sunday	John 21:17 (304)
Monday	Exod 19:12-13 (59)
Tuesday	Matt 3:16-17 (206)
Wednesday	Matt 4:5-7 (207)
Thursday	Luke 5:4-6 (256)
Friday	Luke 5:22-26 (257)
Saturday	Psalm 127:2 (132)

Week of 4 Easter:

Sunday	Exod 32:1a (60)
Monday	Exod 32:1b (61)
Tuesday	Exod 32:1-4 (62)
Wednesday	Col 2:13-15 (378)
Thursday	Col 2:20-23 (379)
Friday	Col 3:3 (381)
Saturday	Psalm 124 (130)

Week of 5 Easter:

Sunday	Luke 7:36-48 (258)
Monday	1 John 3:19-20 (424)
Tuesday	1 John 4:12 (425)
Wednesday	1 John 5:4 (426)

Thursday	1 John 5:19-20 (427)
Friday	Rom 15:7 (338)
Saturday	Psalm 31:16 (117)

Week of 6 Easter:

Sunday	James 1:16-17 (409)
Monday	James 1:19-20 (410)
Tuesday	Luke 11:5-8 (263)
Wednesday	James 1:22-25 (412)
Ascension Day	Psalm 69:1-18 (126)
Friday	Lev 26:42-45 (63)
Saturday	1 Sam 2:6 (92)

Week of 7 Easter:

Sunday	Matt 10:39 (221)
Monday	Joshua 1:6-9 (77)
Tuesday	Ezek 11:19-20 (172)
Wednesday	Mark 7:14-15, 21-23 (246)
Thursday	Luke 10:29-37 (260)
Friday	Luke 10:38-42 (261)
Saturday	Psalm 35:17 (120)
Pentecost	Acts 2:1-11 (307)

Proper 1 (Week of the Sunday closest to May 11):

Sunday	Matt 5:48 (215)
Monday	Matt 6:1-2 (216)
Tuesday	Ezek 20:29 (173)
Wednesday	Ezek 34:7-10 (174)
Thursday	1 John 2:1-2 (421)
Friday	1 John 3:1 (423)
Saturday	Psalm 23:4 (114)

Proper 2 (Week of the Sunday closest to May 18):

Sunday	Luke 13:18-21 (264)
Monday	Matt 7:3 (218)
Tuesday	Matt 7:11 (219)
Wednesday	Matt 11:27-30 (223)
Thursday	Exod 3:2, 6 (51)

| Friday | 1 Cor 1:18 (341) |
| Saturday | Psalm 137:4-5 (133) |

Proper 3 (Week of the Sunday closest to May 25):

Sunday	Matt 13:29-30 (224)
Monday	Matt 13:44-46 (225)
Tuesday	Luke 15:11-32 (265)
Wednesday	Luke 15:12-13 (266)
Thursday	Luke 15:17-24 (268)
Friday	Deut 1:26-27 (68)
Saturday	Psalm 127:2 (132)

Proper 4 (Week of the Sunday closest to June 1):

Sunday	Matt 14:13-21 (227)
Monday	Deut 10:14-19 (70)
Tuesday	Deut 15:1-2 (71)
Wednesday	Eccles 2:1,11 (141)
Thursday	Eccles 2:20-23 (142)
Friday	Eccles 3:14-15 (143)
Saturday	Gal 3:22-25 (364)

Proper 5 (Week of the Sunday closest to June 8):

Sunday	Deut 30:11-16 (72)
Monday	Deut 31:6 (74)
Tuesday	Matt 15:10-20 (228)
Wednesday	Matt 16:25 (229)
Thursday	Song of Songs 2:10-12 (144)
Friday	Song of Songs 2:14-16a (145)
Saturday	Psalm 34:18 (119)

Proper 6 (Week of the Sunday closest to June 15):

Sunday	Num 13:30-14:4 (64)
Monday	Matt 18:21-35 (230)
Tuesday	Acts 1:7 (306)
Wednesday	2 Cor 3:7-11 (355)

Thursday	2 Cor 3:14-16 (356)
Friday	2 Cor 3:17 (358)
Saturday	2 Cor 5:17-21 (360)

Proper 7 (Week of the Sunday closest to June 22):

Sunday	Luke 22:44 (271)
Monday	1 Sam 8:19-22 (93)
Tuesday	Matt 20:1-16 (231)
Wednesday	Num 15:32-36 (65)
Thursday	Acts 4:24-30 (308)
Friday	Acts 5:1-11 (310)
Saturday	Psalm 27:12-14 (116)

Proper 8 (Week of the Sunday closest to June 29):

Sunday	1 Sam 12:20-24 (94)
Monday	Acts 8:22-24 (311)
Tuesday	Acts 9:36-43 (312)
Wednesaay	Num 22:9-32 (67)
Thursday	Luke 23:24 (274)
Friday	Luke 23:43 (276)
Saturday	Luke 23:46 (277)

Proper 9 (Week of the Sunday closest to July 6):

Sunday	1 Sam 17:8-9 (94)
Monday	Luke 23:46 (277)
Tuesday	Deut 34:7-8 (75)
Wednesday	Matt 22:1-14 (233)
Thursaay	Matt 22:15-22 (235)
Friday	Rom 15:7 (337)
Saturday	Psalm 90:7-8 (127)

Proper 10 (Week of the Sunday closest to July 13):

Sunday	Matt 26:33-35 (238)
Monday	Joshua 2:1-21 (78)
Tuesday	Joshua 6:1-5 (80)
Wednesday	Joshua 6:15-25 (81)
Thursday	Gal 4:6 (366)

Friday	Gal 5:6 (368)
Saturday	Gal 5:14 (369)

Proper 11 (Week of the Sunday closest to July 20):

Sunday	Matt 27:46 (239)
Monday	Matt 27:46 (240)
Tuesday	Matt 27:51 (241)
Wednesday	Joshua 24:15 (82)
Thursday	Joshua 24:19 (83)
Friday	Rom 7:15 (326)
Saturday	Rom 7:24 (327)

Proper 12 (Week of the Sunday closest to July 27):

Sunday	Judges 3-5 (84)
Monday	Judges 6:15-16 (86)
Tuesday	Mark 1:40-42 (244)
Wednesday	Isa 40:30-31 (151)
Thursday	2 Cor 5:15 (359)
Friday	2 Cor 5:17-21 (360)
Saturday	2 Cor 1:3-5 (352)

Proper 13 (Week of the Sunday closest to August 3):

Sunday	John 1:12 (280)
Monday	2 Cor 1:20 (353)
Tuesday	2 Cor 2:5-8 (354)
Wednesday	2 Cor 4:6 (358)
Thursday	2 Sam 9:13 (96)
Friday	2 Sam 12:7 (97)
Saturday	Psalm 3:8 (111)

Proper 14 (Week of the Sunday closest to August 10):

Sunday	John 4:13-26 (284)
Monday	Judges 14:6 (87)
Tuesday	Eph 1:3-8 (370)
Wednesday	Gen 2:7 (28)
Thursday	Gen 2:23 (30)
Friday	Rom 12:15 (335)

Saturday	Rom 13:8-10 (336)

Proper 15 (Week of the Sunday closest to August 17):

Sunday	Mark 13:6 (252)
Monday	John 6:37-39 (290)
Tuesday	Gen 50:15-21 (50)
Wednesday	Isa 25:6-9 (148)
Thursday	Jonah 2:2 (187)
Friday	1 Cor 15:19 (350)
Saturday	John 16:7-8 (299)

Proper 16 (Week of the Sunday closest to August 24):

Sunday	John 19:28 (301)
Monday	John 19:30 (302)
Tuesday	Acts 26:14 (313)
Wednesday	Acts 27:20, 40-44 (315)
Thursday	Acts 28:23-31 (316)
Friday	Job 7:11 (106)
Saturday	Psalm 32:1-2,5,10-11 (117)

Proper 17 (Week of the Sunday closest to August 31):

Sunday	Mark 1:14-15 (243)
Monday	Job 12:9-10 (107)
Tuesday	Job 13:4-5, 16:3, 19:2 (108)
Wednesday	James 2:10 (413)
Thursday	James 2:13 (414)
Friday	James 3:8 (416)
Saturday	Gen 37:3-7 (48)

Proper 18 (Week of the Sunday closest to September 7):

Sunday	John 11:35 (294)
Monday	Phil 3:7-11 (375)
Tuesday	Zech 12:10 (198)
Wednesday	Phil 3:20 (376)

Thursday	Matt 13:29-30 (224)
Friday	Jer 17:9 (164)
Saturday	Psalm 42:5 (123)

Proper 19 (Week of the Sunday closest to September 14):

Sunday	John 18:36-38 (300)
Monday	1 Kings 19:4-7 (98)
Tuesday	1 Kings 19:11-22 (99)
Wednesday	1 Peter 1:18-19 (417)
Thursday	Heb 4:14-16 (399)
Friday	Ruth 1:15-18 (88)
Saturday	Ruth 3:11-14 (90)

Proper 20 (Week of the Sunday closest to September 21):

Sunday	Heb 11:3 (407)
Monday	2 Kings 5:14 (100)
Tuesday	Acts 8:22-24 (311)
Wednesday	Gal 2:19-20 (361)
Thursday	Luke 5:4-6 (256)
Friday	Philemon 1:18-19 (396)
Saturday	Psalm 42:7 (124)

Proper 21 (Week of the Sunday closest to September 28):

Sunday	John 3:1-4 (282)
Monday	Hosea 3:1-5 (180)
Tuesday	Hosea 2:16-23 (181)
Wednesday	Hosea 7:14 (182)
Thursday	Matt 10:39 (221)
Friday	Heb 10:32-34 (404)
Saturday	Psalm 38:3-4, 21 (121)

Proper 22 (Week of the Sunday closest to October 5):

Sunday	Gen 3:1-7 (31)
Monday	Gen 3:4-5 (32)
Tuesday	Gen 3:10 (33)
Wednesday	Gen 3:15 (34)
Thursday	Gen 3:17-19 (35)
Friday	Gen 3:21-24 (37)
Saturday	Mark 9:7 (248)

Proper 23 (Week of the Sunday closest to October 12):

Sunday	John 3:30 (283)
Monday	Jonah 1:1-10 (186)
Tuesday	Jonah 4:2 (188)
Wednesday	Jonah 4:9 (189)
Thursday	Phil 1:21 (374)
Friday	Job 7:11 (106)
Saturday	Psalm 25:7 (115)

Proper 24 (Week of the Sunday closest to October 19):

Sunday	Luke 10:25-37 (259)
Monday	Phil. 1:4-7 (393)
Tuesday	Phil. 1:17-18 (395)
Wednesday	Phil. 1:18-19 (396)
Thursday	Ezra 9:15 (103)
Friday	Revelation 21:6 (434)
Saturday	Psalm 39:1-6 (122)

Proper 25 (Week of the Sunday closest to October 26):

Sunday	John 2:9-10 (281)
Monday	Exod 17:2 (57)
Tuesday	Exod 17:6 (58)
Wednesday	Col 1:21-22 (377)
Thursday	John 15:1-5 (297)
Friday	John 15:9-12 (298)
Saturday	Psalm 103:10-12 (128)

Proper 26 (Week of the Sunday closest to November 2):

Sunday	Neh 6:8-9 (104)
Monday	Neh 8:10 (105)
Tuesday	Luke 10:29-37 (260)
Wednesday	Joshua 1:6-9 (77)
Thursday	Gal 5:14 (369)

| Friday | Mark 7:14-15, 21-23 (246) |
| Saturday | Psalm 35:17 (120) |

Proper 27 (Week of the Sunday closest to November 9):

Sunday	Joel 2:25-27 (183)
Monday	Joel 3:18 (184)
Tuesday	Rev 21:1, 3-5 (433)
Wednesday	2 Chron 20:12 (102)
Thursday	Luke 15:12-13 (266)
Friday	Ezek 11:19-20 (172)
Saturday	Psalm 148 (136)

Proper 28 (Week of the Sunday closest to November 16):

Sunday	Mal 3:1-4 (199)
Monday	Luke 10:38-42 (261)
Tuesday	Matt 22:15-22 (235)
Wednesday	Matt 4:5-7 (207)
Thursday	1 John 4:12 (425)
Friday	Luke 23:46 (277)
Saturday	Psalm 139:7-12 (134)

Proper 29 (Week of the Sunday closest to November 23):

Sunday	Nahum 1:7 (191)
Monday	Nahum 1:13 (192)
Tuesday	1 Pet 2:9-10 (418)
Wednesday	1 Chron 13:9-12 (101)
Thursday	2 Chron 20:12 (102)
Friday	Luke 15:11-32 (265)
Saturday	Psalm 139:23-24 (135)

ABOUT MOCKINGBIRD

Founded in 2007, Mockingbird is an organization devoted to connecting the Christian faith with the realities of everyday life in fresh and down-to-earth ways. We do this primarily, but not exclusively, through our publications, conferences and online resources. Five years and 62 contributors in the making, *The Mockingbird Devotional* is our most substantial project yet. Some of our other titles include *Grace in Addiction: The Good News of Alcoholics Anonymous for Everybody*, *This American Gospel: Public Radio Parables and the Grace of God*, *The Merciful Impasse: The Sermon on the Mount for Those Who've Crashed (and Burned)*, and *The Gospel According to Pixar*.

To find out more, visit us at mbird.com or e-mail us at info@mbird.com.

FOR FURTHER READING

Todd Brewer and David Zahl
The Gospel According to Pixar
USA: Lulu Publishing Co. 2010

Robert Farrar Capon
Kingdom, Grace, Judgment: Paradox, Outrage, and Vindication in the Parables of Jesus
Grand Rapids: Wm. B. Eerdmans Publishing Co. 2002

T.S. Eliot
The Cocktail Party
New York: Harcourt, Inc. 1950

Gerhard Forde
On Being a Theologian of the Cross: Reflections on Luther's Heidelberg Disputation, 1518
Grand Rapids: Wm. B. Eerdmans Publishing Co. 1997

Bo Giertz
To Live with Christ: Devotions
St. Louis: Concordia Publishing House. 2008

Sally Lloyd-Jones
The Jesus Storybook Bible
Grand Rapids: Zondervan Publishers. 2007

Martin Luther
The Bondage of the Will
Grand Rapids: Baker Academic Publishers. 2012

Brenna Manning
All Is Grace
Colorado Springs: David C. Cook. 2011

Dorothy W. Martyn
Beyond Deserving
Grand Rapids: Wm. B. Eerdmans Publishing Co. 2007

Ed. Sean Norris
Judgment and Love: Expanded Edition
New York: Mockingbird Ministries. 2009

Walker Percy
The Message in the Bottle
New York: Farrar, Straus & Giroux Publishers. 1984

Ethan Richardson
This American Gospel: Public Radio Parables and the Grace of God
Louisville: Createspace Publishing Co. 2012

Tullian Tchividjian
One-Way Love: Inexhaustible Grace for an Exhausted World
Colorado Springs: David C. Cook Publishing Co. 2013

Leo Tolstoy, Trans. Pevear and Volokhonsky
The Death of Ivan Ilyich & Other Stories
New York: Alfred A. Knopf. 2009

C.F.W. Walther
God Grant It: Daily Devotions
St. Louis: Concordia Publishing House. 2006

Thornton Wilder
Theophilus North
New York: Harper & Row. 1973

Christian Wiman
My Bright Abyss: Meditation of a Modern Believer
New York: Farrar, Straus & Giroux Publishers. 2013

John Z.
Grace in Addiction: The Good News of Alcoholics Anonymous for Everybody
Louisville: Createspace Publishing Co. 2012

Paul F.M. Zahl
Grace in Practice: Theology for Everyday Life
Grand Rapids: Wm. B. Eerdmans Publishing Co. 2007

Paul F.M. Zahl
Who Will Deliver Us? The Present Power of the Death of Christ
Eugene: Wipf & Stock Publishing Co. 2008

And, of course, www.mbird.com

CPSIA information can be obtained at www.ICGtesting.com
Printed in the USA
BVOW09*0434121214

378515BV00002B/3/P